GEORGE MEREDITH

HIS LIFE AND ART

From the photograph by Thomson

GEORGE MEREDITH

HIS LIFE AND ART IN ANECDOTE AND CRITICISM

BY

J. A. HAMMERTON

AUTHOR OF 'STEVENSONIANA'

A NEW AND REVISED EDITION
WITH FIFTY-FIVE ILLUSTRATIONS

HASKELL HOUSE PUBLISHERS LTD.

Publishers of Scarce Scholarly Books

NEW YORK. N. Y. 10012

1971

First Published 1911

HASKELL HOUSE PUBLISHERS LTD.
Publishers of Scarce Scholarly Books
280 LAFAYETTE STREET
NEW YORK, N. Y. 10012

Library of Congress Catalog Card Number: 73-179268

Standard Book Number 8383-1369-8

Printed in the United States of America

PREFACE

As each great writer moves to fame, his way is marked and its stages heralded by a succession of critical utterances. These become, as it were, rallying points and battle-cries of his partisans; discussion crystallises round them; they strike the key-notes for interpreters. Hence the importance, for the biographer and literary student, of histories of critical opinion.

THESE words, taken from an old review, might very well be allowed to stand as an 'apology' for the present volume. They give in happy and convincing phrase an excellent reason for such a work as that here attempted. The author's purpose has been to follow the career of a great figure in modern letters with some measure of critical detachment, that the result might be to disengage from the vast mass of contemporary criticism an even-tempered and well-considered estimate of the man and his work. Such an estimate should be at least as important as the personal opinion of any one critic, no matter how brilliant, and, in some ways, more valuable. But it is not for the writer to say whether he has succeeded in hitting the mark at which he has aimed.

Criticism represents fully one half of the work; yet my efforts to present for the first time in orderly narrative some slight account of Meredith's life and friendships may not, I trust, be considered ill-spent. Clearly, a 'life' of Meredith, in the proper sense of the word, is a matter for some one of his intimate friends or of his own family; a great undertaking and one to test severely the resources of whoever is called upon to achieve it. But what I have done has seemed to me well worth doing, for while I have strictly confined myself to quotation from and reference to already published matter, I have considered it better thus to present a survey of all that has been printed about George Meredith and his art, than to encroach upon the ground of the 'life' which must some day be written, by using any of the unpublished matter that has been offered to me or availing myself of ample opportunity to record many unpublished anecdotes. In a word, I have preferred to attempt a work that would be ' complete ' within the limits set to it, instead of producing a fragmentary biography by attempting something of a more ambitious character.

As it is, the present volume has involved not a little labour. This will be apparent to any intelligent reader. The research work and preliminary reading—in some cases the reading of a whole volume is represented by a passing reference of a few lines—to say nothing of the writing, have occupied much of my scanty leisure during the last five years. One who had not examined the Meredithiana of more than half-a-century would hardly credit what an immense amount of printed matter that represents. The constant difficulty, in seeking to capture the spirit of this, was to keep the present work within the compass of a single volume. The hope of the writer is that, to all Meredithians, it may prove a companionable and useful book, entering into competition with no existing work concerned with the great novelist and poet, but filling a niche of its own.

To the many eminent authors from whom I have had occasion to quote some passage here or there, sometimes of the briefest, or again of considerable length, I gladly acknowledge my great indebtedness. In every case where I have felt it desirable to quote somewhat more than the average proportion of text I have endeavoured to get into communication with the author and to receive his or her permission—always, I need scarcely say, readily granted.

It remains only to add that the completed work had been delivered to the publisher the week before Mr. Meredith was taken with his last illness. In view of his death, it has been necessary to submit the whole to further revision, and certain interesting matters have been touched upon which had previously been ignored, when it was hoped that the present tense would still apply to most that had been written. Although I have now employed the sad tense, there is really no sadness in the passing of George Meredith, whose voice is still strong in his written word.

J. A. H.

P.S.—I add just a word to the above on the occasion of this revised edition. The reception of the work, as indicated by the remarkable cordiality of the reviews quoted elsewhere, is its ample justification. There were only two writers who subjected my book to ill-natured comment. I have nothing but gratitude to the exponents of honest criticism, on whose advice I have made certain emendations.

CONTENTS

LIST OF ILLUSTRATIONS

[*Photo, Silk.*

MEREDITH'S BIRTHPLACE, HIGH STREET, PORTSMOUTH.

[*To face p.* 1.

I

OUTLINE OF LIFE AND WORK

1828–1873

SOMETHING of the author's aloofness to the personages of his fiction, which one feels in the novels of George Meredith, characterises also his relations with the tangible world down to the later years of his life. 'Far off, withdrawn' describes his relativeness to the living world of literature and affairs, certainly until his seventieth birthday is passed. In the later years of his life he seems to have warmed to the touch of his fellow-men in a way that his old-time austerity would never have led us to expect. Newspaper 'interviewers,' curious visitors, pilgrim parties were cordially received, where before one had as lief thought of arranging an interview with the Dalai Lama.

It is no part of my business here to account for this change of attitude, but it must be recorded, as his habit of strict and almost defiant seclusion, to all but his few intimates, extending over fifty years of his working life, has given rise to a mass of legend seldom equalled in the lifetime of an author. The remarkable outburst of newspaper comment which accompanied his eightieth birthday made the pages of the newspaper and periodical press to teem with the quaintest fables of his early life.

When a man has sought and won public distinction, under his own name, yet persists in wrapping the cloak of mystery around himself, that is little short of a challenge to public curiosity. A certain female writer of our time has gained—no doubt unintentionally—immense advertisement by this means. Advertisement was the last thought to enter the mind of George Meredith; of that we are all persuaded. But in a friendly age his long-maintained attitude of detachment from the life around him was bound to be mistaken by some for a pose, by others for a challenge, and, denied the facts, behold the fables of the newspaper writers! I am no apologist for these much-inventing scribes, but I understand them.

After all, no man has a right to make a public appeal who is not ready to face the consequences of having awakened interest in himself. A public writer should be publicly known within the limits of good taste, and all who pretend that the personality of an author is no one's business but his own are either ignorant or posturing critics. As Carlyle reminds us, the book is important, but 'the man behind the book' is important also. Is he a greater or a less personality than his book suggests? Is his book an honest expression of his individuality, or a performance bearing as much relationship to himself as an actor's part to the man discharging it? Does the book square with the man behind it? These are legitimate questions and all of high importance to the function of literary criticism. If an author pleads for purity and holiness and is himself a libertine, we ought to know him as he is. If another thunders for the strong arm and the thirsty sword and is himself a timid, emasculate, slippered thing of the fireside, it is highly important that we should see him undisguised. Men are more important than books, and the 'superior persons' who, in a not unnatural revolt against the worser side of the personal journalism of our age, affect to depise all consideration of an author's personality, must not be mistaken for critics of uncommon penetration.

On the other hand, we are all at liberty to tell just as much of our inner thoughts or our private affairs as we may care to disclose, and where memory awakens pain we may claim the privilege of sanctuary for these old grey years. Let us then be guiltless of any vulgar curtain-lifting in examining even the lives of those whose careers are full of interest to their fellow-men.

George Meredith has chosen to tell us very little of his own early days, and in the absence of exact knowledge we may profitably dismiss all the stories familiar to most of us who are in touch with the literary world of our time. This we know: he was born in Hampshire on February 12, 1828, of mixed Irish and Welsh parentage. I have heard him say to a gathering of admirers, 'If I had the eloquence of a true Irishman I should be making an impression now, but I am only half Irish—half Irish and half Welsh—I halt, therefore, rather on one leg. The Welsh are admirable singers, but bad dancers.'

The name Meredith, of course, is Welsh, and a writer in the *Manchester Guardian* has pointed out that it is invariably pronounced incorrectly by Englishmen. 'Nearly all Englishmen place the accent on the first syllable, whereas no Welshman would dream of placing it anywhere but on the second, in accordance with the iron Welsh law that the accent must always be on the penultimate syllable. It would be interesting to know whether our greatest living novelist gives countenance to the popular mispronunciation of his name.'

I have never heard any of his intimates accentuate the name differently from the common rendering, and I suspect that the novelist, like a philosopher, had long ago accepted the English pronunciation. His case did not call for such self-sacrifice as many Scotsmen have had to bear in adapting their names to English tongues. The poet Mallet, whose name was Malloch, and the inventor Murdock, whose name was Murdoch, are good examples of what I mean.

Always proud of his Welsh origin, any appeal to him that had the support of Welsh sentiment never failed to awaken his sympathy. Thus in his eightieth year he became the honorary president of the Cymmrodorion Society, formed at the beginning of 1908, chiefly by professors of the Liverpool University, with the object of 'forwarding and promoting Welsh studies in the University by means of lectures and discussions.' And on the occasion of the St. David's Day banquet in London, March 2, 1908, the aged novelist wrote as follows to his compatriots:

> It is one, among many regrets incident to advanced age, that I am unable to be with you. St. David is one of the great bonds holding Welshmen together, and they are of a more fervent blood than men of other races. To them there is no dead past. The far yesterday is quick at their hearts, however heartily they may live in the present. It is a matter for rejoicing, to see that Welshmen are in all walks of life making their energies more and more felt.

Meredith's fondness for Wales and the Welsh is frequently to be noted in his fiction, both in comment and in character. In 'Sandra Belloni,' for example, we have Merthyr and Georgena Powys, two very striking—if somewhat priggish—characters, where many are only partially realised and vague, and these two being Welsh have powers denied to others. 'All subtle feelings are discerned by Welsh eyes when untroubled by any mental agitation,' says their creator. 'Brother and sister were Welsh, and I may observe that there is human nature and Welsh nature.'

Yet his Welsh blood came to him through the connection he valued least—his father, a person of the tradesman class, whom he hardly knew, but certain of whose characteristics are embodied in 'The Great Mel.' His mother, an Irish lady of good family, died when George was about five. Though his father lived to an advanced age—lived indeed for many years after he was satirised in his son's novel—the usual relationship did not obtain between father and son. As a boy he was sent by his grandparents to the celebrated Moravian schools at Neuwied on the Rhine, about ten miles north-west of Koblenz, and the influence of the training he there received is very present in his work. 'Farina,' of course, is the first effort to use his Rhineland experience for the colouring of his fiction; but in his subsequent work the feeling of intimacy with German ideas and habits of life and thought is so noticeable that, without being told, it would be plain to the reader the author had early been brought into direct touch with German life.

Neuwied, however, did more for him than that. Whatever his relatives may have been in the matter of sectarian religion, the Moravians, to whose care the youth was committed for a time, are unsurpassed for their courageous devotion to their ideals of the Christian life and their liberal education of the young. The late Professor Henry Morley, who preceded Meredith by a few years as a Neuwieder, continued throughout his life to be intensely interested in his old school, and fifty-five years after he had left it he was editing a magazine which kept the scholars, old and new, of the various Moravian schools on the Continent and in England in touch with each other. Speaking at a gathering of 'old Neuwieders' in London, on January 17, 1889, he paid this beautiful tribute to the school where George Meredith had been educated: 'No formal process of education had acted upon their lives so thoroughly or so much for their good as the little time they had spent at Neuwied. It had taken all the bitterness out of their lives, all envy and hatred and uncharitableness having been so thoroughly removed from them by contact with the gentle spirit of the old Moravians.'

We may reasonably assume that Meredith's school-days at Neuwied represent a period of the utmost importance to his after life, and the scene of this early influence on one of the greatest figures in modern literature is worthy of some little notice, for one so observant and vigilant as Meredith must have been, even as a boy, could not have lived there long before he had absorbed the spirit of the place, and doubtless that passion for long walks and hill-climbing, which later characterised his days of lusty manhood,

NEUWIED ON THE RHINE AS IT WAS IN MEREDITH'S SCHOOLDAYS.

[*To face p.* 4.

first awoke among the historic heights along the right bank of the Rhine from Neuwied to the Drachenfels. The Moravian schools at Neuwied have long been famous throughout Europe, and many notable Englishmen have passed through them. Their origin dates from the time of Prince Alexander of Neuwied—the town was formerly the capital of a little principality—who was a shining example of liberalism in an age of bigotry, and who in 1762, during the religious unrest and intolerance of his time, made free of his little town to all the sects that cared for religion sufficiently to stand by their convictions. Lutherans, Calvinists, Catholics, Moravians, Jews, were all allowed in Neuwied the fullest liberty of thought and worship; being, as an old writer quaintly puts it, 'children of the same Parent, subjects of the same moral government, candidates alike for a future state, they are taught to reflect that the articles in which they agree are of infinitely greater importance than those on which they differ, and that the minutiæ and speculative opinions cannot annihilate the primary duty of brotherly love.' The partisans of each sect were allowed to maintain their own ministers and conform each according to their established convictions, without any form of interference from the state. A little religious Utopia! Out of this grew up the remarkable educational establishment of the Moravians, whence so many of the famous missionaries of that small but energetic body have gone out to the far places of the earth. Neuwied was happy in its princes, the little town was beautifully laid out, industries encouraged, and life must have flowed along there with melodious and purposeful rhythm for generations. When Meredith became a Neuwieder, the town had a population of about 5,000; but to-day it has considerably extended and contains some 11,000 inhabitants. It was the scene of Cæsar's crossing of the Rhine and the district was rich in Roman antiquities, which the care of Prince Alexander first brought together in the museum of his palace, still one of the features of the place.

We may conclude that something of this spirit of liberalism, which must still have been electrical in the air of Neuwied in the earlier years of last century, entered into the young Meredith and conditioned the shaping of his mind.

After his return to England—he left Neuwied when not yet sixteen—he seems to have been engaged for a time on thoughts of a career in the law, the wish of his guardian, it is understood; but by twenty he was pursuing his study of the law with no very fixed notion of maintaining it to a conclusion. His mind was already bent towards authorship, and his first poem, 'Chillianwallah,' appeared in *Chambers's Edinburgh Journal* of July 7, 1849. In this by no means remarkable piece of verse, which has never been reprinted, he celebrated the heroism of the British soldiers who, under Lord Gough, on 'the fatal field of Chillianwallah,' fought one of the most sanguinary battles of the second Sikh War, on January 13, 1849, the British losing 2,400 killed and wounded:

> Chillianwallah, Chillianwallah!
> Where our brothers fought and bled!
> Oh, thy name is natural music,
> And a dirge above the dead!
>
> Though we have not been defeated,
> Though we can't be overcome,
> Still whene'er thou art repeated
> I would fain that grief were dumb.

Although this poem is the earliest of his published writings which the bibliographers have been able to trace, some ten years ago a letter of his turned up, in which he mentioned that previous to the publication of 'Chillianwallah' he had published a paper on Kossuth. There seems to be some doubt, however, as to whether this paper was actually printed and, if so, whether it was before or after the poem, as it has been stated on the authority of Chambers's records that the editor of *Chambers's* had the essay on Kossuth in his hands about the time of the printing of the poem, though it was never published in that journal. This is a point that may be left to the elucidation of some future bibliographer more fortunate than Mr. John Lane, or Mr. A. J. K. Esdaile, whose painstaking work has already been of great advantage to students of Meredith, though incomplete and not free from error.

The year 1849 had not only seen the first small beginning of Meredith's literary work, presently to shape itself into a resolution for the literary life rather than for that of the law, but the same fateful year saw the opening of a tragic chapter in his personal history—a chapter which none but himself had any right to read, and if at all, can be written only by one of his own family, to whom the facts may be known. Perhaps it is better that the story of his first unhappy marriage should remain untold. Here, at least, nothing shall be set down concerning it that might give pain to any living person.

A young man of one-and-twenty, his career quite unsettled, his future a riddle unread, George Meredith in 1849 became the husband of a young widow, Mary Ellen Nicholls, one of the daughters of Thomas Love Peacock, the poet-novelist and friend of Shelley. His own fiction is not without trace of influence from the satiric, intellectual wit of his father-in-law, and a feeling of literary kinship may possibly have had something to do in bringing about the match. Mrs. Meredith is described as 'a singularly brilliant and witty woman,' but happiness did not characterise their wedded life. There is the poignancy of a personal sorrow in some lines of 'Modern Love'; though in no sense else do I suggest that we may look into that wonderful revelation of 'tragic life' for any confession bearing upon the poet's own experience.

Mrs. Meredith lived through the years of her young husband's early attempts to establish himself as a man of letters; he wrote three of his masterpieces in her lifetime. The first two years of his married life were lean in literary achievement and, from the practical point of view, meant absolutely nothing by way of income to the young poet. He was merely an amateur of letters, in the experimental stage; three other short poems, in addition to 'Chillianwallah,' being the sum total of his contributions to *Fraser's Magazine* and the *Leader*, to the end of 1851. But in this year his first book of 'Poems,' a thin volume of 159 pages, including the incomparable 'Love in the Valley,' was published by John W. Parker and Son. He had made his first serious appeal for audience as a new writer. The book bore this dedication: 'To Thomas Love Peacock, Esq., this volume is dedicated with the profound admiration and affectionate respect of his son-in-law. Weybridge, May, 1851.' From this it may be judged that the cloud which later overshadowed the union of Peacock's daughter and George Meredith had not yet begun to lower. The Merediths were then in residence at Weybridge, within easy reach of Peacock's home at Lower Halliford. For forty years Peacock lived at that little riverside town, while Meredith was true to the sister county, the duration of his residence at Box Hill, Surrey, having rivalled that of his father-in-law at Lower Halliford, Middlesex.

The reception of 'Poems' was at least sufficiently warm to encourage the younger author to continue. The *Athenæum*, for instance, in a fairly prompt critique, over two columns in length, in the course of which the writer quoted approvingly and *in extenso* 'Will o' the Wisp' and 'The Death of Winter,' observed: 'Where the 'prentice hand is so manifest as in this little volume, we accept the signs of care and intention which it exhibits as indications of an artistic tendency in the "singer," and to a certain extent as pledges that one day he may become a poet.' Not a very penetrating judgment on a volume containing 'Love in the Valley,' but yet not unkindly.

If the poet had not made a hit, he was at least accepted as a writer of promise, as I shall endeavour to show in a later chapter of this work. Charles Kingsley and Mr. W. M. Rossetti were among those who reviewed his 'Poems' with very considerable enthusiasm, while Alfred Tennyson, who the year before had published 'In Memoriam' and succeeded Wordsworth as Poet-Laureate, wrote to compliment the young poet upon 'Love in the Valley,' saying he was so charmed with it that he went about the house reciting it to himself. Meredith's friend, Sir William Hardman, who recorded this interesting fact some forty-five years ago, blames him for having mislaid the letter, 'for it would be interesting and valuable in future times.' Certainly Meredith had a more encouraging reception for his 'Poems'—and not unnaturally—than Tennyson had for his early efforts, and whatever his feelings may have been, they could scarce be charged with disappointment, in view of what he wrote to Charles Ollier, the veteran publisher and novelist, who had the honour of being publisher to Keats and Shelley. Ollier had complimented him on his first book, and Meredith replied in these words:

> It is the appreciation you give that makes Fame worth asking for; nor would I barter such communication for any amount of favourable journal criticism, however much it might forward the popularity and sale of the book. I prepared myself, when I published, to meet with injustice and slight, knowing that the little collection, or rather selection, in my volume was but the vanguard of a better work to come. . . . The poems are all the work of extreme youth, and, with some exceptions, of labour. They will not live, I think, but they will serve their purpose in making known my name to those who look with encouragement upon such earnest students of nature who are determined to persevere until they obtain the wisdom and inspiration and self-possession of the poet.

As the foregoing was penned before Kingsley's or Mr. Rossetti's reviews had appeared, the writer was evidently expecting no great warmth of welcome from the press, but he must have been persuaded before the end of the year that his first book, however inconsiderable its sale, had not been printed in vain. That he published it with any notion of making pecuniary profit is, of course, unthinkable; but as eleven years elapsed before he again offered a book of poetry to the world, the 'vanguard' of his 'better work'—assuming that

[*From a print of the time when Meredith was writing 'Farina.'*

THE DRACHENFELS.

[*To face p.* 8.

to be in poetry—had presumably not achieved sufficient success for him to hasten up the main body of his forces; and, changing tactics meanwhile, he turned his thoughts to journalism and prose fiction. Yet the 'Poems' of 1851 may be said to have achieved all he had hoped for in the concluding sentence of his letter to Ollier.

Journalism, 'that grisette of Literature,' as Mr. Barrie has happily put it, so often the resource of those who must contrive to earn a livelihood by the pen ere they succeed in making their books financially profitable, was soon to offer George Meredith some material assistance while he persevered with the production of the literature by which he aimed to establish himself among the notable authors of his time. But we are quite without data as to a period of his life in which literary biography is usually full of interest. In the four years and a half that intervened between the appearance of his first book of poetry and 'Shagpat,' three poems—'Invitation to the Country,' *Fraser's*, August, 1851; a sonnet 'To Alexander Smith, Author of City Poems,' the *Leader*, December 20, 1851; and 'The Sweet o' the Year,' *Fraser's*, August, 1852—represent the sum total of his signed contributions to the periodicals. Not for eight years after the publication of 'Poems' do we find his name attached to verse or prose in the periodical press, until, in July, 1859, beginning his connection with *Once a Week*, he became a fairly regular contributor of poetry to the magazines and literary journals of the day. Thus from his twenty-third to his twenty-eighth year the history of George Meredith may be summed up: he published three short poems and wrote 'The Shaving of Shagpat'! We know that a son was born to him during this period. No more. His work as a journalist may have begun before the publication of 'Shagpat,' but we are without evidence. How he earned his livelihood, whether he needed to earn a livelihood, we are not told. We only know his emoluments from literature were practically nil.

'The Shaving of Shagpat' was published by Chapman and Hall at the end of 1855, though dated for 1856, and, among some dozen notices of the work which appeared in the press of the day, George Eliot, who earlier had made the personal acquaintance of the author, wrote two criticisms to which I purpose devoting further attention in the chapter on 'Early Appreciations.' The *Athenæum* gave a long review of two and a half columns to the book, as undistinguished as its critique of the 1851 volume, but distinctly encouraging. 'It is a work which exhibits power of imagination, ability in expression, and skill in construction.' This was almost enthusiasm from the grudging old *Athenæum!* 'Shagpat' quite certainly did not immediately achieve great things for its author, and it is said that this first edition had a poor sale, a considerable part of it being eventually disposed of as a 'remainder.' It contained a short prefatory note, dated December 8, 1855, and as this is absent from subsequent editions, it is interesting enough to copy here:

It has seemed to me that the only way to tell an Arabian story was by imitating the style and manners of the Oriental storytellers. But such an attempt, whether successful or not, may read like a translation: I therefore think it better to prelude this Entertainment by an avowal that it springs from no Eastern source, and is in every respect an original work.

A second edition of 'The Shaving of Shagpat' was not attempted until ten years after the first, when the work was included in Chapman and Hall's 'Standard Editions of Popular Authors,' with the fine frontispiece engraved from the painting of 'Bhanavar the Beautiful' by the novelist's friend, Frederick Sandys. The third was printed in 1872, in the form of the two-shilling 'yellow-backs,' once so popular on railway bookstalls, but long since obsolete as the 'three-decker'—Hawley Smart was, I fancy, the novelist whose works sang the swan-song of the yellow-back. Both the second and third editions contained a preface so interesting as a winder to the dull faddists who cannot read a work of pure imagination without suspecting the author of some hidden didactic purpose, that it is a pity the author—perhaps with the feeling that any explanation to intelligent readers was superfluous—dropped it from all later issues of the book.

It is important to realise how remarkably Meredith comes among the great Victorians in the chronology of his work. We have heard him so often described as the last of the great figures that gave lustre to the mid-Victorian era, that we are apt to accept the statement without quite appreciating its full import.

Swinburne, a greater name in poetry than Meredith, came ten years later with his first book; Mr. Thomas Hardy, certainly as great, perhaps a greater novelist, came twenty years later with his first novel; so that neither began quite in 'the great days.' In the year preceding Meredith's 'Poems,' Dickens gave to the world 'David Copperfield,' Kingsley published 'Alton Locke,' Tennyson 'In Memoriam,' and Thackeray 'Pendennis.' How lean our literary harvests are now, when we think of five such masterpieces issuing from the press in the same year! George Eliot had still to begin her splendid contributions to our national literature, Tennyson had still to write 'The Idylls of the King,' Thackeray had not yet written 'Esmond,' 'The Newcomes,' or 'The Virginians,' nor Browning his masterpiece, 'The Ring and the Book,' and Kingsley's 'Westward Ho!' had still to come. If we extended our survey beyond the limits of imaginative literature, such figures as Carlyle, Ruskin and Darwin would, of course, rise up; but confining the view to the great Victorian novelists and poets who were productive in the 'fifties' of last century the table which I have compiled and reproduce on the following page forms in itself no unimportant chapter in the history of George Meredith.

'There were giants in those days.' And the young poet-novelist found himself pitted against accepted writers in both prose and poetry. Is it any great wonder that he did not achieve immediate fame? The question of his difficulties of style does not yet present itself; that is altogether a later issue. A glance at the table overleaf will show the competition the young writer had to meet during his earlier years, and may induce us to modify our condemnation of the public of that day which is so often thoughtlessly blamed for its sheer neglect of his genius.

But, to return to the chronology of his work and the progress of his life, we have to note that his connection with journalism began somewhere about the time of the appearance of 'Shagpat.' Even here no precise dates are available. All that seems certain is that prior to 1856 or 1857 George Meredith was not a professional journalist or man of letters. He must have looked elsewhere for his livelihood. Whether circumstances may have altered and required his writing for a living, we are not told; but about the period mentioned he became editor of the *Ipswich Journal* and also correspondent of the *Morning Post*. By an odd twist of fate these two, the only papers he ever served, were both strongly Conservative, whereas Meredith was in his political opinions an advanced Radical. It is indeed difficult to account for his connection with the *Ipswich Journal* on any grounds but the need to earn a living. I do not recall any passage of his which would indicate that he considered the journalist might follow the example of the barrister and hire his pen to either side. Yet he was induced to write Tory 'leaders' and criticise the men he most admired in the public life of the time. I have read with some amusement of late not a few accounts of the novelist by professed admirers who sigh sadly at

George Meredith	Robert Browning	Charles Dickens	George Eliot	Charles Kingsley	Alfred Tennyson	W. M. Thackeray
Poems, 1851 The Shaving of Shagpat, 1855 Farina, 1857 Ordeal of Richard Feverel, 1859	Christmas Eve & Easter Day, 1850 Men and Women, 1855	David Copperfield, 1850 Bleak House, 1853 Hard Times, 1854 Little Dorrit, 1857 Tale of Two Cities, 1859	Trans. of Feuerbach's Essence of Christianity, 1854 Scenes of Clerical Life, 1858 Adam Bede 1859	Alton Locke, 1850 Hypatia, 1853 Westward Ho! 1855 Glaucus, 1855 Two Years Ago, 1857	In Memoriam, 1850 Maud, 1855 Idylls of the King, 1859	Pendennis, 1850 Esmond, 1852 The Newcomes, 1853 The Rose & the Ring, 1854 The Virginians, 1859
Evan Harrington, 1861 Modern Love, 1862 Sandra Belloni, 1864 Rhoda Fleming, 1865 Vittoria, 1866	Dramatis Personæ, 1864 The Ring and the Book, 1869	Great Expectations, 1861 Our Mutual Friend, 1865	The Mill on the Floss, 1860 Silas Marner, 1861 Romola, 1863 Felix Holt, 1866 The Spanish Gypsy, 1868 Agatha, 1869	Water Babies, 1863	Enoch Arden, 1864 Holy Grail, 1869	Lovel the Widower, 1860 The Adventures of Philip, 1862 Denis Duval, 1862 Roundabout Papers, 1862
Adventures of Harry Richmond, 1871 Beauchamp's Career, 1875 The Egoist, 1879	Fifine at the Fair, 1872 Red Cotton Nightcap Country, 1873 The Inn Album, 1875 Trans. of Agamemnon, 1877 Dramatic Idylls, 1879	The Mystery of Edwin Drood, 1870	Middlemarch, 1872 Jubal, 1874 Daniel Deronda, 1876 Impressions of Theophrastus Such, 1879	At Last, 1870	Gareth and Lynette, 1872 Queen Mary, 1875 Harold, 1876 The Lover's Tale, 1879	
The Tragic Comedians, 1880 Diana of the Crossways, 1885 A Reading of Earth, 1888	Asolando, 1889				The Promise of May, 1882 The Falcon, 1884 The Cup, 1884 Becket, 1884 Locksley Hall, 1886 Demeter, 1889	

Comparative Chronology of Meredith and six of his great contemporaries, from 1850 till 1889.

the thought that his writings in the *Ipswich Journal* are lost for ever and wish they but knew how these might be recovered. Those gentlemen have not been very wide awake, else they had read, so long ago as March, 1893, Mr. Frederick Dolman's contribution to the *New Review* on 'George Meredith as a Journalist.' Mr. Dolman, instead of sighing, took the pains to search the files of the *Journal* and to institute other researches which provide a contribution of some value to the record of Meredith's life. He was induced to take up the subject because it was rumoured at that time that Meredith was engaged upon a novel to be called 'The Journalist.'[1] Rumour was true to her reputation. If the novelist ever did contemplate such a theme, he would have had to rely more on his imagination than on any actual experience of journalism, for his own connection with the newspaper press was quite exceptional, save in the case of the *Morning Post*. 'The later fifties and the early sixties' is the period which Mr. Dolman, with unavoidable vagueness, assigns to Meredith's work in journalism. He was in journalism for 'seven or eight years.' Since we know that his most important experience was obtained as a war correspondent of the *Morning Post* during the Austro-Italian War of 1866, he evidently became an active journalist in 1858 or 1859, and ceased soon after 1866 what must have been to him distasteful task work. The fact that nothing could make him deviate from the ideals of his art in the books he toiled at during these years, while he placed his journalistic pen at the service of causes in which he had no measure of sympathy, admits of no interpretation other than I have given. And we must remember that in those struggling days he was fighting against burdens of debt, not of his own making.

'And you will not expect me to make money by my pen. Above all things I detest the writing for money. Fiction and verse appeal to a besotted public, that judges of the merit of the work by the standard of its taste—avaunt! And journalism for money is Egyptian bondage. No slavery is comparable to the chains of hired journalism. My pen is my fountain—the key of me; and I give myself, I do not sell. I write when I have matter in me and in the direction it presses for, otherwise not one word!'

The editorship of the *Ipswich Journal*—which we may attribute to some personal influence rather than to the usual process of a county newspaper proprietor advertising for an editor and selecting

[1] Mr. Henry Murray asserts with some show of authority that this novel was finished and put aside for posthumous publication; but the novelist's daughter stated after his death that he had left no finished work of any importance.

one from the many who apply—was held by Meredith under curious circumstances. He did not regularly see his paper to press; the routine of the office was unfamiliar to him. He did his work in his Surrey cottage and posted his 'copy' to Ipswich, where the editor *de facto* produced the paper. In short, he was only an editorial writer, his work consisting of one or two leading articles and an average of about two columns of news-notes each week: a sort of running commentary on the events of the week. Mr. Dolman has made a careful study of these editorial writings and extracted much of real interest to us. It is difficult to conceive George Meredith, the apostle of enlightened liberty, in the rôle of journalistic champion of the South during the American Civil War. Yet how characteristic is this comment on John Bright: 'Mr. Bright, *par exemple*, spoke at the Birmingham Chamber of Commerce on Tuesday. His speech contained the necessary "vindication" of the North. Mere blockade is perfect, wonderful, their greatness should inspire fear, and so forth. We dub him Yankee and bid him good-bye.' His editorial enthusiasm for the South was no doubt palatable to the readers of the *Ipswich Journal*—and he gave them good value for their money—but it must have cost the writer some qualms of conscience. Mr. Dolman considers that it may have been genuine enthusiasm in a wrong cause, but I am inclined to class it with the Tory sentiments which the *Journal* demanded of him if he had to eat its bread. For, having by fell circumstance been forced to the work, Meredith at least was no shirker, and he wrote for his paper just the best 'leaders' and the brightest 'notes' that a brilliant journalist could have written. The work was admirably done, and I shall venture to say that at no time in its existence was the *Ipswich Journal* better served. It is most interesting to observe in these ephemeræ of the press the true touches of what we have long known as the Meredithian style. The politics need engage us no further, but some examples of the humour and satire, gleaned by Mr. Dolman, are certainly worth reproducing, as for instance:

It is stated that the Padre Pantaleo, Garibaldi's fighting chaplain, is in the hands of a British Barnum, who has engaged him to recite the deeds of the hero, by him witnessed, before the day when, like Achilles, he was struck in the heel. This good Padre and most excellent fistic Friar has doubtless been tempted by a mighty sum to come over and make his chieftain small to us. Is it a sign, when the ghostly warrior consents to be farmed out by a Barnum, that the fighting days of the adventurous leader are at an end, and that the Torch of Italy is to smoulder at Pisa?

In the following he pursues a fanciful analogy between the Franchise agitation and the celebration of Guy Fawkes' Day:

> Here is reform coming before us once more with its semi-resuscitated figure, tottering on the shoulders of its lusty supporters. Who cares for it? Do the people shout? It is scarcely possible to picture a more melancholy sight than that presented by the late Reform Conference at Leeds. The veteran, Mr. George Wilson, comes before us with the usual array of figures . . . a letter of Mr. Bright's—a very encouraging and cheerful epistle from that genial reformer—was read. . . . And so Guy was patted on the back, and set up on his right side, and then on his left, and finally made a little blaze, and passed.

There is a fine sense of seriousness in his leading article dealing with the rumour that Lord Palmerston was about to be made a co-respondent in a divorce suit, and its closing words might be given as an example of the dignified treatment of a very delicate subject:

> But rumour is a wicked old woman. Cannot something be done to stop her tongue? Surely one who is an octogenarian might be spared? We are a moral people, and it does not become us to have our Premier, agile though he be, bandied about derisively like a feathered shuttlecock on the reckless battledore of scandal. For ourselves, hearing much, we have nevertheless been discreetly reserved, but now the veil is drawn by a portion of the press, and not so delicately but that the world is taught pretty plainly things concerning the Eternal Youth in office, and the fatal consequences of his toasts to the ladies, which may make some of them blush. We are indeed warned that nothing less than an injured husband has threatened and does really intend to lay an axe to the root of our Premier's extraordinary successes, in a certain awful court. We trust that rumour again lies, but that she is allowed to speak at all, and that men believe her and largely propagate her breathings, is a terrible comment on the sublime art of toasting the ladies as prosecuted by aged juveniles in office. It is a retribution worthy of Greek tragedy. We are determined to believe nothing before it is proved. It is better to belong to the laughed-at minority who decline to admit that the virtue has gone out of our Premier than to confirm a shameful scandal, the flourishing existence of which is sufficient for our moral.

One more quotation should be given, this time from an article on the Prince and Princess of Wales, the last sentence of which could have been written by no other journalist at that time:

> Our ladies wish, they tell us, and we can more decidedly say that every man living who is not a milliner in spirit devoutly desires, that the Princess Alexandra will relieve them from servitude to the Crinoline Empress. The introduction of the crinoline has been in its effects morally worse than a *coup d'état*. It has sacrificed more lives; it has utterly destroyed more tempers; it has put an immense division between the sexes. It has obscured us, smothered us, stabbed us.

The period of Meredith's activity in journalism coincides with the publishing of 'The Ordeal of Richard Feverel,' 'Evan Harrington,' 'Modern Love,' 'Sandra Belloni,' and 'Rhoda Fleming'; that is to say, from 1859 to 1866; the most productive years of his literary career and the most eventful of his life. One of the dearly-cherished fables concerning this period of Meredith's life was thus crystallised into a short paragraph by Mr. Henry Murray, the literary critic, in the course of an address to a London literary circle some years ago:

> There is a legend current in literary circles that Mr. Meredith first started his career as a writer in the possession of one guinea. This he invested in a sack of oatmeal. Since he was too poor to buy fuel to cook it, during the whole of the time he wrote his first work, 'Evan Harrington,' he subsisted on oatmeal and water, in the form of a most unpalatable drink. Even when he had achieved great fame, he never received more than £400 for one of his novels.

It has been some little diversion to me to trace the travels of this paragraph through the newspaper biographies. The abhorred shears must have been busy at the snip when the paragraph first appeared. Journalists who had never read a book of his, but would gaily write you a paragraph or a column biography of the novelist, had all got this 'legend' among their clippings, and out it came on birthdays and on any other occasion when the name of Meredith was particularly before the public. Mr. Murray gave it as a 'legend'; but the newspaper writers have turned it into history. Of course, the slightest examination of the story is sufficient to expose its improbableness. When Meredith was writing 'Evan Harrington'—not his first but his fifth book—he was for the first time in his life making money out of journalism. During the year 1859 he was also a frequent contributor to *Once a Week*, his poems being illustrated there by the greatest artists of the day. His only long contribution in prose, 'A Story-Telling Party: being a Recital of Certain Miserable Days and Nights passed wherewith to warm the Heart of the Christmas Season' (this is wrongly given in Mr. Esdaile's 'Bibliography') was founded on some stories told to him by Sir Francis C. Burnand. This contribution was signed 'T,' but is obviously by Meredith, who at this 'oatmeal and water' time was living in plain comfort in his cottage at Esher, and is spoken of by Sir Francis in his 'Records and Reminiscences' as 'then a rising star.' Nay, more, this starveling author of the cheap journalist's maudlin sentiment was able, *before* 'Evan Harrington' began appearing in *Once a Week*, to give young Burnand an introduction to the proprietors of that journal (who were also the owners of *Punch*), from which began Sir Francis's long association with Bradbury and Evans (later Bradbury, Agnew and Co.). The oatmeal and water fable may be dismissed, even at the loss of a picturesque passage.

That Meredith never received more than £400 for a novel is not at all unlikely and nothing to marvel at; but even this, so stated, is misleading, as most of his novels must have earned, from first to last, sums far in excess of the amount named, and in some cases well into four figures. A novel may be sold for £400 down on a royalty basis, and yet in ten or twenty years may earn for its author several times the original 'advance.'

Reverting to the chronology of Meredith's life and work, we have now to note that 'Farina; a Legend of Cologne,' was published by Smith, Elder and Co. in the autumn of 1857 and attracted considerable attention from the press, being reviewed by George Eliot in the *Westminster Review* of October; but as eight years elapsed before a second edition was included in the publishers' 'Shilling Series of Monthly Volumes of Standard Authors,' that may be sufficient indication of the limited commercial success attending the first publication. In 1859 'The Ordeal of Richard Feverel,' which had been written while the author was staying at Halliford, was published by Chapman and Hall in the three-volume form. The second English edition, altered and condensed, did not appear until nineteen years later, being then issued by Kegan Paul in one volume. 'Evan Harrington' was published serially in *Once a Week*, from February 11 to October 13, 1860, admirably illustrated by Charles Keene, and bearing the sub-title, 'or, He would be a Gentleman.' A pirated edition was brought out in America towards the end of the same year, and in January of 1861 Bradbury and Evans issued the novel in three volumes. No early work of the same author received less attention from the critical press. George Parsons Lathrop, the American writer, who was unreliable in his facts, though an able critic, stated that 'Feverel' (obviously an error for 'Evan Harrington') 'was drawing near the end of its publication as a serial in *Once a Week*, when the conductors of the English periodical made a bid for Hawthorne's "Marble Faun" (then lying finished in MS.) to succeed Meredith's tale. Hawthorne did not accept the offer; but this chance conjunction of the two works in time and place offers an interesting contrast. The romance of the American author, when published, rose to its due place in the monument of his fame which his own genius built for him. The Englishman's novel, published simultaneously, sank into obscurity.' Whether this is correct or not, as regards the conjunction, I cannot say; but there is no doubt that 'Evan Harrington' passed almost unnoticed, though in five years a second edition in one volume was called for. It is worthy of note that Mr. Tinsley, the publisher, who was well versed in the commercial side of books at that time, records that 'Evan Harrington' brought its author 'a fairly large sum of money.'

Here I have to notice a most curious error for which Mr. Arthur Symons, by some strange trick of his memory, usually so correct in its impressions, is evidently responsible. A good many years ago I read in Lathrop's study of Meredith, just quoted, the startling statement that 'his next novel, "Mary Bertrand," is not included in this latest and authoritative edition.' Was it possible, thought I, that it had been left for an American critic to point me to a forgotten novel of George Meredith's with which no Englishman that I knew seemed to be familiar? My efforts to secure a copy of 'Mary Bertrand' by George Meredith were unsuccessful. Later, I read Mr. Arthur Symons's critique of 'Evan Harrington' in *Time*, the magazine conducted by Edmund Yates from 1879 to 1883, and in the course of this I found Mr. Symons writing: '"Mary Bertrand," which should come between "Richard Feverel" and "Evan Harrington," is absent from the list; on what account I am at a loss to conceive.' As this article preceded Lathrop's by three years, it was doubtless the source of his information. Mr. Symons may long ago have discovered why 'Mary Bertrand' was not included. The reason, as I later found for myself, was an excellent one. That novel, published in 1860, was written by a lady named Mary Francis Chapman, whose *nom de guerre* was Francis Meredith! It is well to correct such errors as these, as no author of our time has been the subject of more misstatements than George Meredith, for reasons which, perhaps, are sufficiently obvious.

In 1860 Mrs. Meredith died. For a great part of the twelve years of their married life she and her husband had lived separately. Meredith, now residing at Copsham Cottage, Esher, was thus a widower at thirty-two, with one son, Arthur, who had been born four years after the marriage, and his pride and affection for the lad are the subject of remark by the late Sir William Hardman, who had made the novelist's acquaintance at this time, forming a lasting friendship with him. Meredith was now entering the busiest period of his life. If not already 'reader' to Chapman and Hall, he had certainly acquired that position within a year of this time, on the resignation of John Forster, the friend and biographer of Dickens. He was 'editing' the *Ipswich Journal*, as we have seen, and had begun his connection, lasting for at least six years, with the *Morning Post*, to which he contributed a variety of articles on social and literary subjects. With Swinburne, Dante Gabriel Rossetti, Frederick A. Sandys, the artist, and other notable men, as we shall see later, he had also formed friendships, and towards the end of 1861 he entered into an arrangement with Rossetti to rent a sitting-room in his house at 16, Cheyne Walk, Chelsea, intending to make use of this on his weekly visits to London in connection with his literary and journalistic pursuits. But the scheme does not seem to have worked very well, as he made but little use of Rossetti's house, though his sub-tenancy continued to the end of 1862 at least.

In the spring of that year his second book of poetry, 'Modern Love and Poems of the English Roadside, with Poems and Ballads,' had been issued by Chapman and Hall, and dedicated to the poet's friend, the late Admiral Frederick Augustus Maxse, then a Captain R.N., whose remarkable personality was later to provide Meredith with so rich a study for 'Beauchamp's Career,' and one of whose sons, Mr. L. J. Maxse, is now editor of the *National Review*. The book made even less stir in the world of letters than its predecessor of 1851, and but for the attack upon it appearing in the *Spectator* of May 24, 1862, we should have to chronicle that, like the poet's novel of the previous year, it passed practically unnoticed. Mr. Swinburne's spirited defence of his friend, the author of 'Modern Love,' in his famous letter to the *Spectator*, did not even give the book a fillip, and no less than thirty years were to pass before parts of it were reprinted.

Despite his journalistic and literary engagements, and to some extent in consequence of these, Meredith contrived in those days to make occasional stays on the Continent: in France, Germany, Switzerland and Italy. Sir William Hardman has left us notes of a meeting between them at Paris in 1863 when Meredith was on the way to the Dauphiné. He was now engaged upon 'Emilia in England' (later, and not very happily, re-named 'Sandra Belloni'), which was issued in three volumes in the spring of 1864 by Chapman and Hall, no arrangement for a first serial issue having been made. The press gave the novel a little more attention than the two works immediately preceding it, but nothing, of course, in proportion to the importance of the book. Richard Garnett wrote a long and careful review of it in the *Reader*, a literary journal of that time.

But a matter of more moment in Meredith's life than the publication of another of his books is now to be chronicled, in his second marriage. The second Mrs. Meredith—whose charming portrait, done in chalk by Sandys in 1864, was an item of particular interest at the R. A. Winter Exhibition of 1905—a lady of French descent, named Vulliamy, was happily to prove a worthy companion of the poet-novelist, sympathising with him in every way and fulfilling the need of his strong and steadfast character for a large and satisfying love. An era of joyous, fruitful life now opened for him; the shadows that must hover about the ill-mated and the lonely heart were chased away in the light of this new domestic happiness, and bright children were soon to make Flint Cottage, Box Hill, a very idyll of rural life and happy, successful literary work.

'Rhoda Fleming' was the first novel written after his second marriage, and it also failed to find a serial opening—supposing that to have been sought—as it was published in the autumn of 1865 by Tinsley Brothers. Mr. William Tinsley tells us that it had 'a very poor sale.' The fact that its author was literary adviser to another firm, which would in the usual course have issued the novel, may suggest that Tinsley, who was personally acquainted with the novelist, made a bid for the book, and Chapman and Hall, not yet finding the works of their own 'reader' so profitable as others on their list, had acquiesced. Certainly the tragic tale of 'Rhoda Fleming' marked no advance in the literary fortunes of its author; but with the beginning of 1866 'Vittoria' made its appearance serially in the *Fortnightly Review*, with the editor of which, Mr. John Morley, Meredith was now on terms of intimate friendship. During this year, too, he undertook, as we have heard, the most important commission in journalism he ever discharged, going out to the Austro-Italian War as correspondent for the *Morning Post.*

It has been stated many times in biographical sketches that it was while engaged in this enterprise Meredith secured his 'material' for 'Vittoria'; a difficult feat, forsooth, unless he wrote the novel from month to month, in Venice or elsewhere, as the story had begun in the *Fortnightly* before Italy struck her final blow against Austria by joining forces with Prussia, eventually to secure Venetia by the peace of the Prague. 'Emilia in England' was but the introduction to 'Vittoria,' as a picture of the Italian revolution of 1848, and when the splendid sequel was ready for the *Fortnightly* it had the great advantage of a strong topical interest, in dealing with the events of eighteen years earlier which were now culminating in the last struggle between Italy and Austria. The author, of course, must have made close acquaintance with Italian scenes before 1866.

I have made it my business to examine his letters to the *Morning Post*, and, to say truth, I cannot profess to have found his war correspondence unique or strongly individual. He did not see a great deal of the actual fighting, though he accompanied the Italian forces in some of their movements and marched and camped with them. Most of his reports are given at second-hand, vivid, gripping stories; but no better than many a war correspondent has done before and since. Written most likely in haste to catch the courier, they are remarkably direct in style of narrative and free from involutions of phrase, with only occasional faint echoes of the Meredithian manner. There is little, if anything, in them that is worthy of reprinting.

At the beginning of 1867, hot upon the closing of the serial issue, 'Vittoria' came out in three volumes, Chapman and Hall being the publishers; but its reception by press and public was in no way remarkable, the work not being reprinted for nineteen years. In a grudging notice of the novel on its appearance in the *Fortnightly*, the *Spectator* had spoken of its author as being 'hitherto known as a novelist of some ability and a rather low ethical tone.' In June, however, it was very sincerely praised in a study of 'Le Roman anglais contemporain,' which M. E. D. Forgues contributed to the *Revue des Deux Mondes*, and this was one of the earliest, if not the first, of the references which were to herald the rising of his European reputation. In the same French review greatly abridged versions of 'Sandra Belloni' and 'Richard Feverel' had been published in 1864 and 1865, the former being reprinted in book form in 1866. Of these and later evidences of Continental appreciation, I purpose treating at some length in another chapter.

The connection which he had thus established with the *Fortnightly* in 1866 was to continue for many years. Now shaken free of the *Ipswich Journal* drudgery, and not writing to any extent, I believe, for the *Morning Post*, he contributed many reviews and poems to the *Fortnightly*, which was to have the honour of publishing most of his later fiction. He was no longer unable to secure the great financial advantage of a first serial issue for any new novel, and as this evidence of substantial success dates from his thirty-eighth year we may consider that his days of struggle and stress were overpast at that comparatively early age, though he was still some little way from what we may regard as the great landmark of his literary life—the appearance of 'Beauchamp's Career.'

Towards the end of 1866, during the absence in America of Mr. John Morley, then editor of the *Fortnightly*, Meredith took charge of the review, and his 'Sonnet to ——,' which appeared in the issue of June, 1866, as well as 'Lines to a Friend Visiting America' in the December number, were personal to Mr. Morley. Both these pieces appear in the complete edition of the poems published in 1898, where the blank in the inscription of the sonnet is filled in 'J. M.'

The novelist had again become the father of a son, who had been christened William Maxse Meredith, his middle name in honour of the father's staunch friend, who retired from the service with the rank of Admiral in 1867. The country habit of life was, if possible, growing upon him. Journalism being finally renounced for literature, his need to be in touch with the town might be thought less than ever; his membership of the Garrick Club merely a link to bind him loosely to the thundering metropolis; though, of course, he continued for upwards of thirty years to be reader to Chapman and Hall, an occupation that would call for regular visits to London. Yet he had good reason to remember the city and to go there whenever the mood took him, for it played a great part in his fiction. Oddly, in all the heaped-up criticism of Meredith there is no feature of his work that has been more neglected than this power of London over his imagination; this London in which he was at most no more than a regular visitor; never one of its myriad workers, swinging along in the surge of its daily life; but more than any Londoner, better, a clear-sighted, penetrating observer. It has been left to a writer in the *Manchester Guardian* to touch, most happily, on this aspect of his work, which impinges so considerably on the character of the man and his life. 'More than any novelist save Thackeray,' says the writer in question, 'he pivots his novels in London.'

You do not find in him one-tenth of the painting of London canvases that you have in Dickens, nor one quarter of the wheels and springs of London life that you have in Disraeli. Yet neither of them has Meredith's absolute unconsciousness of any power-generator for life and action, if I may put it so, other than the bubbling of the pot of London—to use his own phrase. Wherever his characters may go, it is London and what their London will think that tweaks them into action—London that pricks Lord Fleetwood like a gadfly, London that sombres Lord Ormont, London that breaks Victor Radnor, London that fights for the hold upon Sandra Belloni, London that tilts the ground under the feet of Diana, London that drives Richmond Roy a-gallop. Other novelists have made deliberate excursions for characters moulded in the placid importance of the county town or the thoroughly anti-London sufficiency of the big manufacturing towns. But it would be hard to find a first-rank character in Meredith that you could see at home in any town but London.

That is the half-conscious, penetrating flavour. The taste can touch the palate more smartly. Take the passage to which the phrase about the London pot is a passing reference. 'London, say what we will of it, is after all the head of the British giant, and if not the liveliest in bubbles it is past competition the largest brothpot of brains anywhere simmering on the hob. . . . Its caked outside of grime, and the inward substance incessantly kicking the lid prankish, but never casting it off.' There are pictures of times of the day in London as classical as Hogarth's. The bluish red of Whitechapel under the north-easter; London Bridge at that particular hour before lunch when most of all the reflective man can savour there the might and majesty of the City gathered into 'London's unrivalled mezzotint'; late afternoon in the western Strand, with London's wild sunset clouds round the cocked hat of 'the most elevated of admirals' in Trafalgar Square; the night (how cunningly chosen!) in the little square of the newspaper world 'where the morrow is manufactured'; the morning walk in the Park in 'Feverel'—these are London possessions, and if Meredith called us also 'the Daniel Lambert of cities,' that is a possession too. Has any one so finely caught the Londoner's pleasure in the Embankment? 'The meeting near mid-winter of a soft warm wind along the Embankment, and dark Thames magnificently coronetted over his grimy flow.' His London fog is perhaps best of all, although it does not offer a phrase, except, of course, the description of one gas-lamp as seen from another—'It was the painting of light rather than light.' But it was he, too, who said, 'This London is rather a thing for hospital operations than for poetical rhapsody, in aspect too streaked scarlet and pock-pitted under the most cumbrous jewelled tiaras.' In truth he has the genuine Londoner's half-brutal love of the place, and even in these later years, when he could no longer go about London with ease, he has not been able to keep away.

In September of 1870 'The Adventures of Harry Richmond' began to appear serially in the *Cornhill*, the romance being illustrated by George du Maurier. For fifteen months the story ran its course —where is the editor now that would accept a serial of more than twelve monthly instalments?—and in the winter of 1871 it was published in three volumes by Smith, Elder and Co. 'Harry Richmond' had rather more attention from the press than any of its author's previous works, though it did not reach a second edition for fourteen years. But the novelist, never swerving from his determination to give of his best, and in his own way, to literature, resolutely went forward without the slightest concession to public taste, showing no inclination to meet the patrons of the circulating library, however much he may have longed for a multitude of readers—and every man that writes would fain have audience of all who read. Of the success of the market-place he himself has said, 'we find we have pledged the better part of ourselves to clutch it, and the handful of our prize cannot redeem it.' Save for 'The Song of Theodolinda,' which doubtless puzzled many readers of the *Cornhill* in September, 1872, he published nothing more until 'Beauchamp's Career' began its sixteen months' course in the *Fortnightly* of August, 1874.

Thus we see him during the years that intervene between 'Harry Richmond' and this date, closely engaged upon the masterpiece which was to mark the turning-point of his literary fortunes. He has now, we must remember, though popular tradition would have it otherwise, long ceased to be an unsuccessful author. In these far-off days of the three-volume novel second editions were much less common than they are in our own day of single volumes. Apart from the fact that money was scarcer among the reading public, and that public vastly smaller, thirty shillings was somewhat more formidable a price for three volumes than six shillings for one! The libraries, of course, were almost the only purchasers; but a single edition of a three-volume romance might be a good deal more profitable than five or six editions of our familiar 'six shilling' novel. Moreover, serials of fifteen or sixteen issues in the *Cornhill* and the *Fortnightly* must have been handsomely remunerated. Assuredly there is no longer occasion to be sentimental over Meredith's literary fortunes after 1870, and we have seen that ten years before that date journalism and literature together, though hard taskmasters both, were by no means barren of recompense to one who was giving them of his best. The return was disproportionate to the service, but the worker would have his own way—not his master's—and though his own way in the end came to be accepted, he suffered only as all self-willed or independent natures must suffer, until he had succeeded in proving that his way was worth having. It is said, but of this I have no proof, that 'Richard Feverel' and 'Rhoda Fleming' were even refused circulation by Mudie's on the ground of their indecency!

His reputation on the Continent had already made some little headway; in America, on the other hand, his name was scarcely known, and it is quite incorrect to credit American critics and readers with any exceptional acumen in awakening earlier than they of his own country to a due sense of his genius. The late Grant Allen, writing twenty years later of Meredith's position at this period of his life, in his *Fortnightly* essay on 'Our Noble Selves,' February 1887, observes:

> Twenty years ago, George Meredith was by far the greatest artist of character and situation in the English language. But only a few appreciative critics at London clubs had yet taken the trouble to crack the hard nuts he set before them, and extract the rich kernel of epigram and wisdom; if the world at large begins to know him now-a-days it is because the few who could grasp his enigmatic meaning have preached faith in him with touching fidelity till at last the public, like the unjust judge, for their much importunity, consents to buy a popular edition of 'Beauchamp's Career' and 'Evan Harrington.' I don't of course mean to say that this deliberate booming was necessary in either case for the recognition of those two great men's real greatness, on the part of the few adapted by nature for duly recognising it. The critics of England would have found out Meredith, the philosophers of the world would have found out Spencer, even without the aid of an occasional laudatory newspaper allusion. But the 'blind and battling' mass around would never have found them out at all; and it is the blind and the battling that constitute society. As it has been possible thus to boom Herbert Spencer and George Meredith, so is it possible

perhaps to boom the hundred best living authors of whose very names the blind and battling are still for the most part contentedly ignorant.

Is all this strictly true? We see Meredith at forty-two the author of ten notable books: six very long novels, two shorter volumes of fiction, and two books of poetry. He has written a great deal of verse and some little criticism in the leading periodicals; he has had three of his longest novels published serially in the best magazines of his day; yet is he known only to 'a few appreciative critics at London clubs.' Doubtless it flattered these few some forty years ago to think so; but it was not strictly true. Even of conditions at the moment of his writing Grant Allen is not more accurate in his account; but we cannot blame him, as his purpose in the article quoted is purely exegetical and he must make his point even thus:

Unstinted praise of living authors, however deserved, is avoided with an almost Greek terror of Nemesis. I have heard dozens of people say in private—what is the obvious truth—that 'The Ordeal of Richard Feverel' is the greatest novel ever written in the English language. But I never saw anybody say so in print, and I know why: because 'Richard Feverel' still remains half unknown, and they are all afraid of getting laughed at by fools who can only appreciate high merit after it has received the final stamp of popular approbation in illustrated two-shilling paper covers.

This was written after Meredith's work had been the subject of the most enthusiastic praise from many writers of greater critical judgment than Grant Allen—James Thomson, W. E. Henley, Richard Garnett, Arthur Symons, W. L. Courtney and others—at a time indeed when excessive and unmeasured laudation was the danger, and not undue reticence. And, by the way, was the statement that 'Richard Feverel' is the greatest novel in the English language not better suited for drawing-room gossip than for the cool deliberation of printed criticism? This, however, is somewhat apart from my present purpose.

We have now been able to follow the life-work of George Meredith, as closely as ascertainable facts have permitted, until he is engaged upon the writing of 'Beauchamp's Career,' and we find him then about forty-four years of age, settled in his unpretentious little cottage at the foot of Box Hill, Surrey, happy in his domestic life, the son of his second marriage a bright little fellow of five or six, and a daughter but recently arrived. The tide is making for his greatest period of joyous and successful literary labour. Visits abroad, long tramps among the downs of his own homeland, increase of friends, the fireside haven of after-work, love and the glow of good health; all these now mark his days, and this period of tranquil delight is to continue for a good many years, and out of it shall come the ripest fruits of his genius.

II

OUTLINE OF LIFE AND WORK

1874–1909

'My dear boy, we read Meredith in the early seventies at Oxford,' the late York Powell once wrote to Professor Oliver Elton. Whatever the common public may have been applauding then, Meredith was by that time one of the prime favourites of the intellectuals: Grant Allen's 'few appreciative critics at London clubs' were mere flies on the wheel of the novelist's admiring and understanding public. He had made his way; he had his own public fast, and the flood-gates of the press were about to open before the greatest title of printed criticism that has signalised the work of any English author, since Dickens, in his own lifetime. Oxford was an early stronghold of Meredith's, and long continued staunch to him, as we may gather from this little personal reminiscence by Mr. F. T. Bettany, whose undergraduate days were about one decade later than those of York Powell:

> We were all madly in love with George Meredith in my undergraduate days at Christ Church, and, thanks to the generosity of a friendly don who presented our Junior Common Room with complete sets of Thackeray, Dickens, Reade, and Meredith, we were able to gratify our enthusiasm. I remember well stealing from the shelves to which those books were to be confined the copy of 'The Egoist' and keeping it a week or more with scandalous selfishness in my own rooms. For us youngsters George Meredith was what Dickens had been to our seniors, and our joy in him was, I fear, just a little enhanced by his being—then, at least—caviare to the general.

'Beauchamp's Career' came out in the *Fortnightly* of August, 1874, and ran until December, 1875, the three-volume issue being published by Chapman and Hall immediately the serial was concluded, but bearing the date of the following year. A two-volume edition by Tauchnitz for Continental readers, in 1876, indicates the widening of the novelist's public. Unless we are to suppose that the *Fortnightly* was wasting its space by printing the story, or that its circulation was of no consequence, we must always reckon the readers of that review as a considerable body in Meredith's following. The published criticism of the book exceeded in volume and appreciation that which had accompanied the issue of any of the author's earlier works.

Dating from this time, and covering a period of almost twenty years, follows the most fruitful epoch of Meredith's literary life, which may be said to close with the publication of 'The Amazing Marriage' in 1895, when he was sixty-seven years of age. According to himself, in creative art a man's best work is done by sixty-five. In his own case he had reached that age at the writing of 'The Amazing Marriage,' a novel that ranks among his best, and what followed from his pen bears out the soundness of his judgment.

After the launching of his first line of battleship in 1875, he set himself to a companion work of equal magnitude in the shape of 'The Egoist,' but in the meanwhile wrote the three shorter tales which, with 'Farina,' make up his collection of 'Short Stories.' Of course the term short story cannot be strictly applied to these; there is nothing more certain in criticism than the inability of Meredith to write a short story. The spirit, no less than the technique, of the *conte* is utterly foreign to his genius. 'The House on the Beach,' published in the *New Quarterly Magazine*, of January, 1877; 'The Case of General Ople and Lady Camper,' in the July number, and 'The Tale of Chloe,' exactly two years later in the same magazine, are all 'little novels.' His essay on 'The Idea of Comedy,' first given as a lecture—the only one he ever gave—at the London Institution, February 1, 1877, was also printed in the *New Quarterly* for April, 1877, while the revised and enlarged version of 'Love in the Valley' was contributed to *Macmillan's Magazine*, October, 1878, and the stately verses of 'The Nuptials of Attila' to the *New Quarterly*, January, 1879.

In the autumn of that year came forth 'The Egoist,' and behold a great stirring of dry bones! James Thomson ('B.V.') joyously throws up his cap at the long-delayed acclamation of the great novelist; the splendid critical sense of W. E. Henley is leading the movement for a wider recognition of the genius of George Meredith, and presently there is no author more discussed in the press than the writer of 'The Egoist.' This may be quoted against my pause in the story of his literary life at the writing of 'Beauchamp's Career,' but while it is true that 'The Egoist' was the book that spread his fame abroad and extended vastly the horizon of his public, it is also true that the novel which immediately preceded it marked the opening of a new epoch in his history, especially from the point of view of contemporary criticism, which regards 'Beauchamp's Career' as the first work wherein the novelist reached the height of his power.

Grant Allen, himself a brilliant journeyman of letters, scarcely an artist, tells us that it was found possible to 'boom' Meredith. Surely this is not correct. The cant word implies a certain deliberate resolve on the part of some person or persons to push an author's personality and work upon the public. Nothing that I can detect in the course of Meredith's history justifies this. Henley was no 'boomster'; a saner, sounder, more even-handed critic never wrote. Not any single article of his on Meredith—and he wrote many—had the least suspicion of the gush of the log-roller. The volume of criticism, not always appreciative, that now began to pour forth from busy pens had no taint of log-rolling. 'Boom' is an unhappy word applied here. Meredith had merely, in the fullness of time and his own powers, awakened the attention he deserved. 'The Egoist' was first published in three volumes by Kegan Paul and Co., and a second edition in one volume was issued by the same firm within a year. It had not appeared in serial form, probably because he was already busy on 'The Tragic Comedians,' of which an abridged version was arranged for the *Fortnightly* from October, 1880, to February, 1881. That complete work appeared in two volumes in the winter of the latter year, and as evidence of growing popularity a two-shilling edition in Ward Lock's series of 'Select Authors' and a Tauchnitz edition came out in the same year.

In the early summer of 1883 'Poems and Lyrics of the Joy of Earth' was published by Macmillan and Co., marking an interlude in the work of the novelist, who had now turned his creative energy to the production of another long novel, 'Diana of the Crossways,' which was to prove perhaps the most popular of all his fictions so far as the taste of the general public is concerned. Little more than half of the story, the first twenty-six chapters, appeared serially in the *Fortnightly*, June to December, 1884, and the complete work in three volumes was issued at the beginning of 1885, 'Inscribed to Frederick Pollock.'

In the course of the same year an undertaking that illustrates far better than anything else the measure of popularity to which

Meredith had now attained as a writer of fiction—his poetry continued the delight of the very few for some years longer—was the beginning of the first collected edition of his novels in ten volumes. 'Diana' was added to this edition only a few months after its appearance in three volumes. Three others were published in 1885, five in 1886, and 'Shagpat' and 'Farina' together in one volume at the beginning of 1887.

But while 1885 was thus a year to be rubricated in his literary history, in his domestic story it was otherwise. In the autumn the shadow of death fell upon his simple home; he stood bereft of a loving and sympathetic wife. The second Mrs. Meredith died on September 17, 1885, and was buried in the churchyard close by Flint Cottage. Her husband's fine epitaph upon her is printed at the end of 'A Reading of Earth':

> 'Who call her Mother and who calls her Wife
> Look on her grave and see not Death but Life.'

For some little time after his great loss he seemed to be growing more of a recluse, the châlet near his cottage, against the fringe of the woods upon Box Hill, had become to him a little haven of meditation, work, and rest; monastic almost. There he pursued the thread of his quiet life, turning again to poetry, the results of which were soon to appear in 'Ballads and Poems of Tragic Life,' published by Macmillan in 1887, and 'A Reading of Earth' issued by the same house a year later. But he had now his vivacious young daughter of seventeen and his son of twenty-two to comfort him; the son of his first marriage, at this time some four-and-thirty years of age, being resident in Italy. Mrs. M. R. F. Gilman, one of the first Americans to advance his fame across the Atlantic, writing in the introduction to her excellent compilation, 'The Pilgrim's Scrip, or, Wit and Wisdom of George Meredith,' published by Roberts Bros. of Boston in 1888, remarks, under date September 1, 1888: 'For the sake of his daughter, of whom Mr. Meredith is devotedly fond, he is now trying to come out from his solitary retirement, and is occasionally present at social festivities. There is no dinner-table in the county where he is not a welcome and honoured guest.' Mrs. Gilman is usually so correct in her statements that one hesitates to doubt the inference of that last sentence. Certainly we cannot imagine any decent dinner-table, anywhere, at any time, at which George Meredith had not been welcome; but the picture of him as in any sort a 'diner out' is less easy to conjure up. His friendships and home life, however, are left for further discussion in a later chapter.

In the year when Mrs. Gilman's book was published the novelist was a notable guest at a public dinner. This was the banquet to Parnell in May, 1888. Mr. Haldane sat on the left of the Irish leader, and next to him was Meredith, with Mr. Morley on his left. A sketch of this unique meeting of these three friends appeared in the *Pall Mall Gazette* of May 10, from the pencil of 'F. C. G.'

One interesting item of personalia falls into place here. I have gleaned it from an article in the *Western Mail*, of Cardiff, for February 12, 1908:

It may not be generally known that some twenty years ago George Meredith paid an extended visit to South Wales, during which time he visited Llanelly, Merthyr, Llandilo, Cardiff, Tenby and Ferndale. At that time Mr. William Maxse Meredith, the son of the novelist, was in partnership with Mr. J. C. Howell, Llanelly, the well-known electrical engineer. During his stay at Llanelly the distinguished novelist paid a visit to the South Wales Steel and Tin-plate Works, then owned by Messrs. E. Morewood and Co. He was intensely interested in what he saw, and his description of the pyrotechnic display from the charging of the steel furnaces is still a vivid memory to Mr. Howell and the other members of the party. A few days later Mr. Meredith visited Ferndale, and while there he went down one of the pits owned by Mr. Fred Davis. The party included the daughter of the novelist and Mr. (now Sir) Frank Edwards, M.P. This was Mr. Meredith's first experience of the miner's life, and he sat down underground and enjoyed a long chat with some of the grimy colliers.

At Llandilo he spent a very enjoyable week, and was struck, as he could not help being, with the magnificent scenery of the Vale of Towy.

Another pleasant experience was the week at Tenby. A gentleman belonging to the party says he will never forget dining with the novelist on a Sunday evening at Tenby. Mr. Meredith was in brilliant form, and on that occasion his great conversational powers were heard at their best, and so absorbed were the party in this feast of reason and flow of soul that it was close on eleven o'clock before any one moved from the table. It was subsequent to this visit to South Wales that Meredith wrote 'One of Our Conquerors,' and a diligent student of Meredith discovered in that book the well-known Welsh expression, 'Ach y fi,' so that Meredith evidently took away something from South Wales!

We have seen that the first collected edition of the novels was begun in 1885 and completed in 1887. It is worthy of note that

From a sketch by Sydney P. Hall in the 'Graphic,' May 18, 1889.

MR. MEREDITH STUDIES CHARACTER AT THE PARNELL COMMISSION.

From a thumb-nail sketch in an old note book of Sir Francis C. Gould.—' Westminster Gazette,' Jan. 4, 1909.

MR. MEREDITH AT THE EIGHTY CLUB BANQUET TO MR. PARNELL.

[*To face p.* 32.

between these dates America awakened for the first time to George Meredith. Too often are we apt to credit our friends of the United States with 'discovering' our geniuses for us. Whenever they are quick and keen to claim the credit, and in the case of writing that signalised Meredith's eightieth birthday the honour was not only frequently claimed, but weakly granted by English writers who knew better. Meredith is not a parallel case with, for instance, that of Philip James Bailey. I am happy to quote a distinguished American journalist and critic, Mr. William Morton Fullerton, now on the Times staff in Paris, in this connection. He contributed to Mr. Richard Le Gallienne's book about Meredith a chapter entitled 'Some Notes in regard to George Meredith in America,' and from it I excerpt a few passages of interest here:

I remember so well when the name of Meredith first became in America a name to conjure with; and most clearly of all do I recall the surprised awakening for some of us when we realised how long this man had been writing, and that we had known nothing of him.

Before the appearance of the first uniform American edition, George Meredith was scarcely known at all in America. For a long time even the great libraries were without a single work by Meredith, except, perhaps, a small, poorly-printed, paper-covered edition of 'Diana,' which did scarcely an appreciable service in making him known in America. And then the first uniform ten-volume edition appeared from Roberts Bros. in Boston, and the triumphal progress began.

Even then it was a long time, however, before 'George Meredith' and 'Owen Meredith' were quite differentiated in the popular mind. . . . At the same time when this edition appeared I was doing work as literary editor of the *Boston Advertiser*. The first volume of the series was 'Richard Feverel,' and it was upon this book that I chanced, after a weary passage over a truly barren, unhappy season of American fiction. . . . I felt that I detected rare qualities of insight and a great and distinguished power of original expression. But the thing was, at that time, to say it.

Once at a dinner-party I found within me the necessary courage of my opinions. There were at the table several people of recognised authority as critics, who held the ears of many men. I had ventured to say a little of what I thought about Meredith. I met with only an incredulous look, born of an utter ignorance of his work. One man, however, came round with a smile and grasped my hand. The incident was typical of the attitude of the public toward Meredith. Either there was utter ignorance or an enthusiasm equally dense and unworthy.

So that when it came to me to notice these books by the *Adver-*

between these dates America awakened for the first time to George Meredith. Too often are we apt to credit our friends of the United States with 'discovering' our geniuses for us. As a rule they are quick and keen to claim the credit, and in the flood of writing which signalised Meredith's eightieth birthday the honour was not only frequently claimed, but weakly granted by English writers who knew no better. Meredith is not a parallel case with Carlyle, or, let us say, Philip James Bailey. I am happy to quote a distinguished American journalist and critic, Mr. William Morton Fullerton, now on the *Times* staff in Paris, in this connection. He contributed to Mr. Richard Le Gallienne's book about Meredith a chapter entitled 'Some Notes in regard to George Meredith in America,' and from this I excerpt a few passages of interest here:

I remember so well when the name of Meredith first became in America a name to conjure with; and most clearly of all I remember the surprised awakening for some of us when we realised how long this man had been writing, and that we had known nothing of him.

Before the appearance of the first uniform American edition George Meredith was scarcely known at all in America. . . . For a long time even the great libraries were without a volume by Meredith, except, perhaps, a small, poorly-printed, Bowdlerised edition of 'Diana,' which did scarcely any service whatever in making him known in America. And then the first uniform one-volume edition appeared from Roberts Bros. in Boston, and the triumphal progress began.

Even then it was a long time, however, before George Meredith and 'Owen Meredith' were quite differentiated in the popular mind. . . . At the same time when this edition appeared I happened to be literary editor of the *Boston Advertiser*. The first volume of the series was 'Richard Feverel,' and it was upon this book that I chanced after a weary passage over a truly barren, unharvested sea of modern fiction. . . . I felt that I detected rare qualities of insight and a great and distinguished power of original expression. But the thing was, at that time, to say so.

Once at a dinner-party I found within me the temporary courage of my opinions. There were at the table several people of recognised authority as critics, who held the ears of many men. But venturing to say a little of what I thought about Meredith, I met with only an incredulous look, born of an utter ignorance of his work. One man, however, came round with a smile and grasped my hand. The incident was typical of the attitude of the public towards Meredith. Either there was utter ignorance or an enthusiasm equally dense and unworthy.

So that when it came to me to notice these books in the *Adver-*

tiser, in somewhat too eulogistic phrase, and I trespassed upon the editorial page instead of disporting myself within the parallel bars of my own more accustomed columns, a mild but waiting scepticism as to my sanity was the least offensive form of a feeling natural enough indeed, but which in its intensity took the shape of absolutely damning belief in my immature and untrained judgment. But the martyrdom was not painfully protracted. With chagrin I soon noticed that I was not to be allowed the selfish pleasure of clinging to an unpopular cause. I had kept the columns as full of allusions to Mr. Meredith, and of editorials upon him, as my editor-in-chief would endure; and as a result had called out a number of responses that kept, as the expression is, the ball rolling. In less than a year in Boston we all read Meredith, and Mr. Niles up there in the bay window on Beacon Hill would have told you that he was contemplating a new and cheaper edition. Philadelphia, meanwhile, and New York had done themselves the honour of Mr. Meredith's company and I hope with all my heart that Mr. Meredith had honest practical proof of it.

Touching the question of flattering Americans by letting them imagine they discover our great writers for us, even Mr. Fullerton might be thought to fall into an error when he goes on to say 'Nothing ever written in America upon Mr. Meredith was so opportune or effective, I may say, as Miss Flora Shaw's article in the *Princeton Review*.' But is not this lady identical with Lady Lugard, who was then on the staff of the *Times?* Is she not Irish, and is it not probable that she wrote her most excellent study of Meredith on this side the Atlantic and sent it out to the *Princeton Review?* Of course, Mr. Fullerton's sentence may be read with that sense.

The collected edition to which Mr. Fullerton refers was, of course, an American impression of Chapman and Hall's first collected edition, and the cheaper edition was also issued jointly in England and America by the same publishers in 1889–90, 'One of Our Conquerors' and 'Lord Ormont and His Aminta' being added to it soon after they appeared in the three-volume form.

'One of Our Conquerors' had begun its appearance in the *Fortnightly* in 1890, when Mr. John Lane published Mr. Le Gallienne's brilliant study of Meredith's art. By that time the tide of Meredith appreciation was flowing strong and sure, though Mr. William Watson had a few months before delivered his memorable attack in the pages of the *National Review*, which periodical was later to come under the editorship of a son of Meredith's old friend, Admiral Maxse. The seriousness of those who were interesting themselves in the study of Meredith may be gauged by the fact that Mr. Le Gallienne's 'George Meredith: Some Characteristics' passed through four editions in as many years, and a fifth and revised edition was issued in 1900. In 1891 came the late Miss Hannah Lynch's 'George Meredith: a Study,' and the tide of critical writing has since continued so steadily to rise that there is now some danger of the writings of the master himself being neglected for the writings of his expositors: 'the fate of the classics overtook him in his own lifetime,' may be the verdict of a later day.

It must be chronicled of 'One of Our Conquerors' that not only was this novel published serially in England and America—where it was given in the New York *Sun*—but that it also appeared as a serial in the *Australasian.* His compatriots of remotest Britain had at long last come into touch with him. Of course, colonial editions of several of his novels had already appeared, but the opening of the pages of the colonial press was a token that a public for his writings existed there. This was indeed late in the day; yet there is some excuse for Australia setting him to 'dine late,' and it is something to remember that the little brochure, 'George Meredith: Poet and Novelist,' by Mr. M. W. MacCallum, professor of Modern Literature at Sydney University, originally given as a lecture and published separately in the autumn of 1892, takes no mean place among the mass of criticism which Meredith's works have called forth.

In the winter of 1888 it was announced in the newspapers that the novelist was engaged upon a stage version of 'The Egoist.' It will be remembered that this was a time when the dramatised novel was coming into vogue. Many novelists had, like R. L. Stevenson, awakened suddenly to the fact that 'the stage is the gold mine'—though R. L. S. did not extract much gold from it—and busied themselves producing stage versions of their stories. Few, indeed, came to anything; yet every novelist still looks upon the stage as his El Dorado, and is open to face the trials of a Candide to arrive there. Whether Meredith ever seriously contemplated dramatising 'The Egoist' I have been unable to ascertain. What we do know is that the play was never produced, and in all likelihood it was never written, as there is little or no evidence in all the works of the great writer that he possessed any genius for dramatic composition. The art of the stage seems as utterly opposed to his slow, deliberate and penetrating method of characterisation as that of the scene-painter to the miniaturist. Instead of essaying a stage-play in his sixtieth year Meredith, as we have seen, wrote 'One of Our Conquerors,' which appeared in the spring of 1892, in three volumes, and little more than a year later his sixth book of poetry, 'Poems: the Empty Purse,' etc., was published.

In the year 1892 the first of the few public honours ever conferred upon the novelist was announced, St. Andrew's University awarding him its honorary degree of LL.D.; and—a straw only, but indicating the way of the wind—it was in the same year that 'Meredith for the Multitude' had become a possible theme for a magazine writer, Mr. Le Gallienne contributing a paper on that subject to the *Novel Review.*

The novelist's only appearance in the witness-box—he had been a keen follower of the Parnell case, attending many of the sittings of the Commission in 1889—took place in December of 1891, in the matter of a libel action by an African merchant against an author who had written a story which Chapman and Hall had published. Meredith, in giving evidence, said that the story in dispute passed through his hands as reader for the publishers. Asked in cross-examination if he thought that the opening of the story relating to the hero's mother did not offend against the canons of good taste, the witness answered that it was the attempt of a writer of a serious mind to be humorous. It might almost be called a stereotype of that form of the element of humour. It was a failure, but still passed with the public. 'A kind of elephantine humour?' asked the judge. 'Quite so,' the witness answered. 'I did not like it, but one would have to object to so much.'

This little incident is not without interest as indicating that Meredith the novelist and Meredith the publisher's reader were fully alive to the need of keeping a sharp distinction between the class of fiction which the one cared to write himself and that from different pens which the other knew to be of the kind that 'passed with the public.'

Meanwhile, the novelist had in hand the last of his works to be issued in the old three-volume form, 'Lord Ormont and His Aminta,' which was published by Chapman and Hall in the summer of 1894—not yet had publishers decreed the summer months as a close time for book production. The book was 'gratefully inscribed to George Buckston Browne, surgeon.' An edition in one volume followed in the succeeding year, when a two-volume Tauchnitz edition was also published, and the novel has, of course, its place in the various collected editions of his works. No sooner could

'Lord Ormont' have been issued from the press than the author must have taken up, conscious of the fast ebbing years and diminishing vitality, the task of his last novel; for 'The Amazing Marriage' began its serial course in *Scribner's Magazine* of January, 1895, and was published in the winter of the same year by Constable and Co., in which firm the novelist's son, Mr. William Maxse Meredith, was now an active partner.

Thus ended forty years of novel-writing with singularly little evidence of failing powers, the same high reach of intellectual cheerfulness and artistic integrity. He was now beyond the limit of age at which, in his own estimation, a man can produce creative work calculated to rank with his best, and save for occasional excursions into the realm of poesy, his pen was now laid aside. The little châlet at Box Hill, where for so many years the good goose quill of the novelist had traced his thoughts by daylight and dusk and far into the solemn rural night, was losing its primal use as a workshop; with the 'seventies' looming over the white head of its occupant, it was becoming rather a little retreat for reflection and twilight ease. For, despite his remarkable vitality of middle life, at sixty-seven he had broken down in health and looked older and more worn than many men of eighty.

Certain work concerning his fiction was still to be done, and many could wish it had not been discharged. I refer to the revision of the novels for the splendid edition of his writings in thirty-two volumes published by Constable in 1896–98. The alterations which he chose to make at seven-and-sixty on a masterpiece he had written at thirty were drastic and much to be deplored. It is an old complaint this, many notable authors have been equally misguided, and there is no redress but to treasure the early editions. 'Richard Feverel' is a masterpiece which George Meredith *ætat* 67 was scarcely capable of writing, and it is a fair contention that he was equally unfitted to alter seriously the work of his dead self. The outlook of a man of thirty and that of the same man at sixty-seven must be so different on many vital points that they are in effect the outlooks of two different persons. Even allowing for a larger measure of consistent and enduring individuality in the character of George Meredith than is usual in most men, he could not have escaped entirely the common lot, and his overhauling of these early novels in his late years is to be regretted, as only less in degree than if some strange hand had done the work.

The success of the first collected edition and then of the 'New

Popular Edition,' in seventeen volumes, which began appearing in 1897, must have been gratifying to the novelist, if under the curling wave of seventy years he had any lingering wish to see his works in demand at the bookshops. Since that was a matter of indifference to him more than thirty years earlier—if we are to accept as autobiographical certain passages in 'Sandra Belloni'—it is probable that the success of these collected editions, as well as of the pocket edition of 1901–1905, was a source of greater gratification to his friends than to the veteran novelist himself.

Perhaps among the few official honours that came to Meredith he valued most that of President of the Society of Authors, to which he was elected on the death of Lord Tennyson in 1892. After all, the only people who can honour a great author are they who form the Republic of Letters, and the Society of Authors, representative as it is both of the leaders and the rank and file, provides in its presidency the most distinguished position any author can be invited to occupy by the suffrages of his fellow-workers. There was not a moment's hesitation as to who should be asked to accept the office after Death had laid his hand on Tennyson.

Six years later Meredith attained his seventieth year and the occasion was marked by the presentation of a congratulatory address signed by a number of men and women of foremost distinction in the arts. The text and signatories are here given.

To George Meredith

Some comrades in letters who have long valued your work send you a cordial greeting upon your 70th birthday.

You have attained the first rank in literature after many years of inadequate recognition. From first to last you have been true to yourself and have always aimed at the highest mark. We are rejoiced to know that merits once perceived by only a few are now appreciated by a wide and steadily growing circle. We wish you many years of life, during which you may continue to do good work, cheered by the consciousness of good work already achieved, and encouraged by the certainty of a hearty welcome from many sympathetic readers.

(*Signed*)

J. M. Barrie.
Walter Besant.
Augustine Birrell.
James Bryce.
Austin Dobson.
Conan Doyle.
R. B. Haldane.
Thomas Hardy.
Frederic Harrison.
"John Oliver Hobbes."
Henry James.
R. C. Jebb.

Edmund Gosse.	Andrew Lang.
W. E. H. Lecky.	Anne Thackeray Ritchie.
M. London.	Henry Sidgwick.
F. W. Maitland.	Leslie Stephen.
Alice Meynell.	Algernon Charles Swinburne.
John Morley.	Mary A. Ward.
F. W. H. Myers.	G. F. Watts.
J. Payn.	Theodore Watts-Dunton.
Frederick Pollock.	Wolseley.

Ten years later, in the midst of all the extraordinary attentions which his eightieth birthday evoked from press and public, it must have been with something of sorrow, mingled with thankfulness for the prolongation of his own quiet eventide of life, that the recipient of that warmly human and unaffected document—in this comparing favourably with the later address—noted that Death had taken toll of no less than eleven out of the thirty who signed the letter, his personal friend, Leslie Stephen, among them. In acknowledging the letter, Meredith had written:

The recognition that I have always worked honestly to my best, coming from the men and women of highest distinction, touches me deeply. Pray let it be known to them how much they encourage and support me.

Nearly twenty years ago a writer who was not without personal knowledge of the novelist said: 'His second wife lies buried in the churchyard close by his cottage, and he speaks with quiet content of soon going to rest beside her.' He had only said good-bye to the 'fifties' then, and he was to live into the 'eighties' through many years of serene and honoured leisure. Indeed he seems to have grown younger in spirit as he passed with failing steps through the later years of life, for we find him delivering himself thus to an 'interviewer':

I suppose I should regard myself as growing old—I am seventy-four. But I do not feel to be growing old either in heart or mind. I still look on life with a young man's eye. I have always hoped I should not grow old as some do—with a palsied intellect, living backwards, regarding other people as anachronisms, because they themselves have lived on into other times, and left their sympathies behind them with their years.

Certainly those who saw him at seventy-four saw him as fresh-spirited as he had ever been, saving the unhappy affliction which had stricken his legs and made him, once so given to long walks and athletic exercise, a prisoner of the chair. In the summer of that year—1902—he even volunteered an invitation to the members of the Whitefriars Club, a literary fraternity of which he had been elected an honorary member the year before, to pay him a visit at Box Hill, where in July 1900 the same literary group had sought and received the privilege of making a pilgrimage to the home of the master. His readiness to entertain such visitors as these—no mere curiosity-hunters, but genuine admirers of the man and artist—seems to have increased in inverse ratio as his strength diminished. Doubtless the feeling that work was done for ever, that the remaining years were a contented waiting for the call, and that, after all, there was some genuine pleasure to come thus into personal touch with men and women whom he had long before fascinated with his written word, threw open the door of Box Hill with a hearty *Salve!*

In the summer following he had a serious illness and many alarmist reports found their way into the papers, always ready to herald the passing of any great contemporary figure and not unwilling to work off their carefully-prepared biographies—already in type, perhaps! One of the morning papers—doubtless the same authority that assured its readers that the second Mrs. Meredith 'lived only a few months after her marriage'—asserted that our illustrious countryman had 'periods of partial consciousness,' so critical was his condition. This drew from the invalid a telegram to the sober *Westminster,* so characteristic that it must be given here:

Dorking report of me incorrect; though why my name should be blown about, whether I am well or ill, I do not know. The difficulty with me is to obtain unconsciousness; but sleep, on the whole, comes fairly. I am going on well enough. This for friends who will have been distressed by the report.

His illness was certainly serious, but it is clear from this that the citadel of his mind was unassailed, as it had ever been, through all the assaults of illness on the body. Humour still dwelt there, and the characteristic phrases came unforced for the telegram, which is at once familiar and literary. Not many months later, his old friend Mr. Theodore Watts-Dunton had the pleasure of addressing him in the following beautiful sonnet, printed in the *Saturday Review* on the occasion of his seventy-sixth birthday:

This time, dear friend—this time my birthday greeting
Comes heavy of funeral tears—I think of you,
And say, ''Tis evening with him—that is true—
But evening bright as noon, if faster fleeting;
Still he is spared—while Spring and Winter, meeting,

After the portrait by G. F. Watts, R.A.] [*Photo: Hollyer.*

GEORGE MEREDITH.

[*To face p.* 40.

Clasp hands around the roots 'neath frozen dew—
To see the 'Joy of Earth' break forth anew,
And hear it on the hillside warbling, bleating.'
Love's remnant melts and melts; but, if our days
Are swifter than a weaver's shuttle, still,
Still Winter has a sun—a sun whose rays
Can set the young lamb dancing on the hill,
And set the daisy, in the woodland ways,
Dreaming of her who brings the daffodil.

The allusion to 'funeral tears' arose from the recent death of Francis Hindes Groome, the famous gypsologist and intimate friend of the poet.

It was about this time that an old rumour as to his being engaged upon his autobiography was revived. There has never been any show of evidence for such a project, much though every admirer of the novelist would have welcomed an autobiographic work. It is likely enough that after seventy the mood of reminiscence had come upon him, but the strength had failed, and all that we have of original work from him in the thirteen years following 'The Amazing Marriage,' save an occasional poem, are 'Odes in Contribution to the Song of French History' and 'A Reading of Life.'

In July 1905 he was appointed by King Edward to the Order of Merit, a distinction which had the whole-hearted approval of the entire literary world, recognising in this a worthier official cachet than the common bourgeoise baronetcy or knighthood. In the October following, the aged novelist met with a serious accident in a very simple way. He was being assisted by his manservant to a chair in his sitting-room when he slipped and broke two bones of his left leg. It was discovered, happily, that the fracture was a simple and not a compound one, and this, together with the calmness and cheerfulness of the patient, whose spirits never drooped under the pain of the fracture or the restraint of the mending, promised a speedy recovery. In consequence of the accident, however—though it is doubtful if he could have gone in any case—he was unable to attend the King's Investiture at Buckingham Palace, so the Registrar and Secretary of the Central Chancery of the Orders of Knighthood proceeded to Leatherhead, by his Majesty's commands, and conveyed to the illustrious prisoner of Box Hill the insignia and Warrant of the Order of Merit.

By Christmas, although not entirely free from the result of his accident, he was about again in his bath-chair making his old familiar journeys along the friendly roads about the hill. The press had now come to take so keen an interest in the patriarch of

English letters that his every movement and utterance had been for some time recorded with the detail which is usually reserved for the Prime Minister or a noted murderer or bigamist. It is odd, for instance, to find the *Daily Mail* growing lyrical, after this fashion, of George Meredith's Christmas Day, 1905:

Bathed in delightful sunshine and favoured with a beautifully mild and clear atmosphere, the neighbourhood of Box Hill yesterday resembled a Riviera resort.

It was doubtless these spring-like conditions that tempted Mr. George Meredith, only just convalescent from his broken leg, to spend over an hour of his Christmas in the famous fir-bordered lane which climbs a tortuous way from the Mickleham Road to the summit of the hill. Warmly clad in a rich fur-lined overcoat and a grey cap, the veteran novelist was gently wheeled by feminine hands in an extended bath-chair, and his face betokened joy at being abroad in his sacred Surrey.

'In such a matchless morning both my man and my donkey are spending their Christmas out of harness,' he explained genially to a *Daily Mail* correspondent, who inquired after his welfare, 'and so, perforce, I had to be wheeled.' As to his general condition the eminent novelist mentioned that during the past few days he had found sleep an unwilling guest. This fact was chiefly due to his injured limb, which had mended less rapidly than was expected, and which still gave him considerable pain, especially at night.

As he himself pointed out, Mr. Meredith will be seventy-eight next year, and the effects of a serious accident at his time of life cannot be easily shaken off. 'But I am glad to be out of doors this Christmas,' he added, drawing himself up in his travelling chair to view the Surrey landscape. 'I should have been sorry to miss a day like this.'

Mr. Meredith continues to take a keen interest in outside affairs, such as the tragic events in Russia and the forthcoming general election.

The last paragraph touches a feature of Meredith's later years that is noteworthy. There was no public question, national or international, engaging the mind of the country, but George Meredith was asked to express his opinion upon it. An episode of the Boer War, the future of Liberalism, the Marriage Question, Anglo-French relationships, the decadence of Athletics, any topic of the day that gave an interviewer an excuse for a run down to Box Hill and a knock at the door of Flint Cottage, and behold the results next morning in a prominent part of his paper. The literary recluse had in his old age become a sort of intellectual umpire to whom both sides applied for counsel, though he did not hesitate to label himself

Radical. The very multiplicity and magnitude of many of the interests which had stirred the public in his later years, to say nothing of the splendid issues of his middle life, leave one wondering how he could ever have so misjudged his age as when, with evident approval, he makes Adrian in 'Richard Feverel' quote Diaper Sandoe, beginning:

'An Age of petty tit for tat,
An Age of busy gabble:
An Age that's like a brewer's vat,
Fermenting for the rabble!'

and ending:

'From this unrest, lo, early wreck'd,
A Future staggers crazy,
Ophelia of the Ages, deck'd
With woeful weed and daisy!'

These verses he wrote in the full tide of his lusty manhood, when he was something of a rebel to his age; but from many utterances of his later years he had unmistakably come to the conclusion that his own age compared well with any that had preceded it, not merely in its magnificent issues, but in its wide and broadening humanism. It is indeed difficult to think that he ever, save for some passing moment, thought of his own time as an age of petty tit for tat, when none was more profoundly interested than he in the great events of European History, to say nothing of the American Civil War, and the freeing of Italy, which last has been so grandly celebrated by him in one of his masterpieces of fiction. Indeed, among the very latest efforts of his pen, written in his eightieth year, were the verses 'For the Centenary of Garibaldi,' appearing exactly forty years after his 'Vittoria.' Thus his latest note is in praise of liberty and also in praise of nature—the two passions of his life—for to the issue of the *Country House,* July 1908, a periodical published by his son's firm, one of the latest products of his pen, a characteristic nature poem, was contributed. For the Milton tercentenary in December of the same year he also wrote some noble lines, still holding aloft the banner of Liberty.

His eightieth birthday was an event of such historic importance that I purpose dealing with it at some length in the next chapter of this work. He was spared to see another birthday, and though he held to life by the merest thread, his mind remained as vigorous as of yore. A chill contracted at the end of the second week in May proved too much for his enfeebled frame, and in the early hours of Tuesday, May 18, 1909, he died of heart failure. He was practically conscious to the last: he had not died 'from the head downwards.' He 'died facing the dawn and his end came in perfect peace,' says one newspaper account. 'He welcomed death as serenely as he had encountered life, and met the end with calm courage.' The decision of the Dean and Chapter against his interment in Westminster was generally regretted and not a little resented, though, truly, George Meredith has left so great a monument of his own creation that the Abbey may be left for the enshrining of lesser men. His remains were cremated at Woking and the ashes were interred at Dorking on Saturday, May 22, the funeral being strictly private. On the same day a memorial service was held in Westminster Abbey.

Having now outlined the leading features of a long and noble life spent in single devotion to great literature, and for that reason lacking in event and movement, the present chapter may be concluded with some words of Meredith's own, in which the aim of his literary life is briefly stated. The passage occurs in a letter to a contributor to the *Harvard Monthly*, who some years ago wrote in that review a study of the novelist which gave him pleasure. Meredith wrote:

> When at the conclusion of your article on my works you say that a certain change in public taste, should it come about, will be to some extent due to me, you hand me the flowering wreath I covet. For I think that all right use of life and the one secret of life, is to pave ways for the firmer footing of those who succeed us; and as to my works I know them faulty, think them of worth only where they point and aid to that end.

In a note on his eightieth birthday the *Spectator* put the historic view of his life into happy phrase when it said: 'Mr. Meredith is the last of a great generation, for, intensely modern as he is in so many ways, he began to publish verse before Wordsworth died, and as a novelist he was the contemporary of Dickens, Thackeray, and George Eliot. His life spanned, indeed, the whole Victorian age. And what an age was that! Inspired by Tennyson and Browning's songs, and depicted by the brush of Watts, its men, its causes, its discoveries, and its revolutions are unsurpassed in history.' In this great generation, George Meredith is assuredly one of the great figures.

III

THE EIGHTIETH BIRTHDAY

A health, a ringing health, unto the king
  Of all our hearts to-day! But what proud song
  Should follow on the thought, nor do him wrong?
Except the sea were harp, each mirthful string
The lovely lightning of the nights of Spring,
  And Dawn the lonely listener, glad and grave
  With colours of the sea-shell and the wave
In brightening eye and cheek, there is none to sing

Drink to him, as men upon an Alpine peak
  Brim one immortal cup of crimson wine,
    And into it drop one pure cold crust of snow,
Then hold it up, too rapturously to speak,
  And drink—to the mountains, line on glittering line,
    Surging away into the sunset-glow.

ALFRED NOYES, in the *Daily Graphic*, February 12, 1908.

IN recent literary annals there have been two events, each unique in its way, and both significant of the remarkable interest taken by the public of our time in the lives of its leading men of letters. The display of public sympathy with Mr. Rudyard Kipling, when he lay at death's door in New York in 1899, was something quite without parallel in the personal history of our literature. The cable tingled with messages and bulletins concerning the young author, as though he had been a reigning monarch and the fate of a dynasty hung upon his life. Mr. Kipling, by some subtle stroke of genius—for it is futile to deny the tremendous power of the man—had got hold of the mob not less than, by sheer craftsmanship, he had captured the literati, and thus an immense public, coterminous with the Anglo-Saxon peoples, was avid of news about one who had stirred it deeply. Hence, perhaps, that wonderful outburst of international sympathy when he was pasing through a crisis of ill-health.

Nine years later the celebration of the eightieth birthday of George Meredith was the occasion of even greater journalistic commotion. But we must not suppose that none of the authors of past times were the subjects of similar solicitude to their contemporaries, though incidents equal in significance to those just described are lacking in our literary chronicles. The publicity of the modern press is a new factor that accounts for much in this connection. We know that so keen was the public interest in the development of Richardson's sluggish romances that when the part of 'Pamela' containing the account of that tearful creature's wedding was published and circulated throughout England there were villages where the church bells were rung as in celebration of an actual marriage. We know that Scott, Byron, Dickens, Thackeray, Tennyson, and many another famous author received in his lifetime public homage of the most remarkable kind; but, all that notwithstanding, we may justly describe the celebration of Meredith's eightieth birthday as one of the most notable events in the history of modern letters.

Acting under a common impulse, every journalist and man of letters in a position to render homage to the most illustrious of living authors took occasion to do so, with the result that what was doubtless in each case a spontaneous act of hero-worship assumed in the mass—so widespread was the celebration—the appearance of having been 'engineered,' to quote the phrase of a cynical critic. It was truly 'the event of the week'; every daily newspaper, from the *Times* down to the least provincial evening sheet, consecrated a leading article to the 'grand old man of letters,' who masqueraded for that day in many a quaint and unusual guise, according to the intimacy of the writers with his work and personality. The news columns of the papers were brisk for days with paragraphs and Meredithiana; the press agencies telegraphed and cabled tiny 'interviews' with the novelist to the ends of earth; a motley crowd of reporters haunted the precincts of Box Hill, as keen as if a murder had been committed at Flint Cottage; the least incident of the birthday of the veteran was telegraphed to head-quarters; photographers had been busy 'snapping' him when he came forth in his donkey-chaise; pages of illustrations—most of them deplorable—were given in the papers; there were numerous 'special memoirs,' in which every writer contrived to quote that old familiar stanza from 'Love in the Valley,' beginning:

> Happy, happy hour when the white star hovers

and the equally hackneyed lines:

> Into the breast that gives the rose
> Shall I with shuddering fall?

Never, in sooth, was so much written and printed in the space of one week about any man who had not achieved the distinction of committing a singularly revolting crime. So magnificent a tribute to mere literary genius and intellectual greatness made one feel that the British press had taken leave of its senses. But we all rejoiced, and some of us who had been at pains to study the works and follow the life-story of the master derived a good deal of amusement from reading many a 'special memoir' that had obviously been written by a journalist whose entire knowledge of his subject was at second-hand. The splendid muddle of indiscriminate praise, the absurdly invidious epithets—such as 'King of Novelists,' 'Last of the Great Victorians,' 'Our One Great Novelist'—flung abroad with the prodigal hand of the journalist who would to-morrow be 'writing up' the latest jewel robbery or the art of Phyllis Dare, was all very embarrassing; but it was a pleasant change.

Of course, there was much solid and valuable appreciation amidst all this froth; all the great London journals of good repute discharging their parts with becoming dignity, and many of the provincial dailies touching the occasion to profitable issue. In short, the press did its duty well by one who in his day had done his duty by the press. If there were any person lingering in darkness as to who and what this George Meredith was, and that person read any newspaper on the 13th of February, 1908, he could not well avoid making some acquaintance with the name at least.

My purpose in this chapter is to compile from the forbidding mass of these newspaper criticisms and reports an account of the eightieth birthday that may possess some permanent value in the future as a record of a notable event in the career of a great author whose earlier and middle life had been as barren of public interest as his old age was embarrassed therewith. From the soberer chronicles of such journals as the *Times*, the *Telegraph*, the *Standard* and the *Pall Mall Gazette* it is possible, I think, to construct a useful record of the event.

In several of the newspaper chronicles of the scene at Flint Cottage on the birthday there is to be noted a similarity of phrase, indicating that while the correspondent wrote as though he alone of the representatives of the press had been admitted to the presence of the novelist, he must have been one of a select few who had received that privilege together; a modification of the American custom which enables a celebrity to be 'interviewed' by a squad of reporters from different papers at the same time. Hence some of the *obiter dicta* which fell from the white-haired philosopher on his birthday are worded somewhat differently in the various accounts;

but the *Telegraph* correspondent, whose long article is in every way excellent and has a richer literary flavour than most of the others, seems to have caught the spirit of the occasion in a way that makes his description worthy of quotation here. After a spirited personal sketch of Meredith, he goes on to say:

Mr. Meredith commenced the day with his customary drive, although he had to shorten it in order to be back to receive the friends who had come down to Box Hill to congratulate him. 'Picnic' was again in the shafts, with Cole at his head, and in the absence of his daughter, Mrs. Sturgis, who is out of England at present, Lady Edward Cecil, who is the daughter of his old friend Admiral Maxse, accompanied him. Shortly before noon Mr. Clement Shorter, with his wife, Dora Siegerson Shorter, and Mr. Edward Clodd, came down from London to present the memorial of congratulation on his eightieth birthday, signed by dozens of his old friends and colleagues, not only in poetry and fiction, but in politics, art, the drama and journalism, in England and America. The presentation, needless to say, was a purely informal function, and Mr. Shorter, after a stay of half-an-hour, left with his friends, declaring that he had not for some years seen Mr. Meredith in better health.

A little later I was received by Mr. Meredith. He was sitting in an arm-chair between the fire and a window that looks on to his beloved downs, surrounded by his books. On every table were dozens of telegrams of felicitation. In each corner of the room and out in the little hall were bouquets of flowers. A wonderful old leonine man, with a face like Hermes grown old, the long, white hair lying loosely about his ears, with a rug round his knees and his hand to his ear, Mr. Meredith was already engaged in conversation, now listening, now speaking. In repose the face took on an almost feminine grace of expression. When he spoke the deep, rich, resonant voice, and the animation of the countenance, seemed to give added stature to the aged frame. Much of what he said had reference to the many friends who had wired to him on his birthday, and was of a purely personal nature. In everything that concerned himself and the homage being paid to him on his birthday Mr. Meredith was characteristically modest.

'I have been climbing the stairs for eighty years,' he exclaimed, 'and I have done with the pulpit.'[1]

Pointing to the sheaves of telegrams lying about him, he had previously exclaimed, 'They make me think too much of myself. It is a kind of harvest that I wish could have been reaped by a younger man.'

But stung, as one might say, by references to affairs of a more

[1] Another version of this epigrammatic phrase is as follows: 'When a man has climbed the steps of eighty years he should not use them as a pulpit.'

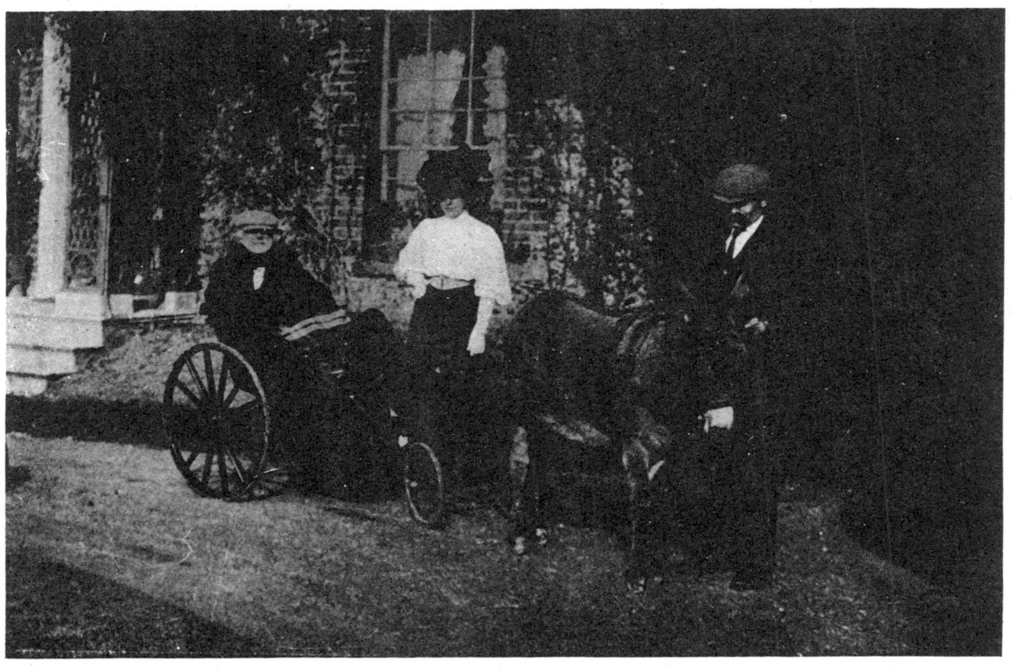

[*Copyright, Illustrations Bureau.*

GEORGE MEREDITH RETURNING FROM HIS DRIVE ON HIS EIGHTIETH BIRTHD.

[*To face p.* 48.

public and less private nature, he launched out with enthusiasm and vigour.

'Suffragists!' said the great [illegible] of [illegible]. 'I have always [illegible] [illegible] [illegible] [illegible] like to see the [illegible] [illegible]. Certainly they should [illegible] [illegible] [illegible]. I am not in agreement with [illegible] their [illegible] strategy. These [illegible] [illegible] way. There is [illegible] [illegible] and women. After [illegible] [illegible] England [illegible] time of pleasure and [illegible] [illegible] to be pleasurable [illegible] [illegible] laughed at soldiering [illegible] uniforms. We need [illegible] onic wars. It is [illegible] friend Mr. Haldane [illegible] further.

'I believe that [illegible] soldiers; the spirit [illegible]

'Life is a long [illegible] bative. Otherwise [illegible] combative; but let [illegible]

'As for me, I do [illegible] you to write much about [illegible] found me sitting [illegible] sentiments.'

One would have [illegible] great novelist [illegible] him, and the habitual [illegible] interrupted with [illegible]. Shortly before [illegible] Zangwill and Mr. [illegible] Seaman, presented [illegible] address of congratulation [illegible] which he is president [illegible] London, Mr. Zangwill [illegible] (Mr. and Mrs. William [illegible] with another literary [illegible]

The subject of [illegible] of the unfinished novel [illegible] the novelist outlined [illegible] Benefactor of the [illegible] the efforts of a man who wanted to improve [illegible] ever getting into quarrels [illegible] not marry the lady he desired [illegible]

'Why don't you write it yourself?' he was asked [illegible] broke into that genial torrential laugh of his that [illegible] every public and less private nature, he launched out with characteristic vigour.

'Suffragists!' said the great delineator of the female character. 'I have always stood up for the intellectual capacities of women. I like to see the combative spirit in them. It is as it should be. Certainly they should be given the use of intellectual weapons. But I am not in agreement with anything that is bad taste and bad strategy. These rowdy scenes! No! Not that. That is not the way. There is a better. I like to see the combative spirit in men and women. After the Napoleonic wars England settled down to a time of pleasure and ease—too much pleasure, too much contentment to be pleasurable and to forget. An Amyclean case! England laughed at soldiering. It was ashamed of seeing its officers in their uniforms. We need to be reminded of these times about the Napoleonic wars. It is an ozone. The Territorial Army! I know my dear friend Mr. Haldane. He is a strong man. But for myself I go further.

'I believe that universal service should be adopted—a nation of soldiers; the spirit of the soldier in every walk of life.

'Life is a long and continuous struggle. It is necessarily combative. Otherwise we cease. Let the struggle go on. Let us be combative; but let us also be kind.

'As for me, I do not wish to talk about myself. I do not want you to write much about me. Say that I am well, and that you found me sitting in my chair, delivering myself freely of very Radical sentiments.'

One would have liked to have put many other 'points' to the great novelist. . . . But the novelist had a trying afternoon before him, and the habitual calm of his home life was being continuously interrupted with the arrival of telegrams, flowers and visitors. Shortly before four o'clock Mr. Anthony Hope Hawkins, Mr. Israel Zangwill and Mr. Herbert Trench, the author of 'Apollo and the Seaman,' presented themselves at the house to hand the novelist the address of congratulation on behalf of the Society of Authors, of which he is president. Mr. Hawkins and Mr. Trench came from London, Mr. Zangwill from Dorchester. They were asked to tea (Mr. and Mrs. William Meredith also being present), and charmed with another literary causerie.

The subject of Mr. Meredith's poetry, of poetry generally, and of the unfinished novel ('The Journalist') again cropped up, and the novelist outlined a new story, to be called, perhaps, 'The Benefactor of the Race,' or some such title, which should deal with the efforts of a man who wanted to improve humanity and was for ever getting into quarrels in endeavouring to do so, and who could not marry the lady he desired to in fulfilment of his System, etcetera.

'Why don't you write it yourself?' he was asked. Mr. Meredith broke into that genial torrential laugh of his that electrifies every one who hears him, and which some one has said is the merry brother of his serious voice. 'They would want me to cut out the excrescences,' he replied. 'No, no! Somebody else must write it. I give them the idea.'

'Let us have it; we want it, "excrescences" and all,' it was persisted. But the great novelist only laughed.

Did his hearers fully realise—did they really believe—that the grand old man before them has far exceeded the allotted Three Score Years and Ten? With the afternoon sun now streaming through the window on to the leonine head and locks, colouring it like to 'a shock of corn that cometh in his season,' were they not illusioned into the vision of the Prophet of Sweet Sanity as he was forty years ago?

For myself, I felt that my own brief interview with him was of that fleeting but wonderful description that only the true spirit of genius—the very presence of the Spirit of Comedy—could have stamped so indelibly, and yet so intangibly, on the mind of a visitor. It was, after all, only an impression.

It was the impression not of a great man, upon whose heart Time had laid its hand to 'deaden its vibrations,' but one to whom the prospect of the near close of life had set up a renewed youthfulness, a renewed ardour, and a renewed response to that Mother Earth and her Children, which he has loved and written about so well.

This is indeed a very pleasant and acceptable picture which the adroit pen of the *Telegraph* correspondent sketches for us. All who saw the novelist and wrote about him on his eightieth birthday express their surprise at his apparent vigour and his cheerfulness, despite his infirmity. A paragraph that concludes the *Daily News'* account of the day indicates how sincere was the admiration which the sage of Box Hill had awakened in the heart of many an unknown student of his works:

All day there has been a silent pilgrimage to Box Hill which Mr. Meredith has not seen or heard of—the pilgrimage of those who know the man only through the leaves of his books. They have come by road and rail; they have stood for a minute or two outside Flint Cottage, registering their tributes in their hearts, and have passed on.

The memorial which was presented to Meredith was mounted on vellum and beautifully bound in dark blue crushed Levant morocco, the monogram 'G. M.' being worked in each corner in gold, while the inside lining was of cream-watered silk. The address read as follows:

To

GEORGE MEREDITH, O.M.

Upon his eightieth birthday.

Dear Mr. Meredith,—Many of your fellow-countrymen will join in felicitating you upon this your eightieth birthday. We desire on our own behalf to thank you for the splendid work in prose and poetry that we owe to your pen—to say how much we rejoice in the growing recognition of this work—and to thank you for the example you have set to the world of lofty ideals embodied not only in books but in life. Most heartily do we wish for you a continuance of health and happiness.

The names of Meredith's old friends and literary colleagues, A. C. Swinburne, Mr. Thomas Hardy, Viscount Morley and Mr. Frederick Greenwood, were inscribed upon the vellum, and there were some 250 other signatures, of which a classified list was given in the *Times*. Among these were so many men and women of the highest distinction that the few who did not exactly add to the weight of the memorial were lost, so to say, in the general brilliance of the throng. One could have wished, however, that the phrasing of the address had taken on a somewhat more literary flavour.

His own countrymen were not alone in their felicitations of the great writer. Although several distinguished Americans had signed the general memorial when in England, a separate address reached him from the United States, the text of which and the signatories were as follow:

To GEORGE MEREDITH

The subscribers, American men and women of letters, desire to unite with their English brethren in offering to you upon your eightieth birthday cordial good wishes for your health and happiness. We are grateful to you for the works with which you have enriched our common literature, and we trust that the remainder of your life may be brightened by the knowledge of the admiration and respect of a multitude of friends, unknown as well as known, in both hemispheres.

Henry Adams, John Burroughs, G. W. Cable, John W. Cunliffe, Richard Watson Gilder, Thomas Wentworth Higginson, Oliver Wendell Holmes, Julia Ward Howe, W. D. Howells, Charles Eliot Norton, Agnes Repplier, Charles G. D. Roberts, F. H. Sykes, Edward Clarence Stedman.

The birthday was an eminently suitable opportunity for certain of the novelist's fellow-writers to pen some appreciative words on the doyen of their craft, and the *Daily News* gathered a little sheaf of such pleasant mementoes of the occasion, some of which were distinctly interesting. Mr. Thomas Hardy excused himself thus:

I have known Mr. Meredith for so long a time—forty years within a few months—and his personality is such a living one to me, that I cannot reach a sufficiently detached point of view to write a critical estimate of his great place in the world of letters.

Madam Sarah Grand wrote:

George Meredith and age! The two ideas are incompatible. You cannot reckon him in years. He has come and he will stay for all time. The great virile voice we know so well and love has spoken truth, and truth is everlasting.

Sir Gilbert Parker thus:

It is given to few men to approach their latter days with an accumulating reputation; but this has been granted to George Meredith. . . . He has been an inspiration to some of the best intellects of our time, and he must remain a fountain from which pure waters may be drawn for generations of lovers of literature yet to come. He has never been a fashion; he is a master and is permanent.

Of peculiar interest was the letter from Mr. William Michael Rossetti, who had known Meredith at the outset of his career and reviewed the 'Poems' of 1851 at the time of their appearance. Thus fifty-seven years after, wrote Mr. Rossetti about the same poet:

With some shame I acknowledge that I am not very well acquainted with the writings of George Meredith, whether prose or poetry; and I regret to say this all the more because at one period of my life I was rather closely associated with him personally. I was, however, one of the early admirers of his first volume of poems, 1851, and I then expressed my admiration in print. I know some of his other writings—especially 'Shagpat,' 'Modern Love,' 'The Egoist,' and 'The Tragic Comedians.'

It has become almost a commonplace by now to recognise—as I do—the supremacy of Meredith in certain qualities: brilliancy, insight, pungency, incisiveness. His discernment is extreme, perhaps excessive, in that it leads him into the constant exhibition of his own 'cleverness,' and makes him rather the student and the dissector of men and women than their sympathetic delineator, and intricates his style into scintillations of epigram, the terms of which are more patent to himself than they always are to his reader.

Mr. Edmund Gosse, who had signed both the memorial of 1908 and the congratulatory letter of 1898, touched upon the loss of old friends which the years had brought to the aged author, and went on to say:

Inevitably, the long advance of years brings solitude, and Mr. Meredith does not fail to suffer from the glory of his old age. But I rejoice to think that few could suffer less. The friends fall off, but in an imagination so vivid and so fresh as his they follow by his side; he is attended by them still in a cloud. And if the early companionships withdraw, as withdraw they must, Mr. Meredith has that vitality of genius, that attractive glow of sympathy, which brings new generations around him. He burns in our midst, a steady flame, and more and more the young, with their moth-like spirits, wheel around in adoration and surround him with a palpitating bodyguard. He may be eighty years old to-day, to calculate by the foolishness of mathematics, but in reality he is just so old as, and no older than, the youngest heart that has responded to his fine appeal.

But perhaps there was no personal tribute so interesting or so quaintly original in expression as that contributed by Mr. Theodore Watts-Dunton to the *Daily Graphic*. At the outset it must have pleased Meredith himself to find, amid all the ecstatics of the press, that Mr. Watts-Dunton had the sobriety to remind the journalistic world that there was a poet of some eminence, named Algernon Charles Swinburne, who was still alive. Meredith, we may be sure, would have been eager to admit that in European literature his was a name that came second to that of Swinburne. Mr. Watts-Dunton gives a humorous but yet a cogent reason for a certain feeling of dubiety that came upon him as he signed the memorial:

Honoured as I must surely feel at being invited to sign such an address, I have to make the confession that I signed it with some dubiety—a dubiety which I should not have felt had the memorial been addressed to an Oriental poet—to a poet of Cathay—to that prince of sonneteers, for instance, the Poet Pin, who, to the great joy of Rossetti, visited London in 1866, and afterwards favoured his guests with his diary. Had the address been to 'the Poet-Laureate and assistant head clerk in the Board of Affairs at Peking, bearing by the honorary licence the button of the third official degree,' who, while lunching at Woolwich Arsenal, 'composed a couple of sonnets in pentameter during the repast,' I should not, I repeat, have had the least hesitation about the good breeding of signing it. But England and the land of Kubla Khan are two very different poetic domains. In the Flowery Land the recipient of such an address would have perfectly understood its import. . . . Throughout Cathay it would have been perfectly understood what such an address meant. For among the Celestials the mere passage of years over any man's head is in itself an honour—in itself a crown of glory. The interest felt in an octogenarian is that of unadulterated reverence. . . . It is pleasant to think that on the Parnassus of the Poet Pin, when one bard meets another, the greatest compliment he can show to his fellow is to improvise a sonnet, a rapturous sonnet, exclaiming, 'Brother Bard, how delightfully old you are looking this morning, older than ever! May your beautiful songs of to-day be worthy of the beautiful ripeness of your years!' . . . The obtuseness of the Anglo-Saxon mind is declared by the way in which English and Americans talk of the old age of a man of genius like Meredith. If it is the fact that no man in health really feels himself to be old, what shall be said about a man of genius like George Meredith, who —as I told one of those who is presenting the memorial—is younger than the youngest now invading his august privacy? The great artist is ever young. . . . All honour then to the youngest writer of our time, except one who is younger still.

Yet the younger writer was the first to pass away; the turf was still loose on Swinburne's grave when the earth was heaped over the coffin of his friend in Dorking churchyard.

No useful purpose would be served by preserving a selection of the anonymous 'leading articles' which appeared in the daily and weekly journals on the eightieth birthday. Most of them met the need of the fleeting hour and were without claim to longer life. But the first paragraph of the *Times* 'leader' stated in well-balanced phrase the proper aspect of the occasion, and indeed the whole article was worthy of the best traditions of a journal which, from the first, had been an ardent and reasonable exponent of the genius of George Meredith:

Mr. George Meredith is eighty to-day, but still with all the youthfulness of heart and the joy in life and vigorous action which have been the burden of his works for well-nigh sixty years. Those—an ever-growing band—who on the threshold of manhood first felt the thrill of his brave words and drank in the glorious meaning which he gave to earth and all its creatures, will rejoice that he is still with us to learn something of our sense of thankfulness. The debt was for many years felt by only a few; for long it was but falteringly expressed; but to-day we all acclaim in him and Mr. Swinburne the two chief glories of our age, the Titans still surviving from that splendid mid-Victorian era of Tennyson and Browning, of Dickens, Thackeray, and William Morris. Moreover, cheap editions of his novels and books written about him bear witness that it is not merely a name that we honour, but that his words, in spite of their difficulty, have made their way home to this English people whom he loves.

One little incident of the day is deserving of a record. Mr. W. Clark Russell, the celebrated writer of sea-stories, sent the following letter to the *Times:*

I was not asked to sign the birthday memorial to our great novelist. I should have been proud to do so. Perhaps I did better. I wrote to him a few lines of respectful congratulation. I beg to send you his letter, which I will ask you to return. Mr. Meredith's reference to quantity is a comment upon what I said—that this is the age of words. The publishers ask for words—not ideas, description, characterisation, and the like, but words, words, words; and they get them. I should be sorry not to make one in the vast crowd whose thoughts and affections were with Mr. George Meredith to-day.

Meredith's letter in reply to that sent him by Mr. Clark Russell was as follows:

Dear Sir,—A kind word to me in my ripe age from a brother of the pen, whose descriptions of bluewater scenes have often given me pleasure, is very welcome. Quantity in production certainly we have, but I notice here and there good stuff, and promise among some of the younger men. Besides, you know the seventh wave. There must be a gathering of the waters before a big surge is thrown on shore. And my observation tells me that the minor work of the present day is altogether superior to that of the mid-Victorian time—and before it. The hour is usually unjust to its own.

Yours very truly,
GEORGE MEREDITH.

BOX HILL, DORKING, *Jan.* 24, 1908.

One is glad that Mr. Clark Russell was omitted from those invited to sign the memorial—to which less eminent names than his were attached—since his own letter to the master-novelist drew forth so charming a reply. Old age is seldom the time of generous sympathy with the new generation, and Mr. Watts-Dunton's denial that genius ever experiences old age is supported by this characteristic Meredithian letter. On his eightieth birthday the heart of the great writer was obviously with the younger men, those who in their careers were where he had been nearly sixty years before them. And as the hearts of these were with the master who has influenced so many of them—not always, alas! to the happiest issues, though the fault is not with him—Meredith must have experienced on the 12th of February, 1908, the pleasantest of all the emotions described by his disciple Stevenson when he wrote, 'I like to fancy that a grateful spirit gives as good as it gets.' Doubtless he had long got over that fear of becoming a celebrity which, twenty years before, in writing to a correspondent, he had entertained.

In every sense, then, was this eightieth birthday memorable: it was worth living for. When we think of the posthumous adulation of great writers, from Dante to Burns, whose lives might have been so sweetened by a mere tincture of the praise and admiration lavished over their ashes, we must conclude that George Meredith was singularly happy in the afterglow of fame which warmed and lighted the long and tranquil evening of his life.

Hater of sham and seeker of true worth,
Wise with your nine-and-seventy summer-tides,
With eye undimmed and youth that still abides
To love the dawn and things of tender birth,
Be with us still to make that mighty mirth
That shook the ass-ear'd crown and cracked his sides
And loosed your Shibli from the Hall of Brides,
To shave all Shagpat follies from the earth.

Still may the loved South-wester fan your face,
The lark and nightingale delight you still,
And corals braid your holly and your yew;
We need your help who found this earth a place
Fit for the training of God's sovereign will,
And taught us by your life the love you knew.

CANON RAWNSLEY, in the *Daily News*.

IV

PERSONAL CHARACTERISTICS

SOME authors are, in their own personalities, greater than their books; others there are whose written works are greater than themselves. It is easier to state this than to illustrate it, since we may assume that the best of a man usually gets into his books. Perhaps the explanation is that certain personalities are so opulent that not all their writings can exhaust them, while others of lesser mould contrive to rise above their ordinary selves under the afflatus of creative literature. The work of George Meredith is so eminent, so vast in its horizon, so profound in imagination, insight, philosophy, in form so rare and individual, that it might be thought a depreciation of its value to place him among the first-named class of authors; yet that is his place. Whatever the future will do or leave undone in respect to his poetry and romance, it cannot ignore the man. His personality, had he never written 'Modern Love' or 'The Egoist,' would still awaken the interest of posterity as that of a great man who moved with firm, sure and stately tread through a great epoch of British history. He will live because he was George Meredith. Dr. Johnson lives by virtue of his splendid insistent personality and not by reason of anything he wrote. How much the greater, then, should Meredith's hold on posterity be, since he has given to it a mass of literature which criticism will never allow it to ignore?

Any attempt at character-portraiture of such a man must have to meet unusual difficulties. His personality is mountainous, and who has ever read a description of Mont Blanc or of Vesuvius that would serve for all the seasons or all its phases of one day, one hour even? So is it with Meredith; no study by one hand, however gifted, can paint the man for us. We need many sketches from different points of view by many different artists, that from the mass we may disengage a general, or a composite, portrait which will serve to each of us as the nearest we can come by of the actual man. Such is the purpose of the present chapter. Fortunately the portfolio whence one may choose these sketches is amply stocked, and in the end we can hardly fail to gather some serviceable notion of his remarkable personality.

There is about all we have read of George Meredith something of that cleansing breeze that blows across the white cliffs of England's 'surge vexed shore.' His very name has the power to image in our mind a wind-blown figure, erect on a gusty day, forward reaching, wholesome. Mr. Barrie, who touched off Professor Blackie in a telling phrase—'Blackie carries his breeze with him,'—might have done as much by Meredith had he known him in his lusty manhood. But I feel that Meredith, too, must have carried his breeze with him. For though he was timid and sensitive as a boy, 'at eighteen,' as he once remarked in conversation, he 'determined not to be afraid again,' and we can well believe he speedily schooled himself to that courageous outlook on life which his clear and steady eye, no less than his written word, suggested. Mr. Justin McCarthy in his 'Reminiscences' has given us a graphic sketch of him in middle life:

I think the first impression which George Meredith made on me was that of extraordinary and exuberant vitality. When I saw him for the first time, he had left his younger days a long way behind him, and yet he had the appearance and the movements of one endowed with a youth that could not fade; energy was in every movement; vital power spoke in every gesture. He loved bodily exercises of all kinds; he delighted to take long brisk walks—'spins,' as he called them—along the highways and the byways of the neighbourhood; and he loved to wander through the woods, and to lie in the grass, and I have no doubt he would have enjoyed climbing the trees. He seemed to have in him much of the temperament of the fawn: he seemed to have sprung from the very bosom of Nature herself.

His talk was wonderful, and, perhaps, not the least wonderful thing about it was that it seemed so very like his writing. Now it was Richard Feverel who talked to you, and now Adrian Harley, and then Beauchamp—not that he ever repeated any of the recorded sayings of these men, but that he talked as one could imagine any of them capable of talking on any suggested subject. . . . He was a man of strong likings and dislikings, in letters and in art; his very prejudices had a charm in them because they gave him such admirable opportunities for scattering new and bewildering fancies around his subject.

Like Matthew Arnold, he had a strong sympathy with the Celtic spirit in poetry and in literature generally; but nobody could be less like Matthew Arnold in his manner and in his expression. He could rattle off humorous verse, especially of the comic or satirical order, at will; and I dare say he felt a certain gratification now and then in utterly bewildering his hearers. . . .

Meredith, as I have said, loved all manner of bodily exercises; and, indeed, it amazed me when I first used to visit him, to see a man, no longer young, indulge in such feats of strength and agility. It delighted him to play with great iron weights, and to throw heavy clubs into the air and catch them as they fell, and twirl them round his head as if they had been light bamboo canes. I remember wondering, indeed, sometimes, whether such exercises and such feats of strength were not taxing too far the physical powers of a man who had already passed his prime, and whether over-taxed nature would not some day show that she had been taxed too far. But, at the same time, the general impression which George Meredith gave one was that of the fawn-like creature, the child of Nature who must always be young, as Nature herself is always young. I do not think I ever met a man in whom the physical and the mental forces were such absolute rivals and equals as they seemed to be in George Meredith at the time when I first had the happiness of knowing him.

Meredith had already entered his sixtieth year when Miss Flora Shaw's (Lady Lugard) brilliant study of his work was published in the *New Princeton Review* of March, 1887. This is one of the earliest glimpses of the man—the walker and talker—that appeared in the press:

At the foot of Box Hill, in one of the lovely valleys of the Surrey downs, a cottage stands, half hidden by encircling trees. A little space of flowers spreads before it, an old yew hedge screens the garden from curious passing eyes. Within, for the privileged who pass the gate, an apple-bordered walk leads up the slope to a terrace underneath some hanging woods, where Mr. Meredith has built himself a study. Here, toward sunset, the fortunate may meet Mr. Meredith himself coming down between the apple-trees. He is serviceably shod, he usually carries a stout stick in his hand, the head—iron-grey now—is held erect, the eyes kindle to light beneath thoughtfully knit brows, the mouth, for those who know him, seems ever ready to break into sonorous speech. He has come down prepared to walk and talk. These walks and talks are among the great enjoyments of his friends, and as round the neighbourhood of Rydal Water in an older generation, so round the neighbourhood of Box Hill now must hang many a lasting association of intellectual pleasure. It was my good fortune to find myself in his company on the turf back of Box Hill one brilliant, breezy morning. Our eyes travelled over the valley where park woods, russet with the changing leaf, clustered beneath the box and juniper of surrounding slopes, and threw into vivid contrast the yews of

Norbury, which are asserted to have held their place for upwards of two thousand years. West of the valley the greens and orange rolled skyward, bearing a tower solitary upon its highest point. Southward, the Weald of Sussex rolled under light October mists to Brighton downs, and legendary glimpses of the sea. And while we mounted, with the horizon widening beneath us, we spoke of the share the intellect has had in human development. Our talk was of the nature of Socratic dialogue, slight and tentative remark on one side serving only to mark the paragraphs of full discourse upon the other.

Following Miss Shaw's slight glimpse of Meredith in his outdoor garb, shod for walking and pouring out brilliant talk on every topic, comes the first, and surely the most charmingly written, account of a visit to him at Box Hill. Signed 'W. M. F.' (William Morton Fullerton), the article appeared in the *Boston Advertiser* (U.S.A.), December 17, 1888. Mr. Fullerton's most admirable essay, following Miss Shaw's brilliant critical review, introduced Meredith to America twenty years ago. It gives a picture of the novelist in the early years of what we may call his period of world-fame, and a pleasanter picture we could not wish to have:

It was an almost Indian summer afternoon which I had taken for this journey, and as we walked down the country road the trees, I noted, had turned colour on the side of the hill. Mr. Meredith met me with his nervous little dachshund at the station. He had his stout walking-stick and his light grey English walking-suit to match, with just a dash of red at the neck, and he was evidently in the midst of the afternoon jaunt which it is his wont to take. Iron-grey hair with ripples in it came out from under his round cloth hat the same material as his coat. A bright eye, a straight nose, a compact, lithe, broad-shouldered figure, a person with fine breeziness in all his movements, and a strong step upon the earth without a touch of uncertainty in it, and all confidence that the ground was sufficient to support him, as he measured it with buoyant stride, and chatted on to the swinging of his cane—that was Mr. Meredith as I first saw him. The first impression was certainly striking. The last impression when, at the fire, head uncovered, he sat in a dark coat after dinner, was not less striking. But until I saw him thus I did not discover how exceedingly handsome as well as animated his face is.

I was immediately impressed with the splendidly healthy tone and superabundant life of the man. There was vigour and sanity at his way of looking at things, and no sentimentalism. One need not talk with Mr. Meredith to discover his hatred of sham and sentimentality; this is the prominent key-note of his work. But I had it anew impressed upon me in a fashion that carried with it at the time all the force of irrefutable demonstration. It is always a nice process, that of moving off from the shore out of the shallows into the full stream of conversation; and in that delicate operation I, when it came to my turn, had done a good deal of futile splashing in the water, making some wholly obvious and commonplace reference to the changing leaves, and the sombreness of their colour in comparison with that of our American foliage, thanks to the maples; and I finished with a platitude about the English hues being more pleasing, as they were less obtrusive and suggestive of the dying year, which meant the flickering of one more series of candles on another Christmas night that would never return. But how axiomatically unfortunate!

Mr. Meredith had no place—and justly too, for I had said what I had said with only a half-hearted sincerity, as some authors pad their books to fill up—Mr. Meredith had no place for sentimentality of that sort. What was there in the thought of the passing years that should be sad? It was life, more life and fuller, for which men should be ever seeking, to be sure. But life was not to be had by whining into a past that had turned tail and fled. Rather, men must look up bravely, planted on the honest present, to the problems of the pressing future, never content to live in a fool's paradise, but always courting activity, and making use of moments as they came, so bravely, so well, that such moments would be quite transformed into the energy of character, not left behind to haunt you like sloughed chrysalises of vanished butterfly hopes and impulses. How eloquently he did crush my poor thought, which was altogether unworthy to be sponsor for such eloquence. I recalled his saying: 'You may start a sermon from stones to hit the stars.' It was refreshing and encouraging. I felt again the full tonic breeze that I had always found blowing through the pages of Mr. Meredith's books.

But Mr. Meredith's fancy ran with that little dog, who was undoubtedly very clever and very ugly. It torments me that I cannot now remember his name. I am sure it was not 'Geist.' He was into everything, like a curious woman with nerves. It was amusing to hear his master talk to him. On the road as we neared the house we met a vagrant fellow, such as we in America would call a 'tramp,' who begged and expostulated by voice and gestures (it could not be said of one who pressed his suit with 'My good sirs' as close upon his heels as he did, that he was a *non sequitur*) that we should give him something. He was on the road to the poor-house, but certainly would not die a natural death on the way; and Mr. Meredith's reply was good political economy: 'I never give to a man I don't know—I never give to a man I don't know.' And so at last the fellow passed us by. The episode was annoying, and there was nothing to do but to whistle up the dog and amuse ourselves with him.

Since in the present chapter we are confined as closely as practicable to matters that concern the individuality of the man, even apart from his home-life, to which our attention will turn in due course, I pass over for the moment Mr. Fullerton's reminiscence of a Box Hill evening, after which he goes on to say:

A room that has once heard Mr. Meredith's voice dominating, among other friends, the talk, and out of which he has gone, is like a Greek theatre that has sounded to the echoes of Æschylean and Aristophanic drama and has lost the voice of the protagonist and the chorus all at the same time. For Mr. Meredith is both of these at once, without stretch of figure. It is not an uncommon thing to say of an author that he talks just as he writes. But that is literally true of Mr. Meredith. If one will recall one of the familiar pages of those novels it will be evident what I mean, and how very remarkable it is that this statement may be made. But more even than this must be said, because the light sparkle on the foam of his chaffing, and the broad gleam of the blue sky reflected on the clear expanse of his deeper utterances, when the conversation is serious and calm, the iterant insistence of an idea by gesture or repeated look, all these qualities can be seen only face to face with this master of eloquent and spontaneous expression. These are the appropriate atmosphere, as it were, through which we look at the most wonderful Gothic structure in England, Mr. Meredith's style. Mr. Meredith's eloquence is simply exhaustless. His memory is as capacious as De Quincey's, and his fund of ideas is almost beyond measure splendid. Drolleries, witticisms, humours, he has, and a wonderful, unique trick of god-like chaffing; but these are nothing in comparison with his fancy and play of ideas. . . . As I look back now upon that evening, one of the chief impressions which I find is left upon me was Mr. Meredith's almost amphitheatrean powers, the prodigality of his genius, like the prodigality of light. Ben Jonson has said of certain obscure writers of his time that 'their writings need sunshine.' Mr. Meredith's writings frequently need sunshine; but his speech never. This is what the personal contact gives, what the voice, the mouth, the eye, and the laugh may assure us—sunshine.

Of all the writers who have been privileged to see Meredith in his own home I find that only one has noted his love of children, and that was Miss Anne Wakeman Lathrop, an American lady, who published an account of her visit to Box Hill in the *Idler* of November, 1893, from which I take this very attractive picture:

Mr. Meredith is fond of children. You remember his vigorous sketches of boys in 'The Ordeal of Richard Feverel,' and are ready to believe that your entertaining host loves child-life, as he has already admitted that he loves the society of young people. With the appearance of after-dinner coffee in the drawing-room, arrives a group of little girls and boys, with their mother. These small visitors range from eight to twelve years of age. Instantly you observe the gentlest side of Mr. Meredith's nature. He adapts himself to the children, with a mingling of man of the world polish, and frank, almost boyish, ingenuousness. He does not tower above them, but treats them like miniature men and women, and always with attentive gallantry. The effect on the children is to make them the more polite and earnest than is usual with childhood. A proposition is made by the little folk to be shown some wonderful red-berried bushes in an adjoining park, to which the Merediths have access. Alas! the key to the gate cannot be found. A disappointed maiden remarks tentatively, 'We cannot go without the key.' On this, Mr. Meredith makes a dance step, throws up his long, slim hands above his head, snaps his fingers as a sort of castanet prelude, and improvises a brief comic ditty, of which the refrain runs, 'But not without the key, says she, oh! not without the key.' This so amuses the children that the song has to be repeated, while their rippling laughter fills all the room. Nor does Mr. Meredith forget to substitute some equally enjoyable treat for his young guests, to make up for their temporary disappointment.

Reverting to Mr. McCarthy's description of Meredith's violent exercises, it is to be feared there is reason for supposing that these bodily exertions in which he indulged, out of sheer high spirits, at a time of life when most men have to observe physical caution, may have had something to do with the permanent collapse of his physique in later years. But even when he could no longer take his walks abroad with swinging stride, he remained 'an outdoor man' and continued, by means of his donkey-chaise, to keep ever in touch with the roads and hedgerows he had loved so well. A writer in *Fry's Magazine*, of November, 1904, made an interesting little study of the novelist from this point of view, in the course of which he wrote:

It is fitting that the greatest living novelist in this vigorous and healthy period should be a prophet of the open air. No one has preached the gospel of the open air more eloquently or more successfully. To the young men who gathered about him like a band of disciples in his early manhood—among whom were Mr. John Morley—the great novelist always gave one sovran piece of advice: '*Live in the open, and study nature.*' Much of the philosophy of our age derived its inspiration from this advice.

And George Meredith is not the worshipper of nature who

believes only in star-gazing or in mooning walks. Solitude is good, and lonely, deep-thinking walks are also good; but games and sports—vigorous and joyful games in the open air are good too. He is a great believer in sport. Everybody, he holds, should learn to delight in outdoor games, and should learn to find pleasure in bodily exercise. Sport is not, according to him, an end in itself, but an important part of Nature's wonderful scheme. You cannot leave it with impunity.

'I have always loved the face of Nature,' he told the writer, 'the dreariest, when a sky was over it—and consented to her spirit. She loves us no better than her other productions, but she signifies clearly that intelligence can make her subservient to our needs: and one proof of that is the joy in a healthy body, causing an increased lucidity of the mind. Therefore, exercise of the body is good, and sport of all kinds to be encouraged. Sport will lead of necessity to observation of Nature. Let us be in the open air as much as possible, engaged in healthy rivalry with our fellows, or with the instructive, elusive game we are after.'

This study of Meredith the outdoor man, from which I have quoted, led a writer in the *Daily Chronicle*—Mr. R. M. Leonard—to pursue the subject further, by examining the works of the novelist to ascertain how far he had expressed his own passion for outdoor life in his fiction. He found, of course, that there is scarcely one of the novels which does not show evidence of sporting tastes and knowledge:

No other novelist is so at home on the cricket-field. Some time ago Mr. E. B. V. Christian called attention to the fact that Dickens is hopelessly at sea in his description of the match between Muggleton and Dingley Dell, while even the author of 'Tom Brown's School Days' fails on examination. (Both Dickens and Meredith were born in Hampshire, 'the cradle of the game.') Mr. Meredith's triumph is to be found in 'Evan Harrington' in his description of the match between Fallowfield and Beckley, when the Countess de Saldar, a daughter of the great Mel, asks to be instructed 'in your creeket.' In 'Diana of the Crossways' we become spectators of a game at Copsley, and Diana admits, reddening, that Redworth looks well in flannels.

Nothing in 'The Amazing Marriage' remains more in the memory than the amazing honeymoon, in which the Earl of Fleetwood drove his bride straight from the church to a prize-fight. Skepsey's creator evidently has a weakness for the little man's enthusiasm for 'the manly art.' 'You are of opinion,' Skepsey is asked (in 'One of Our Conquerors'), 'that the practice of scientific pugilism offers us compensation for the broken bridge of a nose?' 'In an increase of manly self-esteem,' comes the reply. 'I do, sir, yes.' Skepsey is valorous, too, with singlesticks. Mr. Meredith enjoys rustic encounters—perhaps, as in 'Sandra Belloni,' that he may show the great and amazing magnanimity that is in beer.

In 'Rhoda Fleming' he describes a visit to Epsom, and, in the cosy Pilot Inn, Steeve, the Fairly huntsman, expatiates on fox-hunting:

'To kill 'em in cold blood's beast murder, so it is. What do we do? We give 'em a fair field—a fair field and no favour! We let 'em trust to the instincts Nature, she's given 'em; and don't the old woman know best? If they get away, they win the day. All's open and honest, and above board. Kill your rats and kill your rabbits, but leave foxes to your betters. Foxes are gentlemen. You don't understand? Be hanged if they ain't! I like the old fox, and I don't like to see him murdered and exterminated, but die the death of a gentleman, at the hands of gentlemen——' 'And ladies,' sneered the farmer.

Above all, as evidence of his personal taste, we have his frequent allusions to the Alps in his novels. Surely after his own sweet Surrey he has loved no other part of earth quite so well as the glorious mountain land. He 'cannot seem to do without it,' said Dr. E. Dick in a lengthy article on 'The Alps in George Meredith's Novels,' published in the *Alpine Post* at the beginning of 1908, from which the following passages may be taken:

From 'Richard Feverel' down to 'The Amazing Marriage,' the Alps come in at some point or other of the story, frequently with mighty effects on its further development. With him, they are a sort of Presence, like Providence, or Fate, now a souvenir, now a longing, always beautiful, great, friendly.

Meredith has expressed his idea of the proper use and function of the Alps in 'The Adventures of Harry Richmond'; 'Carry your fever to the Alps, you of minds diseased: not to sit down in sight of them ruminating, for bodily ease and comfort will trick the soul and set you measuring our lean humanity against yonder sublime and infinite; but mount, rack the limbs, wrestle it out among the peaks; taste danger, sweat, earn rest: learn to discover ungrudgingly that haggard fatigue is the fair vision you have run to earth, and that rest is your uttermost reward.'

'The Amazing Marriage' is Mr. Meredith's last novel; it is the one in which the Alps loom larger than in any other. Mr. Meredith's language is always rich and of a beautiful transparency when it is about his loved mountains—his readers know how veiled it can be on other topics—their inspiration must have sounded unambiguous, clear peals of purest metals.

It is this love of open-air exercise, this almost obstreperous rejoicing in physical strength, this truly British admiration of the animal man—incongruously present with the intensest intellectuality—that made Meredith so modern and an essential Briton, despite his Celtic temperament. He was intellectually the last eminent man of his time to whom the epithet 'British' might be applied; yet in his outdoor character, he was British and of his time. This is but one of the many perplexities he presents, and it has escaped the attention of most of his critics, with one exception, to which reference will be made when we come to consider his literary characteristics, as this is a matter that concerns more the artist than the man.

But there is a gentler side to the open-air Meredith than that of the lusty pedestrian and rambler of the woodland ways. Like his own 'Melampus' we see him the lover of all the lowly creatures and the simple flowers of the wayside. A charming picture of him as a naturalist is given by the late William Sharp in his chapter on 'The Country of George Meredith,' written for the *Pall Mall Magazine* in 1904, and reprinted in 'Literary Geography':

I doubt if any living writer is an intimate with nature-life, with what we mean by 'country-life.' Certainly none can so flash manifold aspect into sudden revelation. Not even Richard Jeffries knew nature more intimately, though he gave his whole thought to what with Mr. Meredith is but a beautiful and ever-varying background. I recollect Grant Allen, himself as keen and accomplished a student of nature as England could show, speaking of this singular intimacy in one who had no pretension to be a man of science. And that recalls to me a delightful afternoon illustrative of what has just been said. Some twelve or fourteen years ago, when Grant Allen (whom I did not then know) was residing at The Nook, Dorking, I happened to be on a few days' visit to Mr. Meredith at his cottage-home near Burford Bridge, a few miles away. On the Sunday morning I walked over the field-ways to Dorking, and found Grant Allen at home. It was a pleasant meeting. We had friends in common, were colleagues on the staff of two London literary 'weeklies,' and I had recently enjoyed favourably reviewing a new book by this prolific and always interesting and delightful writer. So, with these 'credentials,' enhanced by the fact that I came as a guest of his friend Mr. Meredith, I found a cordial welcome, and began there and then with that most winsome personality a friendship which I have always accounted one of the best things that literary life has brought me. After luncheon, Grant Allen said he would accompany me back to Box Hill; as, apart from the pleasure of seeing Mr. Meredith, he particularly wanted to ask him about some disputed point in natural history (a botanical point of some kind, in connection, I think, with that lovely spring flower, 'Love-in-a-Mist'—for which Mr. Meredith has a special affection, and had and still has fine slips of it in his garden) which he had not been able to observe satisfactorily for himself. I frankly expressed my surprise that a specialist such as my host should wish to consult any other than a colleague on a matter of intimate knowledge and observation; but was assured that there were 'not half-a-dozen men living to whom I would go in preference to Meredith on a point of this kind. He knows the intimate facts of countryside life as very few of us do after the most specific training. I don't know whether he could describe that greenfinch in the wild cherry yonder in the terms of an ornithologist and botanist—in fact, I'm pretty sure he couldn't. But you may rest assured there is no ornithologist living who knows more about the finch of real life than George Meredith does—its appearance, male and female, its song, its habits, its dates of coming and going, the places where it builds, how its nest is made, how many eggs it lays and what-like they are, what it feeds on, what its song is like before and after mating, and when and where it may best be heard, and so forth. As for the wild cherry . . . perhaps he doesn't know much about it technically (very likely he does, I may add! . . . it's never safe with "our wily friend" to take for granted that he doesn't know more about *any* subject than any one else does!) . . . but if any one could say when the first blossoms will appear and how long they will last, how many petals each blossom has, what variations in colour and what kind of smell they have, then it's he and no other better. And as for *how* he would describe that cherry-tree . . . well, you've read "Richard Feverel" and "Love in the Valley," and that should tell you everything!'

Next to the aggressive vitality of Meredith in the prime of his life, which was the subject of marvel to every one who met him before his physical powers had suffered defeat, was his talk: a gift that years and invalidism would seem but to have enhanced. Among the great talkers he must ever have place; for if we may believe all we have been told by his intimates his conversation was always as distinguished as his writing; indeed more brilliant, the play of the eye and face illuminating the quick-flying and ever-changing metaphor in a way impossible to the written word. It is curious to note how every one that has written of Meredith's talk compares his conversation to his writing. We have seen Mr. Justin McCarthy do so in his 'Reminiscences,' and Mr. Fullerton, also. In a privately printed journal Mr. John A. Steuart, author of 'The Minister of State,' writes thus of a meeting with the master:

As he writes, so he talks, brilliantly. Not the tongue alone, but the whole countenance speaks. The eager spiritualised face seems to express the flashing thought, before it can form itself on the tongue, and the eyes, light blue-grey and clear as a child's, look up smilingly and shrewdly. They are worth studying, for they are the keenest eyes of this generation. They look through man and especially through woman (since Shakespeare's there have been no women comparable to Meredith's) as if humanity, the darkest thing on earth, were diaphanous; but they look humorously, sympathetically, and therein lies the secret of their power. The voice is as characteristic as the eye. Carlyle long ago remarked how wonderfully physiognomic is the voice. Hostlers flocked just to hear Burns speak; and one feels there must have been enchantment in the mere tones of Shakespeare. Mr. Meredith's voice is the exquisite instrument of a teeming brain and a great heart. He speaks and your attention is instant. As Johnson said of Burke, if one were by chance to go at the same time with Mr. Meredith 'under a shed to shun a shower,' one would say, 'here is an extraordinary man.' I hope it will not be thought impertinent if I add that the head has the Shakespearian bumps, the bump of sheer intellect no less than the bump of creative imagination—a rarer combination than some good people imagine. Thought transfused by imagination, or imagination transfused by thought—put it as you like—must always be the basis of great, that is to say lasting, work in literature. Goethe said of Byron that when he tried to think, he was a child. If Byron was a child how many noted novelists are babes! In thought, as in imagination, Mr. Meredith is a giant. One feels his strength even in his casual conversation.

The present writer, probably under the flattering delusion that he was the first to describe the likeness between the conversation of Meredith and the colloquies of his fiction, wrote to this effect in a personal sketch of the novelist which was published when its subject was in his seventy-fourth year:

Judging the author of 'Modern Love' from the standpoint of the ordinary reader, I find his poetry presenting a clearness and grace of diction, a simple beauty of words, to which his prose manner is so often foreign. The late Ashcroft Noble has observed with much truth that 'his speaking voice is an affair of organisation; his singing voice is the result of careful training.' In other words, Meredith the novelist tells his story in a manner natural to the man, but in his poetry the conscious artist, under the restraints of his medium, has to rid himself of the perplexing involutions of metaphorical thought which are natural to him and characterise his work in prose.

To hear the great novelist talk is to realise the justice of Noble's criticism, though it may come as a surprise to many to be told that his spoken words resemble curiously his written phrases, with their unexpected epithets and surprising association of thoughts, so that what he has written of his peerless Diana may aptly be said of himself: 'This was like her, and that was like her, and here and there a phrase gave him the very play of her mouth, the flash of her eyes.' Indeed, to have listened to the talk of George Meredith for but one brief hour is to have abandoned entirely the thought that nobody was ever so brilliant in speech as he makes many of his characters to be. We often hear the criticism, 'Nobody in real life sparkles like that.' When this is advanced against the truth of Meredith's personages, let the answer be that the author himself is as brilliant in conversation as any of his heroes or heroines.

Mr. Meredith's face, probably the least familiar among those of our famous authors, as he has ever been shy of the camera, is of that fresh colour which comes from a life spent in the open air. The features are very sharply defined, the mouth large, the forehead wide and square, but the eyes, of a wonderful dark grey, gleaming with tenderness and humour, form the most striking feature. His hair, which is still abundant, is silver white on head and beard, and by contrast with the high, clear colour of his face, produces that fragile look which one had noted long ago in his best-known portrait. Yet, when he speaks, the full volume of his voice, resonant, soft, rich in tone, carries no suggestion of physical weakness. His words are spoken with a relish of the lips not unlike the satisfied smack of the connoisseur sampling a rare vintage. His laugh, too, is lusty and heartsome.

He talks with a touch of that old-fashioned manner which sounds to-day almost like affectation, but none could be freer from a suspicion of such than George Meredith, for the lasting impression which the man leaves on one's mind is that the child's heart has never changed in him, and that he is as lacking in self-consciousness as a boy of twelve. After we have searched laboriously for that unknown, elusive something which constitutes genius, we shall find that it is nothing more than the power to keep in our old age the spirit of our youth, and to retain to the end the great gift of wonder. Assuredly George Meredith has done those things. In his seventy-fourth year we find him as buoyant of spirit, as full of wonder as he can ever have been. Tested further by the severest of tests to which we can put the personality of a man, he comes out triumphant—he can laugh at his own jokes and infect you with his laughter!

'The aim of my work,' he says, 'has been to make John Bull understand himself.'

'And do you think John Bull has the gift of humour?'

'I find but little humour in Anglo-Saxons.'

'You will admit, however, that John has good humour?'

'Ah, you naughty man, you are playing with my words!' and

the hearty laugh rings out again and the grey eyes gleam with delight.

He then goes on to tell a story of how, together with the late W. G. Wills and another friend, he went into the Garrick Club during his early days in London; the three determined for one evening to import a little fun into the dull atmosphere of what was then supposed to be the most amusing club in town. They joked and laughed with so much gusto that at length their fellow-members, drowsing over the *Times*, the *Saturday*, and *Punch*, were whipped into life, and one old fogey declared that he had passed quite a lively evening. This little recollection illustrates well the Celtic character of the man: 'But,' he will say with a merry twinkle of his eyes, and dropping voice, 'I am only half Irish, the other half being Welsh. My mother was an Irishwoman; my father came from Wales.' If it be true that all great men owe most to their mothers, then surely the better part of George Meredith is Irish; and certainly he is all Celt.

From a privately-printed record of a meeting with Meredith in the summer of 1900, written by Mr. Coulson Kernahan, I take this vivid impression of his personal characteristics:

Mr. Meredith's portraits (I had well-nigh written the word in the singular, for the one man every aspect of whose face we all wish to know is the one man who has most set his face against letting his face be known to us) give one no idea of his personality. They are likenesses, it is true. The noble shaping and carriage of the head, the commanding presence, the stern beauty of the features, the touch of hauteur, and even of what I may paradoxically call 'gentle severity,' are all to be seen in his portraits. But, compared with Mr. Meredith himself, the best of his portraits is but a beautiful mask.

Never before have I seen a face at once so strong and so sensitive. It seemed carved in cold steel, but nerved like the nostrils of a racehorse. In moments of repose it struck me as strangely melancholy. Then something was said that brought back the smile—a smile that seemed caused by a light upon the face rather than by the play of the features. The lines which, an instant ago, had been set and severe were now all tenderness--stern tenderness, it is true, as of one who had infinite compassion for humanity, but in whose pity no element of weak laxity could enter. Judgment, self-control, and humour, these are the characteristics which to me seemed most plainly writ upon the face of George Meredith. Humour I take to be the very essence of his being—humour that is touched with gaiety, and humour which deepens into sadness; for though the lips of Humour may smile at the sight of human folly, yet when we look into her eyes we see them sad at the thought of human sorrow. The quality of one's humour is so often a matter of nationality, that some remarks which Mr. Meredith made in my hearing should be recorded. One of our party was, like myself, an Irishman, and when he was introduced to our host, Mr. Meredith exclaimed: 'He bears a name which is surely Irish, and I see, too, that he hath the true Irish eye. Am I mistaken in supposing you to be an Irishman?'

'I am so fortunate,' replied the Irishman.

'You put it well! You put it well!' was Mr. Meredith's comment. 'And I, too, am fortunate in being of Irish blood.'

'Is that so?' replied the Irishman. 'We are proud, indeed, to know that we may claim Mr. George Meredith as a countryman.'

'Ah, but you can only claim the half of me,' was our host's laughing rejoinder. 'My mother was an Irishman, but my father was Welsh.'

Mr. Haldane MacFall did a highly-finished pen-portrait of Meredith for the *Canadian Magazine* of May, 1904. We might call it Meredith's laughing portrait, as laughter is the note of it:

George Meredith faces life a mighty laugher, glad to be alive, glad to walk the fresh, sweet earth, glad to breathe the south-west winds that blow health into the lungs of the race of which he is so proud a being, glad of this splendid wayfaring amid the adventures that make up the journey of life. And what a mighty laugh it is! Right from the deep chest—setting one chuckling at the very merriment of it. The finely-chiselled nose, with the sharp, pugnacious tilt at the end, betrays eagerness for the duel of wit, eagerness to know all, eagerness to be at the very front of life. The leaping energy that lurks behind the dreamy eyelids finds interest in everything. Meredith sees life too exquisitely to be afraid of being accused of regarding small things. His pointed grey beard gives the suggestion to the strong, clean-shaped head of an admiral of our day. He is of the type of the man of action. To hear Meredith talk of the coming youngsters of to-day, asking his keen questions about their personal attainments, their appearance, their promise, his nervous face all alert to know, is to be in the feverish company of an eager youth.

His feet no longer pace the long walk up the grassy slope of the majestic hill that sweeps from his doors upwards into the clouds, but the keen brain is as passionately inquisitive of the world as in the years when his youth took him blithely walking along its ways. There is in the bearing of the man a distinction, a splendour of manners, a perfection of the carriage of the body, as of a great man saying and doing the simple thing with an air that realises the word aristocrat in human shape more vividly than in any living man. He gives a more profound sense of greatness than any one I have ever met.

Mr. Henry W. Nevinson is a journalist of that select class to which Meredith would certainly have belonged had he continued his connection with the craft: a wandering scholar, ever afield for new interests to describe, let the times make for peace or war. In his peaceful and bookish days in England he has had the privilege of several meetings with Meredith at Box Hill, and no one has portrayed the features of the novelist with such cameo clearness of detail as Mr. Nevinson in certain contributions to the press. To the *Book Monthly* of March, 1904, he contributed an article, reprinted in 'Books and Personalities,' from which I take these graphic and noteworthy passages:

It is essentially a Greek head. It might have been modelled upon those statues of mature and powerful manhood which, in the museums of the world, are now vaguely labelled 'a poet' or 'an orator.' If it is a poet's head, it is a Greek poet's. There is no trace of the weakness, the conscious melancholy, or petulant emotionalism which, unhappily, have been too often associated with the modern idea of poetic appearance. It is the head of a man who, like Sophocles, could have commanded a fleet as easily as write a tragedy, and as well. When we see it, we cease to wonder that the Athenians should have expected their great poet to do both as a matter of course. It is the symbol of a tempered intellect, in which there is no flaw of softness or languor—the intellect of a man, and even of a man of action.

There are men of letters who wear a shut-up, indoor look. Their faces are like the windows of a sick chamber; we dimly divine the invalid and delicately-curtained soul within. But the very look of Meredith tells of the open sky, where the sun marches, and the winds pipe, and the thunderclouds mass their battalions.

His is the head of an orator, too—a Greek orator, like Pericles, whose words the historian might have enregistered as an everlasting possession. The great mouth opens almost four-square. It is an Attic mask, a magician's cave. A spirit seems to be speaking, not with it, but through it, and on a broad scale of sound comes the voice, full, unhesitating, and distinct to the last letter, like the voice of one who has spoken much among the waves. We feel that, as Mendelssohn said of Goethe, he should shout like a hundred warriors. Perhaps his slowly increasing deafness had made his utterance even more remarkable when last I saw him; but in earlier days also his words fell rather in superb monologue than in conversation.

There is no effort about the language; the great sentences are thrown out with lavish opulence—the careless opulence of nature at her kindest. There is no pausing for figures, wit, or epigrams; they come of themselves, as water follows water from a spring. It is the style of his books. There is the same concentration, the same

MEREDITH IN HIS DONKEY-CHAISE, WITH HIS DOG 'SANDY.'

[*To face p.* 72.

fulness, and the same irony; but it is all simpler because more unstudied; and whereas some pages of the books have become difficult and dark, the effect of the spoken word when first it is uttered is wholly illumination and delight.

Mr. T. P. O'Connor's thumb-nail sketch does not help greatly but is interesting for its reference to the portrait by the Duchess of Rutland, which, so far as I can ascertain, has never been published in any form:

He is a noticeable man wherever you may see him. Not very tall; not very robust in appearance—rather of the thin and wiry type of physique—with a certain thinness of face, you have to realise the beauties of his eyes before you understand how much of his genius is revealed by his exterior. The only likeness of him I ever saw which gave you a good idea of the wistfulness, the eeriness, and the uniqueness of the face and the expression was that done by the Marchioness of Granby—as she was, the Duchess of Rutland as she now is. The beautiful white hair; the short but beautiful beard; but, above all, that strange, wistful eerie expression of the whole face—all this is brought out with wonderful fidelity and, at the same time, imagination.

There is a vivid touch of actuality in this little pen-picture of Meredith written by M. Charles Legras, the French critic, for the *Journal des Débats* in 1900, and reprinted in 'Chez nos Contemporains d'Angleterre':

When we enter, Mr. Meredith raises his tall figure from a roomy easy-chair that is stuffed with cushions, and supports himself feebly with two walking-sticks, his hands twitching and trembling: like Daudet he has been struck by ataxy. Over his forehead, square and very wide, falls a mass of hair cut *à la chien;* the profile of the face is sharply cut, the eyes of a dark grey, suffused at times by tenderness. His mouth is large and he speaks with much use of gesture. This silhouette of the great writer at the end of his career appears to me to harmonise with his works—long, unrestful, nervous, but still dignified of mien all the same.

The late Moncure D. Conway in his autobiography makes a brief mention of Meredith's conversation. 'In the few times that I have met him,' he writes, 'he was delightful, his imagination putting out his fancy to represent it in sparkling talk that could hardly prepare one for the depth and passion of his poetry. For I always love Meredith's poetry better than his novels, these impressing me as too often containing involved intimations of vital things in order to escape the deletions of Mrs. Grundy, to whom all proofs must be submitted.' A curious judgment on the novels, but a just comparison of the talk and the poetry.

Mr. W. T. Stead wrote a brilliant character sketch of him in the *Review of Reviews* for March, 1904, in which this passage occurs:

'People talk about me,' he said, 'as if I were an old man. I do not feel old in the least. On the contrary,' he went on, in his humorous, sardonic fashion, 'I do not believe in growing old, and I do not see any reason why we should ever die. I take as keen an interest in the movement of life as ever, I enter into the passions of youth, and I watch political affairs and intrigues of parties with the same keen interest as of old. I have seen the illusion of it all, but it does not dull the zest with which I enter into it all, and I hold more firmly than ever to my faith in the constant advancement of the race.

'My eyes are as good as ever they were, only for small print I need to use spectacles. It is only in my legs that I feel weaker. I can no longer walk, which is a great privation to me. I used to be a keen walker; I preferred walking to riding; it sent the blood coursing to the brain, and besides, when I walked, I could go through the woods and footpaths, which I could not have done if I had ridden—now I can only walk about my own garden. It is a question of nerves. If I touch anything, however slightly, I am afraid that I shall fall—that is my only loss, my walking days are over.'

Meredith was then seventy-six, and, as we have seen, his optimism was undimmed when, four years later, the interviewers were inducing the aged master of Flint Cottage to speak to them on the last subject he would have chosen—himself! It is worthy of note, by the way, that there seems to be no evidence of moodiness on the part of Meredith as a talker. About many great men stories are told which would suggest some degree of affectation and even boorishness. Tennyson and Carlyle are often accused of conduct to friends or chance acquaintances that was scarcely in keeping with good manners; Meredith never. There is just one anecdote, which I believe to be authentic, hinting at the possibility of his fountain of talk being sealed at times. A lady who had friends in Surrey who were on terms of some intimacy with the novelist was greatly charmed on one occasion when visiting there to find that Meredith was to be one of the guests at dinner. She prepared herself for a rich ingathering of his celebrated flowers of witty talk, but he was singularly silent throughout the visit, and the only Meredithian phrase the lady could carry away with her was his remark, when reaching across his neighbour for the salt, 'Excuse the pic-nic stretch.'

The first 'interviewer' who sought out the sage at Box Hill was, as we have noted, a literary journalist from Boston. Among the last were two Americans, and in both cases the results were interesting enough to bear some record here. Mr. Charles Frederic Goss does not give a date to his visit, but it was most likely in the summer of 1907, certainly before 1908, as his little account of 'A Visit to George Meredith' was published in the *Book News Monthly* of Philadelphia for March, 1908. After describing the oft-pictured scene of Flint Cottage and the famous châlet, he says:

It was with a sort of reverence that I entered this sequestered spot and rang the bell. An elderly housekeeper answered my summons, took my letter, and left me standing on the steps.

'Well, show him in,' I heard a loud voice say at last—not just as hospitably as I could wish; but a good deal more so than I had expected, from what I had been told of its owner's solitary life.

Entering a narrow hall I passed into one of the brightest and most cheerful sitting-rooms that I had ever seen. The morning sun was shining through the window and falling upon the back of the big, grey head of the old man, turning his hair to a silver aureole. Laying down his morning paper, my host extended his hand, and said, with a deaf man's raucous voice, 'I am always glad to see Americans; among them I have found some of my best and most abiding friends.' And then, without giving me an instant's chance to offer my apologies, he launched into a charming disquisition on the beauties of the region where he lived. From this as a starting-point he began swinging about a vast circle of observations on affairs and men, with the ease and power of a great ship coming around an immense curve.

Here are fragments of his talk for those who care to hear them second-hand:

'I do not produce any longer; or rather, only verse and not for print. I am getting too old. The imagination cools, you know. And then the veterans ought to leave the field to younger men!

'I take a hopeful view of the progress of civilisation, in general; but not so much of Great Britain, at least in the near future. She has been too greedy for power, empire, wealth. She has seized more than she can hold and administer.

'The trouble with society is—the lack of conversational power. Card-playing has stultified, or stupefied, its members.

'The literary outlook seems to me encouraging. There may not be any first-class writers; but the second and third classes are full. There is a great elevation of the rank and file of those who are making books. Multitudes of the very same people who, a few years ago, could not write at all, are writing now with skill, if not with art. In your own country there are many novelists who deserve all praise, among them, Gertrude Atherton, Edith Wharton, and my dear friend Weir Mitchell, a prince of men.

'President Roosevelt is a splendid fellow, but has made a mistake about spelling! He is too *absolutely* democratic. Democracy is good in politics, but bad in literature. The roots of literature are buried so deeply in the past that they cannot be rudely pulled up. He tries in vain to play the school-master. We need castigation, and the man with the birch-rod will come; but the President is not that man, nor his big stick that birch-rod! It must be a colossal man and a colossal stick.'

It requires a great deal of self-denial to leave such a man before you are ejected by the valet or the coachman! I went unaided, but most reluctantly.

There is a characteristic American 'snap' about this little episode that seems to endow Meredith himself with a touch of that Transatlantic quality; but, as the interview was evidently of the shortest and the veteran contrived to say so much and touch so many topics, the little account is valuable as indicating the ready flow of his ideas and the quick-rising flood of his talk at his advanced age.

The other American interviewer was a lady, Miss Catharine Welch, who visited him about his eightieth birthday and wrote a short sketch of her visit in the *Daily Chronicle*, from which the following passages are taken:

'Your being an American,' said he, 'gives you a sure road to my favour. I like Americans, and they have always liked me over there.

'What a man's living to be eighty means,' he went on, 'is, of course, that he is either greedily tenacious of life or else that he is so insignificant the fates have passed him by. . . . It is a misfortune to live to be eighty. A man's life ought to finish when he is five-and-sixty. He must stop working then, or else do work that is inferior. People will praise it at the time and write articles about it, but posterity will know better and see its weakness. You can't fool posterity. . . . No; when a man stops working, nature is finished with him, and when nature is finished with him he ought to go.'

At the conclusion of this gloomy little speech Mr. Meredith chuckled happily, and I realised that he was amusing himself by saying something he did not altogether mean.

He returned to the subject of America. 'I wish I had gone there when I was younger. I had many invitations. I suppose they would have given a lot of dinners to me, and,' he added quaintly, 'the mass of refection would have served to carry out my

[*By permission of the ' Daily Chronicle.*'

THE LAST SKETCH OF MEREDITH.

From a sketch by the well-known French artist, M. Noël Dorville, who visited England some months before the novelist's death and made a series of sketches of distinguished persons for an Entente Cordiale Album issued in France.

[*To face p.* 76.

theory and to remove me [illegible] sixty-five. [illegible] I should have had to [illegible] speeches. I never spoke [illegible] in my life. I can't talk [illegible] and my legs betray my [illegible] them from my chair, [illegible]

Mr. Meredith gave me [illegible] he found most [illegible]

Amongst the [illegible] They both write a [illegible] be mentioned also. [illegible] dith spoke of the [illegible] clear [illegible]

It appears that [illegible] some to him, though he [illegible] allows himself now [illegible] putting his name [illegible] books [illegible] very amusing stories [illegible] to secure his autograph [illegible]

He has sometimes [illegible] novels you must put [illegible] therefore to be impossible [illegible] the fourth or fifth chapter."

In the *Chronicle* [illegible] of Meredith from an [illegible] for its graphic [illegible] as an example of the [illegible] mannerisms of the [illegible] write about him. It was [illegible] one of the many critics who [illegible] but makes use of his [illegible] his, used in such [illegible] personality 'disengages' [illegible] the mass [illegible] about Meredith. The [illegible] like a bell,' nowhere but from Meredith.

You catch the [illegible] that he indoors, in his [illegible] chaise. The hair and [illegible] patriarch, and indeed [illegible] The face is furrowed, [illegible] the eyes. And then Mr. Meredith's voice—[illegible] and melody of youth. [illegible] ing and infective—it [illegible] at you, ringing like a bell. [illegible] Meredith talk is to recall Gladstone's rich voice. [illegible] points occur to one as [illegible] the two men?

Some notice must be taken of Meredith's [illegible] and here seems to be a fitting place since his [illegible] theory and to remove me before I was sixty-five. I suppose, too, I should have had to make speeches. I never spoke in public in my life. I can't talk standing up. The formality of it kills my ideas and my legs betray my brains. But if people will let me speak to them from my chair, I am very happy to talk—and I never stop.'

Mr. Meredith gave me some information as to the modern writers he found most interesting—Americans in particular.

Amongst the novelists he likes Mrs. Wharton and Mrs. Atherton. 'They both write a good, flowing style,' said he. Mr. Henry James he mentioned also. The two men are great friends, and Mr. Meredith spoke of the younger writer as 'my dear Henry James.'

It appears that the physical labour of writing has grown tiresome to him, though he still writes letters to his intimate friends and allows himself now and then to be plagued by his admirers into putting his name in the front of his books. He tells, by the way, very amusing stories about the methods adopted by these enthusiasts to secure his autograph, accompanied by 'a few words.'

He has sometimes tried to dictate. 'But,' said he, 'to write novels you must put your whole self into them. I found dictating therefore to be impossible, and have never been able to get beyond the fourth or fifth chapter.'

In the *Chronicle* of the same day there was a little word-portrait of Meredith from an unknown hand. It may be quoted, not only for its graphic truth, but as an example of the way in which the mannerisms of the master are unconsciously adopted by those who write about him. It was the same with Stevenson. There is not one of the many critics who have written much about Stevenson but makes use of his 'disengage.' This was a favourite word of his, used in such wise as, let us say: A striking and original personality 'disengages' itself from the mass of anecdote gathered about Meredith. The *Chronicle* writer got his 'leaps at you, ringing like a bell,' nowhere but from Meredith:

You catch the flash of that eye immediately you see him, whether that be indoors, in his arm-chair, or out of doors, in his donkey-chaise. The hair and beard are white, and they suggest the patriarch, and indeed Mr. Meredith has always been a prophet. The face is furrowed, too, but youth—perennial youth—gleams from the eyes. And then Mr. Meredith's voice—it has the very sound and melody of youth. It has a great-heartedness which is captivating and infective—it leaps at you, ringing like a bell. To hear Mr. Meredith talk is to recall Gladstone's rich voice, and do not other points occur to one as linking the two men?

Some notice must be taken of Meredith's political convictions, and here seems to be a fitting place since his opinions on affairs may be regarded as a purely personal matter, scarcely affecting his art and, except in later years, evidently without interest to the world at large. He has often, and truthfully enough, been described as a life-long unswerving Radical, and one intelligent writer who mentioned this in February, 1908, spoke of the service he had rendered to the cause as the editor of the *Ipswich Journal!* It was not until he had ceased to be a productive novelist that his opinions on politics of the day began to be courted by the newspapers and his name to assume a political significance it had never before possessed. 'If you meddle with politics you must submit to be held up on the prongs of a fork, soaped by your backers and shaved by the foe,' he writes in one of his novels. But as he did not meddle with politics until he had earned the respect of all men by his literary achievement, he never had to submit to this ordeal, the Conservative press being as urbane to him and considerate of his views as he had been an exponent of its own principles. His genuine Imperialism may account for this friendliness of his political opposites.

His eightieth birthday was made the occasion of a little note of political praise by the *Westminster Gazette*, as follows:

> Liberalism owes much to him; and, while the world of letters is uniting in offering homage to the greatest of living novelists, his services to the Liberal Party may be recalled. The lifelong friend of Mr. John Morley, his political faith is akin to that of the Indian Secretary, and to this we may ascribe his steadfastness at that time of great storm and stress, the Home Rule period. Mr. Swinburne, Radical and Republican—so he liked to style himself—forgot his principles in the passion aroused by Mr. Gladstone's proposals. The mild, academic, Liberalism of Huxley, Tyndall and Tennyson were all lost in the battle of words; but George Meredith stood firm. Considering his long career, the novelist's consistency has been remarkable, for the faith he championed as a political writer in the sixties he is championing to-day.

That is the estimate of a very sober journal of the Liberal faith, but it is doubtful if the invidious comparisons which it makes are altogether justifiable. While Meredith in his later years may have been very pronounced in his utterances and at the election of 1906 had himself conveyed to the polling-booth to record his vote, his Liberalism might also be described as of the academic sort, but not mild. A man of his cast of mind could be nothing else than a Liberal, his very literary style meant Radicalism; but essentially in the way of intellect. 'Beauchamp's Career' is perhaps his greatest service to Radicalism, and even there do we not detect the Celtic note of failure, like the 'sough' of the bagpipe at the end of a rousing slogan? A Liberal thinker Meredith must surely be reckoned, but to say that intellectually he was more consistent than Swinburne is scarcely just to the latter.

Apart from the abundance of Radical sentiment which is to be found in every one of the novels since 'Evan Harrington'—where it is first felt in fullest measure—a political student of Meredith would have little else to work upon until he came to the last ten years of his life. In other words, George Meredith the politician, as distinct from the novelist, is past seventy when we find him 'meddling with politics.' There is preserved a letter of his, written at sixty, which indicates that among his friends, and especially to the younger men, he was then, as at eighty, 'delivering himself of certain very Radical sentiments.' That short-lived genius, J. K. Stephen, who attempted to establish in 1888 a high-class weekly journal under the title of the *Reflector*, had met Meredith, as he seems to have met and impressed most of the notable men of his day. They had discussed politics, and the result is seen in a humorous announcement printed in the advertisement columns of the *Reflector* for January 29, 1888:

The gentleman who recently asked a younger man what the dickens he expected to come to if he started in life as a Tory, is referred to the precedent of Mr. Gladstone.

'That "the gentleman" and "the younger man" were Mr. Meredith and the editor of the *Reflector* respectively,' says Mr. Charles Strachey, 'appears from the next issue of the paper, which contains a poem of eight stanzas by Mr. Meredith, called "A Stave of Roving Tim," prefaced by the following characteristic letter. The reference to "the triolets of the French piano" is an allusion to the large number of poems in triolet form which had appeared in the *Reflector*.'

Sir,—The senior (see your advertisement columns) who met that young Joseph Hofmann of politics, with the question as to the future of the youthful Tory, is impressed by the *Reflector's* repartee, in which he desires to find a very hopeful promise, that may presently dispel strange images of the prodigy growing onionly, and showing a seedy head when one appears. Meanwhile, he sends you a lyric out of many addressed encouragingly to certain tramps, who are friends of his, for the purpose of driving a breath of the country through your pages, though he has no design of competing with the exquisite twitter of the triolets of the French piano which accompanied your birth, and bids fair to sound your funeral notes.

Yours, etc.,
GEORGE MEREDITH.

The first really serious political pronouncement in his own person which we have from Meredith is so recent in date as February 2, 1903, when the *Manchester Guardian* published a long article signed 'H. O.,' in which his opinions on the national position and especially the fortunes and future of the Liberal Party were conveyed in the form of an 'interview.' If any one had ever doubted that in the sage of Box Hill we had a keen and well-informed student of current politics this remarkable article, which was quoted extensively in the press, must have settled the matter, as there was no phase of the political situation on which he had not some illuminating opinion to give, and his Radicalism was whole-hearted. He urged a more democratic ideal for the Liberal Party. '"Forward" must be the cry if the Liberals wish to recapture the heights they once held!' Any defection of the party from Home Rule he deplored. 'I have very little doubt that Home Rule will come, nor do I see any reason why it should not,' were his words. His estimate of Lord Rosebery, in particular, showed how closely he must have followed the perplexing path of that remarkable man. Of Mr. John Morley, Mr. Haldane, and Mr. John Burns, all personal friends of his, he spoke in terms of warm admiration.

John Burns has (he said), I believe, done more good amongst his class than any man in England. In a future Liberal Parliament he should have a voice in the inner council as well as in the party. He would, I think, strengthen any cabinet—a man of infecting energy, and, I believe, absolutely honest. And, not least, John Burns I believe to be a sincere patriot. I had a talk with him once, and I happened to be saying in rather a depressed tone that I thought we were being beaten in the commercial race by other nations, and he said: 'I don't care what you believe. I will bring you instance after instance to show that that is not the case, but that we are holding our own.' Oh yes, John Burns is extremely vigorous in that respect—the fear of contradiction is never before him. There is hope for British democracy when it can produce such men as he. . . .

It was in the course of this same interview that Meredith made the memorable reference to his age which has been so often quoted since, and, somewhat differently phrased and elaborated, we have already read in Mr. Stead's account of a later conversation:

I suppose I should regard myself as growing old—I am seventy-four. But I do not feel to be growing old either in heart or mind. I still look on life with a young man's eye. I have always hoped I should not grow old as some do—with a palsied intellect, living backwards, regarding other people as anachronisms because they themselves have lived on into other times and left their sympathies behind them with their years.

After this famous manifesto it became a stereotype of journalism to have an 'interview' with Meredith whenever some matter of unusual interest was engaging the public mind, while all sorts of Liberal associations took to consulting the oracle of Box Hill. He, who had so long advocated the rights of women, was the ideal man from whom to secure an awakening letter to be read at a meeting of the Dorking Women's Liberal Association in May, 1904. A 'silly season' correspondence in the *Daily Mail*, in the autumn of that year, on 'The Marriage Handicap,' was quite excuse enough to 'draw' the philosopher who, not so long before, could have been induced by no newspaper editor in England to grant an interview for such a purpose. He advocated, as all remember, the modification of our marriage laws, whereby some system of renewable terms might be established between contracting parties; that is to say, a couple might agree to live as man and wife for a period of ten years or so, and each be free to renew the agreement or discontinue it at the end of the time, the State granting all necessary legal protection to the children. 'There will be a devil of an uproar before such a change can be made!' he said. 'It will be a great shock, but look back and see what shocks there have been, and what changes have nevertheless taken place in this marriage business in the past!' 'Love upon a mortal lease,' forsooth! It is difficult to believe Meredith was speaking seriously on this subject; certainly he cannot have looked ahead—his complaint against the English people—to the hopelessness of such a modified marriage law. It would be a case in which the second condition were worse than the first.

A month after this interview had the public by the ears, there was the unhappy affair of the Dogger Bank, and of course the oracle of Box Hill had to be consulted for 'a message to the nation.' Like everybody else, he considered that there had 'never been such justification for an appeal to arms.' In January of 1905 poor Russia is in trouble again; this time at home. There is 'Red Sunday' and the abortive revolution. Down goes the *Chronicle* man to Burford Bridge Station, and next day behold a column beginning: 'In his study at the Cottage at Box Hill yesterday afternoon Mr. George Meredith talked about Russia and the revolution.' Excellent 'copy,' for no leader-writer seemed to focus the situation with anything of the power and direct vision of this old man who protested:

'I live out of the world. Why should people listen to me? I know what is going on only by the newspapers.' Yet his living out of the world had been to some purpose when we read such common-sense criticism as this:

Russia cannot, it is certain, long escape the spirit of Liberalism that has swept over Europe. The sympathy of the British people with the brave fellows who are fighting an uneven, an almost hopeless, battle as it seems, is very great. And it should be practical. Denunciation is useless. . . . Everybody should spare what he can, and the money should be telegraphed immediately to one of the leaders who are not in prison. We must help them, and this is our only way. They cannot expect much help from Germany. Germany ever since 1870 has been an armed camp, waiting behind a fortress to be attacked. But no doubt the German people will sympathise with these poor fellows. France is in a difficult position. She was forced into an alliance with Russia by the Triple Alliance, before she came to a good understanding with us. Her people were attracted by the undeveloped riches of Russia to invest their money in that country. And France has her bondholders to consider. But she has a great spirit of humanity. I do not like the word humanity, but it will be understood—and the French people also will have much sympathy with the aims of the Russian revolutionaries.

His hope that the Russian bureaucracy would have fallen in the course of a year was vain. 'The Fall of the Tsar' was the favourite newspaper heading of the day. The Tsar and the bureaucracy still stand and Russia is still in chains.

A month or two later, and a correspondent—Mr. H. W. Strong, of Newcastle—induces him to a fresh pronouncement on the question of femininism in a letter from which this is a quotation:

Since I began to reflect I have been oppressed by the injustice done to women, the constraint put upon their natural aptitudes and their faculties, generally much to the degradation of the race. I have not studied them more closely than I have men, but with more affection, a deeper interest in their enfranchisement and development, being assured that women of the independent mind are needed for any sensible degree of progress. They will so educate their daughters that these will not be instructed at the start to think themselves naturally inferior to men because less muscular, and need not have recourse to particular arts, feline chiefly, to make their way in the world.

In the same letter the novelist adds that he has no special choice among the women of his books. 'Perhaps,' he says, 'I gave more

[*From a drawing by William Hyde.*

FLINT COTTAGE, BOX HILL.

[*To face p.* **82.**

colour to "Diana of the Crossways" and Cl[illegible] of the "Egoist," and this on account of their position.

Next comes the Fiscal Question and a sporting [illegible] of the great protagonist, in which Meredith asks [illegible] Chamberlain's 'clean, keen mind and adventurous [illegible] what is from time to time possessed of one idea [illegible] it with tremendous energy. He will never [illegible] of his [illegible] would be a demented country that [illegible] him.' If the [illegible] advocates of tariff reform had been able to lay [illegible] very anti-Cobdenite sentiments which appeared in the [illegible] the *Ipswich Journal* somewhere about 1860 they [illegible] sport at the expense of Mr. Chamberlain's [illegible].

Russia is still an [illegible] which [illegible] Mr. G. H. Perris—[illegible] Hill, [illegible] on the situation comes [illegible] 9, 1905. Then comes the [illegible] Election of [illegible] to Liberals. He [illegible] way from Box Hill to [illegible] on Friday, [illegible] may vote for the Liberal candidate [illegible] the last time I shall [illegible] he gets home, after his [illegible] In April of the same year [illegible] Association, with Meredith's [illegible] chair, is honoured [illegible] Holyoake, recently dead, [illegible] as two [illegible] to the Speaker about the [illegible] recluse of Box Hill [illegible] delivering himself [illegible] Only a few of many [illegible] have been chosen [illegible] sufficient surely to prove what I have written [illegible] publicity of his old age; and [illegible] despite his protests, this was [illegible] man of letters. In a long [illegible] Nevinson, reported in the *Daily Chronicle* of [illegible] we find him saying:

> Since my last illness I have felt a peculiar disinclination for work of all kinds. The thought of taking up a pen is [illegible] abhorrent. I am as receptive as ever. I read and enjoy [illegible] new thing. But my mind seems now as if it could not give out [illegible] wrote to our dear friend Clodd, whom I call Sir [illegible], for his trick in beguiling me to my first and only speech in public, a [illegible]

colour to "Diana of the Crossways" and Clara Middleton of the "Egoist," and this on account of their position.'

Next comes the Fiscal Question and a scathing criticism of its great protagonist, in which Meredith asks us to observe in Mr. Chamberlain's 'lean, long head and adventurous nose,' a man who is from time to time possessed of one idea and advances it with tremendous energy. He will have none of his Protection: 'it would be a demented country that believed him.' If the journalistic advocates of tariff reform had been able to lay hands on certain very anti-Cobdenite sentiments which appeared in the editorial columns of the *Ipswich Journal* somewhere about 1860 they might have had some sport at the expense of Mr. Chamberlain's unsparing critic!

Russia is still an anxiety to Europe when a disciple of Tolstoy—Mr. G. H. Perris—goes down to Box Hill, and one more interview on the situation comes out in the *Westminster Gazette* of February 9, 1905. Then comes the General Election of 1906 and more letters to Liberals. He is even conveyed in his little donkey-chaise all the way from Box Hill to Leatherhead on Friday, January 26, that he may vote for the Liberal candidate for Epsom. 'I hope it will be the last time I shall have to vote against Protection,' he says, when he gets home, after his remarkable and much-applauded undertaking. In April of the same year the annual dinner of the Rationalist Press Association, with Meredith's close friend, Mr. Edward Clodd, in the chair, is honoured with a long letter in praise of George Jacob Holyoake, recently dead; a month or two later he is writing to the *Speaker* about the Russian Duma; in short, Meredith the invalid recluse of Box Hill seemed to be far more in the public eye and busier delivering himself of opinions than some of our active politicians! Only a few of many instances have been chosen for mention; but sufficient surely to prove what I have written about the curious publicity of his old age, and one is also left with the impression that, despite his protests, this was not altogether distasteful to the aged man of letters. In a long and noteworthy talk to Mr. Henry W. Nevinson, reported in the *Daily Chronicle* of July 5, 1904, we find him saying:

Since my last illness I have felt a peculiar disinclination for work of all kinds. The thought of taking up a pen is quite abhorrent. I am as receptive as ever. I read and enjoy hearing of new things. But my mind seems now as if it could not give out any more. As I wrote to our dear friend Clodd, whom I call Sir Reynard, for his trick in beguiling me to my first and only speech in public, a visit to me now will give you but a wizened old hen instead of the plump pullet he looks for whenever his sagacious nose is laid to earth.

Besides, who really cares for what I say? The English people know nothing about me. There has always been something antipathetic between them and me. With book after book it was always the same outcry of censure and disapproval. The first time or two I minded it. Then I determined to disregard what people said altogether, and since that I have written only to please myself. But even if you could tell the world all I think, no one would listen.

This, of course, must not be taken too literally. The best minds in England have always been ready to listen to Meredith, and if the multitude has been slower in giving him its ear, the blame does not rest entirely with it.

V

FRIENDSHIPS AND HOME LIFE

WHILE many lesser men in the history of letters seem to cut a more considerable figure in the popular eye by reason of their distinguished and well-chosen friendships, it is only natural that in the case of George Meredith we do not find him deriving anything of fame from such connections. It is the other way round; for there are not a few who will be remembered chiefly because they have had the good fortune to be reckoned among his intimates. He gives all and receives nothing—nothing, that is to say, except friendship, which is all he ever asked for. Perhaps he has not always received that, as we find that every great man of letters attracts to him certain of the parasitic breed, whose sole desire it is to be esteemed one of his circle. With all such the question of true friendship does not arise. 'Certain tramps, who are friends of his,' wrote Meredith of himself in 1888, and we may suppose that in his earlier prime he had many a friendship with the vagrom folk of his countryside worthy of chronicling. But the pose of rustic friendships for later biographical effect, not unknown to some gentlemen of the pen, was the last notion to enter Meredith's mind. Until the last ten or fifteen years of his life he did his work and lived his own life, never studying the public effect of his doings, so that such records of his friendships as we may gather from legitimately accessible sources reveal to us a man and not a mirror-watching actor.

So little did he care for 'literary friendships,' as such, that William Davis Ticknor, the celebrated Boston publisher and man of letters, who died in 1864, and who was one of his early friends, did not know for some years after the beginning of their acquaintance that Meredith had written a book! The friendship of tramps is a wholesome corrective to the friendships of the drawing-room and the club. It signifies character on the search for character. It is what we would naturally look for in the prophet of Mother Earth; but it is the unrecorded part of his friendships, and we must turn to his relationship of a more conventional kind to discover this phase of his life. Even so we find the life of Meredith rich in true and memorable friendships, though the merest tittle of what might be told of these has, so far, been put on record.

We have seen that one of his earliest friends was Thomas Love Peacock, whose daughter he married; but no account of their intercourse exists, nor are we likely to have any information on this connection of his early life, unless at some distant date there may be letters forthcoming. The friends of his youth are unknown to us, and none but himself could have recalled them. This he has not chosen to do. He is a man of thirty, the author of 'Poems' (1851), 'The Shaving of Shagpat' and 'Farina,' before his circle of friends begins to take shape in the available personalia of his life. Already Mr. William Michael Rossetti is friendly with him, George Eliot and G. H. Lewes are among his acquaintance. Doubtless Mr. Rossetti's greater brother had by this time come into touch with the young poet-novelist, though it is a little later that we have evidence of their intimacy. But the great and enduring friendship of his early life was formed with a man, as remarkable as Meredith himself, and five years his junior. In any account of his friendships, Frederick Augustus Maxse (1833–1900), to whom 'Modern Love' was 'affectionately dedicated' on its appearance in 1862, must have the first place. But, above all, does not Maxse live for ever as the hero of 'Beauchamp's Career'? He entered the navy as a lieutenant in 1852, becoming captain three years later, and retiring with the rank of admiral in 1867. He was a political thinker and writer of an advanced type, and, though the younger of the two, his personality must have had some influence on the mind of Meredith. Very little indeed has been put on record concerning this notable man, but Mr. T. P. O'Connor has penned a graphic little sketch of him, which helps us to realise the personality of Meredith's old comrade:

Here was one of the remarkable and yet little appreciated and little known figures of his own time; who would have been forgotten—even now, but a few years after his death—if George Meredith had not given him immortality by painting his portrait in his book. But there was a time when there was no name better known or more honoured in England. He was a sailor during the Crimean War; did a deed of tremendous daring; and all the world echoed with it; and everybody naturally expected that he was beginning a glorious career. There was nothing that he was not considered capable of doing, and of reaching.

But Admiral Maxse lived and died in something like obscurity, or in a certain notoriety that was almost as killing as death and obscurity. He began by becoming a politician, and of an advanced Radical type, which in the 'sixties' was regarded as scarcely reputable—especially in one that was an officer in the Navy. I remember still the mild horror with which people spoke of this man who, while wearing the officer's uniform of Her Majesty's Navy, spoke with such merciless disrespect of so many things then held in honour; many of them have since passed away, to everybody's relief. Indeed, so advanced were Admiral Maxse's views that he never was able to get into Parliament. Then, when possibly his chance was coming, he suddenly turned round; left the Liberal Party over Home Rule; quarrelled, and even bitterly, with an old friend like John Morley; and, in short, ended a forlorn and rather desolate figure. Even in his profession, in which he had had such a magnificent start, Admiral Maxse never did much after his first year; he gained his title ultimately by seniority rather than by service.

I remember seeing him at Carlsbad, and often, of course, in London—a thin, rather sickly, though distinguished-looking man, with a certain air of detachment and of disappointment. The story of Beauchamp's career is sad and touching as it is told by George Meredith; it would have been even more touching, and certainly sadder, if it had been described as it was in the original from whom the story was drawn.

It is to the late Sir William Hardman, for eighteen years editor of the *Morning Post* and Recorder of Kingston, that we owe the most intimate knowledge we have of Meredith's home-life and friendships at the beginning of the 'sixties.' Hardman, engrossed though he was in literary life and public service, contrived to find the leisure for keeping a diary and gathering materials for his memoirs, from which some appetising passages, edited by Mr. Frederick Dolman, were published in *To-day* at the end of 1893 and the beginning of 1894.

As Hardman was one of the novelist's most intimate friends for close on thirty years, some notes of his career may be set down before we proceed to his Meredithian reminiscences. He was a grandson of the William Hardman of Bury Hall, Lancashire, who was associated with Sir Robert Peel, the father of the statesman, in his great industrial enterprise. Although, after quitting Cambridge, he studied for the bar at the Inner Temple, and was called in due course, he did not practise professionally. But he found a highly useful channel for his legal knowledge as Chairman of the Surrey Sessions in criminal cases, which onerous and unpaid office he filled from about 1865 until his death, September 12, 1890. He was knighted in 1885 for his valuable public service in this position, and not for his political work, as one sometimes finds it stated, distinguished though that had been. For a number of years Hardman was the owner of Norbiton Hall, Kingston, but in 1872, when he accepted the editorship of the *Morning Post*, he settled again in London, and until his death was eminent in the higher literary and political circles of the metropolis. His friendship with Meredith had begun in 1861, when, being the occupant of Littleworth Cottage, Esher, he discovered himself a near neighbour of the author of 'The Shaving of Shagpat,' for which book he had so intense an admiration that the offer of a common friend to introduce him to the creator of the immortal Shibli was eagerly accepted, and so began one of Meredith's closest friendships.

Sir William Hardman was the original of Mr. Blackburn Tuckham, in 'Beauchamp's Career,' and a glance at his portrait will show how vivid is the novelist's humorous description of his friend:

It was amusing to find an exuberant Tory in one who was the reverse of the cavalier type. Nevil and he seemed to have been sorted to the wrong sides. Mr. Tuckham had a round head, square flat forehead, and ruddy face; he stood as if his feet claimed the earth under them for his own, with a certain shortness of leg that detracted from the majesty of his resemblance to our Eighth Harry, but increased his air of solidity; and he was authoritative in speaking. 'Let me set you right, sir,' he said sometimes to Colonel Halkett, and that was his modesty. . . . On the question of politics, 'I venture to state,' he remarked, in anything but the tone of a venture, 'that no educated man of ordinary sense who has visited our colonies will come back a Liberal.' As for a man of sense and education being a Radical, he scouted the notion with a pooh sufficient to awaken a vessel in the doldrums.

Let us turn now to Sir William's reminiscences, which yield us the richest store of Meredithiana and are here quoted by kind permission of Lady Hardman, to whom I am indebted for a number of valuable notes. Owing to the entire lack of dates in the published passages, the time of their writing can only be fixed by certain references which occur in them. The character of the man that may be caught up from Hardman's impressionist pages is most engaging, in every sense our hero.

The first meeting of Meredith and Hardman is thus described, and took place in some time in 1861, when 'Evan Harrington' was appearing serially:

GEORGE MEREDITH WITH HIS SON ARTHUR IN 1861.

This rare photograph, here published for the first time, was taken by Sir William Hardman in 1861, and is reproduced by permission of Lady Hardman.

[*To face page* 88.

During our stay at Esher we have made the acquaintance of George Meredith, the author of 'The Ordeal of Richard Feverel,' 'Evan Harrington,' etc. He is very clever, original, and [illegible] We soon became great allies. He is a widower [illegible] a boy of eight years—one of the finest lads I [illegible] probably enclose you copies of the portraits I took of Meredith and his 'little man,' as he calls him. He is intensely proud of this boy, and the boy is well worthy of his father's pride and affection. Your father and sister [illegible] at our country cottage, and were much amused by him, for, contrary to the usual habit of authors, he is not a silent man, and when he is present conversation goes glibly [illegible] quite like an old one. He showed me the place [illegible] and wrote the poem [illegible] surrounded by pines and [illegible]

> New from [illegible]
> Now the [illegible]
> Now the [illegible]
> And the [illegible]

Meredith and I [illegible] have made the [illegible] convinced me that [illegible]

Besides being a [illegible] man, Hardman [illegible] open-air enthusiast, [illegible] quick growth of his friendship with Meredith [illegible] references to their [illegible] one of these rambles [illegible] may be dated January [illegible] refers was never published [illegible]

Meredith chaffs me [illegible] (Cobbett) whose biography [illegible] opinion is, that I come [illegible] rhapsodies with frequent morsels of [illegible] him with a stolid request [illegible] crepancies between his most recent sentence and [illegible] The consequence of this is that we get into long arguments, and it was only last Sunday, during one of our country rambles, that in spite of the raw, inclement January day, we stopped a long time at a stile, seated on the top of which he lectured me, [illegible] effectually, on his views of the future destinies of the human race. I should so like you to know him; you would like him immensely and disagree with him constantly.

Somewhat later, but possibly to the same year, belongs the

During our stay at Esher we have made the acquaintance of George Meredith, the author of 'The Ordeal of Richard Feverel,' 'Evan Harrington,' etc. He is very clever, original, and amusing. We soon became great allies. He is a widower of thirty-two, with a boy of eight years—one of the finest lads I ever saw. I shall probably enclose you copies of the portraits I took of himself and his 'little man,' as he calls him. He is immensely proud of this boy, and the boy is well worthy of his father's pride and affection. Your father and sister met Meredith at dinner at our country retreat, and were much amused by him; for, contrary to the usual habit of authors, he is not a silent man, and when he is present conversation goes glibly enough. Although only a new chum, he is quite like an old one. He showed me the place where he composed and wrote the poem beginning as follows—it was on an eminence surrounded by pines on the St. George's Hill estate:

> Now from the meadow floods the wild duck clamours,
> Now the wood-pigeon wings a rapid flight,
> Now the homeward rookery follows up its vanguard,
> And the valley mists are curling up the hills.

Meredith and I had an argument as to whether he ought not to have made the second and fourth line to rhyme, and I think he convinced me that the plan he had adopted was the better one.

Besides being a Surrey man, Hardman was something of an open-air enthusiast, delighting in country rambles, and hence the quick growth of his friendship with Meredith. He has many references to their wayfaring, and, as we shall see later on, describes one of these rambles at considerable length. The following passage may be dated January, 1862; the 'life' of Cobbett to which Hardman refers was never published, I believe:

Meredith chaffs me, and says I resemble in many ways the man (Cobbett) whose biography I have undertaken. The reason of his opinion is, that I come down in the midst of his many poetical rhapsodies with frequent morsels of hard common-sense. I interrupt him with a stolid request to define his terms. I point out discrepancies between his most recent sentence and some previous one. The consequence of this is that we get into long arguments, and it was only last Sunday, during one of our country rambles, that, in spite of the raw, inclement January day, we stopped a long time at a stile, seated on the top of which he lectured me, quite ineffectually, on his views of the future destinies of the human race. I should so like you to know him, you would like him immensely, and disagree with him constantly.

Somewhat later, but possibly to the same year, belongs this

pleasant anecdote of Meredith in his playful humour: 'Tuck' was his nickname for Hardman—hence, perhaps, 'Blackburn Tuckham':

George Meredith has a fancy for writing to me the wildest letters you ever read. Not infrequently they contain a short poem, as in the following example. This was written in consequence of having been obliged to postpone a promised visit to Copsham Cottage. (Mem. 'The Mound,' line 6, is a conspicuous eminence hard by the cottage.)

Since Tuck is faithless found, no more
  I'll trust to man or maid;
I'll sit me down, a hermit hoare,
  Alone in Copsham shade.
The sight of all I'll shun,
  Far spying from the mound,
I'll be at home to none,
  Since Tuck is faithless found.

I told him I would immortalise the words by setting them to music, but he begged me not to as he would rather write me something fit to read. No, I would not be persuaded, and I have yesterday composed the music in madrigal style for three voices.

In 1861 the friendship between Rossetti and Meredith was budding, as we shall learn presently from the reminiscences of Mr. W. M. Rossetti. The painter-poet evidently esteemed the novelist as something of a celebrity, for we find him writing to Alexander Gilchrist, the art critic and author of the 'life' of Blake, under date November 19, 1861, eleven days before poor Gilchrist died:

My dear Gilchrist: Two or three (friends) are coming here on Friday evening at eight or so—George Meredith I hope for one. Can you look in? I hope so—nothing but oysters, and of course the seediest of clothes.

Meredith had evidently introduced Hardman into the Rossetti circle about this time. Indeed the particular evening mentioned in Rossetti's invitation to Gilchrist was most probably identical with that to which Hardman refers in the following passage:

Yesterday I went with George Meredith to see Rossetti, the celebrated pre-Raphaelite painter. He had, unfortunately, no finished works in his studio, but his collection of sketches and studies was most interesting and beautiful. He is a very jolly fellow, and we had a most amusing visit. I am going on Friday to his place again, to a social re-union of artists and literary men, short pipes and beer being, I am given to understand, the order of the day.

Though the date and certain other details of the following anecdote are lacking, the story is perhaps the most charming of the many rescued from oblivion by Sir William Hardman, to whose memory all Meredithians owe a kindly thought for what his diligence has preserved of the personal portraiture of the master:

The widow of Andrew Crosse, the celebrated electrician, was there, a very lively and talkative lady, who chaffed Meredith immensely about a passage in 'Richard Feverel' which had prejudiced her against our friend. M. A. overheard this conversation, but did not catch the words of the offending passage, so, when the ladies retired to the drawing-room, she boldly asked Mrs. Crosse what it was. She was somewhat surprised at the reply. It was, 'Kissing won't last, but cookery will,' as a piece of advice to 'persons about to marry.' On the drive home we discussed it with Mrs. Meredith (George riding outside, smoking a cigar), and she said that when she was going to be married, an old aunt wrote her a letter of *dis*couragement and *en*couragement, saying *inter alia* that she had read somewhere, years ago, in a book whose title she had forgotten, that 'kissing won't last, but cookery will.' Was not this singular, when she was going to be married to the very man who had written it?

We may venture to date Hardman's next sketch of a visit to Copsham Cottage in the early spring of 1862, as the poem, 'Grandfather Bridgman,' which he mentions, is one appearing in the collection of 1862, published in the month of May:

We have just returned from a charming little country run of two days and one night. Yesterday morning we left the Waterloo Station at 9.15 for Esher. All our mutual requirements were condensed into a little black bag, which I carried, and we started from the station at Esher triumphantly, regardless of vehicles, for a walk of two and a half miles to Copsham Cottage. We were going to stay all night with our good friend George Meredith. The heartiest of welcomes awaited us at the really humble cottage—for it makes no pretensions to anything, but performs a vast deal more than many great houses that promise so much. Meredith is a man who abhors ceremony, and 'the conventionalities.' After our first greetings were over, we turned out for an hour and a half before lunch. We had exhausted all our superlatives in extolling the day and the walk between the station and the cottage, but we had to begin again now. The scent of the pine-woods, the autumn tints on the elms and beeches, the brilliant sunlight exalted us to a climax of ecstasy. We were children again. Luncheon on our return consisted chiefly of home-made products—bread, honey, jams, marmalade, etc., most delicious. Then came a general lighting of pipes and cigars, and off we started for another walk through lanes and wood to Cobham, a good six-mile business. We got back at five o'clock and dined at six. What appetites we had! Gracious goodness! Meredith's two other guests left at eight, to walk home to Walton-on-Thames, and then we put a log of wood on the fire and sat down for a cosy talk. Meredith read some poems which are to form part of a volume shortly to be published. So passed the time till 10.30, when to bed we went, thoroughly prepared to sleep soundly, as you may easily imagine. Up at seven, and away went Meredith and myself for a brisk walk of three or four miles, after taking a tea-cup of hot soup and a slice of bread. After breakfast Meredith retired to work at his book of poems, while we went to call on some friends in the neighbourhood. On our return he read to me the result of his morning's work—portion of a very pretty idyll called 'Grandfather Bridgman.' . . . We left Esher by the four o'clock train, carrying with us a pot of honey for consumption in Gordon-street. Hadn't we enjoyed ourselves!

It was evidently on the occasion of the visit just described that Meredith gave Hardman the book and the story concerning it with which he deals in the following anecdote:

Meredith insisted upon giving me a copy of 'Over the Straits,' by Mrs. Meredith—no relation of his whatever—but he gets all books published by Chapman and Hall for nothing, being in some way connected with that firm. This Mrs. Louisa Meredith resides in Tasmania, and wrote to our friend asking if he was not her husband's long-lost brother; she was with difficulty persuaded that this was not the case. Her letters were impassioned and full of entreaty; she and her husband were dying to take him into their arms. At last our friend favoured them with a sketch of his life and origin by way of explanation. This settled the doubts, and extinguished the hopes of the Tasmanian Merediths, and the correspondence terminated with a hope that if they were not relations they might at least be friends. I should not say 'terminated,' for he still hears occasionally from Mrs. Meredith.

How much would not some Meredith collectors give to-day for that letter in which he has told his own story of his origin! It is possibly still in existence and the matter of it may be attainable, for it would certainly be regarded as a treasure by the lady who received it six and forty years ago, and by her relatives to-day, if Mrs. Lousia Meredith be no more.

The most important of Sir William Hardman's records of his intercourse with Meredith is a spirited sketch of 'A Country Walk with George Meredith' which took place in the second last week-end of May, 1862, the date being fixed by the *Spectator* of May 24, 1862, which contained the attack on the newly-issued 'Modern Love' volume. It is an ideal picture of wholesome, happy friendship that Hardman's sketch brings before us; the two robust and hearty Englishmen, footing it along these Surrey roads and lanes as merry and care-free as children, yet every now and then breaking into discussion of graver things—sober in their mirth. The reference to aphorism-making for 'The Pilgrim's Scrip' is somewhat puzzling, as 'The Ordeal of Richard Feverel' had been published three summers before. It could not be until the altered edition of 1878, or just sixteen years later, that Meredith would be able to work in these aphorisms he had composed in 1862:

> After dining together at his cottage at Copsham, Meredith and I started about seven o'clock one May evening, intending if we failed to obtain beds at Mickleham, to walk on to Burford Bridge. I had no bag or pack of any kind, carrying all my necessaries in the capacious pockets of a shooting jacket. Meredith had what the Germans call, I believe, a 'ruck sack,' a sort of bag slung by a strap over the back and hanging under the left arm—a most convenient article. In it he carried, besides toilet necessaries, a 'Murray's Handbook to Surrey,' and some capital brandy.
>
> I may as well mention here that we never addressed each other by our real names. He called me 'Tuck,' and I called him 'Robin.' Having enjoyed a good dinner before starting, we walked at a pace befitting the victuals, steady and sober, enlivening the way with snatches of song, reminiscences of overtures, frequent bursts of laughter, and absurd rhymes, as occasion suggested. The evening looked dubious and stormy, and the sunset was red and lowering, but on we went, nevertheless. We avoided Leatherhead by a cut across the fields, coming into the main road by the church. It was quite dark when we reached Mickleham, about twenty minutes past nine. The landlady of the inn was most obliging, and promised us the accommodation we required. After making arrangements, we strolled out to listen to the nightingales in the meadows on the banks of the Mole. While enjoying the cool air, drinking in their music, 'the monotonous clattering of the brown eve-jar,' and all the varied sounds of a summer night, Meredith recited Keats' 'Ode to the Nightingale,' one of Robin's favourite poems. We returned to our inn, singing my music to Robin's madrigal addressed to myself, 'Since Tuck is faithless found,' amid peals of laughter. After large potations of soda-water, flavoured with the brandy aforesaid, we retired to rest about eleven o'clock. Our bedrooms communicated by a passage, and we lay shouting to each other, and joking about the joviality of the whole affair, neither of us getting to sleep for an hour or so. Nevertheless, at 5.30 a.m. Meredith

enters my room with a suggestion that we should get up. I recommended him to go to bed again, and he did so. We eventually got up about seven, and strolled out to see the immediate neighbourhood while breakfast was being got ready.

The church is nearly opposite the inn, and into the churchyard we went. A pet lamb came to us, expecting, as Robin put it, a gratuity of some kind, but got nothing, as we had nothing to give it. Beyond the churchyard a stile-road leads across some meadows up the Mickleham Downs. Meredith declares that here may be obtained one of the most perfect bits of rustic scenery in this country, and consequently in any other. The church spire is seen embedded in rich foliage, backed by the hills crowned by Norbury Hall, with all the noble trees placed by dear old Evelyn, of the 'Diary.' The most critical artist—and Meredith has an artist's appreciation of landscape—need not modify one iota of the view; every tree in its place, and the spire of the church just where it should be. Higher up the scene broadens, and with all the varied greens of May made another view of great beauty. In the midst of our enthusiasm the church clock chimed eight, and warned us of our waiting breakfast.

After breakfast I wrote a short note to my wife ('Demitroia,' as we call her), for which I was duly chaffed by Meredith, who called me 'an uxorious old Tuck,' and finally wrote a note to her himself to tell her that I never thought of writing till I had eaten I know not how many chops, kidneys, eggs and the etceteras. I posted the letter at nine, and on we went for our day's walk. Striking into the meadows by the Mole we crossed the bridge near the 'Swallows,' and so back into the road near Burford Bridge, revelling in the glory of the morning and the lovely scenery. We followed the high-road to Dorking for some distance, and then struck into a by-path across the fields into the town. After making vain efforts to obtain a *Saturday Review* or any other 'weekly,' we went on towards Guildford. Presently a sudden descent brought us to 'The Rookery,' the birthplace of Malthus, a quaint old house embedded deep in foliage. Soon after this we lost our way, but Meredith made inquiry of certain tillers of the field, and by dint of scrambling over hedge and ditch we at length found ourselves on the right road. Our mishap occurred in consequence of the interest taken by Robin in Malthus's birthplace. In order to get a better view of the house we had turned into a lane which passed quite close to 'The Rookery.' Coming to the little village of Shere, we turned into the inn for a rest, and some ale and bread and cheese.

Soon after leaving Shere we began an abrupt descent into a place called Combe Bottom, one of the most lovely spots in creation. It is in the shape of a basin hollowed out of the chalk, with almost precipitous sides, covered with short grass at the base, but crowned with the most luxurious foliage in every variety of tint. On a bare projecting knob we lay down and smoked our pipes while enjoying the surroundings. Here Robin overhauled his note-books and read to me a number of aphorisms hereafter to be published in 'The Pilgrim's Scrip,' by Sir Austin Feverel, edited by Adrian Harley. We discussed them at our ease, for such terse sayings naturally provoke conversation. As Sir Austin says, 'A proverb is the half-way house to a thought.' Having finished our aphorisms and our pipes we descended to the bottom and crossed to the opposite side, on to the Merrow Downs, along which we walked as far as Newland's Corner. Immediately on our left lay Albury, where, as Meredith reminded me, the author of 'Proverbial Philosophy' resides.

Getting once more on to the main road we made for Guildford, where, on arriving, we ordered a cold dinner and proceeded to the railway station to get copies of the *Saturday Review, Public Opinion,* and *The Spectator* (May 24, 1862). The last-named journal contained an article on Meredith's Poems and 'Modern Love,' etc., and a regular stinger it was! Robin was naturally annoyed, for the review was most unreasonable, and was, in my opinion, written with decidedly personal feeling. Meredith did not agree with me in this, and eventually concluded that the review was written by a woman. The disagreeable topic did not interfere much with our pleasure, we were too much determined to enjoy ourselves, and Robin's annoyance soon passed off.

After our cold collation we started again for Godalming, intending to pass through that town and sleep at a place two miles beyond. The evening was very fine, and defying the critic of the *Spectator,* we found the walk most exhilarating. In passing through Godalming we could not help noticing the number of patriarchal dogs lying about on the doorsteps! Robin was much tickled by my styling one in particular as an 'ancient dog,' he said it sounded so very old. At a small inn near the village of Milford we found a civil and obliging hostess, who recollected Meredith, he having stayed there the summer before with Maxse. She said she could give us beds, so we ordered tea, and took a stroll to an eminence on the wild common adjoining, from which we obtained a fine but desolate view. It was now nine o'clock, and as we had been on our feet for twelve hours we were not sorry to rest. The house filled with hilarious rustics, who sang old tunes with very dolorous choruses. It was Saturday night. They kept it up till midnight. Our bedrooms were very plain, for the house was a small and poor one, but they were clean, and the beds aired. The following morning (Sunday) we were both up by seven o'clock, took a stroll in the garden, and awaited our coffee, chops, and unlimited bread and butter. Our hostess was very reasonable in her bill, only 3*s.* 6*d.* each. We gave sixpence to the little maid who waited upon us, and she was greatly pleased.

We stopped only once in our ramble from Milford to Haslemere. We lay down on the summit of Hindhead, smoking several pipes, and enjoying a prospect of from fifteen to thirty miles in every direction. About noon we started down towards Haslemere, so as to get there by one o'clock, when folks would be out of church and inns open. We knocked at the hostel of the White Horse about ten minutes to one, and had a cut at the family dinner, a breast of veal, washed down by copious draughts of the best pale ale Meredith and I had ever tasted. After dinner we sat on a wall in the garden and smoked. About three we started—' ignominiously,' as Robin would have it—in a four-wheel chaise for Godalming to catch the train at 5.15, there being no train from Haslemere before 7.20. I arrived in town about seven o'clock, having dropped Meredith at Esher.

Another very attractive glimpse of Meredith is afforded by Hardman's description of a visit to Drury Lane pantomime on Boxing Night of 1862. Here again the date can be fixed with certainty, as Edmund Falconer, the actor-dramatist, began his management at Drury Lane on that day:

George Meredith comes up to-morrow morning with his son to spend Christmas Day with us, and go to a pantomime on Boxing Night. He says, ' Arthur is ardent for a jolly clown, a pantaloon of the most aged, the most hapless, a brilliant columbine, and a harlequin with a waving wand.' The father is ' for Drury Lane or Covent Garden, for uproar, a pit reeking with oranges, gods that flourish pewter-pots, and picks that stick and show their mortality at starting.' Falconer, who opens the theatre on Boxing Night, is said to have spent £10,000 on his pantomime and decoration, etc. . . . We went to Drury Lane on Boxing Night, and such a pandemonium I have rarely witnessed. The first piece was acted in dumb show, not a word could we hear. The fights in pit and gallery were frequent. The shower of orange peel from the gods into the pit was quite astounding. The occupants of the latter place made feeble efforts to throw it back again, but, of course, never got it any further than the first tier of boxes. I was glad to see the thing once, but you won't catch me there again.

The last of Hardman's reminiscences of Meredith end with August of 1863 and take the form of some jottings of three days in Paris:

Paris, August 21.—Letter from George Meredith announcing his approach. He left *via* Newhaven last night, and ought to have been in Paris about 11.30. He stopped at Rouen to see the *Joan of Arc,* and to call on an author who had submitted certain work to the Chapmans. He arrived about 2.30. Joyful greetings. We dined by Robin's request at Vefour's, a great mistake. Between Vefour's and the Trois Frères there's as much difference as between the Uni-

SIR WILLIAM HARDMAN.

Editor of the *Morning Post*, 1872-1890. An intimate friend of Meredith's, and the original of Blackburn Tuckham in 'Beauchamp's Career.'

[*To face p.* 96.

versity Club and the 'London' (corner of Chancery Lane). Meredith and I strolled along the Champs Elysées in the evening—very pleasant, and not offensive, like our Haymarket. He brought me *Once a Week*, containing my article on 'America: An Imaginary Tour,' published August 15, and also put Renan's 'Life of Jesus' into his bag for me. We think him not looking well—his son Arthur's accident has naturally been a matter of great anxiety.

Paris, August 22.—Chartered two carriages, and drove about, visiting the Louvre and other places. Dined at Trois Frères', Robin and I going first to order the dinner, and then returning to our hotel. We were the merriest of parties. Charles, the waiter, was an admirable type of the aristocracy of waiters. We have nothing of the kind in England. The tender interest which he displayed in every dish, the manner in which he delicately urged M. A. to have a morsel of dishes which she would fain have let pass, the respectful way in which he offered advice and suggestions, all concurred in proving that we had before us the very acme and pinnacle of waiters. We arranged for a carriage to take us to Versailles to-morrow—which is a *fête* day—and we afterwards all had a walk up the Champs Elysées. Meredith is going to-morrow evening to Grenoble to meet 'Poco.' They then proceed to Dauphiné, and eventually to Chamouni.

Paris, August 23 (Sunday).—We went to Versailles by the Avenue de Passy, through Sèvres, and arrived safely at eleven o'clock. Could not get Meredith past the more modern French pictures of battles. . . . We had a delightful drive back through St. Cloud and the Bois de Boulogne. Expressions of admiration at the beauty of the drive were exhausted. Truly the Emperor is a wonderful Œdile. Meredith left us at 6.15 for Grenoble.

Sir William Hardman died in 1890, and it is clear from these reminiscences that by his death Meredith lost a true friend and admirer. There is the gusto of the hero-worshipper in many of his references to the novelist, and in the little circle of those who were loyal to Meredith long before it had become fashionable to admire him, Hardman must always have an eminent place. But we suspect that Sir William, who was probably nothing of a Bohemian, did not grow into any intimacy with the Rossetti segment of Meredith's circle, for although the novelist's relations with Rossetti had ripened during the years covered by Hardman's reminiscences, we find only one slight reference to Rossetti in his jottings. Meredith had been on terms of increasing acquaintance with Rossetti for some three years before 1861, but it was in this year that they became intimate. Frederick A. Sandys, the artist, who did the fine decorative picture of 'Bhanavar among the serpents of Lake Karatis' and painted

Mrs. Meredith's portrait, also came into the Rossetti group about the same time; and of course there were Swinburne and Mr. W. M. Rossetti, and, somewhat later, I fancy, Mr. Theodore Watts-Dunton and Burne-Jones.

Joseph Knight, in his 'Life of Rossetti,' thus describes the circumstances of the taking of the house at 16, Cheyne Walk (Tudor House), where, towards the close of 1862, Meredith became one of Rossetti's sub-tenants:

After the death of his wife, Rossetti found the chambers he occupied with her too charged with painful memories to be tolerable. He went for a short period to stay with his friend, Mr. Madox Brown, at Highgate Rise; then, after a brief residence in Lincoln's Inn Fields, he took a lease of the house at No. 16, Cheyne Walk, possession of which he retained until his death. Though unprovided with a studio that fully answered his requirements, this fine old building, with its handsome iron gates, its frontage commanding the river, and its extensive garden, formed an almost ideal residence for him. The conditions under which it had been taken had, however, no element of possible permanency. Joint occupants with Rossetti were Mr. Swinburne, Mr. George Meredith, and Mr. William Rossetti. That four men of individualities so potent, and, in some senses, so aggressive, or at least assertive, as those of the men named, should be able to live together in closeness of continuous intimacy, from which there was scarcely an escape, was barely conceivable. Mr. George Meredith, accordingly, made no long stay. Next after him Mr. Swinburne departed. The two brothers held on, as was natural, for some time longer, the younger, in this, as in every other case, assisting the elder with counsel, not always followed, and in the early days with money.

There are numerous stories as to the cause of Meredith's departure, chiefly designed to reflect on the habits of Rossetti—the artist's breakfast of 'five poached eggs that had slowly bled to death on five slabs of bacon,' which he 'devoured like an ogre,' is an example—but we may dismiss these as mere gossip, for, as we shall see, though far from uncritical of the man, Meredith remained loyal to Rossetti. Indeed 'A Note on Cheyne Walk' which he wrote to the editor of the *English Review* in January, 1909, proves this amply. He there admits the grain of truth contained in the story, for Rossetti's habits were prejudicial to his health, but not to friendship. 'Devotion to his work in contempt of our nature killed him.' He adds, 'No other subject have I spoken of this dear fellow but with the affection I felt.' One thing is certain: that Meredith was a somewhat irregular visitor at Cheyne Walk even when paying his share of the expenses, as we find Rossetti himself, in a letter to Mrs. Anne Gilchrist, January 3, 1863, writing:

By the bye, I have been a martyr to unsatisfactory servants here, and have been asking all my friends if they know any desirable ones. Our household consists of four men, two of whom only, myself and Mr. Swinburne, are at all constant inmates.

But Mr. William Rossetti in the 'Letters and Memoirs' naturally devotes considerable attention to this period of Rossetti's life, and here we find Meredith's association with the historic group at Cheyne Walk described with the accuracy and detail of one who was privy to all that happened. He writes:

For the Cheyne Walk house a new plan had meanwhile been determined. Rossetti was to be the tenant, paying a rent (assuredly a very moderate one) of £100 a year, besides—if I remember right—a premium of £225 upon entry. As his sub-tenants for defined portions of the building there were to be three persons—Mr. Swinburne, George Meredith, and myself. Of course, each of us three was to pay something to Dante; though the latter did not wish me, and in fact did not allow me, to continue any such payment after affairs had got into their regular course. We were all to dine together, if present together in the house. Mr. Swinburne was generally present, Mr. Meredith much less constantly. I came on three fixed days of the week, but not on any others unless some particular occasion arose. Swinburne, and I think Meredith, had their respective sitting-rooms, in which they received their personal visitors. I had, and required, a bedroom only. Dante Rossetti was by this time familiar with Mr. Meredith, whom he had seen increasingly for some three years past, and whose talents and work he seriously, though not uncritically, admired; familiar, yet by no means so much so as with Mr. Swinburne. . . .

Mr. Meredith and Rossetti entertained a solid mutual regard, and got on together amicably, yet without that thorough cordiality of give-and-take which oils the hinges of daily intercourse. It would have been difficult for two men of the literary order of mind to be more decisively unlike. The reader of their works—not to speak of the students of Rossetti's paintings—will not fail to perceive this. Rossetti was not at all a mere recluse, incapable of taking very good care of himself in the current transactions of life; he had, on the contrary, a large share of shrewdness and of business aptitude, and a quick eye for 'the main chance' in all contingencies where he chose to exercise it. He understood character, and (though often too indulgent to its shadier side) he knew how to deal with it, and had indeed a rather marked distaste for that inexpert class of persons who waver on the edge of life without ever throwing themselves boldly into it, and gripping at the facts. But Mr. Meredith was (or I should rather say, is) incomparably more a man of the world and man of society, scrutinising all sorts of things, and using them as his material in the commerce of life and in the field of intellect. Even in the mere matter of household routine, he found that Rossetti's arrangements, though ample for comfort of a more or less off-hand kind, were not conformable to his standard. Thus it pretty soon became apparent that Mr. Meredith's sub-tenancy was not likely to stand much wear and tear, or to outlast the temporary convenience which had prompted it. I could not now define precisely how long it continued—perhaps up to the earlier days of 1864. It then ceased, without, I think, any disposition on either side that it should be renewed. Friendly intercourse between the two men continued for some few years, and gradually wore out without any cause or feeling of dissension. In Mr. Joseph Knight's pleasant 'Life of Dante Gabriel Rossetti' I find some observations made by a 'friend, himself a poet,' which I unhesitatingly (let me hope not rashly) attribute to our pre-eminent novelist. I quote them here less as throwing light on the character of Rossetti—highly deserving though they are of attention in that regard—than as pointing to the sort of relation which subsisted between the two during their joint sojourn in Cheyne Walk:

'I liked him much, though I was often irritated by his prejudices, and his strong language against this or that person or subject. He was *borné* too, somewhat, in his interests, both on canvas and in verse, and would not care for certain forms of literature or life which he admitted were worth caring for. However, his talk was always full of interest and of rare knowledge; and he himself, his pictures, and his house, altogether, had I think an immense influence for good on us all, and on English art and work—being not insular, yet not un-English, and bringing into our world new and delightful subjects, and a personal character very striking and unusual and lovable.'

Mr. Swinburne remained in Tudor House for some considerable while after Mr. Meredith had left.

The most lasting monument of the companionship of Tudor House is, perhaps, Swinburne's famous letter to the *Spectator* of June 7, 1862, in reply to the criticism of 'Modern Love' mentioned above by Hardman in his account of his week-end ramble with Meredith. Swinburne is valiant in defence of a friend as few men could be, and whenever the friendships of poets are in discussion this spirited protest of his against a stupid and unjust criticism of his friend's great poem must be remembered:

Sir,—I cannot resist asking the favour of admission for my protest against the article on Mr. Meredith's last volume of poems in the *Spectator* of May 24. That I personally have for the writings, whether verse or prose of Mr. Meredith, a most sincere and deep admiration, is no doubt a matter of infinitely small moment. I wish only, in default of a better, to appeal seriously on general grounds against this sort of criticism as applied to one of the leaders of English literature. To any fair attack Mr. Meredith's books of course lie as much open as another man's; indeed, standing where he does, the very eminence of his post makes him perhaps more liable than a man of less well-earned fame to the periodical slings and arrows of publicity. Against such criticism no one would have a right to appeal, whether for his own work or for another's. But the writer of the article in question blinks at stating the fact that he is dealing with no unfledged pretender. Any work of a man who had won his spurs and fought his way to a foremost place among the men of his time, must claim at least a grave consideration and respect. It would hardly be less absurd, in remarking on a poem by Mr. Meredith, to omit all reference to his previous work, and treat the present book as if its author had never tried his hand at writing before, than to criticise the *Légende des Siècles*, or (coming to a nearer instance) the *Idylls of the King*, without taking into account the relative position of the great English or the greater French poet. On such a tone of criticism as this, any one who may chance to see or hear of it has a right to comment.

But even if the case were different, and the author were now at his starting-point, such a review of such a book is surely out of date. Praise or blame should be thoughtful, serious, careful, when applied to a work of such subtle strength, such depth of delicate power, such passionate and various beauty, as the leading poem of Mr. Meredith's volume; in some points, as it seems to me (and in this opinion I know that I have weightier judgments than my own to back me), a poem above the aim and beyond the reach of any but its author. Mr. Meredith is one of the three or four poets now alive whose work, perfect or imperfect, is always as noble in design, as it is often faultless in result. The present critic falls foul of him for dealing with 'a deep and painful subject on which he has no conviction to express.' There are pulpits enough for all preachers in prose; the business of verse-writing is hardly to express convictions; and if some poetry, not without merit of its kind, has at times dealt in dogmatic morality, it is all the worse and all the weaker for that. As to subject, it is too much to expect that all schools of poetry are to be for ever subordinate to the one just now so much in request with us, whose scope of sight is bounded by the nursery walls; that all Muses are to bow down before her who babbles, with lips yet warm from their pristine pap, after the dangling delights of a child's coral, and jingles with flaccid fingers one knows not whether a jester's or a baby's bells. We have not too many writers capable of duly handling a subject worth the serious interest of men. As to execution, take almost any sonnet at random out of this series, and let any man, qualified to judge for himself of metre, choice of expression and splendid language, decide on its claims. And, after all, the test will be unfair, except as regards metrical or pictorial merit; every section of this great progressive poem being connected with the other by links of the finest and most studied workmanship. Take, for example, that noble sonnet, beginning:

> We saw the swallows gathering in the skies,

a more perfect piece of writing no man alive has ever turned out; witness these three lines, the grandest perhaps of the whole book:

> And in the largeness of the evening earth,
> Our spirit grew as we walked side by side;
> *The hour became her husband, and my bride;*

but in transcription it must lose the colour and effect given it by its place in the series; the grave and tender beauty, which makes it at once a bridge and a resting-place between the admirable poems of passion it falls among. As specimens of pure power, and depth of imagination at once intricate and vigorous, take the two sonnets on a false passing reunion of wife and husband; the sonnet on the rose; that other beginning:

> I am not of those miserable males
> Who sniff at vice, and daring not to snap,
> Do therefore hope for Heaven.

And, again, that earlier one:

> All other joys of life he strove to warm.

Of the shorter poems which give character to the book I have not space to speak here; and as the critic has omitted noticing the most valuable and important (such as the 'Beggar's Soliloquy,' and the 'Old Chartist,' equal to Béranger for completeness of effect and exquisite justice of style, but noticeable for a thorough dramatic insight, which Béranger missed through his personal passions and partialities), there is no present need to go into the matter. I ask you to admit this protest simply out of justice to the book in hand, believing as I do that it expresses the deliberate unbiassed opinion of a sufficient number of readers to warrant the insertion of it, and leaving to your consideration rather their claims to a fair hearing than those of the book's author to a revised judgment. A poet of Mr. Meredith's rank can no more be profited by the advocacy of his admirers than injured by the rash or partial attack of his critics.

A. C. Swinburne.

I make no apology for giving Swinburne's letter in full; it is of such literary importance, even apart from its great personal interest to the present narrative, that no reader can reasonably object to the full text of it here, even if he is already familiar with it. We are told, moreover, that had not Swinburne written his spirited protest another, whose name is inseparable from Swinburne's, would have plied his pen to the same purpose. Mr. James Douglas in his work on Mr. Theodore Watts-Dunton writes:

Not in the least interesting among the beautiful friendships between Mr. Watts-Dunton and his illustrious contemporaries is that between himself and George Meredith. Mr. William Sharp can speak with authority on this subject, being himself the intimate friend of Mr. Meredith, Mr. Swinburne, and Mr. Watts-Dunton. Speaking of Swinburne's championship, in the *Spectator*, of Meredith's first book of poems, Mr. Sharp, in an article in the *Pall Mall Magazine* of December, 1901, says:

'Among those who read and considered' (Meredith's work) 'was another young poet, who had, indeed, already heard of Swinburne as one of the most promising of the younger men, but had not yet met him. . . . If the letter signed "A. C. Swinburne" had not appeared, another signed "Theodore Watts" would have been published, to the like effect. It was not long before the logic of events was to bring George Meredith, A. C. Swinburne, and Theodore Watts into personal communion.'

The first important recognition of George Meredith as a poet was the article by Mr. Watts-Dunton in the *Athenæum* on 'Poems and Lyrics of the Joy of Earth.' After this appeared articles appreciative of Meredith's prose fiction by W. E. Henley and others. But it was Mr. Watts-Dunton who led the way. The most touching of all the testimonies of love and admiration which Mr. Meredith has received from Mr. Watts-Dunton, or indeed, from anybody else, is the beautiful sonnet addressed to him on his seventy-fourth birthday.

In the course of time, and for no positive reason, Meredith's intimacy with the Pre-Raphaelite circle gradually lessened, until, even while all the members of the original group remained alive, it had ceased to be more than the occasional renewal of an old acquaintanceship. In the 'Memorials of Edward Burne-Jones,' for instance, we read:

In the course of this year (1897) he and George Meredith met again, having seldom seen each other since the Rossetti days, and their meeting was thus described by Edward: 'I met Meredith the other day. "What shall we talk of," said he, "politics or art?"

"Politics I never think of," said I, "and art I never talk of." "Let's begin on Epps' cocoa," said he, and so we started and had a fine time of it.'

The likelihood is that Meredith began to drift away from the Rossetti circle early in 1864, largely because he was becoming an extremely busy man, with very little time for the social side of life, and none at all for artistic Bohemia. He was finishing 'Sandra Belloni,' planning 'Rhoda Fleming,' and also doing a good deal for the *Morning Post*, in addition to his work for the publishing house to which he was 'reader.' But there was another reason: his home was at Esher; London he visited only once a week on business, and that did not afford much opportunity for maintaining relations with the Chelsea group. The Cheyne Walk scheme must have been impracticable from the first, so far as Meredith was concerned. But it is his one London landmark; all other reminiscences of him are to be looked for in Surrey: at Esher and Box Hill. It was at Esher that Sir Francis C. Burnand first made his acquaintance, as he narrates in his own jaunty style in his 'Records and Reminiscences.' This must have been in 1860, if Sir Francis is correct in thinking it was at the time when 'Evan Harrington' was appearing in *Once a Week*. The future editor of *Punch* was then a young man of twenty-four, reading law at Lincoln's Inn, but full of enthusiasm for the drama. He was a friend of Maurice Fitzgerald, younger brother of the better-known Gerald, and nephew of the famous Edward. Maurice lived then at Esher and was on intimate terms with Meredith, though Sir Francis is not supported by the novelist himself in suggesting that the 'Wise Youth' was studied from the brilliant young Fitzgerald. It was through a visit to Fitzgerald at Esher that Sir Francis became acquainted with Meredith, the circumstances being thus vivaciously pictured:

'I thought,' he (Maurice Fitzgerald) observed, breaking off in the midst of a vivid description of the beauties of the Box Hill and Dorking country, 'I thought we should have met George.'

'Who is George?' I asked.

'George Meredith,' he answered. 'I forgot to tell you that he is stopping with me, or I am with him. It doesn't much matter. We've been together for some time. You know him?'

No, I didn't.

'You know,' Maurice put it to me inquiringly, 'his "Shaving of Shagpat" and his poems?'

I regretted to say that, owing to my studies having been for the last year or more on subjects removed far away from modern literature, I had scarcely looked at any new books for the past eighteen months.

'Ah!' said Maurice reflectively; 'you must read his "Richard Feverel." I've got it and the others at home.'

Then we saw a figure standing in front of a white gate on our left, about a quarter of a mile distant, waving to us.

'There he is,' said Maurice quietly (he was always quiet); 'we shall meet him where the roads join at the corner.'

As we neared the 'crossways' (no 'Diana' there as yet), George Meredith was shaking hands with a stoutish, jovial-looking, rubicund-visaged, white-haired gentleman, who, if he had only been attired in gaiters, might there and then have been easily taken for the original of Phiz's delineation of the immortal Mr. Pickwick.

George Meredith and this genial elderly gentleman waved their hands encouragingly to one another as the latter disappeared within the gate, and George strode towards us. George Meredith never merely walked, never lounged; he strode, he took giant strides. He had on a soft, shapeless wide-awake, a sad-coloured flannel shirt, with low open collar turned over a brilliant scarlet neckerchief tied in loose sailor's knot; no waistcoat; knickerbockers, grey stockings, and the most serviceable laced boots, which evidently meant business in pedestrianism; crisp, curly, brownish hair, ignorant of parting; a fine brow, quick, observant eyes, greyish—if I remember rightly—beard and moustache, a trifle lighter than the hair. A splendid head; a memorable personality. Then his sense of humour, his cynicism, and his absolutely boyish enjoyment of mere fun, of any pure and simple absurdity. His laugh was something to hear; it was of short duration, but it was a roar; it set you off—nay, he himself, when much tickled, would laugh till he cried (it didn't take long to get to the crying), and then he would struggle with himself, hand to open mouth, to prevent another outburst.

Two more delightful companions for a young man, trembling on the brink of literature and the drama, it would be difficult to imagine. They were both my hosts. I was at home at once.

'Who were you talking to as we came up?' asked Maurice.

'That,' said George, 'why, you've met him'—no, Maurice didn't remember—'that's Evans, dear old "Pater" Evans.'

And it was in this company, in these circumstances, that I first set eyes on Mullet Evans, second partner in the old publishing firm of 'Bradbury and Evans,' then known all over the world as 'the proprietors of *Punch*.' At this time they had among other ventures started *Once a Week* as a rival to Dickens's *All the Year Round*, and George Meredith was writing for this opposition his 'Evan Harrington.' George scouted the suggestion that his novel should be called 'Bradbury-and-Evans Harrington.'

Our near neighbours were the Duff-Gordons, at whose house

George was a *persona grata.* As Maurice did not affect society, and as I was 'a person of no importance,' neither of us, though formally introduced, was included in the invitations sent to George Meredith, then a rising star, by Sir Alexander and Lady Duff-Gordon.

A far more congenial person to our Bohemian tastes was Frederick Chapman, who had taken a small house in the meadows by the little river Mole, not far from Cardinal Wolsey's tower. Very pleasant company we met there, and it was a delightful summer-time walk from Esher Common to this cottage. Through this association I obtained my first introduction to the Bouverie Street publishers. Thus it happened. I had told George Meredith some stories which he found sufficiently amusing to warrant him in placing them, told in his own inimitable language and style, before the public in the pages of *Once a Week.* Now George never informed me of his design, and made use of them without a 'with your leave, or by your leave.' It was after our trio at Esher was broken up that I found these stories of mine in *Once a Week,* whereupon, seeing a point to be scored for myself, I wrote to George, asking him, as a set-off against the 'honorarium' he had received for my stories ('only infinitely better told'), to recommend a story of mine to the editor. George replied, expressing his regret, excusing himself by saying that he never thought I was going to make capital out of them (here he was right), and that he would have great pleasure in submitting my story to the *Once a Week* editor. *Ainsi dit, ainsi fait*, and my first appearance in magazine form was as the author of a story about a practical joke (its title I have forgotten), admirably illustrated by Charles Keene, whose acquaintance, years afterwards, I was to make at the '*Punch* Table.' So George and myself cried quits. This introduction was of some use to me as acquainting Mark Lemon, who, as Mr. Punch's editor, was *au courant* with all the *Once a Week* affairs, with my name, of which, indirectly, he was soon to hear from a totally different quarter. Mark Lemon, as he long afterwards informed me, had been very much amused by the story.

Sir Francis Burnand, who continued for many years on the most cordial relations with Meredith and must be numbered among the lifelong friends of the novelist, has another anecdote to relate which illustrates Meredith's delight in the jovial humour of the song with a 'lilt' to it, as we have already seen from Sir William Hardman's recollections of their country walks. Sir Francis writes:

I had just come from hearing the new burlesque 'The Lady of Lyons' at the Strand Theatre, written by Henry J. Byron, and one of the songs had got hold of me so fast that I found myself constantly humming the tune and singing a verse or two. During our ountry walks, and in the quiet evenings, George Meredith would call' for this song, and I used to comply with the request by iving, as I fear, a rather maimed version of it. What, however, sed to delight George was the 'swing and go' of it, and the catch f the rhythm. It was sung, through his nose, by Clarke as *eauséant*, and ran thus:

I've hit on a trick they can't see through, not were they Argus-eyed, Oh!
As soon as possi*bel* Miss Deschap*elles* shall be my lovely bride, Oh!

nd the lilt of this to some old American jingle called 'Skid-a-ma-k' used to take George Meredith's fancy. I should doubt whether t any time George Meredith cared much for the drama, that is the tage representation of it, even in its highest comedy or its deepest ragedy, while as for farce or burlesque I should not be very much urprised to learn that he had never seen either one or the other.

A few years later than the time recalled in Sir Francis Burnand's eminiscences, Meredith formed a friendship of which there is no ublished record, but concerning which we would fain hope some-hing may yet be forthcoming. We know that Leslie Stephen was ne of his intimates from about the year 1865 to the time of his eath, yet in the 'Life and Letters' of Stephen this is all that his rilliant biographer, the late Professor F. W. Maitland, has to say bout Stephen's friendship with the novelist, a friendship that nspired one of the most lovable and attractive of Meredith's haracters:

At Vienna there is not much to be seen, except Mr. George Meredith: an exception of importance to Stephen, for then began friendship that lasted until his death; an exception of importance lso to those who would know Stephen, for, though the Comic Spirit reates and never copies, there is no denying that she had looked vith kindly eyes at Leslie Stephen when she created Vernon Whitford.

Fortunately Meredith himself wrote a brief appreciation of Stephen in the *Author* of April, 1904, from which we can catch a eeting glimpse of both of them, with other select companions, on heir wayside ramblings:

When that noble body of scholarly and cheerful pedestrians The Sunday Tramps, were on the march, with Leslie Stephen to lead hem, there was conversation which would have made the presence f a shorthand writer a benefaction to the country. A pause to it ame at the examination of the leader's watch and Ordnance map nder the western sun, and word was given for the strike across ountry to catch the tail of a train offering dinner in London, at the cost of a run through hedges, over ditches and fallows, past proclamations against trespassers, under suspicion of being taken for more serious depredators in flight. The chief of the Tramps had a wonderfully calculating eye in the observation of distances and the nature of the land, as he proved by his discovery of untried passes in the higher Alps, and he had no mercy for pursy followers. I have often said of this lifelong student and philosophical head that he had in him the making of a great military captain.

Perhaps the most familiar of Meredith anecdotes is that connecting his name with Carlyle which is given thus in a letter of the late York Powell to Professor Elton in 1896:

> The story is that Mrs. Carlyle begged Carlyle to read 'Richard Feverel.' He did so, and said, 'Ma dear, that young man's nae fule. Ask him here.' When he came, as Meredith himself told me, he talked long with him on deep things, and begged him to come often. He said, 'Man, ye suld write heestory! Ye hae a heestorian in ye!' Meredith answered that novel-writing was his way of writing history, but Carlyle would not quite accept that. He did not argue about it, but rather doubted over it, as if there were more in it than he had thought at first.

Mr. J. M. Barrie had told the same story, in part at least, some years earlier, and it is, no doubt, quite an authentic anecdote. Meredith's acquaintance with Tennyson was a little more intimate than that with Carlyle, which was of the most casual nature. It has also yielded a story which the late L. F. Austin, in his posthumous volume, 'Points of View,' thus relates:

> Mr. George Meredith tells an amusing story of a walk he took with Tennyson one day when the bard was very silent and gloomy. They walked several miles, and suddenly Tennyson growled 'Apollodorus says I am not a great poet.' This critic was a Scottish divine, and neither his name nor his opinion was of much consequence. Mr. Meredith said something to that effect; and Tennyson retorted, 'But he ought not to say I am not a great poet.' This was the entire conversation.

Apollodorus was, of course, the Scottish divine and critic, George Gilfillan, and there is little doubt that the story is authentic. It has long been current among literary gossips, varying somewhat in detail and perhaps to the heightening of its humour; but as Austin has told it we may let it pass, though not without protest against his slight to Gilfillan, who was no dolt in criticism.

It was after settling at Box Hill that the late William Tinsley, the shrewd old publisher who issued 'Rhoda Fleming' in 1865, spent a day with Meredith, which he describes in his 'Random Recollections' as follows:

It was in the spring time. . . . I remember I went down by an early train, because it was agreed we should have a good walk before an early dinner; I never was a strong or a fast walker, but Master Meredith at that time seemed able to walk any distance, and in quick time. After some light refreshment, we started to climb Box Hill; that was a task for me, and about as far as I wanted to go. However, after looking down upon Dorking and some very picturesque places under the hill and around, my guide proposed we should strike off the hill to the left, where there was some very pretty scenery and peeps into the distance, and one way and another Master Meredith enticed me several miles away from his house, and he was still as fresh as paint when I was a good deal knocked up; now and then I sat down on a bank to rest, and he walked on, and when some distance away called out, 'Come on, Tinsley.' However, in time we came in sight of his house, and then I said, 'You go on; I shall be with you in time for dinner, be sure of that.' It was a lovely walk, but on such occasions the two pedestrians should be about equal in walking powers.

Mr. Justin McCarthy would also seem to have come into personal touch with the mighty walker about this time, but in his 'Reminiscences' he presents to us the indoor man rather than the breezy creature of the downs, when he writes:

A more genial host never entertained the passing stranger. George Meredith loved to make his guests happy in his house, and was never tired at his table of suggesting to them new qualities in food and drink to give their palates a fresh chance of satisfaction. He had an exquisite fancy for dainty dishes of all kinds, and could create a new and refined taste in the system of even a city alderman by the manner in which he dilated on the peculiar delicacy of this or that article of food. To dine with George Meredith was to find dinner converted into a feast of intellect and fancy, and no longer left to be either a mere satisfaction of physical craving or the indulgence of an epicure's appetite. He had a charming little châlet in his grounds, which he used as a study when he wanted to be quite alone with his work, and where he sat and talked with a friend now and then when his work was put away for the moment and he and his companions could smoke and talk, and watch the clouds in the sky, and the shadows on the grass, and only a very prosaic person could fail to find something of the poetic in himself under such an influence.

Mr. Comyns Carr's friendship with Meredith dates back to 1876, and in that most engaging volume of reminiscence, 'Some Eminent Victorians,' which Mr. Carr issued in 1908, there is a modest reference to his intimacy with the great writer that calls for quotation in this record of friendships:

The hours that I have spent with George Meredith in and around his simple home at Box Hill count among the most delightful of my life. I met him first at the house of a dear friend of both, Frederick Jameson, in the year 1876, and it was, I think, about that time that I had published in the *Saturday Review* a criticism of his novel, 'Beauchamp's Career,' which I think must have pleased him, for I find a phrase of his in a letter written to me at that date in which he says, 'Praise of yours comes from the right quarter.'

It was not long after that that we became intimate friends, and it was his hospitable custom to invite me to breakfast with him on the little lawn in front of his cottage, and then, after the repast, light and dainty after the fashion of the French *déjeuner*, we would start for a long ramble over Box Hill, returning, often but just in time for dinner, to continue or to renew the talk that had made the afternoon memorable. Meredith could talk and walk after a fashion that I have known in no one else. Sometimes he would occupy the whole of our ramble in a purely inventive biography of some one of our common friends, passing in rather burlesque rhapsody from incident to incident of a purely hypothetical career, but always preserving, even in the most extravagant of his fancies, a proper relevancy to the character he was seeking to exhibit.

On one occasion I remember he traced with inimitable humour, and with inexhaustible invention, a supposed disaster in love encountered by an amiable gentleman we both knew well; and as he rambled on, with an eloquence that never halted, he became so in love with his theme that I think he himself was hardly conscious where the record of sober fact had ended and where the innocent mendacity of the novelist had begun. And then, at the immediate summons of some beauty in the landscape around us that arrested his imagination, he would pause in the wild riot of the imagined portrait and pass, in a moment, to discourse, as eloquent but more serious, on some deeper problem of life or art. Not that he ever sought, either in the lighter or the deeper vein, to talk so as to absorb the conversation. In single companionship there was no better talker, as, indeed, there was no better listener; and in either mood he was singularly stirring and inspiring.

From the strictly literary point of view, perhaps, the friendship with R. L. Stevenson is the most interesting of the associations of Meredith's middle life; for none with whom we associate his name in the way of friendship has shown such distinct evidence of the master's influence in his work and his ideals of art. Stevenson was a young man of twenty-eight when first he sat at the feet of Meredith, as we learn from an article by Mrs. J. E. H. (Alice) Gordon in the *Bookman*, January, 1895:

Some time in the 'seventies' (1878) Robert Louis Stevenson came with his mother and took up his abode for a summer at the romantic little inn at the foot of Box Hill known as the Burford Arms. At that time we were living about ten minutes' walk from the little hostel, and among our most honoured and best beloved friends was the sage of Box Hill, George Meredith. A publisher friend wrote to us from London and begged my mother to make the acquaintance of Mr. Louis Stevenson, requesting her if possible to invite him to meet George Meredith. Thus it came to pass that Robert Louis Stevenson, then entirely unknown to fame, would occasionally drop into our garden and sit at the feet of the philosopher and listen with rapt attention and appreciative smiles to his conversation.

I well remember the eager, listening face of the student Stevenson, and remember his frank avowal that from henceforth he should enrol himself 'a true-blue Meredith man.' He was an inspiring listener, and had the art of drawing out the best of Mr. Meredith's brilliant powers of conversation, so that those were halcyon days. . . . My sister, I remember, was much interested in Stevenson, and even in those early days expected great things from him in the future. And I well remember her satisfaction one afternoon when, after he had taken his departure from our circle, and one of us was idly wondering why our friend, the publisher, was so hopeful about young Stevenson's future, Mr. Meredith trumpeted down our feeble utterances by informing us that some day he felt sure we should all be proud to have known him, and prophesied success and fame for him in the future.

The acquaintance thus begun quickly ripened into a friendship that endured to the end, though mountains divided and 'the waste of seas.' Stevenson was indeed a 'true-blue Meredith man,' as we have ample proof in his letters, and also in his essay on 'Books which have influenced me.' There was nothing in literature he thought to be beyond the range of his master. In the 'Vailima Letters,' for instance, we find him writing in this strain about the difficulty of dealing in any unhackneyed and dignified way with love in fiction:

The difficulty in a love yarn which dwells at all on love is the dwelling on one string; it is manifold, I grant, but the root fact is there unchanged, and the sentiment being very intense, and already very much handled in letters, positively calls for a little pawing and gracing. With a writer of my prosaic literalness and pertinacity of point of view, this all shoves toward grossness—positively even towards the far more damnable closeness. This has kept me off the sentiment hitherto, and now I am to try: Lord! Of course, Meredith can do it, and so could Shakespeare.

The sequence of the names of the two master-writers may be remarked! It indicates the superlative degree of his faith in Meredith, but he was rather inclined to superlatives; for although the music of 'Love in the Valley' haunted him and the stanzas beginning 'When her mother tends her' made him 'drunk like wine' and he could remember 'waking with them all the hills about Hyères'—this was early in the 'eighties'—he could confess to W. E. Henley some years later, after reading a new book of poetry by his old friend and collaborateur, that he had not received the same thrill of poetry since Meredith's 'Joy of Earth' and 'Love in the Valley,' adding: 'I do not know that even that was so intimate and deep.' Praise from Meredith was as much like wine to Stevenson as the poetry of his hero. Mr. Graham Balfour in the 'Life' writes:

Soon after the issue of 'Prince Otto' (October, 1885), Stevenson wrote to Mr. Henley: 'I had yesterday a letter from George Meredith, which was one of the events of my life. He cottoned (for one thing), though with differences, to Otto; cottoned more than my rosiest visions had inspired me to hope; said things that (from him) I would blush to quote.' Mr. Meredith's letter unfortunately has disappeared, but in another from the same source there occur these words: 'I have read pieces of "Prince Otto," admiring the royal manner of your cutting away of the novelist's lumber. Straight to matter is the secret. Also approvingly your article on style.'

Mr. W. M. Fullerton, who visited Box Hill, as we have heard, in the winter of 1888, mentions R. L. S. and Mr. Henry James as the subjects of some talk with Meredith:

Going up the footpath across the slope we got upon the subject of Mr. James and Mr. Stevenson. For Mr. James, both as man and writer, Mr. Meredith has a very warm regard; but Mr. Stevenson, who was undoubtedly a sort of protégé of Meredith, he thinks a very great artist. 'I knew Stevenson,' he said, 'long before he was known to you all. I saw what was in him and knew that he would do good work.' Mr. and Mrs. Stevenson are frequent visitors at the Box Hill Cottage, where Mr. Stevenson's favourite point of vantage, I understand, is the steps in front of the door.

FLINT COTTAGE, BOX HILL.

[*To face p.* 112.

There are several interesting photographs of him in the home; and they evidently like to have him there as much as he enjoys coming.

There is one particular letter of Stevenson's that should be included; it was written in the last year of his life and after his friendship with Meredith had endured for fully twenty years:

VAILIMA, SAMOA, *April* 17, 1894.

My dear Meredith,—Many good things have the gods sent to me of late. First of all there was a letter from you by the kind hand of Mariette, if she is not too great a lady to be remembered in such a style; and then there came one Lysaght with a charming note of introduction in the well-known hand itself. We had but a few days of him, and liked him well. There was a sort of geniality and inward fire about him at which I warmed my hands. It is long since I have seen a young man who has left in me such a favourable impression; and I find myself telling myself, 'O, I must tell this to Lysaght,' or, 'This will interest him,' in a manner very unusual after so brief an acquaintance. The whole of my family shared in this favourable impression, and my halls have re-echoed ever since, I am sure he will be amused to know, with 'Widdicombe Fair.'

He will have told you doubtless more of my news than I could tell you myself; he has your European perspective, a thing long lost to me. I heard with a great deal of interest the news of Box Hill. And so I understand it is to be enclosed! Allow me to remark, that seems a far more barbaric trait of manners than the most barbarous of ours. We content ourselves with cutting off an occasional head.

I hear we may soon expect 'The Amazing Marriage.' You know how long, and with how much curiosity, I have looked forward to the book. Now, in so far as you have adhered to your intention, Gower Woodsere will be a family portrait, age twenty-five, of the highly respectable and slightly influential and fairly aged 'Tusitala.' You have not known that gentleman; console yourself, he is not worth knowing. At the same time, my dear Meredith, he is very sincerely yours—for what he is worth, for the memories of old times, and in the expectation of many pleasures still to come. I suppose we shall never see each other again; flitting youths of the Lysaght species may occasionally cover these unconscionable leagues and bear greetings to and fro. But we ourselves must be content to converse with an occasional sheet of notepaper, and I shall never see whether you have grown older, and you shall never deplore that Gower Woodsere should have declined into the pantaloon 'Tusitala.' It is perhaps better so. Let us continue to see each other as we were, and accept, my dear Meredith, my love and respect.

ROBERT LOUIS STEVENSON.

P.S.—My wife finds joins me in the kindest messages to yourself and Mariette.

The lady referred to by Stevenson at the beginning of the letter and in the postscript is Meredith's daughter, now Mrs. Sturgis, and Mr. Sidney R. Lysaght is, of course, the novelist and poet, author of 'The Marplot,' which had just appeared before his visit to Vailima, and 'One of the Grenvilles,' published in 1898. As regards the portraiture of Gower Woodsere in 'The Amazing Marriage,' that is no doubt modelled upon Stevenson in the earlier chapters, but later the modifications do not in any way leave the finished character 'a family portrait.' Poor Tusitala, who had looked forward so eagerly to Meredith's last novel, was dead before it began to appear serially in *Scribner's Magazine*.

Touching the portrait of Stevenson in 'The Amazing Marriage,' an anonymous writer in the *Sketch* of November 27, 1895, has an interesting note on the subject, from which I quote the following:

Gower is the son of a cobbler, and his Bohemianism is all to match. Perhaps Gower's hat is not worse than the one which Mr. Gosse was so anxious to abolish from the head of 'R. L. S.'; but his shirts! Indeed, it must not be the plural. 'Gower's one shirt' (when he was staying with Admiral Fakenham) 'was passing through the various complexions, and had approached the Nubian, on its way to the negro.' Gower himself, by the way, describes his shirt as 'resembling London snow.' To the housekeeper who promises him one 'more resembling country snow,' he retorts, 'it will save me from buttoning so high up.' And in that retort, if not in that shirt, you discern the ownership of 'R. L. S.' It is the Stevenson of the donkey journey that Mr. Meredith has reproduced, with his own transformings; but, despite the transformings, the vital Stevenson is there. He is met, a youth of twenty-three, upon a mountain, with a sprain in his leg which 'at each step pronounced a negative to the act of walking,' and so you get the word from his own lips, 'this *donkey* leg.' Gower's profession of faith is soon made: 'I slept beside a spring last night, and I shall never like a bedroom so well.' The landladies of the 'Inland Voyage,' who were always taking the Voyager and Cigarette, his companion, for pedlars, have their counterparts in the pages of Mr. Meredith. When, with Lord Fleetwood for comrade, Gower responds to that 'invitation of the road' for ever singing in Stevenson's ears, it is Mr. Meredith's British baronet, Sir Meeson Corby, who is abashed by the spectacle of a peer 'tramping the road, pack on back, with a young nobody for his comrade, who might be a cut-throat, and was avowedly next to a mendicant. Hundreds of thousands a year, and he was tramping it like a pedlar, with a beggar for his friend.' When Woodsere calls at a great house, the butler 'refused at first to take his name to his master,' and when he relents, he relents 'in spite of the very suspicious, glib, good English spoken by a man wearing such a hat'—of course, the very hat which Mr. Gosse wanted to destroy, when he lured Stevenson into the hatter's, and, turning round, found him not. You have everything but the episode in the pages of 'The Amazing Marriage.'

Another of Meredith's literary friendships, but by no means so intimate as any we have been concerned with so far, was that with 'B. V.,' the ill-fated James Thomson, a countryman of Stevenson's and author of 'The City of Dreadful Night.' From Mr. H. S. Salt's excellent 'Life' of Thomson we may glean some interesting details of the intercourse between Meredith and 'B. V.,' which was chiefly in the way of correspondence, as Thomson only met his hero twice:

In July, 1879, through Mr. Foote's introduction, Thomson became engaged in a correspondence with Mr. George Meredith, for whose genius he had long felt and expressed the utmost respect and admiration; and he had now the great satisfaction of learning that his own writings were held in high esteem by one whose good opinion he probably valued above that of any living critic. 'I am glad,' wrote Mr. Meredith, 'to be in personal communication with you. The pleasant things you have written of me could not be other than agreeable to a writer. I saw that you had the rare deep love of literature; rare at all times, and in our present congestion of matter almost extinguished; which led you to recognise any effort to produce the worthiest. But when a friend unmasked your initials, I was flattered. For I had read "The City of Dreadful Night," and to be praised by the author of that poem would strike all men able to form a judgment upon eminent work as a distinction.'

Meredith must have read Thomson's great poem in the *National Reformer,* where it was first printed in four parts in the year 1874, and in 1879, when the poet was at work revising it for issue in book form, Meredith wrote to him:

The reviewers are not likely to give you satisfaction. But read them, nevertheless, if they come in your way. The humour of a situation that allots the pulpit to them, and (for having presumed to make an appearance) the part of Devil to you, will not fail of consolation. My inclination is to believe that you will find free-thoughted men enough to support you.

The reception of 'The City of Dreadful Night,' when it came out in book form at the beginning of 1880, proved the wisdom and prescience of Meredith's opinion. He himself wrote to Thomson from Box Hill, under date April 27, in terms of warmest praise and frank admiration.

My friends could tell you (he wrote) that I am a critic hard to please. They say that irony lurks in my eulogy. I am not in truth frequently satisfied by verse. Well, I have gone through your volume, and partly a second time, and I have not found the line I would propose to recast. I have found many pages that no other poet could have written. Nowhere is the verse feeble, nowhere is the expression insufficient; the majesty of the line has always its full colouring, and marches under a banner. And you accomplish this effect with the utmost sobriety, with absolute self-mastery. I have not time at present to speak of the City of Melancholia. There is a massive impressiveness in it that goes beyond Dürer, and takes it into upper regions where poetry is the sublimation of the mind of man, the voice of our highest. What might have been said contra poet, I am glad that you should have forestalled and answered in your 'Philosophy'—very wise writing. I am in love with the dear London lass who helped you to the 'Idyll of Cockaigne.' You give a zest and new attraction to Hampstead Heath.

So far the two poets had not met each other, and fifteen months later they had yet to meet; but Meredith was evidently anxious to know the poet of pessimism more closely than by correspondence, as we gather from the following letter of Thomson's to his good friend Miss Barrs, under date August 6, 1881:

Finding, when I called at Reeves' (my publisher), that George Meredith had been there lately and inquiring after me, I took occasion to write him a note on Thursday about a little matter I had before lazily thought of writing about. My conscience, which, as you have doubtless perceived already, is always my only law, forbade me conclude without putting in some lines to the following effect (words pretty exact):

'I found a man in Leicester who has all the works of yourself and Browning, and appreciates them. Need I say that I gave him the grasp of friendship. I preached you to the dearest little lady (What impudence! you cry), and fairly fascinated her with Lucy and Mrs. Berry. Richard she heartily admired in the headlong imperiousness of his love, and you will be as grieved as I was to learn that she could not be brought to even the faintest moral reprobation of his unscrupulous fibbing (as in the cases of going to hear the popular preacher, and introducing to his uncle "Miss Lætitia Thomson"); while she exulted heartlessly in the tremendous thrashing of poor faithful Benson. Such are women, even the best! But neither she nor any other woman, and scarcely any man, will ever forgive you the cruel, cruel ending.'

Such is the judgment your own wicked judgment has brought upon you. As I have no reply this morning, Mr. M. may be off holiday-making (people have the queerest infatuation for holidays in these times: they ought to know that work is so much pleasanter as well as nobler than idleness—see my moral essays on 'Indolence' and 'A National Reformer in the Dog-Days'); but even if he is now in vacation (*i. e.* emptiness!) your punishment can be delayed only for a month or two. Therefore tremble in the meantime. Should he demand your name in order to publicly denounce you, of course I shall feel conscientiously bound to give it. And if he has not yet gone off, or, having been off, has returned, I may have to spend a day with him: and then what a terrible tale I shall have to tell by word of mouth!

Thomson's first meeting with Meredith took place a month later, as described in a letter to Miss Barrs, dated Thursday, September 15, 1881:

Tuesday I spent with George Meredith at Box Hill; a quiet, pleasant day, cloudy but rainless, with some sunshine and blue sky in the afternoon. We had a fine stroll over Mickleham Downs, really park-like, with noble yew-trees and many a mountain-ash ('rowan,' we Scots call it) glowing with thick clusters of red berries, —but you have some at Forest Edge. . . . We had some good long chat, in which you may be sure that Forest Edge and its inmates, as well as certain Leicester people, figured. M. read me an unpublished poem of considerable length, which, so far as I can judge by a single hearing (not like reading at one's leisure), is very fine, and ought to be understood even by that laziest and haziest of animals, the general reader. He says that, having suspended work on a novel, poems began to spring up in his mind, and I am glad that he thinks of bringing out a new collection.

Ever ready to exert himself on behalf of any friend, Meredith set about to secure for poor Thomson a proper opening for his great literary powers, so much of which had been spent on mere hack work for *Cope's Tobacco Plant,* and that had ceased publication early in 1881. He introduced him to Mr. John Morley, then editing the *Pall Mall Gazette* and the *Fortnightly Review;* but, alas! it was too late, for the irregularities of Thomson's life had become so pronounced that he could not be relied upon to discharge with punctuality any literary commission for a daily paper, and the good offices of Meredith were in vain. A few months later—June 3, 1882 —the tragic life of James Thomson had closed. Meredith's estimate of the unfortunate genius, whose late years had been brightened by the friendship and appreciation of him whom Thomson revered above all the authors of his day, must be quoted in any record of his friendships :

> I had full admiration of his nature and his powers. Few men have been endowed with so brave a heart. He did me the honour to visit me twice, when I was unaware of the extent of the tragic affliction overclouding him, but could see that he was badly weighted. I have now the conviction that the taking away of poverty from his burdens would in all likelihood have saved him, to enrich our literature; for his verse was a pure well. He had, almost past example in my experience, the thrill of the worship of moral valiancy as well as of sensuous beauty; his narrative poem, 'Woddah and Om-el-Bonain,' stands to witness what great things he would have done in the exhibition of nobility at war with evil conditions.
>
> He probably had, as most of us have had, his heavy suffering on the soft side. But he inherited the tendency to the thing which slew him. And it is my opinion that, in consideration of his high and singularly elective mind, he might have worked clear of it to throw it off, if circumstances had been smoother and brighter about him.

Some three years after the death of Thomson another Scotsman 'of pairts' had settled in London, and was soon to win universal fame as the interpreter of the lowly life of his native land, and later to become the most successful of contemporary writers for the stage. Mr. J. M. Barrie was a Meredithian from the first, and one of the finest studies of the novels which have been published was that contributed by him to the *Contemporary Review* in 1888. He, too, in due time became a friend of the great author whose work he so warmly admired, and among the few privileged ones who dined with the veteran on his eightieth birthday was the author of 'A Window in Thrums.' Mr. Barrie is credited with a quaint story of his first sight of Meredith, which may or may not be true. His enthusiasm for the works of the master took him down to Box Hill, soon after he had settled in London, in the hope of catching a glimpse of the novelist. 'He sat down outside the house and waited,' so the story goes. 'Presently the fine face appeared at the window. Mr. Barrie trembled. A few moments and the door opened. George Meredith himself appeared and walked down to the garden gate. Consternation seized Mr. Barrie; in utter panic he fled—back to London.'

But of all the friendships of Meredith it is on that with Mr. John Morley we should most care to have some light, and some day there may be much that is of deep interest to tell us concerning the long relationship of two men who have had so marked an influence on the thought of their time. Meanwhile we know almost nothing but the baldest facts of what must have been one of the most interesting of all literary friendships. Mr. John Morley—the pen is somehow rebel to 'Viscount Morley'—had made friends with Meredith in the 'sixties,' and, as we have seen, it was so long ago as 1867 that Meredith acted as his *locum tenens* on the *Fortnightly*, where, in June of that year, he printed the sonnet to 'J. M.', which breathes the spirit of true admiration and confidence in his friend:

> Thou, fighting for poor humankind, wilt feel
> The strength of Roland in thy wrist to hew
> A chasm sheer into the barrier rock,
> And bring the army of the faithful through.

In the character sketch of Mr. Morley which Mr. W. T. Stead, who was his colleague and successor on the *Pall Mall Gazette* and knows him intimately, contributed to the *Review of Reviews* for November, 1890, the influence exerted by the novelist on the mind of the statesman is noted:

> No living person would hold a higher place in the list of those who had contributed to fashion his mind than Mr. George Meredith. In the early days, before he became famous, Mr. George Meredith, then himself neither so popular nor so widely known as he is to-day, took him with a friendly hand. He used to stay with Mr. Meredith in a remote country village, and in the evening Mr. Meredith would read over the work he had done in the day—the chapter or the poem. It was Mr. Meredith who awoke in him the feeling for nature which has ever since remained as one of the great pleasures of his existence, as well as imparting to him a larger concern for the wisdom of life. For many years the long walks across the Surrey commons, where the south-west wind blows, and when Mr. Meredith's genius was at its best, were the delight of Mr. Morley's life. 'Much, and very much,' Mr. Morley once told me, 'did he owe to the wise and stimulating friendship of George Meredith in the impressionable times.'

When Mr. Morley was a candidate for the lord-rectorship of Glasgow University in 1902, Meredith penned a brief, personal tribute to the integrity and statesman-like qualities of his old friend. There is a sentence in it of curious interest in view of the most familiar complaint against the writer's own literary style:

As an orator and as an author Mr. Morley is comprehensible to the simplest of minds (he wrote), while he satisfies the most exacting critical taste and adds to our stores of great speeches and good literature. It is not too much to say of such a candidate that in receiving a distinction he confers one.

With the name of Lord Morley among the friends of Meredith that of Morley's intimate and ally, James Cotter Morison, should be mentioned. Morison had been at Lincoln College, Oxford, with Morley, and the two friends became very frequent visitors at Copsham Cottage. The author of 'The Life and Times of St. Bernard,' that masterpiece of the dusty shelves, was also an intimate of the Hardmans. Morison, though something of a visionary, was a delightful talker, so, what with the sparkling wit and gusty laughter of their host and the brilliant qualities of the three visitors named, their *parties carrées* at Copsham must have been ambrosial nights.

Here I would introduce some interesting extracts from the writings of two French visitors to Box Hill—the late Marcel Schwob and Madame Daudet. Marcel Schwob, who died in the spring of 1905, was one of the rarest spirits of modern French letters, though but little known to the ordinary reading public, even in his own country. A man of vast learning and the most remarkable command of languages, his was a great talent, perhaps, rather than genius. Stevensonians will recall his brilliant essay on 'R. L. S.,' unrivalled among the many that have been devoted to the study of that author. He visited Meredith in 1895, most likely, as 'Spicilège,' the book in which he records his impressions of the novelist, was published in 1896. From his most charming and characteristic chapter I translate the following:

Near Dorking, at the foot of Box Hill, facing the golden Surrey meadows, sown over with thick-set trees, dotted here and there with tiny eminences of a soft emerald green, amidst elms and ash trees, nestles the house of George Meredith, close by the fertile slope. Higher up, on the side of the hill, above groups of cornflowers and wild poppies, there stands a small two-roomed cottage. It is in this cottage that Mr. Meredith does all his work. In times gone by he used even to sleep there. He shuts himself up in it from ten o'clock in the morning till six at night. On pain of his greatest displeasure, he has forbidden any one to disturb him during these hours of the day. Even Cole, his faithful valet, 'the best in England,' who has served him for thirty years, would not dare to face the storm resulting from an intrusion. If there is really need for him, some one from his house gives Mr. Meredith particulars by means of an electric bell and a telephone.

JAMES COTTER MORISON.

Author of 'The Life and Times of St. Bernard.'

[*To face p.* 120.

When I saw Mr. Meredith coming towards me immediately on leaving the page he had just begun, I was struck with the physical traces of his mental efforts. Mr. Meredith is tall, his hair and beard are grey, his head is erect, handsome and impressive, his eyes are deep blue; but these wonderful eyes of his, I noticed in the first few seconds of our interview, were literally *ivrés de pensée.*

While he was leading me towards his 'cell,' Mr. Meredith remarked to me: 'People say that the brain grows jaded. Don't believe them. The brain never grows weary. It is one's stomach that overrides feeling. And I, unfortunately, was born with a weak stomach,' he added, laughing.

In the room in which he works there is a large bay-window opening out on to the wide pastures and clusters of thick low trees characteristic of the fat land of Surrey; facing another small window, from which one can see a dark coppice of pine trees on the hill-side, stands Mr. Meredith's writing-table. 'The brain needs darkness so that thought may spring forth and grow freely,' he said to me.

He had been closely watching a bird which was flying tirelessly, hither and thither, across the sky. 'Look at that bird,' Mr. Meredith said. 'It interests me very greatly; every day it flutters about, never alighting, never stopping: we call it a swift. Whenever I see it I think that its restless movement is like the indefatigable flitting of the brain, which never ceases, never rests.'

In some casual way I began to speak about the old castle at Utrecht whose bell tolls only on the death of a king. 'And I wouldn't have them toll even then,' cried Meredith. 'I loathe the bells, with their persistent monotony. At Bruges, I remember, they kept me from thinking the whole night long; oh, I loathe them!'

When we think of his mind so constantly at tension, we cannot fail to understand how his characters and their voices are vividly realistic to him. Balzac had tears in his eyes when he broke the news of the death of his Lucien de Rubempré to his visitors. Mr. Meredith has lived in his cottage in an actual existence with the persons who have sprung from his imagination.

In that cloistral solitude, seated before that dark window, he wrote long ago at their dictation. 'When Harry Richmond's father first met me,' he said to me, 'when I heard him tell me in his pompous style about the son of a duke of royal blood and an actress of seventeen years of age, I perfectly roared with laughter!' Again, when we were discussing Renée in 'Beauchamp's Career,' he asked me, 'Was she not a sweet girl? I think I am a little in love with her yet.'

'Death?' Mr. Meredith said to me. 'I have lived long enough; I am not afraid: it's only the inside and the outside of the door.'

And I shall always hold in my mind the picture of George Meredith's tall figure, with his fine face and his grey hair, as he stood at the door of his charming little house, and watched the carriage that took me away along the green roadway from Box Hill.

It was less than three years before his death, which occurred on December 16, 1897, that Alphonse Daudet paid his first and only visit to England. He was accompanied by his wife and family, and despite the paralysis of his legs he contrived to meet many of our celebrities. Whether he was of the party that visited Meredith at Box Hill does not appear from Madame Daudet's narrative, but he was probably present at the Piccadilly dinner party which she also describes. In any case, Madame Daudet's vivacious 'Notes sur Londres' in the *Revue de Paris*, of January 1, 1896, contain no more interesting pages than those in which she pictures the life at Flint Cottage and the characteristics of its master as observed by her during her fleeting visit in the spring of 1895. I translate the following:

There were several of us who visited George Meredith, the poet and novelist, in a certain county of England, which resembles greatly our Dauphiné, with its peaceful green valleys, its gently-sloping hollows. He himself was waiting for us at the station, attired in light holiday suit. His appearance is that of a poet and gentleman, his manners are perfect, his face is distinguished-looking and mobile. His eyes are of a clear keen blue, Saxon eyes; his step, though, is now not so free, and so that we might not notice that he was tired and perhaps suffering in consequence of his fatigue, he was humming almost cheerfully an improvised tune.

We noticed from our carriage that his garden, surrounded by tall trim box trees, was sheltered from the strong wind, cold but healthy, which blew from the north. It is a well-kept garden on a sloping piece of ground, and in it were growing in this particular English spring, which is more backward than ours, clusters of yellow laburnum and lilac, while some lilies of the valley, of a milky whiteness, showed from amidst their tender green. At the end of our visit the ladies of our party were presented with bouquets of these lilies, as sweet if quickly-perishing souvenirs of our short stay.

There is a wonderful energy shown in Mr. Meredith's fine artist face, sunken, perhaps, but so lighted up by his eyes, whose depths are often pierced by his flashes of wit and the sparkling of little lights. His daughter was there in the narrow drawing-room, also the daughter of Admiral Maxse, Lady C. (Edward Cecil), daughter-in-law of Lord S. (Salisbury)—two pretty types of fair-haired beauty, with clear velvety skins, both of whom stay in the neighbourhood.

Leaving his residence, we climbed the hill to the châlet where he works: it contains two small rooms. In these rooms the books are everywhere, piled on the table, overflowing the bookshelves, books English and foreign; among them are 'Mireille' and 'Calendau,' well worn, showing the delight taken by one poet in the works of a brother poet. The other room contains a small iron bedstead in case his work is specially exacting and necessitates some rest.

My feeling of awe as I entered this privileged sanctuary was tinged with curiosity, as I mused on his habits of thought, the pauses in his dreaming or his reading, and of those characters who have engaged his mind. I thought of Zola's study, with its florid candelabra, reminiscent of glowing Catholic altars, with its precious and rare trinkets, and of Edmond de Goncourt's library with its ceiling decorated in Japanese relief, its shelves packed with the rarest editions of rare books, from his windows a glimpse of roses and the choice greenness of his Auteuil garden,—or again, of Mistral's home, from which one looks out to a horizon of cypress trees across borders of evergreens and Alpine blues,—I thought of these other places and of what the rest of the eyes and a methodical abode contribute to inspiration. What strikes me in Meredith's case is his need of solitude, his shelter on the little hill overlooking his house, and literature aside from life.

From the châlet we climb to the top of a hillock, covered with that short fine turf, yielding to the touch, which is so common in England. We could see, as the wind dispersed the clouds, rolling away deep shadows or bright lights on the near neighbourhood, a village, with clustering houses, on the land opposite. Then we descended with Meredith, and after tea and the mild excitement which followed as our chat became brisker and more animated, we took leave of the writer, carrying away with us the most delightful impression of him.

Of her later meeting with Meredith at a fashionable mansion of the West-end, Madame Daudet relates:

In response to a kind invitation, and to see Meredith once more, we went to dine with the family of a rich manufacturer whose works we had seen a few days previously not far from the Crystal Palace. These friends live in a Piccadilly mansion. We were cordially and magnificently received; the table, set for fifteen, was ablaze with every variety of rose—among which 'La France' roses reared their heavy heads, beautiful proud roses. 'La France roses in honour of Madame Daudet,' the owners of the house said several times. The young hostess was handsome and kindly, robed in black velvet; her dress was cut low over an under-vest of lace, which made her round curl-crowned head like one from an old Italian picture. She had magnificent eyes, frank, blue, and very slightly uneven. She paid great attention to Meredith, in a way that showed she was in full sympathy with this great man of genius.

We lost none of our admiration for the poet as seen at an evening party, though I had first seen him in the rustic setting of his 'cottage.' He had the same brave simplicity, the same smile, in which we can discern triumph over suffering. We then had a little talk, and some music in a cheerfully-furnished drawing-room, with rounded windows. A talented violinist played, one whom my children soon after met again at Lord B——'s house, the manager of the *Morning Post*, one of the leading London dailies [the late Lord Glenesk, of course]; a house which is a meeting-place for all the nobility, and in which Lord Byron once lived—a door is shown even now through which he escaped, not only from the building, but from marriage itself, and fled towards that life which was to be free but stormy for him in after years.

In some notes with which the *Tablet* commented upon Meredith and Catholicism on the occasion of the eightieth birthday celebration, I find a reference to a meeting between the novelist and Cardinal Manning that should be preserved, though it can scarcely be classed under the head of 'Friendships.' The *Tablet*, by the way, did not consider Meredith had done justice to the resumed importance of Catholicism in the life of his time; but went on to say:

One sonnet of Mr. Meredith's shows, however, his alert appreciation of Catholic actuality as presented by the career of Cardinal Manning. It is the sonnet beginning:

> I, wakeful for the skylark voice in men,

which he addressed to Cardinal Manning at the time of the London Dock strike. Novelist and Cardinal were strangers personally when that noble tribute to nobility was offered; but an exchange of letters followed; and one of the many memories which cling to old Archbishop's House, and one which adds to our regret in its going, is that of a meeting, within its ever friendly walls, between the Cardinal and the greatest literary creator of his time.

To follow all the friendships of George Meredith would be to contemplate a work of greater proportions than the present undertaking,—considerable though this promises to be,—despite the fact that the chronicles are so meagre where they might be so rich. I must therefore content myself by mentioning mere names where I should have liked to pursue my researches after something more substantial. To those whose names appear in the present chapter we must add Mr. Frederick Greenwood, long a favoured visitor at Box Hill, Mr. Edward Clodd, Mr. Haldane, Mr. John Burns, Lady Lugard, and, of course, the family of Admiral Maxse. Grant Allen was an intimate friend of the novelist, as we would gather from William Sharp's reminiscence, and Sharp himself, when his wanderings brought him back to England, was a welcome guest at Box Hill. W. E. Henley was probably never on terms of great intimacy, but as both had a common friend in Stevenson, Henley was bound to come into some friendly relations with Meredith, though I have found no record of these. There exists, however, a beautiful memorial to Henley, in the shape of the tribute written by Meredith and read at the unveiling of the bust by Rodin in the crypt of St. Paul's Cathedral, July 11, 1907. This is perhaps the best evidence of friendship we could wish to have. Henley is therein described as 'one of the main supports of good literature in our time,' and the tribute concludes in these words:

> Deploring we have lost him, we may marvel that we had him with us so long. What remains is the example of a valiant man; the memory of him in poetry that will endure.

Mention has just been made of Mr. Edward Clodd. It was this old friend of Meredith who beguiled him into his one and only speech,—for his lecture on Comedy at the London Institution in 1877 could hardly be regarded as a 'speech.' The occasion of Meredith's only after-dinner speech was a dinner of the Omar Khayyam Club, held at Burford Bridge Hotel, near Box Hill, in July, 1895. Dr. Robertson Nicoll described the event at some length in his 'London Letter' to the New York *Bookman* of August. Mr. Meredith was too feeble in health at the time to attend the dinner, but he joined the company of distinguished literary men after the meal, being 'received by the company standing, and with every demonstration of enthusiasm and respect.' Dr. Nicoll writes as follows:

> As Mr. Meredith came into the room he graciously recognised several of his old friends. Mr. Shorter conducted him to the seat of honour on the right hand of the chairman, and he made a striking figure against the sunshine streaming through a window half-covered with green boughs. He exchanged hearty greetings with Mr. Hardy, who was on Mr. Clodd's left hand, and after a little the President welcomed him in the name of the Club. Mr. Clodd's speech was singularly happy, light, and graceful, but with more than a trace of deep feeling. We hardly ventured to expect a formal reply, and were taken by surprise when Mr. Meredith, with a very good grace, rose to his feet and informed us that he was now making his maiden speech. He did not say much, but what he said was exquisite in form, and benignant in feeling. It must have cheered the veteran after his long, hard fight to have such an emphatic proof of the affection and veneration with which he is regarded by literary England. . . .
>
> We then had speeches from Mr. Hardy and Mr. Gissing. Both of them made the same speech, although each in his own way,

Mr. Hardy told us Mr. Meredith read the manuscript of his first book, and gave him friendly encouragement. Mr. Meredith was at that time reader for Messrs. Chapman and Hall, and a more conscientious, patient, and encouraging reader never lived. What a treasure his reports on manuscripts would make! Mr. Hardy modestly described his first attempt as 'very wild,' on which Mr. Meredith ejaculated 'Promising.' Mr. Hardy went on to say that if it had not been for the encouragement he received then from Mr. Meredith he would never have devoted himself to literature, and that from the time of their first meeting he and Mr. Meredith had been friends. It is well known that Mr. Meredith firmly believes that Mr. Hardy is beyond comparison our best novelist. Mr. Gissing had a similar experience to relate. His first novel, 'The Unclassed,' was read by Mr. Meredith. Mr. Gissing told us how he had an appointment with the reader of Messrs. Chapman and Hall, who amazed him with his accurate knowledge of the manuscript. He did not know at the time that his critic was no less a man than George Meredith.

Touching the 'promising' first effort of Mr. Hardy's, there are more stories than one; but it is generally understood that the book was strongly tinged with satire and unlikely to be popular with the public. It is said to have been entitled 'The Poor Man and the Lady,' but, whatever it was, its author did not hesitate to accept the judgment of Meredith upon it and into the fire it went, Mr. Hardy then producing 'Desperate Remedies,' in 1871, the same year that 'Harry Richmond' was published.

The home life of the novelist has been reflected indirectly in many preceding passages, since it is always difficult to detach a man entirely from his environment. But some aspects of the domesticities of Box Hill remain to be noted, especially certain glimpses into the famous châlet that stands on the terrace above Flint Cottage. Describing a pilgrimage of the Whitefriars Club to Box Hill, Mr. John A. Steuart gives this little vignette of the châlet:

The visit to the famous châlet, where 'The Egoist' and half-a-dozen other masterpieces were written, had a particular interest. The cottage conforms to Mr. Ruskin's idea of a work-place; small, with a pleasant outlook. Standing high on the hill-side, it affords wide views of green heights and valleys. Below, embowered in flowers and trees, is the dwelling-house, a minute's walk away. The library in the châlet is a workman's library, and the writing-table bears the same practical appearance. The books, as might be expected, are pleasantly cosmopolitan; classics of all ages and countries, not excluding English. French works are conspicuous, and there is more than a tincture of German philosophy. But one thinks less of the books than of the brooding hours and joyous flights of the creative spirit in that lonely wind-swept garden-house. Many a midnight hour has the great novelist and poet spent there, giving 'to airy nothings a local habitation and a name' that must remain to fascinate long, long after the shaping hand shall have vanished. In that time to come, say, a century hence, when the Whitefriars of the day, tempted, perhaps, by curiosity, turn over musty records to read our unremembered names, the love of Richard and Lucy and the folly of Sir Willoughby will still be potent to charm and warn and purify. One can fancy, too, those remote successors going to Box Hill and saying 'Here and here walked, and talked, and worked, the novelist of his age,' and for a certainty they will envy us the privilege of holding converse with him in the flesh. Mr. Meredith says he will write no more novels, so that already the châlet belongs to history.

Of the same occasion Mr. Coulson Kernahan has this souvenir to offer us:

I shall not soon forget my first glimpse of the home where so much of his life has been passed. One of Mr. Meredith's contemporaries speaks of that sense of human story which haunts the mind when one looks upon some quiet English country house and remembers its human associations. 'Many a simple home will move one's heart like a poem, many a cottage like a melody.' If one can feel so at sight of a cottage, the very name of whose tenant is unknown to us, how much more must we be moved when we look, for the first time, upon the walls which have sheltered him whose words have so long made their home in our hearts! That there should have been to us anything of strangeness in what, to him, has been so familiar, seemed to me almost incongruous. 'Surely I know that "wet bird-haunted English lawn!"' I said to myself. 'And that shoulder of green upland where, even now, two lovers stand out clearly against the line of sky—it must be that I have looked upon it before.'

The present writer gave a very slight but somewhat more detailed picture of the châlet in a magazine article some five years ago, from which the following may be reprinted:

Flint Cottage lies in a hollow by the roadside, around it spreads its owner's well-loved gardens, and perched on the hill behind is the châlet in which most of his writing for over thirty years has been done. This is a plain little structure of two rooms, one formerly equipped as a bedroom so that he might sleep here when writing into the night, the other and larger used as a study. The well-stocked bookshelves are heavy with what the literary man would call working books, but a large proportion are the familiar paper-bound French novels, of which Mr. Meredith has been a great reader. Here and there one notes presentation copies from admirers, one of these being an autograph copy of 'A Window in Thrums.' The poets are in abundance on these shelves, and the interest of the novelist in his father's people is indicated by a Welsh dictionary. There are few adornments, no luxuries at all, and among the few fading photographs over the mantelpiece are those of James Russell Lowell and John Morley. In a corner stands the desk whereon the master-hand has written so long, but the quills lie dry, the ink-bottle empty. From the window is obtained a spacious view of the green hills of Surrey, gentle in outline, soft and peaceful, strangely unsuggestive of the rugged grandeur of the master's work, and yet this scene, noted daily by his eye in all the changing moods of nearly two score years, must have played its part in the moulding of his mind.

Mr. W. T. Stead, who must be numbered among the friends of Meredith, has on several occasions written with some intimacy of his causeries with the veteran at Box Hill. Thus, we find him writing in the lengthy character-sketch which he published in the *Review of Reviews* for March, 1904:

From his eyrie on the hill-side Mr. Meredith ever keeps a keen look-out upon the world and its affairs, and there are few things occurring at home or abroad in which he does not take a keen, sympathetic interest. From old time he has ever been a diligent student and a great admirer of French literature. The day I was there a copy of the *Journal des Débats* was lying on his table; and the literary side of French journalists, with its peculiar delicate irony, appeals to him much more than the less urbane and more bludgeon-like methods of their English *confrères*. . . .

But Mr. Meredith has ever been on intimate terms with the editors who have from time to time conducted the journal which was first of all Greenwood's *Pall Mall Gazette*. Mr. Frederick Greenwood has been, and is still, one of the favoured visitors at Box Hill. Mr. Morley, of course, may be said to be, in one sense, one of George Meredith's disciples, and he still remains an intimate friend. For myself, from the time I succeeded Mr. Morley at Northumberland Street, I found in Mr. Meredith the kindest and most encouraging of sympathising friends. He frequently contributed to the *Pall Mall Gazette*, and I count among the golden days of my editorial experiences the times when we drove over to Box Hill, and spent some delightful hours in listening to the large and luminous discourse of Mr. Meredith, who combines the acumen of the philosopher with the quick intuition and insight of the poet.

A charming anecdote illustrating the simplicity of the novelist's life in his later days is told by Mr. T. P. O'Connor as follows:

[*From a photograph by the author.*

THE SWISS CHÂLET AND GARDEN AT FLINT COTTAGE.

[*To face p.* **128.**

His son's wife, who was staying at the house, was recovering from an illness, and during the period of convalescence she used to take drives in a little donkey-carriage. It would hardly be thought that in this could be found a source of amusement [illegible] genius, but I am told that Meredith used to [illegible] delight in having the little donkeys, from [illegible] was made, brought outside his hut in order [illegible] them grazing, while at the same time, [illegible] conversed with the lady who had charge of the animals.

In turning from the personal aspect of George Meredith, [illegible] better conclude the present [illegible] able but anonymous writer in the Daily Telegraph, [illegible] with the description of the scene on his birthday, for a [illegible] veteran's home life in the evening of his days:—

Old age has planted [illegible] Mr. Meredith. [illegible] it has wrinkled his [illegible] his hair. [illegible] use of his limbs, he [illegible] for his morning outing [illegible] to a point where [illegible] England—spreads [illegible] the half-distinguished [illegible] journey—a matter of [illegible] he has perforce consented [illegible] morning alike, be the [illegible] Meredith may be seen leaving Flint Cottage [illegible] driven by 'Picnic,' the donkey he [illegible] and led by Cole—the faithful attendant for [illegible] most occasions, his kindly nurse, Miss [illegible] of the little car. Every day, [illegible] to the cottage for lunch. [illegible] and letters, and the rest [illegible] bed.

The week-end is [illegible] but [illegible] the cottage is so [illegible] part put up at the well-known Burford Bridge [illegible] friends in art and literature [illegible] tion is the same. [illegible] satire, rich with [illegible] is to be alternately dazzled by [illegible] ledge, or to be irresistibly shaken into laughter by [illegible] lightheartedness and mirth.

Our last look at the man [illegible] something of his ardent and unwavering optimism. [illegible] be judged by his own gospel, how [illegible]

K

His son's wife, who was staying at the house, was recovering from an illness, and during the period of convalescence she used to take drives in a little donkey-chaise. It would hardly be thought that in this could be found a source of amusement for a man of genius, but I am told that Mr. Meredith used to take the greatest delight in having the little army of donkeys, from which the selection was made, brought outside his house in order that he might watch them grazing, while at the same time, leaning over his gate, he conversed with the lads who had charge of the animals.

In turning from the personal aspect of George Meredith I cannot better conclude the present chapter than by drawing upon the very able but anonymous writer in the *Daily Telegraph* who was charged with the description of the eightieth birthday, for a final sketch of the veteran's home life in the evening of his days:

Old age has planted no wrinkle in Mr. Meredith's mind, howbeit it has wrinkled his face and whitened his hair. Deprived of the use of his limbs, he still, as he has done for forty years past, goes for his morning outing up the Box, with its mounting ridge of firs, to a point where the panorama of Surrey—one of the finest in England—spreads itself before him, to the gap of Shoreham and the half-distinguished Sussex coast. Years ago he walked the journey—a matter of four or five miles—but for some years past he has perforce enjoyed the outing in his donkey-chaise. Every morning alike, be the weather wet or fine, cold or sunny, Mr. Meredith may be seen leaving Flint Cottage promptly at 10.40, driven by 'Picnic,' the donkey he rescued from less easeful labour, and led by Cole—his faithful attendant for thirty years—with, on most occasions, his kindly nurse, Miss Nicholls, walking at the side of the little car. Every day, at ten minutes to one, the party returns to the cottage for lunch. Then follow books and newspapers and letters, and the calls of friends, till tea-time and early supper and bed.

The week-end is still an institution; but the accommodation of the cottage is so restricted that the novelist's friends for the most part put up at the well-known Burford Bridge Hotel near by. His friends in art and literature are legion. To one and all the fascination is the same. His company is a feast of vivacity, humour, and satire, rich with worldliness and unworldliness. To hear him speak is to be alternately dazzled by his eloquence, amazed at his knowledge, or to be irresistibly shaken into laughter by his pure, boyish lightheartedness and mirth.

Our last look at the man is thus well calculated to infect us with something of his ardent and unwavering optimism. If a man is to be judged by his own gospel, how splendidly does the prophet of the joy of earth stand the test! The personal life ot him is attuned so clearly to the virile ring of his philosophy that we cannot but suppose a full and intimate account of his friendships and home life, written with the necessary authority and the 'inner knowledge,' would be an immensely valuable contribution to literary history. It is sincerely to be hoped that such a work may be undertaken. If John Morley had not been swallowed up into politics and the peerage, he had possibly given us a monograph on Meredith that would have ranked high in his literary achievement. This we may be sure, that though Meredith's works are his best biography, there is bound to be in the future an immense and deepening interest in his personal character; the man himself is fully as worthy of study as his work.

VI

SOME EARLY APPRECIATIONS

THERE is good excuse if one repeats that George Meredith met with appreciation from the first; for the fable of his 'long years of neglect' survives lustily to-day in newspaper offices and places where men write, and his own words have encouraged it. Seldom does a journalist pen a paragraph about Meredith into which he does not contrive to weave 'long years of neglect'; a catchy phrase. More than most authors, Meredith had intelligent and cordial appreciation from the beginning, and that from the critics whose opinion he had best reason to value. Though an anonymous writer in the *Spectator* did describe him in 1862 as 'an author with a somewhat low ethical tone,' that was a mere incident in the rough-and-tumble of criticism, which every author, great and small, must experience; his prose and poetry had already been the subject of numerous sane and satisfactory reviews in the critical journals. Moreover, was the *Spectator* stupidity not well worth having for the sake of Swinburne's splendid reply? Meredith was only thirty-four at the time, and the attack ruffled him for a moment, according to Sir William Hardman; but he had to face far more drastic criticism in his later years of 'popularity' than he ever met in his days of 'neglect.' To secure serial publication in a high-class weekly in 1860, when 'Evan Harrington' appeared in *Once a Week*, was a much greater distinction to a novelist than it would be to-day; to have a long novel published in the *Fortnightly Review* in 1866, when 'Vittoria' ran through that review, also implied more honour to the writer than it would to-day. Meredith was not yet forty, and literary success before that age was then rarer than it is to-day. Briefly, from his first publication of 'Poems' in 1851 he never lacked appreciation, and if he never caught the ruck of readers he never set out to catch them. Far too much has been made, parrot-wise, of the thoughtless story about the frosty reception his earlier works met with at the hands of critics and readers.

In this chapter my purpose is not to examine all the early

appreciations of his prose and poetry. It is doubtful whether a review of these long-forgotten reviews would be a profitable undertaking, though I have studied them for my own satisfaction. Anonymous criticism is, on the whole, of so little value, that it deserves the dusty tomb of the back-number as thoroughly as the other unidentified remains reposing there. In compiling a contemporary estimate of any noteworthy person or event, anonymous criticism, except in rare instances, and these chiefly where the criticism is bellicose and brutal, has astonishingly little to contribute. Hence I pass over here all such early writings on Meredith and his works, and that the more willingly as there exists material of the greatest possible interest, by reason of its writers no less than its subject, which must engage our attention.

It is no mean distinction to have been the first writer in the press to welcome into the republic of letters so worthy a citizen as George Meredith. But that fifty-seven years after the publication of a famous book, the author and his first appreciative critic should still be surviving, is surely a fact unique in literary history. The lives of literary journals are brief, however, and the medium of Mr. William Michael Rossetti's criticism of George Meredith's 'Poems' is long since dead. It was to the *Critic* of November 15, 1851, that the younger brother of Dante Gabriel contributed the first signed article on Meredith's poetry. In later years Mr. Rossetti may have re-read his little study with misgivings, for it has some of those faults of youth which he discovers in the poet—it is not without amusement that we may note the paternal air of the critic in referring to the author, the one being twenty-two years old at the time and the other twenty-three!—but allowing for the limited range of the work under review, the criticism shows genuine insight and sound appreciation. It begins in the somewhat stiff and formal style of the period, now curiously suggestive of the literary debating society, essaying to establish a definition of 'the full poet' as a 'thoroughly balanced compound of perception and intellect,' Keats being quoted as the perfect example of the perceptive poet, who 'saw loveliness in nature; or found it the incentive to lovely thoughts,' and 'rested in the effect.' Meredith is a 'kind of limited Keats'; an estimate which the young critic endeavours to make good on these grounds:

Scarcely a perceptive, but rather a seeing or sensuous poet. He does not love nature in a wide sense as Keats did; but nature delights and appeals closely to him. In proportion, however, as his sympathies are less vivid, excitable, and diffusive, he concentrates them the more. He appropriates a section of nature, as it were; and the love which he bears to it partakes more of affection. Viewing Mr. Meredith as a Keatsian, and allowing for (what we need not stop to assert) the entire superiority of the dead poet—we think it is in this point that the most essential phase of difference will be found between the two: and it is one which, were the resemblance in other respects more marked and more unmixed than it is, would suffice to divide Mr. Meredith from the imitating class. The love of Keats for nature was not an *affectionate* love: it was minute, searching, and ardent; but hardly personal. He does not lose himself in nature, but contemplates her, and utters her forth to the delight of all ages. Indeed, if we read his record aright, he was not, either in thought or in feeling, a strongly affectionate man; and the passion which ate into him at the last was a mania and infatuation, raging like disease, a symptom and a part of it. It is otherwise with Mr. Meredith. In his best moments he seems to sing, because it comes naturally to him, and silence would be restraint, not through exuberance or inspiration, but in simple contentedness, or throbbing of heart. There is an amiable and engaging quality in the poems of Mr. Meredith, a human companionship and openness, which make the reader feel his friend.

Mr. Rossetti then goes on to speak of Keats's treatment of women as lacking 'the language of individual love,' and seems inclined to the same view of Meredith, though he quotes at length the first version of 'Love in the Valley,' which appeared in the book under review. Striving, I fear, after the manner of the youthful critic, to display great subtlety of analysis, Mr. Rossetti leads us by a somewhat tangled track to a conclusion that is reasonable enough. But as the first noteworthy criticism of 'Love in the Valley,' his words call for quotation at some length:

Surely, it may be said, there is passion enough here, and of a sufficiently personal kind. True, indeed: this is not a devotion which sins through lukewarmth, and roams uncertain of an object. It will not fail to obtain an answer, through dubiousness of quest: and if it shocks at all, it shocks the delicacy, not the *amour-propre*. But its characteristics are, in fact, the same at which exception was taken in the case of Keats. The flame burns here, which there only played, darting its thin, quick tongue from point to point; but the difference is of concentration only. The impressionable is changed for the strongly impressed—the influence being similar. Here, again, the love, like our poet's love of nature, has the distinct tone of *affection*. It is purely and unaffectedly sensuous, and in its utterance as genuine a thing as can be. We hear a clear voice of nature, with no falsetto notes at all; as spontaneous and intelligible as the wooing of a bird, and equally a matter of course.

The main quality of Mr. Meredith's poems is warmth—warmth of emotion, and, to a certain extent, of imagination, like the rich mantling blush on a beautiful face, or a breath glowing upon your cheek. That he is young will be as unmistakably apparent to the reader as to ourself; on which score various shortcomings and crudities, not less than some excess of this attribute, claim indulgence.

To 'The Rape of Aurora,' 'Daphne,' and 'Angelic Love,' the young critic takes exception, but the graceful lyric 'Under Boughs of Breathing May' he classes with 'Love in the Valley,' quoting the whole of it, and 'The Daisy now is out' he copies in full, to illustrate the poet in one of his 'most exclusively descriptive pieces,' observing that the emotional quality is stronger than the descriptive. His estimate of the new poet, based on the quality of his first book of verse, is thus summed up:

We have assigned Mr. Meredith to the Keatsian school, believing that he pertains to it in virtue of the more intrinsic qualities of his mind, and of a simple enjoying nature; and as being beyond doubt of the perceptive class in poetry. In mere style, however, he attaches himself rather to the poets of the day; the pieces in which a particular bias is most evident being in a Tennysonian mould—as the 'Olive Branch,' and the 'Shipwreck of Idomeneus'—while some of his smaller lyrics smack of Herrick. He has a good ear for melody, and considerable command of rhythm; but he seems sometimes to hanker unduly after novelty of metre, attaining it, if there be no other means to his hand, by some change in length or interruption of rhyme, which has a dragging and inconsequent effect. That his volume is young is not his fault: nor are we by any means sure that it is its misfortune. Some jingle-pieces there are, indeed—mere commonplace and current convention, which mature judgment would exclude: but the best are those whose spirit is the spirit of youth, and which are the fullest of it. We do not expect ever quite to enrol Mr. Meredith among the demi-gods or heroes; and we hesitate, for the reason just given, to say that we count on greater things from him; but we shall not cease to look for his renewed appearance with hope, and to hail it with extreme pleasure, so long as he may continue to produce poems equal to the best in this first volume.

On the whole, it will be admitted this was no unworthy review of George Meredith's 'Poems,' allowing for precisely those qualities in the critic which he allowed for in the poet. That he was too timid in his estimate of the promise held out by the little volume we have all known for many years, but he was in no sense ungenerous.

He was not so enthusiastic about Meredith as the latter was about Alexander Smith, a lesser man, in his sonnet in the *Leader* of December 20, 1851. But enthusiasm is not the highest attribute of the critic. In that same December, however, a writer already of high distinction, with the 'Saints' Tragedy' and 'Alton Locke' to his credit and 'Yeast' but newly issued, heralded the coming of the new poet with greater confidence, yet with more searching criticism, being in his riper judgment surer of the weak places and quicker to discern the strength of the young writer. Charles Kingsley contributed to *Fraser's Magazine* of December, 1851, a review of the poetry of the year, under the title of 'This Year's Song Crop,' and a considerable part of his paper was devoted to Meredith's 'Poems.' The article is of so great interest to every student of the poet, and so characteristic of the lusty, wholesome, kindly author of 'Westward Ho!' that I purpose quoting in entirety all the passages touching the subject in hand:

This, we understand, is his first appearance in print; if it be so, there is very high promise in the unambitious little volume which he has sent forth as his first-fruits. It is something, to have written already some of the most delicious little love-poems which we have seen born in England in the last few years, reminding us by their riches and quaintness of tone of Herrick; yet with a depth of thought and feeling which Herrick never reached. Health and sweetness are two qualities which run through all these poems. They are often over-loaded—often somewhat clumsy and ill-expressed—often wanting polish and finish; but they are all genuine, all melodiously conceived, if not always melodiously executed. One often wishes, in reading the volume, that Mr. Meredith had been thinking now and then of Moore instead of Keats, and had kept for revision a great deal which he has published; yet, now and then, form, as well as matter, is nearly perfect. [Here he quotes the songs, 'The Moon is Alone in the Sky' and 'I cannot lose Thee for a Day.'] In Mr. Meredith's Pastorals, too, there is a great deal of sweet, wholesome writing, more like the real pastorals than those of any young poet whom we have had for many a year. . . . Careless as hexameters; but honest landscape-painting; and only he who begins honestly ends greatly.

Kingsley next quotes the first three stanzas of 'Love in the Valley,' and continues:

What gives us here hope of the future, as well as enjoyment on the spot, is, that these have evidently not been put together, but have grown of themselves; and the one idea has risen before his mind, and shaped itself into a song; not perfect in form, perhaps, but as far as it goes, healthful, and consistent, and living, through every branch and spray of detail. And this is the reason why Mr. Meredith has so soon acquired an instinctive melody. . . . To such a man any light which he can gain from æsthetic science will be altogether useful. The living seed of a poem being in him, and certain to grow and develop somehow, the whole gardener's art may be successfully brought to bear on perfecting it. For this is the use of æsthetic science—to supply, not the bricklayer's trowel, but the hoe, which increases the fertility of the soil, and the pruning-knife, which lops off excrescences. For Mr. Meredith—with real kindness we say it, for the sake of those love poems—has much to learn, and, as it seems to us, a spirit which can learn it; but still it must be learnt. One charming poem, for instance, 'Daphne,' is all spoilt, for want of that same pruning-knife. We put aside the question whether a ballad form is suitable, not to the subject—for to that, as a case of purely objective action, it is suitable—but to his half-elegiac, thoughtful handling of it. Yet we recommend him to consider whether his way of looking at the Apollo and Daphne myth be not so far identical with Mr. Tennyson's idea of 'Paris and Ænone,' as to require a similar Idyllic form, to give the thoughtful element its fair weight. If you treat external action merely (and in as far as you do so, you will really reproduce those old sensuous myths) you may keep the ballad form, and heap verse on verse as rapidly as you will; but if you introduce any subjective thought, after the fashion of the Roman and later Greek writers, to explain the myth, and give it a spiritual, or even merely allegorical, meaning, you must, as they did, slacken the pace of your verse. Let Ovid's 'Fasti' and 'Epistles' be your examples, at least in form, and write slowly enough to allow the reader to think as he goes on. The neglect of this rule spoilt the two best poems in 'Reverberations,' 'Balder' and 'Thor,' which, whatever were the faults of the rest of the book, were true and noble poems, and the neglect of it spoils 'Apollo and Daphne.' Mr. Meredith is trying all through to mean more than the form which he has chosen allows him. That form gives free scope to a prodigality of objective description, of which Keats need not have been ashamed; but if he had more carefully studied the old models of that form—from the simple Scotch ballads to Shakespeare's 'Venus and Adonis'—a ballad and not an idyll,—he would have avoided Keats' fault of too-muchness into which he has fallen. Half the poem would bear cutting out; even half of those most fresh and living stanzas, where the woodland springs into life to stop Daphne's flight—where

> Running ivies, dark and lingering,
> Round her light limbs drag and twine;
> Round her waist, with languorous tendrils
> Reels and wreathes the juicy vine,

By permission of Messrs. Smith, Elder & Co.] [*From the drawing by George du Maurier in the 'Cornhill.'*

ROY CARRYING HARRY AWAY FROM RIVERSLEY.

Sometimes his father whistled to him, or held him high and nodded a salutation to him, as though they had just discovered one another.—*Harry Richmond*. Chapter II.

[*To face p.* 136.

Crowning her with amorous clusters;
Pouring down her sloping back
Fresh-born wines in glittering rillets,
Following her in crimson track.

Every stanza is a picture in itself, but there are too many of them, and therefore we lose the story in the profusion of its accidentals. There is a truly Correggiesque tone of feeling and drawing all through this poem, which is very pleasant to us. But we pray Mr. Meredith to go to the National Gallery and there look steadily and long, with all the analytic insight he can, at the 'Venus and Mercury,' or the 'Agony in the Garden'; or go to the Egyptian Hall and there feast, not only his eyes and heart, but his intellect and spirit also, with Lord Ward's duplicate of the 'Magdalen'—the greatest Protestant sermon on 'free justification by faith' ever yet preached; and there see how Correggio can dare to indulge in his exquisite lusciousness of form, colour, and *chiaroscuro*, without his pictures ever becoming tawdry or overwrought—namely, by the severe scientific unity and harmonious gradation of parts which he so carefully preserves, which make his pictures single glorious rainbows and precious stone—that Magdalen one living emerald—instead of being, like the jewelled hawk in the Great Exhibition, every separate atom of it beautiful, yet as a whole utterly hideous.

One or two more little quarrels we have with Mr. Meredith—and yet they are but *amantium iræ*, after all. First, concerning certain Keatsian words—such as languorous, and innumerous, and such like, which are very melodious, but do not, unfortunately, belong to this our English tongue, their places being occupied already by old and established words; as Mr. Tennyson has conquered this fault in himself, Mr. Meredith must do the same. Next, concerning certain ambitious metres, sound and sweet, but not thoroughly worked out, as they should have been. Mr. Meredith must always keep in mind that the species of poetry which he has chosen is one which admits of nothing less than perfection. We may excuse the roughness of Mrs. Browning's utterance, for the sake of the grandeur and earnestness of her purpose; she may be reasonably supposed to have been more engrossed with the matter than with the manner. But it is not so with the idyllist and lyrist. He is not driven to speak by a prophetic impulse; he sings of pure will, and therefore he must sing perfectly, and take a hint from that microcosm, the hunting-field; wherein, if the hounds are running hard, it is no shame to any man to smash a gate instead of clearing it, and jump into a brook instead of over it. Forward he must get, by fair means if possible, if not, by foul. But if, like the idyllist, any gentleman 'larks' his horse over supererogatory leaps at the coverside, he is not allowed to knock all four hoofs against the top bar; but public opinion (who, donkey as she is, is a very shrewd old donkey, nevertheless, and clearly understands the difference between thistles and barley) requires him to 'come up in good form, measure his distance exactly, take off neatly, clear it cleverly, and *come well into the next field.*' . . . And even so should idyllists with their metres.

In the foregoing there is wise and kindly counsel of a sort that young poets of promise have seldom received, and had Meredith taken this advice to heart we cannot but think his later poetry had benefited appreciably; but his is a rebel spirit, and neither friendly criticism nor unfriendly was likely to affect him; certainly neither did. Kingsley's counsel was even more needful forty years later than at the time it was first given. But it is clear that Kingsley felt the ichor of greatness pulsing in those early poems of Meredith, and his words to-day sound almost prophetic: 'Only he who begins honestly ends greatly.'

On the whole, George Meredith had no reason to be disappointed by the reception of his first volume of verse at the hands of the critics, and if the public was cold, when, since the palmy days of Byron and Moore, has it been otherwise to the new poet?

Four years had passed before the poet offered himself again to the critics, and now it was with a work in which poetry and prose intermingle and render the task of criticism none too easy. 'The Shaving of Shagpat,' published at the end of 1855, but dated 1856, received almost as much attention from the critical press of the time as any other new work of note. It was by no means 'neglected.' Of chief interest to us, however, is the fact that the author's friend and admirer, George Eliot, was the writer of two of the criticisms—an early and mild example of 'multiple reviewing.' One of her reviews appeared in the *Leader*, January 5, 1856, and the other in the *Westminster Review*, April, 1856. George Eliot had been assistant editor of the latter periodical from 1851 to 1853 and was still a contributor; but, of course, she had not yet made her pen-name a household word, as it was only in 1856 that she wrote the first of her 'Scenes of Clerical Life,' which, appearing in *Blackwood's* in 1857, was the beginning of her literary fame. Her journal bears the entry: 'Dec. 30, 1855.—Read "The Shaving of Shagpat" (George Meredith's).' So she must have penned her appreciation hot foot on her reading, in order that it might be printed in the *Leader* of January 5.

No act of religious symbolism (she wrote) has a deeper root in nature than that of turning with reverence towards the East. For almost all our good things—our most precious vegetables, our noblest animals, our loveliest flowers, our arts, our religious and philosophical ideas, our very nursery tales and romances have travelled to us from the East. In an historical as well as in a physical sense, the East is the land of the morning. Perhaps the simple reason of this may be that when the earth first began to move on her axis, her Asiatic side was towards the sun—her Eastern cheek first blushed under his rays. And so this priority of sunshine, like the first move in chess, gave the East the precedence, though not the pre-eminence in all things; just as the garden slope that fronts the morning sun yields the earliest seedlings, though these seedlings may attain a hardier and more luxurious growth by being transplanted. But we leave this question to wiser heads.

Felix qui potent rerum cognoscere causas.

(Excuse the novelty of the quotation.) We have not carried our reader's thoughts to the East that we may discuss the reason why we owe it so many good things, but that we may introduce him to a new pleasure, due, at least indirectly, to that elder region of the earth. We mean 'The Shaving of Shagpat,' which is indeed an original fiction just produced in this western island, but which is so intensely Oriental in its conception and execution, that the author has done wisely to guard against the supposition of its being a translation, by prefixing the statement that it is derived from no Eastern source, but is altogether his own.

'The Shaving of Shagpat' is a work of genius, and of poetical genius. It has none of the tameness which belongs to mere imitations manufactured with servile effort or thrown off with sinuous facility. It is no patchwork of borrowed incidents. Mr. Meredith has not simply imitated Arabian fictions, he has been inspired by them, he has used Oriental forms, but only as an Oriental genius would have used them who had been 'to the manner born.' Goethe, when he wrote an immortal work under the inspiration of Oriental studies, very properly called it *West-ostliche*—West-eastern—because it was thoroughly Western in spirit, though Eastern in its forms. But this double epithet would not give a true idea of Mr. Meredith's work, for we do not remember that throughout our reading we were once struck by an incongruity between the thought and the form, once startled by the intrusion of the chill north into the land of the desert and the palm. Perhaps more lynx-eyed critics, and more learned Orientalists, than we, may detect discrepancies to which we are blind, but our experience will at least indicate what is likely to be the average impression. In one particular, indeed, Mr. Meredith differs widely from his models, but that difference is a high merit; it lies in the exquisite delicacy of his love incidents and love scenes. In every other characteristic —in exuberance of imagery, in picturesque wildness of incident, in significant humour, in aphoristic wisdom, 'The Shaving of Shagpat' is a new Arabian Night. To two-thirds of the reading world this is sufficient recommendation.

According to Oriental custom the main story of the book—'The Shaving of Shagpat'—forms the setting to several minor tales, which are told on pretexts more or less plausible by the various *dramatis personæ*. We will not forestall the reader's pleasure by telling him who Shagpat was, or what were the wondrous adventures through which Shibli Bagarag, the wandering barber, became Master of the Event and the destroyer of illusions, by shaving from Shagpat the mysterious identical which had held men in subjection to him. There is plenty of deep meaning in the tale for those who cannot be satisfied without deep meanings, but there is no didactic thrusting forward of moral lessons, and our imagination is never chilled by a sense of allegorical intention predominating over poetic creation. Nothing can be more vivid and concrete than the narrative and description, nothing fresher and more vigorous than the imagery. Are we reading how horsemen pursued their journey? We are told that they 'flourished their lances with cries, and jerked their heels into the flanks of their steeds, and stretched forward till their beards were mixed with the tossing manes, and the dust rose after them crimson in the sun.' Is it a maiden's eyes we are to see? They are 'dark, under a low arch of darker lashes, like stars on the skirts of storm.' Sometimes the images are exquisitely poetical, as when Bhanavar looks forth 'on the stars that were above the purple heights and the *blushes of inner heaven that streamed up the sky*,' sometimes ingenious and pithy: for example, 'she clenched her hands an instant with that feeling which knocketh a nail in the coffin of a desire not dead.' Indeed, one of the rarest charms of the book is the constant alternation of passion and wild imaginativeness with humour and pithy, practical sense. Mr. Meredith is very happy in his imitation of the lyrical fragments which the Eastern tale-tellers weave into their narrative, either for the sake of giving emphasis to their sententiousness, or for the sake of giving a more intense utterance to passion, a loftier tone to description.

George Eliot then goes on to quote many of the lyrics from the story of 'Bhanavar the Beautiful,' which she describes as 'the brightest gem among the minor tales, and perhaps in the entire book.' She also gives most of the tale of 'The Punishment of Khipil' to illustrate the author's 'skill in humorous apologue,' and concludes:

We hope we have said enough to do justice to 'The Shaving of Shagpat,' enough to make our readers desire to see it. They will find it, compared with the other fictions which the season has provided, to use its own Oriental style, 'as the apple tree among the trees of the wood.'

Writing to Miss Sara Hennell, on January 18, 1856, George Eliot makes a reference to her article in the *Leader*, saying, 'If you want some idle reading get "The Shaving of Shagpat," which I think you will say deserves all the praise I gave it.'

George Eliot's second notice of 'The Shaving of Shagpat' was rather incidental than particular, occurring in a twenty-five page article on 'Art and Belles Lettres,' contributed to the *Westminster Review* of April, 1856, in the course of which she dwelt on Wilkie Collins's 'After Dark,' Kingsley's 'Heroes,' 'Noctes Ambrosianæ,' and a variety of French and German books. It is a very graceful and generous tribute, well worthy of a place in any collection of Meredithiana. I quote the reference in full:

We turn from the art which most of us must leave our homes to get even a glimpse of, to that which has at least the advantage of visiting us at our own firesides—the art of the romancer and novelist; and the first work of fiction that presents itself as worth notice is 'The Shaving of Shagpat,' an admirable imitation of Oriental tale-telling, which has given us far more pleasure than we remember to have had even in younger days from reading 'Vathek' —the object of Byron's enthusiastic praise.

Of course, the great mass of fictions are imitations, more or less slavish and mechanical—imitations of Scott, of Balzac, of Dickens, of Currer Bell, and the rest of the real 'makers'; every great master has his school of followers, from the kindred genius down to the feeble copyist. 'The Shaving of Shagpat' is distinguished from the common run of fictions, not in being an imitation, but in the fact that its model has been chosen from no incidental prompting, from no wish to suit the popular mood, but from genuine love and mental affinity. Perhaps we ought to say that it is less an imitation of the 'Arabian Nights' than a similar creation inspired by a thorough and admiring study. No doubt, if a critical lens were to be applied, there would be found plenty of indications that the writer was born in Western Europe, and in the nineteenth century, and that his Oriental imagery is got by hearsay; but to people more bent on enjoying what they read than on proving their acumen, 'The Shaving of Shagpat' will be the thousand and *second* night which they perhaps longed for in their childhood.

The author is alive to every element in his models: he reproduces their humour and practical sense as well as their imaginativeness. Shibli Bagarag, the barber, carries a great destiny within him: he is to shave Shagpat the clothier, and thus to become Master of the Event. The city of Shagpat, unlike the city of London, regards shaving, and not the beard, as the innovation; and Shagpat is a 'miracle of hairiness, black with hair as he had been muzzled with it, and his head, as it were, a berry in a huge bush by reason of it,' and when the countenance of Shagpat waxed fiery it was as 'a flame kindled by travellers at night in a bramble bush, and he ruffled and heaved and was as when dense jungle-growths are stirred violently by the near approach of a wild animal.' Moreover, among the myriad hairs of Shagpat is the mysterious 'Identical' which somehow holds the superstition of men in bondage, so that they bow to it without knowing why—the most obstinate of all bowing, as we are aware. Hence, he who will shave Shagpat, and deliver men from worshipping his hairy mightiness, will deserve to be called Master of the Event; and the story of all the adventures through which Shibli Bagarag went before he achieved this great work—the thwackings he endured, the wondrous scenes he beheld, and the dangers he braved to possess himself of the magic horse Garaveen, the Lily of the Enchanted Sea, and other indispensable things, with his hairbreadth escapes from spiteful genii—all this forms the main action of the book.

Other tales are introduced, serving as pleasant landing-places on the way. The best of these is the story of Khipil the Builder, a humorous apologue, which will please readers who are unable to enjoy the wilder imaginativeness of Oriental fiction; but lovers of the poetical will prefer the story of Bhanavar the Beautiful. We confess to having felt rather a languishing interest towards the end of the work; the details of the action became too complicated, and our imagination was rather wearied in following them. But where is the writer whose wing is as strong at the end of his flight as at the beginning? Even Shakespeare flags under the artificial necessities of a *dénouement*.

'Farina; a Legend of Cologne,' being published the year after 'The Shaving of Shagpat,' George Eliot was again the critic of her friend's work in the pages of the *Westminster*, her review of 'Farina' appearing in the issue of October, 1857. Naturally the book did not move her to the enthusiasm which the author's former work had produced in his admirer, and in her estimate of the story we can see personal liking struggle with the critical sense, the latter proving the stronger in the result. Where she accuses the novelist of sacrificing 'euphony and almost sense, to novelty and force of expression,' we have one of the earliest expressions of what has grown into a volume of adverse criticism of style, unexampled in the case of any other famous writer of prose or poetry. George Eliot was certainly no blind admirer, but her sane and tempered praise, coming at so critical a period in the fortunes of the young author, and from one whose judgment he must have respected, could hardly fail to be heartening to him.

An abridgement of the review by George Eliot is here given:

The author of 'Farina' has exposed himself to a somewhat trying ordeal. Last year he treated us to a delightful volume of well-sustained Oriental extravagance, and we remember our friend Shibli Bagarag too well to be easily satisfied with any hero less astonishing. It was refreshing to leave the actual and the probable for a time, and follow Mr. Meredith's lead into the bright world of imagination. The hope of such another enchanted holiday prepared us to welcome his new tale with all due honour and cordiality. It was with something like disappointment, therefore, that we found ourselves brought down to the vulgar limits of time and place, and our appetite for the marvellous entirely spoilt by scenes which challenge prosaic considerations of historical truth and the fitness of things.

The title, 'Farina; a Legend of Cologne,' will naturally carry the reader's mind to those ungainly-shaped bottles, with which the British tourist is sure to return laden from the city of evil smells. Mr. Meredith is pleased to bestow a high antiquity on the famous distillation, and his hero, doubtless the first of all the Jean Maries, is invested with the dubious honours of a dealer in the black art, on account of his suspicious collection of bottles and vases, pipes and cylinders. But when the Devil is beaten in single combat on the Drachenfels, and returns from whence he came, entering to his kingdom under the Cathedral Square, and leaving behind him a most abominable stench, Farina's perfumed water does good service. The kaiser, six times driven back by the offence to his nostrils, is enabled to enter the good city of Cologne, and then and there reward the restorer of a pure atmosphere with the hand of his long-loved bride.

For the rest, the story is sufficiently slight. We have the blonde and bewitching heroine, Margarita, and her troop of lovers, who prove their devotion by such strenuous interchange of blows in her honour, that there is not one of them who is not black and blue; and we have *the* lover, Farina, tender and true, brave as Siegfried, and worshipping his 'Frankinne' with such fanatical homage, as 'Conrad the Pious' might have sung. Margarita's father, Gottlieb Groschen, the rich Cologne citizen, is a characteristic specimen of the prosperous mediæval Rhinelander. . . .

Much clever and vigorous description is to be found in the narrative, and Mr. Meredith has been very successful in setting before us a vivid picture of the coarse, rough manners, the fierce, warlike habits, and the deep-seated superstition of the 'good old times' of chivalry. The character of the jovial Squire Guy the Goshawk is especially well done.

As a whole, we think 'Farina' lacks completeness, and the ghostly element is not well worked in. The combat between Saint Gregory and the Devil is made ludicrous by its circumstantiality. It was not as a jeering satirist that the old monkish legends set forth

Sathanas, and there is a clumsiness in the whole affair which accords ill with the boldness and skill displayed in other portions of the tale. We must also protest against Father Gregory's use of the nominative case 'ye' instead of accusative 'you,' monk though he be, and privileged, doubtless, to speak bad grammar at will; nor can we admire many passages in which the author has sacrificed euphony, and almost sense, to novelty and force of expression. With these blemishes, 'Farina' is both an original and an entertaining book, and will be read with pleasure by all who prefer a lively, spirited story to those dull analyses of dull experiences in which the present school of fiction abounds.

When an author has 'arrived,' and particularly when his sun is setting in a peaceful glory, there are always many ready to claim that they had first given him a friendly greeting in the chill, grey dawn of his rising, and we cannot find fault with this very human weakness; next to being a great man is the acumen of knowing one when you see him. Thus the *Times* not unnaturally found occasion to observe in its 'leader' on Mr. Meredith's eightieth birthday: 'This journal may perhaps claim a special pleasure in bearing testimony to-day to Mr. Meredith's achievements, inasmuch as we believe the first public attempt to appreciate him was in a three-column review which we gave to "The Ordeal of Richard Feverel" in 1859.' Whether this is strictly correct may be left to the judgment of my readers with the facts of the earliest appreciations now before them. The *Times* article was certainly worthy of those traditions which are still the glory of that journal. In any case, this is further evidence in favour of my contention that Meredith was not coldly eyed in the high places of journalism in the early stages of his career. A three-column article in the *Times* on a writer of a new book was supposed to be good for the sale of a whole edition fifty years ago.

Reference has already been made to A. C. Swinburne's very spirited and characteristic letter to the *Spectator* of June 7, 1862, defending his friend Meredith from the attack of an anonymous writer in that journal on the appearance of 'Modern Love.' That letter has further value as indicating the position to which Meredith had attained in the year 1862, when Swinburne himself had only published 'The Queen Mother and Rosamund.' 'One of the leaders of English literature,' 'the very eminence of his post,' 'a man who has won his spurs and fought his way to a foremost place among the men of his time'; these and like phrases applied to Meredith by a writer so intimate with the literary world of his day as Swinburne

By permission of Messrs. Smith, Elder & Co.] [*From the drawing by George du Maurier in the 'Cornhill.'*

HARRY RICHMOND'S MEETING WITH THE PRINCESS OTTILIA.

She waited for us to march by, without attempting to conceal that we were the objects of her inspection, and we in good easy swing of the feet gave her a look as we lifted our hats.—*Harry Richmond.* Chapter XV.

[*To face p.* 144.

in 1862, should [illegible] apt [illegible] in late years, which [illegible] some [illegible] Meredith's long period [illegible] and [illegible] an early and valued [illegible] writing [illegible] 'Reminiscences

I think I was [illegible] was borne as [illegible] and original force [illegible] greatly mistaken [illegible] contributed the first [illegible] Meredith to the [illegible] I do not mean to [illegible] on George Meredith [illegible] of weekly and of [illegible] magazines; but [illegible] having been the [illegible] appeared in one of [illegible] the *Westminster Review* [illegible] Chapman. Chapman [illegible] Meredith [illegible] immense admiration [illegible] genius, and yet [illegible] my suggestion to [illegible] about a man as [illegible]

The article to [illegible] a Purpose,' which [illegible] reprinted in the [illegible] later. Quotation [illegible] preferred to utilise [illegible] as the estimate of [illegible] thinking himself [illegible] quarterlies; indeed [illegible] though numerous [illegible] none dealt with Meredith [illegible] reference to his [illegible] Mr. McCarthy's memory [illegible] what blurred impression [illegible] to publish an article [illegible] Meredith's novels [illegible] Chapman's [illegible] had already published [illegible] those by George [illegible] the same issue as Mr. McCarthy's own contribution [illegible] that the novelist's name was far from unknown [illegible] and in 1862, should be noted, for memory is apt to play strange tricks in late years, which may account for some of the stories of Meredith's long period of obscurity. Thus I find Mr. Justin McCarthy, an early and valued friend of Meredith, writing in his most engaging 'Reminiscences':

> I think I was among the earliest of those into whose minds it was borne as a fact that with George Meredith an entirely new and original force had arisen in English literature. If I am not greatly mistaken, I think I am entitled to boast of the fact that I contributed the first long and elaborate study of the genius of George Meredith to the pages of a regular quarterly review. Of course, I do not mean to say that other writers had not contributed articles on George Meredith full of appreciation and rapture, to the pages of weekly and of daily journals, and, probably, too, of monthly magazines; but I hope I am entitled to claim the distinction of having been the writer of the first essay concerning him which appeared in one of the quarterlies. The essay which I wrote was for the *Westminster Review*, then edited by my friend the late Dr. John Chapman. Chapman knew George Meredith intimately, had an immense admiration for him, and a thorough appreciation of his genius, and yet it was not without some hesitation that he accepted my suggestion to write an article altogether, or almost altogether, about a man at that time so little known to the general public.

The article to which Mr. McCarthy here refers is 'Novels with a Purpose,' which appeared in the *Westminster*, July, 1864, and was reprinted in the author's volume of essays 'Con Amore,' four years later. Quotation from it would be quite in place here, but I have preferred to utilise it in other chapters of this work, and chiefly as the estimate of a fellow-novelist. Mr. McCarthy is correct in thinking himself the first to write of Meredith in one of the quarterlies; indeed he is too modest in his claim, for, prior to 1864, though numerous articles had appeared in periodicals of all kinds, none dealt with Meredith's prose as a whole; all had some particular reference to his latest book; but what sounds strange, and where Mr. McCarthy's memory may conceivably have given back a somewhat blurred impression, is the recollection of Chapman's hesitancy to publish an article largely, but not exclusively, devoted to Meredith's novels. Under Chapman's editorship the *Westminster* had already published four reviews of Meredith's works, including those by George Eliot, and had one of 'Emilia in England' in the same issue as Mr. McCarthy's own contribution, indicating that the novelist's name was far from unknown to its readers, and, unless Swinburne's epithets of two years earlier date were greatly exaggerated, or were merely the affected knowledge of the literary elect—which we have no reason for supposing them to be—Meredith was, even in 1864, and apart from Chapman's personal friendship, an entirely suitable subject for the *Westminster.* All honour to Mr. McCarthy for his first weighty article, but *was* the 'general public' of 1864 really more ignorant of Meredith and his work than that of to-day? Even at the time of his death he was no more than a name to the 'general public'; the intelligent reading public is larger, but hardly better informed, than it was forty-five years ago; and it has never been the business of quarterly reviews to choose their topics on the principle of interesting any but the select public of readers, to whom I have endeavoured to show Meredith has always been familiar, if not as an author whom they have read, at least as one with a reputation commanding their respect.

My contention seems to receive further support from the opening passages of the thoughtful criticism of 'Emilia in England' which the late Dr. Richard Garnett contributed to the *Reader*, April 23, 1864. Dr. Garnett was clearly addressing a public that was aware of the eminence of George Meredith when he wrote in this strain:

The announcement of a new work by Mr. George Meredith is necessarily one to provoke much curiosity and expectation, since even a modest approximation to the end he has been wont to propose to himself implies ability of an unusual description. Mr. Meredith belongs to that select band of humorists who mainly rely for effect upon the pungency and piquancy of their diction, whether uttered in their own character or placed in the mouths of their *dramatis personæ.* Few writers, indeed, could dispose of resources adequate to so sustained a display of intellectual pyrotechnics as that which has now lasted Mr. Meredith through nine volumes. It is comparatively easy to devise humorous situations; but this is farce. Mr. Meredith's works are the best modern representatives of the genteel comedy of a hundred and fifty years since. Incident and character are not neglected; but both are subordinate to dialogue. The personages have their prototypes in nature, but are still somewhat idealised: they are like and not like people we have seen. They are rather types of character than individuals. Maskwell in Congreve's comedy, for example, is a really scientific combination of the chief traits of a designing villain; but we may perceive at once that these have been ingeniously put together in the study, not copied from the living model. It is a significant circumstance that all Congreve's plays were composed at an age when Mr. Meredith had hardly begun to write. The latter's experience of life is consequently much wider, and there is that in the genius of his time which causes him to be more solicitous about the truth of things. Nevertheless, next to the intellectual brilliancy of his writings, their most salient feature is their artificial aspect. A principle of intelligent selection seems to have presided over their genesis and development. The story is carefully chosen for the sake of some favourite idea snugly bedded in the centre of it—a Psyche-germ, swathed in a rich cocoon of illustration. The personages are all selected with a similar view, and their sayings and doings meted out with the nicest accuracy. The style again is highly *recherché*, spiced with epigram, and elaborated even to obscurity. It might easily be surmised that Mr. Meredith experienced considerable difficulty in arraying his thoughts in their appropriate garment of speech, and that the frequent harshness of his exposition was the evidence of a victory won by a vigorous growth over an unkindly soil. Thus rich, original, strained, and artificial, the general effect of one of Mr. Meredith's novels is very much that of a fine landscape seen through tinted glass—a pleasing variety, so long as there are plain windows in the house. To read Mr. Meredith in his turn is to season the feast of literature with an exquisite condiment; to read nobody but Mr. Meredith would be like making a dinner of salt—Attic, of course.

'Emilia in England' is fully equal to the author's former works in humour and power, and only less remarkable in so far as it is less original. The plot is a variation on the theme of 'Evan Harrington.' The comedy of that admirable novel turned on the struggle of three sisters, upheaved into a higher than their natural sphere, with the demon of Tailordom; their frantic efforts to entomb the monstrous corpse of their plebeian origin beneath the highest available heaps of acted and spoken lies; the vigorous resistance of that ghastly being to this method of disposing of him, and his victorious assertion of his right to walk the earth. The more serious interest arose from the entanglement of their straightforward brother in their web of imposition, not without the participation of the mischievous deity of Love. In 'Emilia' we have three sisters again—the Misses Pole—Pole, Polar, and North Pole, or, as the profane have entitled them, Pole, Polony, and Maypole. The situation is fundamentally the same, but so far varied that the ladies have no chance of concealing their mercantile origin, of which, indeed, to do them justice, they are not ashamed. They simply wish to get higher, and, by way of justifying their ambition to themselves, have set up a fanciful code of feelings supposed to be proper to the highest circles, to which, by way of demonstrating their fitness for the same, they make it the study of their lives to conform. That is, they lived by a conventional rule, just as the baronet in Mr. Meredith's first novel brought up his own son upon system. Mr. Meredith appears to entertain a special detestation for anything cut and dried, and the gist of his present work is a sarcastic but quiet exposure of the evil these ladies wrought against their better nature.

Emilia Belloni, the heroine, is an entire contrast to the Miss Poles. She is in some respects the repetition of Rose Jocelyn in 'Evan Harrington'—a pattern of pure nature, perfect guilelessness, absolute unreserve, and entire surrender to self-oblivious passion. She combines the unembarrassed purity of an antique statue with the fire of a painting of the modern school. She is most pathetic in her confiding simplicity—in her frankness perfectly irresistible. This complete self-abandonment is powerfully contrasted with Wilfrid Pole's merely sentimental feeling for the beautiful stranger, and paralleled with Merthyr Powys' devotion to the cause of Emilia's country. Here are the materials of an excellent drama; and, though the interest of the book does not mainly depend upon the incidents, there are sufficient to prevent it from flagging to any great extent. The chief obstacles to its success will probably be found in the peculiarity of the style, the quaintness (so pleasant to those who have once learned to relish it) of Mr. Meredith's habits of thought, and the idealisation of the characters. There is a soul of truth in them all; but it is sometimes rather grotesquely incarnated. A hostile criticism might enlarge on their unlikeness to ordinary mortals. The reply must be that they are meant to embody certain types of thought and feeling, and consequently rather made to order than sketched from life. This employment of Mr. Meredith's talents is perfectly legitimate, especially after the proofs he has given of his ability to reproduce actual character with unimpaired effect. Observation alone could have furnished material for such vivid delineations as those of Mrs. Chump, in whose vicinity sentiment is barely possible, and Mr. Pericles, Greek millionaire, musical bear, and beneficent ogre. Perhaps the scenes where he appears are the richest in a work scintillating throughout with wit and humour.

In strict point of time we may have travelled some distance beyond the 'early' appreciations of the poet and novelist. When an author has produced seven notable works, three of them unusually long three-volume novels—the 'nine volumes' to which Dr. Garnett refers—and has been acknowledged by the best judges of his time a leading figure in contemporary letters, it is scarcely correct to qualify further criticism of him with the epithet 'early'; especially when we remember that in 1864 'The Ordeal of Richard Feverel' had been published for five years. But as Meredith's last novel was not written until thirty years later, we may be permitted to characterise a longer period of his earlier work as 'early' than would apply in the case of one whose literary life had been less protracted. Even so, I can hardly urge that an article written so late as 1876 would naturally fall within this chapter of the present work. But James Thomson, the author of 'The City of Dreadful Night,' has some claim to be regarded as one of the early admirers of Meredith's genius, though others had anticipated him in the printed expression of their opinions. Touching this point, I find the following entries in Thomson's diary for the year 1879:

> *Saturday, Nov.* 1.—*Athenæum;* openg. article on Egoist. The first critique on any of George Meredith's books I have ever come across, in which the writer showed thorough knowledge of his works, and anything like an adequate apprec. of his wonderful genius.
>
> *Saturday, Nov.* 8.—*Athenæum*, advt. of Egoist: cordial praise from *Athenm., Pall Mall, Spectr., Examr.* At length! Encourg.! A man of wonderful genius and a splendid writer may hope to obtn. something like recogn. after working hard for thirty years, dating from his majority!

There is something here of the natural exaggeration of a warm-hearted admirer, not unmixed with a suspicion of the pride of one who supposes himself to have long appreciated a pearl to which the grosser mob is indifferent. Thomson's earliest appreciation of Meredith did not appear until June, 1876, in *Cope's Tobacco Plant*, and in the *Secularist* about the same time he also wrote his 'Note on George Meredith, on the occasion of Beauchamp's Career,' which is reprinted in his 'Essays and Phantasies.' Now, in the opening passage of this 'note,' which I reprint below, he indicates quite clearly what we all know: how thoroughly Meredith's genius was appreciated by those best qualified to judge: whereas, in his diary three years later we have seen him making one of these somewhat rash statements so curiously common among writers on Meredith. He had not been sufficiently wide-awake, else he had 'come across' many a critique of earlier date than November 1, 1879, in which no grudging praise and no blundering judgment was passed on the object of his literary idolatry. In some way the present chapter has been designed to prove this, but had I cared to quote at length from the considerable mass of anonymous criticism, dating from 1851 to 1879, there had been no difficulty in showing how wrong was Thomson's impression—an impression that has become a tradition of modern literature and is like to last as long as the fame of Meredith.

Certainly no critic before Thomson, and none since, has written of Meredith with greater insight, but in admitting thus much one does not homologate his every statement, nor in reading his critique do we fail to detect something of the haughty spirit of the 'superior person' disengaging itself from the swinging rhythm of his invective, when he speaks of the dolts who are not wearing out their knees before the Meredithian shrine. His 'note' here follows:

George Meredith stands among our living novelists much as Robert Browning until of late years stood among our living poets, quite unappreciated by the general public, ranked with the very highest by a select few. One exception must be made to this comparison, an exception decidedly in favour of the novelists and novel readers; for whereas Tennyson, the people's greatest poet, is immeasurably inferior to Browning in depth and scope and power and subtlety of intellect, George Eliot, the public's greatest novelist, is equal in all these qualities, save, I think, the last, to her unplaced rival, while having the advantage in some deservedly popular qualities, and the clear disadvantage in but one, the faculty of conceiving and describing vigorous or agonistic action,—in the fateful crises her leading characters are apt to merely drift.

The thoughtful few have succeeded in so far imposing their judgment of Browning upon the thoughtless many, that these and their periodical organs now treat him with great respect, and try hard to assume the appearance of understanding and enjoying him, though doubtless their awkward admiration is more genuine in the old sense of wonder or astonishment than in the modern of esteem or love. But the thoughtful few are still far from succeeding to this extent in the case of George Meredith. Even literary men are unfamiliar with him. For having in some freak of fun or irony specified only two of his other books, and these among the earliest, on his title-page, leaving etc's. to represent 'Farina,' 'Evan Harrington,' 'Rhoda Fleming,' 'The Adventures of Harry Richmond,' 'Modern Love and Other Poems,' with his great masterpieces, 'Emilia in England' and its sequel 'Vittoria'; he has reaped the satisfaction of learning that many of his well-informed reviewers manifestly know nothing of these obscure writings. For the rest, the causes of his unpopularity are obvious enough, and he himself, as he more than once lets us know, is thoroughly aware of them. . . . Not only does he appeal to the conscience residing in thoughtfulness, he makes heavy and frequent demands on the active imagination—monstrous attempts at extortion which both the languid and the sentimental novel reader bitterly resent, and which, indeed, if they grew common with authors (luckily there is not the slightest fear of that!) would soon plunge the circulating libraries into bankruptcy.

The late Charles Dickens, who coincided at all points with the vulgar taste as exactly as two triangles of the fourth proposition of the first book of 'Euclid' with one another, carried to perfection the Low-Dutch or exhaustive style of description, which may be termed artistic painting reduced to artful padding; minutely cataloguing all the details, with some exaggeration or distortion, humorous or pathetic, of each to make them more memorable, so that every item can be checked and verified as in an auctioneer's inventory, which is satisfactory to a business-like people. George Eliot, with incomparably higher art, paints rich and solid pictures that fill the eyes and dwell in the mind. But George Meredith seldom does this, either in the realm of Nature or in that of Humanity, though the achievement is well within his power, as none of our readers can doubt who studied, being fit to study, those magnificent selections from his 'Vittoria' in the *Secularist* (No. 10, March 4), entitled 'Portrait of Mazzini' and 'Mazzini and Italy.' He loves to suggest by flying touches rather than slowly elaborate. To those who are quick to follow his suggestions he gives in a few winged words the very spirit of a scene, the inmost secret of a mood or passion, as no other living writer I am acquainted with can. His name and various passages in his works reveal Welsh blood, more swift and fiery and imaginative than the English. And he says in 'Emilia,' with fair pride of race: 'All subtle feelings are discerned by Welsh eyes when untroubled by any mental agitation. Brother and sister were Welsh, and I may observe that there is human nature and Welsh nature.'

If his personages are not portrayed at full length, they are clear and living in his mind's eye, as we discern by the exquisitely appropriate gesture or attitude or look in vivid moments: and they are characterised by an image or a phrase, as when we are told that the profile of Beauchamp 'suggested an arrow-head in the up-flight'; and of Renée: 'her features had the soft irregularities which run to varieties of beauty, as the ripple rocks the light; mouth, eyes, brows, nostrils and blooming cheeks played into one another languidly; thought flew, tongue followed, and the flash of meaning quivered over them like night-lightning. Or oftener, to speak truth, tongue flew, thought followed: her age was but newly seventeen, and she was French.' And as with the outward so with the interior nature of his personages. Marvellous flashes of insight reveal some of their profoundest secrets, detect the mainsprings and trace the movements of their most complete workings, and from such data you must complete the characters, as from certain leading points a mathematician defines a curve. So with his conversations. The speeches do not follow one another mechanically adjusted like a smooth pavement for easy walking: they leap and break, resilient and resurgent, like running foam-crested sea waves, impelled and repelled and crossed by under-currents and great tides and broad breezes; in their restless agitations you must divine the immense life abounding beneath and around and above them; and the Mudie novice accustomed to saunter the level pavements finds that the heaving and falling are sea-sickness to a queasy stomach. Moreover, he delights in elaborate analysis of abstruse problems, whose solutions when reached are scarcely less difficult to ordinary apprehension than are the problems themselves; discriminating countless shades where the common eye sees but one gloom or glare, pursuing countless distinct movements where the common eye sees only a whirling perplexity. As if all these heavy disqualifications were not enough, as if he were not sufficiently offensive in being original, he dares also to be wayward and wilful, not theatrically or overweeningly like Charles Reade, but freakishly and humoristically, to the open-eyed disgust of our prim public. Lastly, his plots are too carelessly spun to catch our summer flies, showing here great gaps and there a pendent entanglement; while his catastrophes are wont to outrage that most facile justice of romance which condemns all rogues to poverty and wretchedness, and rewards the virtuous with wealth and long life and flourishing large families.

In exposing his defects for the many I have discovered some of his finest qualities for the thoughtful and imaginative few, and need now only summarise. He has a wonderful eye for form and colour, especially the latter; a wonderful ear for music and all sounds; a masterly perception of character, a most subtle sense for spiritual mysteries. His dialogue is full of life and reality, flexible and rich in the genuine unexpected, marked with the keenest distinctions, more like the bright-witted French than the slow and clumsy English. He can use brogue and *baragouinage* with rare accuracy and humorous effect; witness the Irish Mrs. Chump and the Greek Pericles in 'Emilia.' Though he seldom gives way to it, he is great in the fiery record of fiery action; thus the duel in the Stelvio Pass, in 'Vittoria,' has been scarcely equalled by any living novelist save by Charles Reade in that heroic fight with the pirates in 'Hard Cash.' He has this sure mark of lofty genius, that he always rises with his theme, growing more strenuous, more self-contained, more magistral, as the demands on his thought and imagination increase.

His style is very various and flexible, flowing freely in whatever measures the subject and the mood may dictate. At its best it is so beautiful in simplest Saxon, so majestic in rhythm, so noble with noble imagery, so pregnant with meaning, so vital and intense, that it must be ranked among the supreme achievements of our literature. A dear friend said well when reading 'Vittoria': 'Here truly are words that if you pricked them would bleed.' For integral grandeur and originality of conception, and for perfectness of execution, the heroine of his 'Emilia' appears to me the sovereign character of our modern fiction: in her he has discovered a new great nature, whom he has endowed with a new great language.

In fine I am aware of no other living English writer so gloriously gifted and so little known and appreciated except Garth Wilkinson: and Garth Wilkinson has squandered his superb genius in most futile efforts to cultivate the spectral Sahara of Swedenborgianism, and, infinitely worse, the Will-o'-the-Wisp Slough of Despond of Spiritism;

By permission of Messrs. Smith, Elder & Co.] [*From the drawing by George du Maurier in the 'Cornhill.'*

RICHMOND ROY WITH HIS SON IN 'HIGH GERMANY.'

My father smoked his cigar peacefully. He had laid a guitar on his knees, and flipped a string, or chafed over all the strings, and plucked and thrummed them as his mood varied.—*Harry Richmond.* Chapter XVIII.

[*To face p.* 152.

while George Meredith has constantly devoted himself to the ever-fruitful fields of real living nature and Human Nature.

Apart from its intrinsic value as a contribution to the contemporary appreciation of Meredith, the foregoing critique is of especial interest regarded merely as the opinion of one man of genius concerning another; but where it lacks the touch of logic, characteristic of Thomson's countrymen with less of the Celtic strain than he had, is in its fulmination against the patrons of the circulating library for neglecting Meredith, while assuring us that Meredith cares not a jot for such brainless readers! This is an attitude common to many of Meredith's expositors. It could even be argued that Thomson's criticism places Bunyan and Scott, both of whom are not altogether unworthy to rank with Meredith, among the authors who have written for the common herd and so partake of its grossness. Dickens he thrusts forthright into the gutter; yet Dickens was not quite a blockhead. George Eliot he seems to consider the exception that proves his rule. But we need not pursue this subject here, as it will present itself for more extended treatment in another chapter; and enough has been accomplished if we have realised that in the earlier years of his literary career George Meredith was neither destitute of friends, nor denied the solace and inspiration of appreciative and intelligent criticism.

VII

LITERARY CHARACTERISTICS

If we have not been greatly embarrassed with personal details of George Meredith, it is far otherwise when we turn to criticism of his work. Embarrassment is here a pale and feeble word. For we find ourselves smothered in a veritable avalanche of writing, and how to force a passage through to daylight is a puzzle to exercise the most ingenious mind. That I shall win through to daylight I dare not hope, but, struggling dimly lightwards, I may yet succeed in presenting, in this and the following chapters, some serviceable notion of how Meredith's art has been regarded by the criticism of his own time. Six books have been published, devoted exclusively to the exposition of his art; magazine and newspaper articles in hundreds have had the same end in view; and there are numerous works on modern prose or poetry in which at least one chapter is consecrated to Meredith. In short, the mass of critical writing about him is appalling, and it has been no light task to examine it with care and consideration.

'Thank God I have never written a word to please the public,' Meredith once said to York Powell. We know very well that he never pleased the public and that he never will. Let us then discover whom it is he has pleased, and by what qualities. It is also a moot question whether he could have pleased the public had he greatly tried. Here and there in his novels we seem to see him just a little envious of the lesser men who have the knack of pleasing the public. Do not let us be party to the detestable affectation that he scorned to see his works passing into new editions. No professional author ever wrote a book who did not hope to sell as many copies as people could be induced to buy, and we have no reason for supposing that Meredith was superbly superior to all considerations of the publishing department before or after he had produced his new manuscript for its exploitation. The iron fact of his lack of popularity is simply that he had been denied by the fairies, who had given him so many other gifts, the power of writing 'a tale which holdeth children from play and old men from the chimney corner.' Among the writers of his own time there are scores with not a fraction of his genius who possess this gift and use it to excellent purpose. There is manly recognition of this, and none of the puling bitterness some of his 'appreciators' display in their gibes at the public, in this passage from 'Beauchamp's Career':

We will make no mystery about it. I would I could. Those happy tales of mystery are as much my envy as the popular narratives of the deeds of bread-and-cheese people, for they both create a tideway in the attentive mind; the mysterious pricking our credulous flesh to creep, the familiar urging our obese imagination to constitutional exercise. And oh, the refreshment there is in dealing with characters either contemptibly beneath us or supernaturally above! My way is like a Rhone island in the summer drought, stony, unattractive and difficult between the two forceful streams of the unreal and the over-real, which delight mankind—honour the conjurors! My people conquer nothing, win none; they are actual, yet uncommon. It is the clockwork of the brain that they are directed to set in motion, and—poor troop of actors to vacant benches!—the conscience residing in thoughtfulness which they would appeal to; and if you are there impervious to them, we are lost: back I go to my wilderness, where, as you perceive, I have contracted the habit of listening to my own voice more than is good.

Are we not to infer from this frank confession that Meredith lacks the story-telling gift? Surely. Twenty years after he penned these words he concluded his last novel with a final avowal that he was not a teller of tales. Thus ends 'The Amazing Marriage':

So much I can say: the facts related, with some regretted omissions, by which my story has so skeleton a look, are those that led to the lamentable conclusion. But the melancholy, the pathos of it, the heart of all England stirred by it, have been—and the panting excitement it was to every listener—sacrificed in the vain effort to render events as consequent to your understanding as a piece of logic, through an exposure of character! Character must ever be a mystery, only to be explained in some degree by conduct; and that is very dependent upon accident: and unless we have a perpetual whipping of the tender part of the reader's mind, interest in invisible persons must needs flag. For it is an infant we address, and the story-teller whose art excites an infant to serious attention succeeds best; with English people, assuredly, I rejoice to think, though I pray their patience here while that philosophy and exposure of character block the course along a road inviting to traffic of the most animated kind.

Let Mr. Thomas Lloyd (in the *Evening Standard*), and many another who sought to flatter the veteran on his eightieth birthday by assuring him that, an he would, he could have made himself the most popular novelist of his time, digest the foregoing. Thus Mr. Lloyd:

By choosing simpler weapons, stones instead of lightning and light, he could have made an impression on the forces arrayed against him. By forfeiting the respect of the few, who could not produce him a large income, he might have brought the multitude to his feet, rich offerings in their hands. To stories, plain stories, they would have succumbed, and occasionally the temptation to win at once must have been dazzling. For here was a writer who could have told a plain story with the best, only he desired to give something more. Nothing less than the putting of 'brain stuff' into fiction was his aim—'brain stuff' the weapon with which he desired to strike. He persisted along his own line. The victory was deferred. What the postponement meant in sacrifice of ease and prosperity, in loyalty to conviction and inspiration, Mr. Meredith, and he alone, knows.

What Meredith knew was that he couldn't do it. In one of Edmund Kean's great scenes, when he was acting with his son Charles, and had the whole theatre breathless with excitement, he whispered, 'We're doing the trick, Charlie!' Meredith had never been able to 'do the trick,' and perhaps his good sense is seen in the fact that he never attempted it. He once said: 'Capacity for thinking should precede the art of writing. It should. I do not say it does. Capacity for assimilating the public taste and reproducing it is the commonest.' But he himself lacked this common capacity: Shakespeare had it, Scott, Dickens, Thackeray, George Eliot had it. Hence the universality of their appeal.

Now, we have to settle in our own minds a point of some perplexity to criticism before we go one step further in the consideration of this great writer, who is so honest a critic of himself. All who are familiar with the modern French drama and its criticism will know how Francisque Sarcey maintained for well-nigh forty years a consistent and unfailing fight for *la pièce bien faite*. He set himself up a standard of what a drama should be, a convention, a sort of machine-made model from which any departure in form meant falseness to his ideal and merited his condemnation; yet all the while men of great gifts were producing plays which did not conform to his model, but were instinct with qualities immensely greater than mere form. They were not *des pièces bien faites*, and so to the dogs with them! It is precisely this one-eyed criticism, which often comes, as in Sarcey's case, of an insensate devotion to the classic models, that condemns Meredith as 'an artist, but no novelist.' But it is a narrow convention that insists that a novel must be a story 'with a beginning, a middle, and an end.' The most flexible of all literary forms, as we are pleased to regard the novel, is to become, forsooth, a rigid mould for the man of genius who makes use of it! And the journeyman hack who conforms to its conventions, and brightens his tale with never one little flash of intellect or observation, is the real right novelist! So would hide-bound criticism have it. None the less, it is so that popularity may be achieved, and the man of genius who either disdains to conform or cannot, try as he may, conform to the convention, must discover some other way of fascinating 'the infant' he addresses, and if he does not hold that infant from play the blame is with him. As Meredith's substitute for story is the minute analysis of character, long sustained and remorselessly inquisitive, it is scarcely surprising that the children have not been holden from play, and that the old men have dozed by the chimney corner, while his 'poor troop of actors to vacant benches' have played their parts to here and there a spectator who can understand and appreciate life in symbolism. For, being inspired of the comic muse, Meredith has to present his reading of life not in actual characters, deftly exaggerated, as Dickens did, but in types and symbols. That is the ineluctable method of comedy, and Meredith is nothing if not a writer of comedy. Here and there we find a Mrs. Berry, or a Tom Cogglesby—essentially Dickensian characters—but how curiously do his chief personages pale into abstractions, and leave the mind with the sense of having grasped some aspect of life rather than having made friends with a group of characters, who will live with us as Dugald Dalgetty, Sam Weller, Micawber, Becky Sharp, and so many others, live with us. On the score of exaggeration, which the 'superior' critics find such a barrier to their appreciation of Dickens, what about Mrs. Chump, that impossible buffoon, whose preposterous figure can raise not 'laughter of gods,' but only melancholy, 'in the background' of high comedy?

While character is the concern of Meredith, it is not character for its own sake, but in the bulk, as interpretive of life. And here we touch another of the reasons for failure with the public. The 'infant' does not care a straw for character in the abstract, it asks for persons, 'quaint and curious,' good or bad, but interesting as persons. The writer of comedy troops out his symbols of Egoism, of Youthful Conceit, of Social Ambition, of Intellectual Wit, of Parental Unwisdom, and 'the infant,' though these all bear names far more alluring than Christian, Faithful, Giant Despair or Mr. Worldly Wiseman, finds Bunyan's actual characters, though labelled with the names of abstractions, more fascinating than Meredith's abstractions labelled with the names of persons.

It is also because his personages are parts of a philosophy of life rather than our fellow-creatures that Meredith himself seldom seems to warm into friendship with them. Now and then he is obviously writing of them with gusto; he likes Nevil Beauchamp, Mrs. Mel, Dr. Shrapnel, Diana and a few more, but it is noteworthy that he is apt to be most in love with his most artificial characters. We can understand his liking Diana and Beauchamp, but Mrs. Mel or Shrapnel! It is no injustice to say that he is, broadly speaking, aloof from his own personages, and this is fatal to all illusion, which is surely of the essence of great fiction. This aloofness has, in my judgment, been better explained on temperamental grounds by Mr. W. C. Brownell, the talented American critic, in his 'Victorian Prose Masters,' than by any other writer, and I turn to him at this stage for a valuable contribution to Meredithian criticism.

The defect one feels most sensibly in Mr. Meredith's organisation is his lack of temperament (writes Mr. Brownell). It is this that extracts the savour from his originality. . . . It is through temperament that character organises its traits into a central and coherent efficiency. Temperament, in a word, is energy accentuating personality. Original—and indubitable—as Mr. Meredith's genius is, his personality is what we never feel in it. . . . Distinction is so marked and constant a quality of Mr. Meredith that to ascribe inferiority of any kind to him would be ludicrous—except in so far as, for example, his particular order of critical implies an inferiority of constructive talent. He is the ideal dilettante in virtue of the completeness and the catholicity of his devotion to the delectable. He finds it everywhere—everywhere, that is to say, where it exists in intellectual combination. And this, I think, gives him his extraordinary relief against his English environment, in which his temper and interests are rarely to be encountered. He has inexhaustible curiosity. What he calls 'the human mechanism' attracts him distinctly as a mechanism. Within certain limits he explores its intricacies with wonderful ardour. He treats an eccentric type a little as if it were a new toy. . . .

Note that his detachment is not that of an artist. It is a deachment of spirit, not objectivity in treatment. He is often enough on the stage himself. His observations *in propria persona* are constant. He is never absorbed either in his subject or in its delineation. On the contrary, he keeps it at arm's length when he is most interested in it, and speculates copiously about it. He gives the reader his impression of it—often pungent, generally prolix. His tongue submits to no objective restraint in uttering the thoughts that arise n him regarding it. If these thoughts were sufficiently charged with feeling he would appear as a moralist or a sentimentalist, but as they have no temperamental alloy, no purpose, it is less obvious hat his attitude is not artistically, but only emotionally, detached. We are accustomed, in other words, to the artist whose presentation of his subject is supplemented by his personal commentary, but not o him whose commentary, though constant, is thoroughly impersonal. The latter is the case with Mr. Meredith; and it constitutes no mall part of his originality that even his essential aloofness should be no help to him in the artistic presentation of his subject unconused with talk about it. . . .

He turns his subject round and exhibits it as a collector does an interesting possession—a bit of cloisonné or a figurine. Except hat he does so in large fashion, without pettiness or partisanship or other limitation, and that his 'specimens' have indubitable significance, the parallel would be perfect. But in his large and penerating way he lectures at great length on his finds. . . .

Mr. Meredith's world, however, is not a real world. It is a antastic one treated realistically. It is not simple enough to be eal; *he* is not simple enough. It is so little representative that it acks illusion. Any one who should base upon it his notion of the world of English society—society in the large sense, I mean—would et not only an incomplete but a distorted idea, though Mr. Mereith's world is as multifarious as it is populous. It is, like his enius, thoroughly *sui generis*, and it is peopled for the most part with figures of which the large or piquant conception is far more efinite than the realisation. Dickens's world, too, is *sui generis*. But it is everywhere intensely real and definite. You recall his haracters vividly often without remembering in which books they ccur. In the case of Mr. Meredith, you recall the books, not the haracters.

Mr. Brownell then goes on at some length, and with perfect coniction, to show us how Meredith fails to enthral the reader, leaving im with a disheartening sense of the author's tyranny over his haracters and his determination to do with them what he chooses, nstead of allowing them to work out their own salvation; so that hey become puppets foredoomed to their creator's caprice and not ersonages with whom he is on terms of intimacy and to whom he ust allow such freedom of action as will bring them humanly through the mazes of his plot. The American critic also points out with some subtlety that the Meredithian characters do not suffer solely because they are so often symbolic of certain well-defined qualities, just as I have chosen above Bunyan's everlasting, because living realities, by way of contrast. Mr. Brownell writes:

George Eliot's genius for generalisation is, considering its scope and its seriousness, certainly not inferior to Mr. Meredith's, but she is mistress of it, and though it limits the elasticity of her characters, it is never allowed to dilute their individuality. On the contrary, it intensifies it. Tito illustrates an idea as completely, as exclusively, as Mr. Meredith's 'Egoist' does, for example; but he incarnates it also. You get so much of the idea that you would perhaps be glad of a diversion, but it is because Tito himself is so interpenetrated with it that it is an idea active, moving and alive. Patterne is in comparison a symbol. Setting aside the fact that the whole question is begged by describing him as vastly more winning than he is shown to be, half his psychology is commentary, and before long the reader is admiring the penetration of the author into human character in general, his detection of egoism under its multifarious disguises, the justice he renders the quality even in exposing it, and so on. Tito, on the other hand, has the actual, almost palpable force of the traditional 'awful example.' As for Maggie Tulliver or any of George Eliot's notablest successes, none of Meredith's are at all in the same class with them any more than they are with Thackeray's. His discursiveness and his kind of discursiveness are fatal obstacles.

In short, we have in Meredith the curious spectacle of a novelist who, rightly enough, has decided that the telling of a straightforward story is not the sole purpose of the novel—which is a literary form that may legitimately be made to do the work of the philosopher, using character as the medium of his philosophy—failing to grip the reader on the very issue he has chosen for his appeal to him: the interest of character. And this because the author himself does not always warm to the character he is portraying. Some such opinion as this seems to run through all that has been written in criticism of the novels, though, of course, it is a proposition that is subject to numerous exceptions in detail. Even the least temperate applauders of his genius make so many reservations as to his distinct failures in character that the weight of their opinion does not disturb the balance of the general proposition more than all generalisations may be disturbed by advancing particular cases which weigh to the contrary.

Mr. W. L. Courtney in his careful study of the novels, in the

By permission of Messrs. Smith, Elder & Co.]

[*From the drawing by George du Maurier in the 'Cornhill.'*

ROY RE-INTRODUCES HARRY TO OTTILIA AT OSTEND.

'It is I, my friend,' she answered. 'And you?' 'With more health than I am in need of, dearest princess.' 'And he?'

[*To face p.* 160.

Fortnightly Review, June, 1886, was inclined to insist on the telling of a story as the novelist's first duty, giving second place to the psychological instinct, on the ground that 'the first is creative, spontaneous, original, while the second is introverted and critical.' This may be held to colour somewhat Mr. Courtney's attitude to Meredith's fiction, whereas no such discount could be taken from Mr. Brownell's criticism, which, as I read it, accepts Meredith's own notion of fiction as its basis. But Mr. Courtney's judgment is unassailable on any other ground, and he arrives at precisely the same destination as Mr. Brownell by a different route.

So far the criticism has been scarcely of the 'appreciative' order. There has been so much of that, and we shall yet have so many occasions to indulge in it, that we need not be impatient to give the signal to the orchestra of praise, always so ready to energise with drum and cymbal, and not always wisely. No; rather let us regard our Meredith as a veritable island of a man, with tangled forests, swamps and waste places, as well as a domed and glittering citadel, and make our way to that citadel through prickly paths and over rough wastes. But here I quote a eulogistic passage from Professor M. W. MacCallum's lecture on Meredith (published at Sydney in 1892), not with approval, but for a purpose that will presently appear:

His material is not only spiritual and intellectual, it is *mind* in the fullest sense of the term; he is concerned with the brains as well as with the hearts of his persons, he traces not only their feelings but their thoughts. 'Be wary,' he tells us in Diana, 'of the disrelish of brainstuff. Brainstuff is not lean stuff; the brainstuff of fiction is not internal history, and to suppose it dull is the profoundest of errors. . . . A great modern writer of clearest eye and head, now departed, groaned over his puppetry—that he dared not animate them, flesh though they were, with the fires of positive brainstuff.' Meredith has had no such timidity as he here attributes to Thackeray—if Thackeray it be,—and in the face of thirty years' neglect, persevered at his Shakespearian task of portraying men and women in the whole of their conscious life. When we remember that the phenomena of consciousness are just the most complex and intricate of all, we need not wonder that he is often hard; nor, for the most part, does he resemble George Eliot, who may be said to have attempted something of a similar kind, in helping us with explanatory disquisitions on his characters. He studies them in activity, not in repose; he does not dissect them motionless before him while the narrative is motionless too, but shows us thought following thought in the rapids of the mind. His analysis is given in, not apart from, the story. He seldom forgets that the duty of a narrator is to narrate; even his apparent pauses, like the reflective passages in Shakespeare, generally help on the plot; like all good story-tellers he avoids preaching, avoids even unprogressive description, and the story itself is his first care. But as the story is less of physical event than of mental process, this very obedience to his art increases the difficulties of his readers. His objects are remote from our ordinary points of view, and it is hard to see remote objects distinctly; but when these will not stay still, but are ever on the wing, it becomes a great deal harder.

Professor MacCallum is, in the main, a sound critic, but like the late Miss Hannah Lynch he is quite capable of allowing his admiration for Meredith to lead him into assertions utterly unsupportable. Could anything be more incorrect than the statement that the novelist 'seldom forgets that the duty of a narrator is to narrate'? If there is any 'duty' incumbent upon the novelist which Meredith is apt to forget it is precisely this one. He never hesitates to hang up his story when he wishes to deliver his opinions on any subject under or in the heavens. This is 'as plain as way to parish church,' yet a good critic is ready in the interest—as he conceives it—of his admired writer, to deny the fact. It needs no apology, for a novelist who does not submit himself to the public merely as a narrator is entitled to do as he chooses, to be a law unto himself—but not to complain if the public prefers writers who observe other laws. No good purpose is served by claiming for Meredith qualities which he does not possess, and instead of taking us straight through to the aforesaid citadel, Professor MacCallum has only landed us into another prickly place; for we pass naturally from the question of narration to that of construction, and here assuredly is one of the tangled forests of the Island Meredith. I find that Mr. Ernest Newman, in a temperate and closely-reasoned study of the novels, in the *Free Review*, August, 1894, has devoted his attention to Meredith's shortcomings in the matter of construction.

His excellences (writes Mr. Newman) are mainly excellences of detail; the novels would come under the Voltairean characterisation of 'some fine moments, but some bad quarters of an hour.' In 'Beauchamp's Career' anti-climax after anti-climax weakens the interest of the novel, and the ending is lamentably feeble. It reminds us of the sudden descent to bathos in the old Scotch popular legend of 'The Shifty Youth,' who, after many admirable adventures, one day died accidentally, without any apparent reason for such an abrupt proceeding. 'Richard Feverel,' though not a well-constructed novel, is not a noticeably ill-constructed one; but 'Evan Harrington' is truly deplorable. It shows Mr. Meredith at his worst in everything that is worst in him—his bad social sentiment, his feeble construction, his dummy characters, and an evident attempt to rival Dickens on his own ground in the characters of Mr. Raikes and the Cogglesby brothers. But the entire work is a mass of bad articulation. The whole handling of the two brothers, the fictitious devices by which Evan is maintained in ease and idleness, the sudden and inexplicable elevation of Mr. Raikes to fortune, the intercepting of a letter from Evan to Rose, the contents of which are communicated to her by Evan himself a few pages after, thus rendering the whole episode futile; the fictitious bankruptcy of the brothers, the inconceivably clumsy scheming to have the Harrington family under the one roof in Lymport, in order that the final scenes may be brought about—are only some of the worst faults of the book.

The jerkiness and inarticulation of the novels as a whole reappear in the individual characters. Setting aside the obviously dummy characters, whom not even Mr. Meredith's brilliant writing can galvanise into life, it is evident at times that his hold on his main personages is by no means certain. A careful tracing of their springs of action shows that they change inexplicably; sometimes, like the caterpillar, they commence as one being and end as another. This weakness is undoubtedly due to Mr. Meredith's small power of organic construction. His novel grows together from many peripheral points, so that having developed one set of characters with fair consistency, he finds that the exigencies of construction at this point compel him to make certain other characters act in a way for which there is no warrant from their previous conduct. Yet so skilful is he in psychologising that he can frequently almost persuade us against our better judgment that the character is compact and consistent. To see the process of change clearly, however, and the preparatory psychologising by which Mr. Meredith paves the way for the change, an excellent example may be had in the episode of the robbery of the gold by Anthony Hackbut in 'Rhoda Fleming.' It it utterly inconceivable that the Anthony of the previous chapters should act in such a way; he only does it because Mr. Meredith wants him to do it for the sake of his story. And, conscious that the change of character is wholly unjustifiable, Mr. Meredith tries to cover his retreat by writing a preparatory dissertation on 'A Freak of the Money-Demon,' and does it so dexterously that only on second thoughts do we detect the device, and the purpose it is meant to serve. . . . Mr. Meredith is always weak in the 'jineing of his flats.'

If we mean to be perfectly honest with ourselves, there is no blinking the fact that the critic who wrote the above puts his finger unerringly on Meredith's cardinal sin as a novelist, judged by the canon of criticism we must apply to the writing of fiction. We may, therefore, without more ado, decide that among his literary characteristics the writing of fiction according to established notions of the art does not appear, and the sources of his literary pre-eminence are to be looked for elsewhere. Nowhere in his novels do we feel a great and inevitable catastrophe impending; we often enough are aware oppressively, as of thunder in the air, that something is bound to happen presently, but we know it is something he will himself make to happen, like the writer of melodrama, not necessarily the inevitable, as we have experienced so many of his arbitrary 'catastrophes' that we have long since ceased to expect the inevitable or to guess even dimly what it may be. He will step in whenever *he* feels inclined and dispose of his people, perhaps only to continue the play by hauling up the curtain again forthwith, as he has thought of something more he would like his 'poor actors to vacant benches' to say for him.

The late George Parsons Lathrop, another American critic who wrote of Meredith with insight that rivals the best of his English critics, has a notable passage on this subject in his study in the *Atlantic Monthly*, February, 1888, which I am constrained to add to Mr. Newman's indictment:

A cardinal fault in Meredith's novels is that they are lame in movement. He lacks, on the whole, narrative and dramatic skill, although he shows, in places, that he can command it. He is too much like a biographer. We look for a novelist, and find an annalist. The mere bulkiness of his novels cannot wholly account for our disappointment; because some of George Eliot's books are just as bulky, but do not oppress us so severely by their size. The difficulty consists rather, I think, in the fact that Meredith tries to give an epic largeness to every history that he undertakes. The result is a want of proportion; just as it is when painters choose a canvas too large for their composition, or, conversely, paint figures which are too large for the canvas on which they are placed. This was the case with Madox Brown's 'Work,' and with the 'Rest' of George Watts. It was also the case with some of the Russian Verestchagin's early paintings. The effect of disproportion found in these paintings of the Russian, and of two English artists representing a certain school, meets with a curious correspondence in the disproportion of Meredith. We discover the same thing again in Tolstoy's Anna Karenina. Russian and English! It is curious that these two peoples, so opposed politically, should develop the same uncouth disproportion artistically. One does not perceive the defect in

Daudet or Zola, however heavy their outlines or gross their delineation may be. They, at least, preserve the sense of proportion.

In Tolstoy the waste of space and material is less annoying, because it seems to proceed from unsophistication. Meredith sins like Tolstoy; but it is not through unsophistication. Nor is it through wilfulness entirely, but rather by the weakness of a too great self-consciousness, the pride of a brilliant, superior mind, which wants to make itself instantly felt by squandering superfluous treasures of diction and of sententious statement, instead of waiting to be slowly recognised at last. The crudities and disproportion in Meredith seem, at first glance, to ally him with the extreme so-called Realists, who believe that nature stunted and dwarfed is truer than nature carried to the largest development. He says, somewhere, 'Romances are the destruction of human interest.' But, in fact, Meredith, while realistic in certain ways, is highly romantic. He never hesitates to give a free rein to the impulses of human nature, however sentimental or extravagant they may be. He is also very romantic in his manner of heightening effects and idealising emotions or actions. Possibly it is just this mixture of the two tendencies in him which has led to his missing popular approbation in his day. He is like a richly-freighted boat that, launched on an eddy formed by the meeting of two rivers, is stranded at the very point of junction, and loses the momentum of both currents.

As Mr. Courtney has said, 'If only Mr. Meredith had sometimes followed the advice of his admirable Mrs. Berry! What a comfort it would be if he would allow us sometimes to picture him as praying God and walking forward!' This is assuredly the feeling of his genuine admirers when they return critically to his works after the first glamour of his philosophical comedy has passed away.

One of Meredith's characteristics which accounts for the delight with which the literary man may read him while it bores the ordinary patron of the circulating library, is his evident delight in being 'literary.' He seems never to have mastered the art that conceals art. He is always conscious that he is a literary man with a pen in his hand, pleased that less clever labourers in the same field should see how he does his work. The machinery of his novel interests him a great deal too much, and he invites us to examine it, as some newspaper publishers allow their patrons to come into their printing works to see how the newspaper is produced. The ordinary reader of the newspaper has only the vaguest notion of how the thing is made: type, formes, matrices, stereo-plates, and rotary machines are meaningless terms to him, and remain so even after he has been admitted to the mystery of the actual production, but it flatters him to think he knows how his morning sheet is printed, and he is delighted to have a peep at the mysteries. It is not so with a story. He wants the novelist to tell his story and not to be pausing ever and again to explain how difficult is the task, or to invite inspection of his machinery. 'Cut the cackle and cotton to the narrative' is his sentiment, and Meredith refuses to 'cut the cackle.' Take 'Sandra Belloni,' for example. The jerks and spasms of the story must be intolerable to any reader who is not intimate enough with the novelist to discount his mannerisms, as one makes allowance for the foibles of a dear friend. There is the absurdly inartistic chapter entitled 'A Chapter interrupted by the Philosopher,' in which that stage-property figure is introduced, as elsewhere, when the author is in a fix, and allowed his say, after which the novelist goes on *in propria persona:*

> Now this is good teaching: it is indeed my Philosopher's object—his *purpose*—to work out this distinction; and all I wish is that it were good for my market. What the Philosopher means, is to plant in the reader's path a staring contrast between my pet Emilia and his puppet Wilfrid. It would be very commendable and serviceable if a novel were what he thinks it: but all attestation favours the critical dictum, that a novel is to give us copious sugar and no cane. I, myself, as a reader, consider concomitant cane as an adulteration of the qualities of sugar. My Philosopher's error is to deem the sugar, born of the cane, inseparable from it. The which is naturally resented, and away flies my book back at the heads of the librarians, hitting me behind them a far more grievous blow.
>
> Such is the construction of my story, however, that to entirely deny the Philosopher the privilege he stipulated for when, with his assistance, I conceived it, would render our performance unintelligible to that acute and honourable minority which consents to be thwacked with aphorisms and sentences and a fantastic delivery of the verities. While my Play goes on, I must permit him to come forward occasionally. We are indeed in a sort of partnership, and it is useless for me to tell him that he is not popular, and destroys my chance.

It will be noted that the Philosopher does not protest against the novelist's splitting his infinitive, and the whole device is artificial and ruinous to illusion. Again, in the chapter which 'Contains a Further Anatomy of Wilfrid,' where 'the Philosopher' has another innings, and is really the novelist *in excelsis*, running to confused and impenetrable wordiness about the tremendous subtleties of Wilfrid's character, the novelist pretends to intervene after this fashion:

This waxes too absurd. At the risk of breaking our partnership for ever, I intervene. My Philosopher's meaning is plain, and, as usual, good; but not even I, who have less reason to laugh at him than anybody, can gravely accept the juxtaposition of suffering and cigars. And, moreover, *there is a little piece of action in store.*

How futile is this make-believe! I have italicised a phrase that indicates the legitimate fear which has arisen—too late, alas!—in the mind of the novelist. 'Little pieces of action' doled out now and then, after long slabs of soliloquy and chapters of stagnation, are not sufficient to move a great novel along to a heart-searching climax. Perhaps Meredith is nowhere so artificial as in the novel in question and its sequel, 'Vittoria,' though in the latter there are numerous passages of great power and beauty, flooded with sunshine, moving in description and intense in passion, which bring it within sight of what a great novel should be. But there is no gainsaying the fact that Meredith never masters the art of telling a story in a natural and forceful style, which a novelist of far inferior powers, such as Wilkie Collins, could do to perfection. And this matter of well-knit narrative surely touches the question of art, leaving the great writer who has been unable to master it so much less the artist. In the case of Meredith, his other qualities are so great that the discount is the less.

There is, however, a certain kind of unity in all the Meredith novels, which Mr. Brownell has pointed out and defined in this passage:

> Each book is the elaboration of an idea, the working out of some theme taken on its intellectual side. Sometimes this is very specific, as in 'Diana' or 'Feverel,' but it is always perfectly defined. The book is a series of deductions from it. Its essential unity, therefore—spite of excrescent detail—is agreeably unmistakable. But it is hardly necessary to point out that it is not the unity of a sympathetic image of life immediately beholden in its entirety. It is a mathematical, that is to say an artificial, unity.

While that is not the unity that makes for popular favour, it is at least a characteristic of Meredith's fiction which must be recognised in endeavouring to get at the novelist's own point of view, the mark he aims at, without which endeavour criticism can only be partial. But the difficulties of arriving at any clear notion of Meredith's literary characteristics seem to increase the closer we inquire into them. He is weak in construction, lame in narrative, he relies largely upon character for interest, yet he pursues analysis of character and motive to issues so fine that sometimes, indeed often, the broad, telling effects are ruined.

Though character is so eminent a feature of his work, romance is there hardly less, and the two are not always friends: the one or the other absent and a step had been taken towards simplicity or unity of form. George Meredith's, however, being a personality in which a dozen other personalities seem to flash like the darting to and fro of swallows over an evening, shining pool of summer, his works have to take on this inevitable complexity which is so characteristic of the man; it is mentally impossible for him to be simple and direct, as Bunyan and Defoe are simple and direct; he sees too clearly in detail every character he is portraying, and in his effort to force up his description to the minutely-lighted details of his vision he is apt to raise only confusion where a less laboured and a simple outline would have realised a far more enduring result. He gets his picture out of focus, so to say, by insisting upon these crannies of character which none but his all-searching vision would ever have noticed. All this refers to his novels as analysis of character. But, of course, they are not deficient in drama, which springs from character; though it is not the splendidly-sustained drama that characterises Mr. Hardy's novels, but rather episodic or spasmodic, as it is, perhaps, in life itself. Readers of R. L. Stevenson will recall this passage from 'A Gossip on Romance,' which he wrote in *Longman's Magazine*, November, 1892:

> The last interview between Lucy and Richard Feverel is pure drama; more than that, it is the strongest scene, since Shakespeare, in the English tongue. Their first meeting by the river, on the other hand, is pure romance; it has nothing to do with character; it might happen to any other boy and maiden, and be none the less delightful for the change. And yet I think he would be a bold man who should choose between these passages. Thus, in the same book, we may have two scenes, each capital in its order: in the one, human passion, deep calling unto deep, shall utter its genuine voice; in the second, according circumstances, like instruments in tune, shall build up a trivial but desirable incident, such as we love to prefigure for ourselves; and in the end, in spite of the critics, we may hesitate to give the preference to either. The one may ask more genius—I do not say it does; but at least the other dwells as clearly in the memory.

We may not be willing to endorse Stevenson's superlatives, but the reason for quoting this passage is to illustrate how appreciative

By permission of Messrs. Smith, Elder & Co.]

[*From the drawing by George du Maurier in the 'Cornhill.*

RICHMOND ROY MEETS SQUIRE BELTHAM.

My father stood up and bowed, bareheaded. My grandfather struck his hat and bobbed. 'Mr. Beltham, I trust I see you well.' 'Better, sir, when I've got rid of a damned unpleasant piece of business.' 'I offer you my hearty assistance.' 'Do you? Then step down and come into my bailiff's.' 'I come, sir.'—*Harry Richmond.* Chapter XL.

[*To face p.* 168.

criticism of Meredith nearly always turns on praise of episodes and not on dramatic entities. One could give whole pages of such laudation of scenes and episodes from the novels, in which no novel as a whole is bepraised. In a letter to his biographer, Professor Elton, York Powell says, 'Mention the early morning walk in "The Amazing Marriage," the splendid scene in the Scala, of "Vittoria," the voice in the wood at even in "Sandra."' It is always so; from the novels certain scenes detach themselves and, standing away from all context, become in the memory the novel itself, or at least we must think of them before we can remember anything of the novel, whereas it should be exactly the reverse. We seem to remember 'Pendennis' as a whole, 'Adam Bede,' even 'Jane Eyre,' with all its melodrama, leaves in the mind the impression of an organic whole, yet it is doubtful if they are more so than 'The Egoist,' 'Richard Feverel,' 'Beauchamp's Career,' 'Evan Harrington,' or 'Rhoda Fleming,' though in the case of each of these novels there are parts that do not seem to foreshorten properly but attract the eye of the mind before the picture as a whole can be recalled. The explanation may be that the glory of the whole is apt to be dimmed by the greater glory of the parts! But the fact remains and must be recognised in any study of Meredith's literary characteristics.

Another perplexing feature of his fiction is touched upon by the late Miss Hannah Lynch in a short study contributed to the *Bookman*, November, 1899, though she is in no way perplexed by it. She writes:

> There is one distinctive feature in Mr. Meredith's work which, while common in that of a great many writers in different degree, reaches in him an absolute supremacy. Landscape lights up most English fiction and English poetry, but where will you find it so richly, vividly, variously portrayed as in the unique work of this writer? Whether it be in verse or prose, you can never forget the world of nature into which you have entered under his magic guidance. All his books glow and throb with the love and perfect understanding of nature. It is not mere landscape painting, which any one may try his hand at, the sort of thing William Black did by the yard, with all the skill and originality and diversity of the signboard painter. It is the very life of the earth made visible to us; its mysteries and secrets are seized and unrolled before us with the utmost cunning of design, an amazing precision of eye, of ear, of senses. Mr. Meredith does not drag in sunset effects into a novel as a suitable background for a flirtation, nor are woods solely described that the lovers may wander in them. Whether he invites us out of doors at home or abroad, he will make us see and understand scenery by means of a vigorous beauty of description, and such

an intensity and originality of revelation as no other writer I can think of ever has achieved. Here he drops all affectation and obscurity of utterance. The wild cheery tree he arrests us under blooms and scents the air about us. We stand with Dacier and Diana among the rocks and roaring waters of Italian hills, and we are filled with envy of Dacier's bath in those sunny solitudes, so quick and vital is the landscape to our vision. We enter the enchanted woods of verse, and hold our breath for awe. Yes, here is the magician, here is the poet, here is the writer of splendid prose. Elsewhere he may exasperate; here only does he enchant. Elsewhere the persistently blinding quality of his brilliance leaves us ill at ease, but here we surrender ourselves gladly to his charm. In his company out of doors we are at home with George Meredith, no longer doubtful of his meaning, afraid of the ferocity of his intuition, of the eagerness and mercilessness of his intellect.

All this is perfectly true, but the strangeness behind the truth is the fact that no novelist of our day has less attachment to place. If we except 'Sandra Belloni' and its sequel, and 'The Tragic Comedians,' to what extent can we localise any of the other novels? We feel that they might have happened anywhere. Have we any absolute vision of Wilming Weir, or Oxshott Woods, or Lymport? The action might have taken place anywhere, so little does environment affect the drama. Yet Miss Lynch does not overrate the perfection of Meredith's 'landscape.' Come fresh from Italy and read 'Vittoria,' how the book lights up with the soft glow of evening sunshine memory's pictures of that enchanting land, but all the landscape might be deleted without detracting in any degree from the story as a whole. Again we seem to touch Meredith's indifference to, or incapacity for organising, his 'material.' No great writer is so deficient in 'local colour.' Perhaps that may be accounted an attribute of his greatness; certainly some critics praise him for less praiseworthy characteristics.

But if we talk of perplexity in regard to the landscape of Meredith's fiction, what shall we say of the naturally perplexing subject of love? His treatment of the passion is essentially characteristic, no other novelist is remotely like him in his attitude towards the love of man and woman. Yet to set down in any general terms what that attitude is would baffle the shrewdest critic. Mr. W. C. Brownell comes nearest to the mark, I think, when he writes:

There is infinite talk in Mr. Meredith's books about love. He has written a sonnet series on 'Modern Love,' indeed, most interesting in its intricacies. But love as a passion he treats mainly, one may say, in trituration. There are express experiments in the other direction. The idyl of Richard Feverel and Lucy is as pretty, as charming as its slightly eighteenth-century atmosphere, its Ferdinand and Miranda conceits, the playful but palpable aloofness of the author, will permit. The gondola courtship of Nevil Beauchamp is more than promising, but the experienced reader of Meredith is not surprised to encounter later even less than non-fulfilment. The love of Rosamund Culling for her husband's nephew is caressingly sketched because it is recondite, but it is distinctly a minor and incidental element of the story. In general, anything properly to be called passion is presented with diluting playfulness. Even in seriousness, its weakness, not its force, is the side most emphasised. Mr. Meredith seems to care rather more for Nevil Beauchamp than for most of his characters, but he is so interested in preserving him from heroism, in his theoretic fashion, that he makes his passion not only the least persistent but the least intense phase of his energy, which is otherwise depicted as extravagant. Through the representativeness of Nevil's character, which is much insisted on, one is made to reflect on the transience and lack of depth in the passion of the average young man, however ebullient he may be. Can anything be tamer than the love-making of 'Diana,' or more debonair than that in 'Harry Richmond,' or more insubstantial than that in 'The Egoist'?

But 'The Tragic Comedians' furnishes the most striking of Mr. Meredith's disposition to psychologise love out of all passionate intensity. If 'The Tragic Comedians' had been sustained to the end it would assuredly have been the fine thing it just misses being.

This means, in effect, that Meredith's craving for 'brain stuff' has led him away from the heart; the relationship is always one where intellect enters more than passion, to which intellect should be subordinated. As Mr. Ernest Newman says, 'his women with brains are sometimes so intolerable as to make men even long again for the old ideal of woman—the "veiled virginal doll" of the sentimentalists.' But it is Meredith, and we must take him with his 'brain stuff' if we wish to have him at all, and we do wish most heartily to have him, with all his impedimenta. He cannot 'get rid of the baggage of his own psychology,' and if he could perhaps we should care for him the less. What we have to realise is that he is great in spite of many inequalities and not because of them, as certain perfervid advocates of his would have us believe. We have touched upon many of these loose stones in his structure, and before we turn to the consideration of the most remarkable of his literary characteristics, his extraordinary style, we may look for a moment at his points of strength.

The two great weapons in which Meredith excels are satire and humour (writes Dr. W. J. Dawson). The satire is never less than excellent, for in the mere literary finish of his biting epigrams he is unsurpassed by any writer of English, either past or present. The fault of the satire is that it is not kindly, and it can be cruel. It is as keen as a surgeon's knife, and as cold. It lays bare all the hidden disease of the human soul, and cuts relentlessly, and almost savagely, through the intervening filaments. . . . But when it is allied with humour it is delightful. It is then the smack of the sea-salt that gives edge to the sunny breeze. His humour . . . runs through a hundred variations, from the keenest to the broadest; it smacks of Jingle and of Falstaff; it is sometimes roaring farce, at others finished comedy; it is acute, genial, caustic; it is now hilarious with boyish buoyancy and good spirits, now the product of masculine good sense and piercing insight, now a shaft of laughter playing round a fountain of tears: and, widely as it differs, running through the gamut from the verbal quip to the profoundly human delineation, from merely comic to half tragic laughter, it is a persuasive element with which all his books are lavishly endowed. As a mere humorist Meredith is as superior to those ephemeral writers who pass as such to-day as is Shakespeare to Douglas Jerrold.

Further on we shall have occasion to dwell at some length on the aspect of Meredith as inspired of the Comic Muse, which is in truth the countervailing quality that makes up and over for all the literary graces we have so far sought in vain. Had he been less intellectual his comedy had been still greater, for the worst of all his faults, if, indeed, it be not father of them all, is his excessive activity in matters of pure intellectuality, keeping him always at more than arm's length from us, away from the love we give so readily to lesser men of warm heart and homely voice. Miss Lynch expresses this very successfully in the following passage from her *Bookman* study, from which I have quoted already :

In music Mr. Meredith's tastes are old-fashioned and Italian, which is odd, seeing how opposed his genius is to that of the dulcet conventional school of Italian music. To be consistent, Mr. Meredith should be a furious Wagnerite. I would not have it thought that I could compare, except in a very relative degree, the operas of Wagner with the novels of George Meredith. The influence of the former is universal, while that of the latter is purely local. But there are unmistakable links between the two natures. Take, for instance, that incomparable masterpiece of gaiety and fantastic humour, the 'Meistersingers.' Has not Mr. Meredith in many instances caught a like large spirit of mirth? Might not Beckmester shake hands in fraternity with many of Meredith's grotesque characters? There is in the 'Meistersingers' an interpretation of the fun and the quaintness of things that alone among living writers George Meredith reveals in his work. And many of the orchestral surprises of Wagner have their equivalent in the rare and astounding utterances of the novelist. But where resemblance ceases is in the tragic note. Mr. Meredith is too intellectual to sink into the extreme and moving depths of simplicity and poignant, naked passion that Wagner reaches in the glorious death-scene of Tristan. He could never send us to Rome with conviction so sincere and soul so naïvely penitent as Wagner does when we hear the great pilgrims' march of the 'Tannhauser.' For that is Mr. Meredith's great vice. He is too ruthlessly intellectual. He soars too obviously above us and above the life he portrays. He is too witty, too laboured, too satirical, too humorous. He dwells with too much gusto on the failings of his characters. From very force of understanding human nature so well, he is too aloof from us, too little part of ourselves to inspire us with confidence. We are afraid of him, and when we meet the man in the flesh, we remember the writer, and still continue to be afraid of him. Speaking from personal experience, I know this too well. The mere presence of Mr. Meredith, and the fact that he was addressing me, sufficed to turn me into a complete idiot. I was like Heine in the presence of Goethe, who thought he ought to talk Greek, and when he hunted for an inspired phrase, could find nothing to say but that the Saxony plums were fine. I do not think I mentioned the Saxony plums or even Jersey pears, but I found it impossible to lift myself out of a state of mental hebetude, in my frightful anxiety to utter only appropriate speech. Genius should be more simple and more sincere. I do not say that the work of Mr. Meredith is not sincere. It is too generous and too just not to be sincere, and then it is the expression of the man himself. But simple it is not, and hence the kind of inexplicable terror it inspires in us.

It was in his review of 'The Egoist' in the *Athenæum* of November 1, 1879, afterwards revised and reprinted in 'Views and Reviews,' that the late W. E. Henley, at once Meredith's frankest critic and sanest advocate, began in earnest that discussion of his literary style, to which there has been no end, nor is there like to be an end. Mention of Meredith is almost equivalent to mention of literary style in general and his own in particular. But before we see what Henley had to say, let us discover Meredith's own convictions in the matter of style, for 'manner is a great matter,' as Philip James Bailey observes. To Mr. George Bainton, who in 1890 compiled a work on 'The Art of Authorship,' consisting of letters written to him by eminent authors of the day, for reading to a group of young men in a course of lectures on literary art, Meredith wrote:

. . . I have no style, though I suppose my work is distinctive. I am too experimental in phrases to be other than a misleading guide. I can say that I have never written without having clear in vision the thing put to paper; and yet this has been the cause of roughness and uncommonness in the form of speech.

Your theme is well chosen. Impress on your readers the power of the right use of emphasis, and of the music that there is in prose, and how to vary it. One secret is, to be full of meaning, warm with the matter to be delivered. The best training in early life is verse. That serves for the management of our Saxon tongue. . . . Explain that we have, besides a Saxon, a Latin tongue in our English, and indicate where each is to be employed, and the subjects which may unite them; as, for example, in the wonderful sweep of a sentence of Gibbon, from whose forge Macaulay got his inferior hammer. Warn against excessive antithesis—a trick for pamphleteers. Bid your young people study the best French masters. I think it preferable, especially in these days of quantity, to be largely epigrammatic rather than exuberant in diction; therefore I would recommend the committing to memory passages of Juvenal. And let the description of a battle by Cæsar and one by Kinglake be contrasted for an instance of the pregnant brevity which pricks imagination and the wide discursiveness which exhausts it. Between these two, leaning to the former, lies the golden mean.

I note with personal satisfaction the last sentence of the first paragraph, which may be held to confirm the opinion advanced earlier in this chapter, as to the very intensity of Meredith's vision and his valiant effort to make the reader see it with his own clearness of detail being, at times, the actual cause of confusion in the reader's mind. The obscurity is nearly always in the reader's mind only, as a second and closer study of the words will show him, when the meaning of the author will come up suddenly and beautifully as the partly-developed picture on a sensitised plate appears suddenly perfect after it has been dipped again into the bath. But perhaps his style has never been better described than in his words, wherewith, in 'Beauchamp's Career,' he describes the style of Carlyle:

His favourite author was one writing on Heroes, in (so she esteemed it) a style resembling either early architecture or utter dilapidation, so loose and rough it seemed; a wind-in-the-orchard style, that tumbled down here and there an appreciable fruit with uncouth bluster; sentences without commencements running to abrupt endings and smoke, like waves against a sea-wall, learned dictionary words giving a hand to street-slang, and accents falling on them haphazard, like slant rays from driving clouds; all the pages in a breeze, the whole book producing a kind of electrical agitation in the mind and joints. This was its effect on the lady.

And that is the effect of Meredith on his intelligent readers—'a kind of electrical agitation in the mind and joints.' His style has this tonic quality; those who have once been electrified by it are keen to have further experiments, knowing they will be the better for them, despite certain shocks that may set their teeth on edge for a moment. It is not a style that makes for popularity, but that is rather to its credit, for while the public is right in demanding a 'story,' it has no sense of literary fitness and will accept the style of a William Le Queux or a Marie Corelli as readily as that of a Hawthorne or a Stevenson.

In a message to a Liberal Colonial Club a few years before his death Meredith wrote: 'The mother of a young giant must learn to take pride in her, but she relapses into timidity, *i. e.* Conservatism. *I use the metaphorical to avoid the long-winded.*' The phrase I have italicised might stand as the novelist's reason for his prose style; but whether he succeeds in avoiding the long-winded is a point on which there may conceivably be two opinions. We shall see. Thus writes W. E. Henley in 'Views and Reviews':

Mr. Meredith is one of the worst and least attractive of great writers as well as one of the best and most fascinating. He is a sun that has broken out into innumerable spots. The better half of his genius is always suffering eclipse from the worst half. He writes with the pen of a great artist in his left hand and the razor of a spiritual suicide in his right. He is the master and the victim of a monstrous cleverness which is neither to hold nor to bind, and will not permit him to do things as an honest, simple person of genius would. . . . He is tediously amusing; he is brilliant to the point of being obscure; his helpfulness is so extravagant as to worry and confound. That is the secret of his unpopularity. His stories are not often good stories and are seldom well told; his ingenuity and intelligence are always misleading him into treating mere episodes as solemnly and elaborately as main incidents; he is ever ready to discuss, to ramble, to theorise, to dogmatise, to indulge in a little irony or a little reflection or a little artistic misdemeanour of some sort. . . . Not infrequently he writes page after page of English as ripe and sound and unaffected as heart could wish; and you can but impute to wantonness and recklessness the splendid impertinences that intrude elsewhere. To read him at the rate of two or three chapters a day is to have a sincere and hearty admiration for him and a devout anxiety to forget his defects and make much of his merits. But they are few who can take a novel on such terms as these, and to read your Meredith straight off is to have an indigestion of epigram.

While the foregoing was suggested to Henley after a reading of 'The Egoist,' the following, written eight years later, appeared originally in his *Athenæum* review of 'Ballads and Poems of Tragic Life':

On the whole, I think, he does not often say anything not worth hearing. He is too wise for that; and, besides, he is strenuously in earnest about his work. He has a noble sense of the dignity of art and the responsibilities of an artist; he will set down nothing that is to his mind unworthy to be recorded; his treatment of his material is distinguished by the presence of an intellectual passion (as it were) that makes whatever he does considerable and deserving of attention and respect. But unhappily the will is not seldom unequal to the deed; the achievement is often leagues in rear of the inspiration; the attempt at completeness is too laboured and too manifest—the feat is done but by a painful and ungraceful process. There *is* genius, but there is not felicity. . . . But he has charm as well as power, and, once his rule is accepted, there is no way to shake him off. The position is that of the antique tyrant in a commonwealth once republican and free. You resent the domination, but you enjoy it too, and with or against your will you admire the author of your slavery.

The paradox of George Meredith has never been better explained. Henley was probably the greatest critic that ever wrote upon Meredith and his art, and in his own virile, clear-eyed way he states the case with irresistible force. His 'appreciation' is the real stuff; no slobber of unctuous praise, but a manly recognition of the defects to which criticism cannot honestly turn a shut eye, and a no less manly admission that, spite these grave defects, there is a mighty personality working through all the writings of Meredith which commands our respect and holds us in thrall, even when it may irritate. It is useless to speculate how mightily Meredith would have moved his generation had he purged himself of the literary sins which Henley so unerringly lays bare. We have to take the rose with its thorns.

Mr. Andrew Lang has in a few sentences summed up the charge against Meredith, laid so candidly by Henley, and shown how the novelist was himself to blame for limiting his audience:

Mr. Meredith may err in a wilful obscurity, in a too eager search for points and epigrams, in the leaps and bounds of too agile a wit,

By permission of Messrs. Smith, Elder & Co.] [From the drawing by George du Maurier in the 'Cornhill.

SQUIRE BELTHAM HAS HIS LAST INNINGS.

'She's the person—one of your petticoat "Government"—who paid—do you hear me, Richmond?—the money to help you keep your word: to help you to give your balls and dinners too.' . . . My father touched the points of his fingers on his forehead, straining to think, too theatrically but in hard earnest, I believe.'—*Harry Richmond.* Chapter LIII.

[*To face p.* 176.

and these things have [illegible]
like the crudeness [illegible]
an inner circle of [illegible]
good gifts, but [illegible]
to pass away the [illegible]
occasionally a humor[illegible]
or wander by the [illegible]
Black.

But it has been [illegible]
ing to say a [illegible]
that while we may [illegible]
to be the "mark [illegible]
find delight and [illegible]
that first repels [illegible]

Mr. Meredith's [illegible]
pulator of words [illegible]
It was by this [illegible]
was valuable to [illegible]
many in my case [illegible]
It was his very [illegible]
intelligence—that [illegible]
self. Youth can [illegible]
But youth is [illegible]
prehended. That [illegible]
case. We puzzled [illegible]
of some complexity [illegible]
innertime. Fortunately [illegible]
editions had not yet [illegible]
or youth is conceit[illegible]
mass of its contempor[illegible]
ion in us, and som[illegible]
the passage of years[illegible]
appreciation, in our [illegible]
was also a great [illegible]

Coventry Patmore [illegible]
on "Distinction" [illegible]
the monstrous clever[illegible]
of his style.

Distinction [illegible]
Meredith when the [illegible]
to think of anything [illegible]
epigram has no [illegible]
whisked away from [illegible]

and these things have harmed, and will harm, his popularity. But, like the crudeness of Mr. Browning, they only endear him more to an inner circle of admirers. The fairies of literature gave him all good gifts, but added a Celtic wilfulness. We do not read him to pass away the hour, as many read Mr. Besant, always a skilled, occasionally a humorous story-teller, or as more read Miss Braddon, or wander by the stream-side and kill grilse with Mr. William Black.

But it has been left to Mr. George S. Street, in his 'Quales Ego,' to say a new thing of Meredith's style, which goes to show that while we may admire an ideal widely different from what seems to be the 'mark' with which Meredith would 'wed,' we can still find delight and stimulus, as well as artistic satisfaction, in prose that first repels us:

Mr. Meredith is often neither musical nor easy. But as a manipulator of words to express complexity of thought he has no peer. It was by this complexity, this subtlety of penetration of his, that he was valuable to me when first I read him. I imagine there must be many in my case, to whom he was, above all things, an educator. It was his very obscurity—another name, so often, for a higher intelligence—that was the stimulating force in him for such as myself. Youth can rarely appreciate an achievement of art as such. But youth is keen to grind its intellect on the stone of the uncomprehended. That was the service of Mr. Meredith to those in my case. We puzzled and strove, and were rewarded by the discovery of some complexity of thought or some subtlety of emotion imagined aforetime. Fortunately for us, advance of years and multiplying editions had not yet earned him the homage of the average reviewer; for youth is conceited, and does not care to accept the verdict of the mass of its contemporaries. Mr. Meredith was sometimes an affectation in us, and sometimes the most powerful educator we had. In the passage of years, as we grew from conceit of intelligence into appreciation, in our degrees, of things artistic, we perceived that he was also a great artist, and sympathy was merged in admiration.

Coventry Patmore was another friendly critic who, in his essay on 'Distinction' in the *Fortnightly*, June, 1890, had to admit that the monstrous cleverness of Meredith detracted from the distinction of his style.

Distinction (he wrote) is also manifest in the prose of Mr. George Meredith when the cleverness is not too overwhelming to allow us to think of anything else; but, when the nose of epigram after epigram has no sooner reached the visual nerve than the tail has whisked away from it, so that we have had no time to take in the body, our wonder and bedazement make it sometimes impossible for us to distinguish the distinction, if it be there.

'Epigram after epigram' is certainly not an ideal of English prose, nor does the art of the epigram rank high among literary values. Oddly enough his dexterity in this direction is often chosen by writers on Meredith as the chief proof of his distinction. Even Viscount Morley in the very few words he has ever penned for print on his old friend makes his aphoristic ingenuity the subject of his praise. 'One living writer of genius,' he says in his lecture on 'Aphorisms,' published in 1887, 'has given us a little sheaf of subtly-pointed maxims in "The Ordeal of Richard Feverel," and perhaps he will one day divulge to the world the whole contents of Sir Austin Feverel's unpublished volume, "The Pilgrim's Scrip."'

Though not entirely apropos to the matter in hand, Viscount Morley's only other printed remark upon Meredith, with which I am familiar, may be given here. It occurs in his essay in the *Fortnightly*, April, 1873, on the Poems of Walter Pater, where he says: 'We have one man of genius who is as great a master of subtle insight into character as Mr. Pater is of analysis of beautiful impressions; Mr. Meredith, like Mr. Pater, is not always easy to follow, and for the same reason. After all, the plain men are at least as much in fault as those who touch them with perplexity.'

Mr. J. M. Barrie shows the sound judgment which those of us who are familiar with his essays in criticism always expect from him in his reference to Meredith's style in the article he contributed on 'Mr. George Meredith's Novels' to the *Contemporary Review* of October, 1888:

Mr. Stevenson has said that if Shakespeare could have read 'Rhoda Fleming' he would have cried, 'Here's a fellow!' Carlyle, I happen to know, was acquainted with 'Richard Feverel'; his wife read it aloud to him, and he was so pleased that he said, 'This man's no fule.' This is not the whole story. First Mrs. Carlyle read the book herself, and many times she flung it aside in irritation before becoming reconciled to Mr. Meredith's yoke. Such is the common experience of readers, who fall back before the showers of epigrams or resent the fantastic phraseology. It is the law of the land that novels should be an easy gallop, but Mr. Meredith's readers have to pant uphill. He reaches his thoughts by means of ladders which he kicks away, letting his readers follow as best they can, a way of playing the game that leaves him comparatively free from pursuit. Too sluggish to climb, the public sit in the rear, flinging his jargon at his head, yet aware, if they have heads themselves, that one of the great intellects of the age is on in front.

Phrase-making is Mr. Meredith's passion. His books are as over-dressed as fingers hidden in rings. . . . Were I to pick out Mr. Meredith's triumphs in phrase-making I could tattoo the *Contemporary* with them—to use one of his own phrases. He has made it his business to pin them to his pages as a collector secures butterflies. He succeeds, I believe, in this perilous undertaking as often as he fails. He must have the largest vocabulary of any living man. . . . If to avoid the conventional in phrases he puts words to fantastic uses, he shows that language which had become cold may still be beaten red-hot, and in the process he strikes out numberless sparks of thought. This thinking over words puts new life into literature.

Mr. Zangwill, another novelist who has the critical faculty in no mean measure, is not so judicial as Mr. Barrie, for in 'Without Prejudice' he remarks:

The two great writers of our day who have sinned most against the laws of writing are Browning and Meredith, the one in verse, the other in prose. I speak not merely of obscurities, to perpetrate which is in every sense to stand in one's own light, but of sheer fatuities, tweakings-of-the-nose to our reverend mother-tongue, as either might have expressed it.

Since every real admirer of Meredith has well-grounded reasons for the faith that is in him, and more especially as his friendly critics have been the least sparing in exposing his eccentricities, no apology is needed for giving some examples of the extremes to which his tireless and so often successful search for the new, image-awakening phrase, has led him at times. I quote from Mr. Ernest Newman's careful study in the *Free Review:*

The quickly-concentrative imagination of Keats is possessed by Mr. Meredith, and is answerable for some of his woeful distortions of language. Mannerisms he displays in abundance. His ladies never walk: they swim. Mrs. Doria swims to meet Richard Feverel; Mrs. Mount swims 'wave-like to the sofa'; Lady Rosely swims 'sweetly' into the room; Mrs. Lovell 'swims into the general conversation'; Madame d'Auffray swims to meet Beauchamp; Diana is always swimming,—on one occasion she swims 'to the tea-tray.' Still more extraordinary are some of his other expressions. There is a 'combustible silence' in 'Farina'; when Hippias Feverel is asleep, his door is a 'somnolent door'; a hooked fish comes, we are told, to 'the gasping surface'; Adrian 'opens his mouth to shake out a coil of laughter'; when Mrs. Berry weeps we hear that 'the black-satin bunch careened to a renewed deluge'; the Countess de Saldar 'rambles concentrically'; Caroline sits down 'with her hands joined in pale dejection'; Cornelia's eyelids 'shed a queenly smile'; Dahlia 'eyes' Edward 'a faint sweetness'; Robert Eccles 'flings a lightning at him.' As time went on this tendency in Mr. Meredith became almost irresistible. When he wishes to convey to us the idea of a woman in the days before she became man-like, he tells us, 'Yet was there an opening day when nothing of us moustached her.' When she does become somewhat masculine, we are 'amazed by the flowering up of that hard rough jaw from the tender blooming promise of a petticoat.' Sometimes the very artificiality of the style is not without a charm, as in the description of Sir Willoughby about to embrace Clara: 'the gulf of a caress hove in view like an enormous billow hollowing under the curled ridge. She stooped to a buttercup, the monster swept by.' But gradually we come to the thoroughly distorted style that dominates the later works. It begins on the opening page of 'The Egoist,' although that novel as a whole is of remarkable purity of phrase: 'Who, says the notable humorist, in allusion to this book, who can studiously travel through sheets of leaves now capable of a stretch from the Lizard to the last few pulmonary snips and shreds of leagues dancing on their toes for cold, explorers tell us, and catching breath by good luck, like dogs at bones about a table, on the edge of the Pole.' In 'One of Our Conquerors' the degeneration is complete. Not to mention the celebrated phrase of Dr. Peter Yatt about 'feeling a rotifer astir in the curative compartment of a homœopathic globule,' we have expressions of such elegance as this: 'The word "Imposter" had smacked her on both cheeks from her own mouth'; and this: 'She called on bell-motion of the head to toll forth the utter night-cap negative.' In the face of so much perversity and affectation, can we sum Mr. Meredith up better than in his own chastened and elegant sentence: 'A fantastical plangun-cula enlivened by the wanton tempers of a nursery chit!'

It would be difficult to better this collection of verbal monstrosities, though easy to extend it. Yet the critic who has been at pains to compile it is careful to remind us that Meredith's 'defects are the almost inevitable correlatives of his qualities, the peculiarly vivid imagination that has empowered him to write pages of the most virile and suggestive prose in the language, is the same imagination that has decoyed him into some of his deplorable experiments with our tongue.' And he further points out that 'his excellences and beauties of style are so great and so many that quotation is almost a work of supererogation.' Which unnecessary work he proceeds to discharge with as much success as he has just acquitted himself with, in an opposite direction. All this really weighs for Meredith's greatness, as none but a veritable giant in literary power could offend as he does and still command our homage. As Mr. James Oliphant puts it in his 'Victorian Novelists,' 'no one has ever tried to make words convey so much meaning as Meredith, and very few have had so much meaning to express.' It is this effort to compress so much into his phrases that Mr. W. C. Brownell considers to be the weakness and not the strength of his style.

His perversity is a natural bent toward the artificial (writes Mr. Brownell). Its delight is in disappointing the reader's normal expectations. Simplicity is its detestation. If the idea is simple, its statement is complicated. If it is particularly subtle, its expression is correspondingly succinct. . . . But his style is not obscure in the general sense of the word. He has a wonderful gift of expression, and can not only say clearly the most recondite things, but give a recondite turn to things essentially quite commonplace. He does not love the obscure, but hates the apparent. He has that 'horror of the obvious' so long ago as Longinus censured as hostile to the sublime. And as one cannot always avoid the obvious, especially if one is also extremely prolix, he does his best to obscure it. His vocabulary is never at a loss for a telling word when one is really called for. He can be crispness or curtness itself at need, often indeed wonderfully vivid, sometimes within and sometimes without and sometimes on the verge of the confines of taste, in his pursuit of vividness; for example, 'He read and his eyes became horny'—of Dacier's horror and amazement at the evidence of Diana's treachery. He makes few phrases that one remembers, however. He loads a phrase with meaning, but it is apt to be compression without pith, and often, in greater extension, it becomes rhetorical rather than pungent, though rhetoric that is never tinctured with insincerity. But where he cannot be telling, and even in cases where he might so easily be that he has an opportunity perversely to disappoint you by not being, he is exasperatingly evasive.

Dr. Robertson Nicoll seems to incline to Mr. Brownell's notion as to the perversity of Meredith's style being deliberate, though he does not say this in so many words in his 'Notes on English Style in the Victorian Period' which he contributed to the *Bookman* of New York, December, 1899. In this way he submits what he regards as '*the* problem on the solution of which Meredith's future among English authors depends':

That his is a personality singularly rich, complicated, intense, and outstanding, the most careless reader will perceive. Does that personality find its true expression in his style, or has the artist deliberately set himself to bewilder readers? If the style is a natural style, it will always be studied, and will always repay study. If it is not, then in spite of the immense treasures in his works they will be on the whole neglected, discovered every now and then by some shrill and eager spirit, but as a whole they will be sealed books.

Let me put the question in a concrete form. I take no account of his later books, because the acquired style becomes the natural style. But if—remember I say if—in his earlier days Meredith wrote two versions of his books, the first easy, clear and Thackerayan, and then translated this into Meredithese, this would put him among the second rank of writers. We have, I regret to say, one example at least where we can trace this process at work. In his volume of poems, published in 1851, Mr. Meredith wrote one of the most charming, rhythmical and melodious of love songs, 'Love in the Valley.' For months after he read it Tennyson could not get the lines out of his lips. For a long time they were hidden, and then not many years ago they were republished in Meredithese. Even in the present form some vestige of their former beauty may now and then be seen, but they are intolerable to any reader fortunate enough to possess the first copy.

The caution and poise of Dr. Nicoll's words add to the seriousness of this critical judgment, which, even less guardedly phrased, would still have been important as coming from so ripe a student of literary style. Even so ardent a Meredithian as Mr. James Douglas, in his critical biography of Mr. Theodore Watts-Dunton, has to write on the same subject with misgivings, for in the end this question of style will be the determining factor in the permanence of Meredith's works.

No one adores the work of Mr. Meredith more than I do (says Mr. Douglas), though my admiration is not without a certain leaven of distress at his literary self-consciousness. I say this with all reverence. Great as Meredith is, he would be greater still if, when he is delivering his priceless gifts to us, he would bear in mind that immortal injunction in 'King Henry the Fourth'—'I prithee now, deliver them like a man of this world.' I can imagine how the great humorist must smile when the dolt, who once found 'obscurity' in his most lucid passages, praises him for the defects of his qualities, and calls upon all other writers to write Meredithese.

To be a classic—to be immortal—it is necessary for an imaginative writer to deliver his message like 'a man of this world.' Shakespeare himself, occasionally, will seem to forget this, but only occasionally, and we never think of it when falling down in worship before the shrine of the greatest imaginative writer that has ever lived. Dr. Johnson said that all work which lives is without eccentricity. Now, entranced as I have been, ever since I was a boy, by Meredith's incomparable romances, I long to set my imagination free of Meredith and fly away with his characters, as I can fly away with the characters of the classic imaginative writers from Homer down to Sir Walter Scott. But I seldom succeed. Now and then I escape from the obsession of the picture of the great writer seated in his châlet with the summer sunshine gleaming round his picturesque head, but illuminating also all too vividly his ink-stand, and his paper and his pens; but only now and then, and not for long. If it had pleased Nature to give him less intellectual activity, less humour and wit and literary brilliance, I feel sure that he would have lived more securely as an English classic.

Perhaps the most searching examination of Meredith's style is to be found in Mr. J. M. Robertson's study in 'Preciosity' in the *Yellow Book*, April, 1897, where he writes:

> There can be no dispute, I think, over the judgment that Mr. Meredith's style is the most pronounced outbreak of preciosity in modern English literature. There, if ever, we may allow ourselves a quasi-Pantagruelian protest. It is indeed impossible for a reader who respects Mr. Meredith's genius to read him—or at least his later works—without irritation at his extraordinary ill-usage of language. Old admirers, going back to his earlier works, never free from the sin of preciosity, recognise that there has been an almost continuous deterioration—the fatal law of all purposive preciosity. In the earlier novels there were at times signal beauties of phrase, sentences in which the strain towards utterance was transmuted into fire and radiance, sentences of the fine poet who underlay and even now underlies that ever-thickening crust of preciosity and verbal affectation. Even in 'One of Our Conquerors' there seemed, to the tolerant sense, to be still some gleams of the old flame, flashing at long intervals through the scoriæ of unsmelted speech. But in 'Lord Ormont and his Aminta' neither patience nor despair can discover in whole chapters aught but the lava and cinders of language. . . . With the exception of Zola's 'La Terre'—hard reading for a different reason—'One of Our Conquerors' was the hardest novel to read that I ever met with; but I have found 'Lord Ormont and his Aminta' easy enough. After a few chapters I no longer sought to read Mr. Meredith. I made a hand-to-mouth *précis* of nearly every page, and soon got over the ground, only pausing at times to reassure myself that all was ill.
>
> Hardly once, so far as I have read, do we find an important sentence really well written; never a paragraph; for the perpetual grimace of expression, twisting the face of speech into every shape but those of beauty and repose, is in no sense admirable. Simple statements, normal reflections, are packed into the semblance of inspired fancies and brilliant aphorisms.

Yet notwithstanding this vigorous denunciation of the Meredithian sins, Mr. Robertson is by no means blind to the virtues. He considers Meredith 'a novelist, if not of the very first rank, yet so powerful and so independent that to apply to him the term second-rate is not allowable,' and he declares that he must be classed by himself 'as a master with not worse limitary prejudices than those of Bàlzac; with more poetic elevation than any novelist of his day; a true modern in many things, despite a fundamental unrealism in his characters and an almost puerile proclivity to old-world devices of circumstantial plot.' Admitting thus much, he next sets himself to explaining 'the egregious vice of style' on the grounds of 'individual self-will, defiance of censure, persistence in eccentricity, and self-absorption in isolation.' It seems to me, however, when Mr. Robertson argues that Meredith pushed his natural mannerisms to unnatural extremes as a sort of defiance of those who failed to appreciate him, he is leaving criticism for speculation and advancing a charge of wilful pettiness against an author in whom he has discovered certain large and splendid qualities. If Meredith is an artist he could never have behaved like a spoilt child. To say that an author, out of spite at lack of appreciation, 'put an antic disposition on' in his later writings, is to raise doubts of his sanity. Why seek to get away from Buffon's '*le style c'est l'homme*'? It is, and Meredith's style *is* Meredith, for good or ill. None the less Mr. Robertson's theory is of interest to all students of the master and we may follow it further, when he writes:

The prompt appreciation of the few good readers did not teach him to look on the reading-public as what it is, a loose mass of ever-varying units, in which even the dullards have no solidarity; he entrenched himself in the Carlylean and Browningesque manner, personifying the multitude as one lumpish hostile entity, or organised body of similar entities. Thus when, after an interval of silence, he produced 'The Egoist,' and the accumulating units of the new generation, the newer minds, appreciated the novelty of the problem and the solution so generally as to make the book the success of its year, he was understood to be cynical over the praise given to a work which was in his opinion inferior to its predecessors. The new generation has since proceeded to read those earlier works; but Mr. Meredith had fixed his psychological habits, and no sense of community with his generation could now avail to make him treat language as a common possession, which any one may rightly improve, but which no one may fitly seek to turn into impenetrable jungle for his own pleasure. Ill health may have had something to do with Mr. Meredith's æsthetic deviation from 'the general deed of man'; and his contemporaries have their share of responsibility; but we must recognise in him what we have recognised behind all

By permission of Messrs. Smith, Elder & Co.] [*From the drawing by George du Maurier in the 'Cornhill.'*

JANET ILCHESTER WITH HARRY AND HIS FATHER.

'Harry!' Janet said softly. I knelt to her. 'My own and only Janet!' 'Do not awaken him,' she whispered. 'No, but I am home.' 'I am glad.' One hand she was obliged to surrender. I kissed it. She seemed startled at my warmth.
—*Harry Richmond*. Chapter LV.

[*To face p.* 184.

forms of preciosity—a specific limitation or one-sidedness, a failure to develop equally and in healthy relation to all the forces of the intellectual life. . . . What he long ago confessed of himself in 'Beauchamp's Career'—that he had acquired the habit of listening too much to his own voice—is now too obvious to need confessing. It all goes to produce, not only that defect of relation to current life which we see in his unhappy style, but that further defect which consists in his lapses into unreality as a novelist.

But after the worst has been said, and every fault laid bare, it must be confessed there remains some subtle magic in Meredith's style that cannot be defined so easily as his mannerisms and their excesses can be defined; that charms us almost against our better judgment; that makes us feel, when we have applied all possible tests of criticism, that criticism does not meet the case and nothing but joyful submission to the spell of that magic will enable one to do full justice to Meredith's style. Mr. Richard Le Gallienne in his enthusiastic little book, 'George Meredith: Some Characteristics,' is clearly under the spell, though he writes as follows in terms of grave and reverend criticism:

Mr. Meredith's method is, indeed, that of the poets and all great imaginative workers. His style may be said to be the result of that process expressed in 'Pippa Passes' of following in one art an ideal conceived in another, a process with which we are familiar in the relations of poetry and painting, and to which, doubtless, we owe some other products of our new imaginative prose. Such a style was the only possible medium for his matter—matter too intricate for verse, and too elusive for 'pedestrian' prose. Nothing but vivid metaphor could light up for us such strange, untrodden regions of the subjective as those into which he loves to take us; for we can only, of course, understand the unfamiliar in terms of the familiar, and if 'our flying minds cannot contain a protracted description' of the objective, how much less can we hope to hold the elusive impressions of the subjective by such means. As well hope to take down the rapid words of a fluent speaker in longhand. The essential quality, then, of Mr. Meredith's work, in his prose as in his verse, is a great metaphor. One wishes above all things to avoid over-accentuation in this present heyday of the superlative, but one can hardly help asking whether, since Shakespeare, there has been a handling of imaginative phrase more truly masculine than Mr. Meredith's. Greater artists, both in prose and verse, of course, there have been, but in that one quality of flashing a picture in a phrase, of, so to say, writing in lightning, who are Mr. Meredith's rivals?

That Meredith's metaphor is deliberate, and not entirely a habit of thought, Mr. Le Gallienne seems to suggest when he goes on to say that the master 'is capable of putting it aside altogether—as in

"Vittoria" or "Rhoda Fleming"—and writing Saxon simple as a song.' Perhaps the consensus of opinion would be that Meredith thinks in metaphor and writes in the terms of his thoughts.

It will be granted that I have shown no inclination to urge the case for Meredith's unique mastery of literary expression; I have, indeed, called hostile witnesses more often than partisans, and this for a reason I have endeavoured to make clear. But I am persuaded that after any one has devoted much study to Meredith's style, it is such appreciation as Mr. Le Gallienne's that makes one's heart warm to the writer.

For my own part, I am not prepared to say whether Meredith will stand or fall on the merits or demerits of his style. That style is the great preservative of literature, its veritable salt, I firmly believe; but it is obvious that 'style' cannot be a fixed and readily ascertainable quality, since 'it is the man.' Now, Meredith's style is surely George Meredith, inimitable, himself even when most self-conscious, and Meredith is an intellectual force with which the future, as well as his own generation, is bound to reckon. Wordsworth speaks of an order of great writers who create the taste by which they are judged; to this order Meredith belongs. Hence the futility of comparative criticism in respect to him; his style not less. Later on we shall see what contemporary criticism thinks of his chances with posterity; that is not the concern of the moment.

Before leaving the present subject, let me give an anecdote on the authority of the *Outlook*, which may possibly be authentic, but is in any case amusing. 'In an unrecorded conversation,' says the anonymous writer, 'Mr. George Meredith once asked a friend and neighbour how he had enjoyed the reading of "Beauchamp's Career"; and, in spite of a very appreciative verdict, Mr. Meredith confessed to a sense of serious disappointment. His admirer, like many others, had failed to notice his translation of *tête-à-tête;* and Mr. Meredith was prouder of his phrase "a you-and-me" than of the achievement of the novel.'

I do not recollect this use of 'you-and-me' in the novel named, but I do recall a phrase of the kind in 'The Tragic Comedians'—'The carrying on of a prolonged and determined you-and-I in company intimates to those undetermined floating atoms about us that a certain sacred something is in process of formation, or has formed.' Fortunately, the novelist never became so enamoured of his you-and-me's or his you-and-I's as he did of his swim, swam, and swimming, else a new and greater terror had been added to his style!

VIII

IN PARODY AND CARICATURE

It is a commonplace that the more individual the style of an author the better is he suited to the needs of the parodist. True, Mr. Henry James has a style that is all his own and yet so elusive that to succeed in parodying it, as Mr. Owen Seaman has succeeded, is no slight achievement. But the characteristics, we might almost say the tricks, of Mr. Meredith's manner, in all his later prose and poetry, lie so open to the salty winds of satire that the surprise is to find him so rarely the subject of parody. Of course, the parodist usually selects an author whose work is fairly familiar to the general mass of readers, and that may be a reason. Another, possibly, is that so many imitative writers exist who unconsciously parody the Meredithian style in their works that conscious burlesque is scarcely called for! At all events, the fact remains as stated; and outside the pages of *Punch* but little has been written where so much might have been expected. Some of the very ablest literary criticism of our time has taken the form of parody. Mr. Owen Seaman has often shown us that by an ingenious imitation of an author's mannerisms a far more searching criticism may be achieved in a very few lines than a long essay would have established.

The earliest effort to invoke the comic muse against the greatest of her modern devotees was made, I believe, by Mr. R. C. Lehmann, no bungling hand at the delightful art of parody, though his first shot was scarcely a bull's-eye. Clever and amusing it was, but not exactly comic imitation, which is the essence of parody. As burlesque, however, it would pass readily. It appeared in the series which he contributed to *Punch* in 1890–91, 'Mr. Punch's Prize Novels,' the third being 'Joanna of the Cross Ways.' It was supposed to be written by George Verimyth, Author of 'Richard's Several Editions,' 'The Aphorist,' 'Shampoo's Shaving Pot'—not a very happy set of comic inversions, by the way. The action was based on the frequent charge against the novelist of his failure to realise his characters, his inability to make them act up to the expectations he claims for them as wits and aphorists. Thus:

> Many are the tales concerning Joanna's flashing wit. There appeared many years back, in a modest shape that excited small interest among the reviewing herd, a booklet whereof the title furnished little if any indication to the contents. *The Spinster's Reticule*, for so the name ran, came forth with no blare of journalistic trumpets challenging approval from the towers of critical sagacity. It appeared and lived. But between its cardboard covers the bruised heart of Joanna beats before the world. She shines most in these aphorisms. Her private talk, too, has its own brilliancy, spun, as it was here and there, out of a museful mind at the cooking of the dinner or of the family accounts. She said of love that 'it is the sputter of grease in a frying-pan; where it falls the fire burns with a higher flame to consume it.' Of man, that 'he may navigate Mormon Bay, but he cannot sail to Khiva Point.' The meaning is too obvious it may be, but the thought is well imaged.
>
> She is delightful when she touches on life. 'Two,' she says, 'may sit at a feast, but the feast is not thereby doubled.' And, again, 'Passion may lift us to Himalaya heights, but the hams are smoked in a chimney.' And this of the soul, 'He who fashions a waterproof prevents not the clouds from dripping moisture.' Of stockings she observes that, 'The knitting-needles are long, but the turn of the heel is a teaser.' Here there is a delightful irony of which matrons and maids may take note.
>
> Such, then, was our Joanna—Joanna Meresia Spratt, to give her that full name by which posterity is to know her—an ardent, bubbling, bacon-loving girl-nature, with hands reaching from earth to the stars, that blinked egregiously at the sight of her innocent beauty, and hid themselves in winding clouds for very love of her.

There is hardly any attempt here—certainly no success—to mimic the Meredithian phraseology, though the burlesque idea is well enough maintained. Joanna's husband, Sir John Spratt, is intended for a comic presentment of Sir Austin Feverel, and their mock tragedy, though in no way a comic comment on Meredith, is sufficiently amusing of itself to be worthy of quotation:

> They sat at table together. Binns, the butler, who himself dabbled in aphorisms, and had sucked wisdom from the privy perusal of Sir John's note-book, had laid before them a dish on which reposed a small but well-boiled leg of one that had trod the Southdowns but a week before in all the pride of lusty life. There was a silence for a moment.

Punch, *December* 19, 1891.

Punch, *July* 28, 1804.

TWO CARICATURE SKETCHES FROM 'PUNCH.'

Reproduced by permission from Messrs. Bradbury, Agnew & Co., Proprietors of 'Punch.'

[*To face p.* 188.

'You will, as usual, [illegible],' queried Sir John.

'Lean for me [illegible],' [illegible], with [illegible] dashes.

'Nay, nay,' said [illegible] which assigns to [illegible].'

Joanna pouted [illegible] were not her aphorisms [illegible] cold face of Sir John [illegible] them with one wave [illegible] pork, and caper sauce [illegible] Binns, gasping in [illegible] had disappeared [illegible] above calling on her [illegible] had been fairly scraped [illegible] trembling fingers [illegible] the mercy of an august [illegible].

But the world [illegible] Joanna's freak. [illegible] with her dashes [illegible] was [illegible]. But in Sir John's [illegible] it was written that [illegible] Boot is but a [illegible]. [illegible] drawn [illegible] better.'

Far happier, and [illegible] was unsurpassed [illegible] the Meredithian style, was [illegible]. By George [illegible] I understand, by Mr. [illegible] *Punch*, December [illegible] dith had shortly before appeared [illegible] witness [illegible] brought against an action [illegible] lishers, Chapman and Hall. [illegible] the point. The story [illegible] tine humour: 'It was [illegible] An admirable opening [illegible] the published report [illegible] between the Judge [illegible] and Mr. Meredith. [illegible] is asked to [illegible] more clearly:

Mr. George Meredith: 'My Lord, I will put it with a [illegible] brevity, not indeed a [illegible] brevity [illegible] bling recluse, who [illegible] grey London [illegible] ward at break of naked [illegible] of compassing clouds [illegible] is denied to his external [illegible] vision [illegible] brevity of a rotifer [illegible] pathic globule—so, if humorously perceptible [illegible] sallow——'

'You will, as usual, take the fat?' queried Sir John.

'Lean for me to-day,' retorted Joanna, with one of her bright flashes.

'Nay, nay,' said her husband, 'that were against tradition, which assigns to you the fat.'

Joanna pouted. Her mind rebelled against dictation. Besides, were not her aphorisms superior to those of her husband? The cold face of Sir John grew eloquent in protest. She paused, and then with one wave of her stately arm swept mutton, platter, knife, fork, and caper sauce into the lap of Sir John, whence the astonished Binns, gasping in pain, with much labour rescued them. Joanna had disappeared in a flame of mocking laughter, and was heard above calling on her maid for salts. But Sir John, ere yet the sauce had been fairly scraped from him, unclasped his note-book, and with trembling fingers wrote therein, 'Poole's masterpieces are ever at the mercy of an angry woman.'

But the world is hard, and there was little mercy shown for Joanna's freak. Her husband had slain her. That was all. She with her flashes, her gaiety, her laughter, was consigned to dust. But in Sir John's note-book it was written that, 'The hob-nailed boot is but a bungling weapon. The drawing-room poker is better.'

Far happier, and in its way unsurpassed as a parody on the Meredithian style, was the biting satire 'By George!' written also, I understand, by Mr. Lehmann in *Punch*, December 19, 1891. Meredith had shortly before appeared as a witness in a libel action brought against an author whose book he had read for the publishers, Chapman and Hall. His evidence was very short and to the point. The story, he admitted, was written in a sort of elephantine humour: 'it was a failure, but still passed with the public.' An admirable opening here for Mr. Punch, who proceeds to amplify the published report of the matter by a dialogue of some length between the Judge, Sir Charles Russell (counsel for the prosecutor) and Mr. Meredith. The witness is asked to explain himself a little more clearly:

Mr. George Meredith. 'My Lord, I will put it with a convincing brevity, not indeed a dust-scattering brevity fit only for the mumbling recluse, who perchance in this grey London marching Eastward at break of naked morn, daintily protruding a pinkest foot out of compassing clouds, copiously takes inside of him doses of what is denied to his external bat-resembling vision, but with the sharp brevity of a rotifer astir in that curative compartment of a homœopathic globule—so, I humorously purposeful in the midst of sallow——'

The Judge. 'One moment, Mr. Meredith. Have you considered——'

Mr. G. M. 'Consideration, my Lord, is of them that sit revolving within themselves the mountainously mouse-productive problems of the overtoppingly catastrophic backward ages of empurpled brain-distorting puzzledom: for puzzles, as I have elsewhere said, come in rattle-boxes, they are actually children's toys, for what they contain, but not the less do they buzz at our understandings and insist that they break or we, and, in either case, to show a mere foolish idle rattle in hollowness. Nor have the antic bobbings——'

Sir Charles Russell (cross-examining). 'Really, Mr. Meredith, I fail to follow you. Would it not be possible——'

Mr. G. M. 'Ay, there you have it. In truth, the question looks like a paragraph in a newspaper, upon which a Leading Article sits, dutifully arousing the fat worm of sarcastic humour under the ribs of cradled citizens, with an exposure of its excellent folly. For the word. That is it. The word is Archon, with extended hand summoning the collaboratorically ordained, misbegotten brood of shock-shilling pamphlets to his regal presence——'

The Judge (testily). 'No doubt that would be so, but it brings us no nearer to a decision upon the question of humour in the particular passage of the book which contains the alleged libel.'

Here Sir Charles is supposed to interfere with several passages from 'One of Our Conquerors,' hackneyed failures of the Meredith style long familiar to us all, which read as comic as Mr. Lehmann's inventions, and the incident ends with the judge praising the clarity of the witness's evidence and throwing a phrase of his own in his teeth when he says that he may become 'a trebly cataphractic Invisible.' The whole is cleverly done: genuine parody. Mr. Lehmann made a bull's-eye at the second shot, which is not bad shooting.

The humorist had now got the trick of the Meredithyramb as clean as the pot-stroke at billiards, and when we next find Mr. Lehmann contributing to *Punch* in 1894 a longish parody (appearing three consecutive weeks) there is perfect confidence in the manner of it, every paragraph is a hit. 'Lord Ormont's Mate and Matey's Aminta' was the title, and a brief passage will give the savour of the whole:

Matey then was Lord Ormont's secretary. A sad dog his Lordship; all the women on bended knees to his glory. Who shall own him? What cares he so it be a petticoat? For women go the helter-skelter pace; head-first they plunge or kick like barking cuckoos. You can tether them with a dab for Sir Francis Jeune. He will charge a jury to the rightabout of a crapulous fallow-ball, stiff as Rhadamanthus eyeing the tremblers. But Matey had met this one before. Memories came pouring. He gazed. Was she, in truth, Lord Ormont's? The thought spanked him in the face. A wife? Possibly. And with an aunt—Aminta's aunt. She has a nose like a trout skimming a river for flies, then rises a minute and you not there, always too late with rod and line for sport. But there was danger to these two, and Lord Ormont was writing his Memoirs. A mad splashing of unnecessary ink on the foolscap made for his head, never more to wear the plumed cocked hat in a clash of thunder-bearing squadrons.

Mr. Lehmann's three parodies were accompanied by comic pictures, by Mr. E. T. Reed and Mr. E. J. Wheeler. Mr. Wheeler's little caricature of 'George in the box' appeared in *Punch* of December 19, 1891, and gives a good likeness of the great author, doubtless based on one of the few existing photographs. Mr. Reed's caricature, published first in *Punch* of July 28, 1894, is a bolder attempt, showing Meredith as a bull in the literary china shop, demolishing the vases of Grammar, Construction, Syntax and Form, with very vigorous hoofings. The likeness here also is excellent and most probably had the same source as Mr. Wheeler's.

But here enters Mr. Max Beerbohm, our only English caricaturist in the full sense of the word, and *Vanity Fair* of September 24, 1896, published from his brush the solitary caricature of any importance that exists. Opinions will differ as to the taste of this, but none who have studied the art of caricature will question its great merits. 'Max' may have studied his victim from the life. If not he has rendered with remarkable fidelity the impression that one retains of the head of Meredith.

The pinkish-ruddy effect of the skin, the dove-like, silvery whiteness of the hair and head, the dominance of the large up-looking eyes, the thinness of the neck, the general feeling of gentleness—all are exaggerated with the very perfection of the caricaturist's art, and it would not be too much to say that here is a better pictorial impression than any of the serious portraits. Meredith was sixty-eight years old at that time, and it may be questioned whether the caricaturist was quite kind to the ageing author; but kindness and caricature do not go hand in hand. Kindness is usually the only virtue of the incompetent; it is, for that reason, not greatly in evidence in the writings of Meredith himself; and there is fitness in the fact that the comic muse, inspiring an artist of the pencil, has given us so truthful a portrait of one whose life was passed before her shrine.

Naturally, one who had lived a life so withdrawn from public pryings had largely escaped the pencil of the caricaturists, who must deal with features familiar to a wider circle than the following of George Meredith, so that it is not surprising to find that these three caricatures just described represent the sum-total of pictorial parody of the man himself; but we are by no means at the end of the literary parody.

To the witty 'Max' must be ascribed not only the credit of the one important caricature of the man, but also of the most successful parody of the novelist. This, Mr. Max Beerbohm contributed to the *Saturday Review*, Christmas Number, 1896, a few months after he had produced his *Vanity Fair* caricature. It was one of a set of equally ingenious parodies of eminent authors, and had for title 'The Victory of Aphasia Gibberish'—in itself a little triumph of satire. The piece is a perfect gem of prose parody, and quoted passages scarcely give an adequate notion of the sustained cleverness of the whole. But I must be content to offer a few specimens only:

In the heart of insular Cosmos, remote by some scores of leagues of hodge-trod arable or pastoral—not more than a snuff-pinch to gaping tourists' nostrils accustomed to inhalation of prairie-winds, but enough for perspective—from these marginal sands, trident-scraped, we are to fancy, by a helmeted Dame Abstract, familiarly profiled on discs of current bronze, price of a loaf for humbler maws disdainful of Gallic side-dishes for the titillation of choicer palates, stands Ghibberish Park, a house of some pretension, mentioned at Runnymede, with the spreading exception of wings given to it in latter times by Dædalean monsters not to be baulked of billiards or traps for Terpsichore, and owned for unbroken generations by a healthy line of procreant Gibberishes, to the undoing of collateral branches eager for the birth of a female. Passengers in cushioned chambers flying through space, top-speed or dallying with obscure platforms not alighted at apparently, have had it pointed out to them, as beheld dimly for a privileged instant and then forgotten, for the most part, as they sink back behind crackling barrier of instructive paper, with a 'Thank you, sir,' or 'Madam,' as the case may be.

Here, again, in the most comic Meredithese, is a portrait of Aphasia:

She had breadth. Heels that sent ample curves over the ground she stood on, and hands that could floor you with a clinch of them, were hers. Brown eyes looked down at you from swelling temples

By permission of the Proprietors of 'Vanity Fair.'] *[From the Cartoon by Max Beerbohm in 'Vanity Fair.'*

'OUR FIRST NOVELIST.'

To face p. **192.**

that were lost in a ruffling copse of hair. Square chin, cleft centrally, gave her throat the look of a tower with a gun protrudent at top. Her nose was virginal, with hints of the Iron Duke at most angles. Pink Oyster covering pearls must serve for her mouth. She was dressed for church, evidently, but seemed no slave to Time. Her bonnet was pushed to the back of her head, and she was handling the ribbons. One saw she was a woman. She inspired deference.

The lover is Sir Rhombus, and he is with her on Christmas morning, lingering while the rest of the Gibberish family have gone to church. Aphasis and Sir Rhombus talk of going also:

'You have Prayer-Book?' he queried.

She nodded. Juno catches the connubial trick.

'Hymns?'

'Ancient and Modern.'

'I may share with you?'

'I know them by heart. Parrots sing.'

'Philomel carols.' He bent to her.

'Complaints spoil a festival.' She turned aside. There was a silence as of virgin Dundee or Madeira susceptible of knify incision.

'Time speeds,' said Sir Rhombus, with a jerk at the clock.

'We may dodge the scythe.'

'To be choked with the sands.'

She flashed a smile.

'Lady! Your father has started.'

'He knows the aphorism. Copy-books instil it.'

'It would not be well that my Aphasia should enter after the Absolution,' he pursued.

She cast her eyes to the carpet. He caught them at the rebound.

'It snows,' she said, swimming to the window.

'A flake. Not more. The season claims it.'

'I have thin boots.'

'Another pair! . . .'

'My maid buttons. She is at church.'

'My fingers?'

'Twelve on each!'

'Five,' he corrected.

'Buttons. . . .'

'I beg your pardon.'

She saw opportunity. She swam to the bell-rope and grasped it for a tinkle. The action spread feminine curves to her lover's eye. He was a man.

Obsequiousness loomed in the doorway. Its mistress flashed an order for Port—two glasses.

Sir Rhombus sprang a pair of eyebrows on her. Suspicion slid down the banister of his mind, trailing a blue ribbon. Inebriates were one of his studies. For a second, she was sunset.

'Medicinal!' she murmured.

'Forgive me, madam! . . . A glass. Certainly. 'Twill warm us for worshipping.'

The wine is discussed in the most diverting mock Meredithese, and Sir Rhombus the while is warming to the sipping, his glass needing frequent refilling, until 'he swam to the decanter unsteadily.'

He filled. 'Here's to you!'

'No heel-taps!' she sparkled.

'With your permission!' he said, refilling. 'Finish it under table. Genius of Port demands it. . . . Pretty carpet. . . . Revolving pattern.'

When the craze for the dramatisation of novels set in some ten years ago, and every sort of book except Webster's Dictionary seemed about to have a 'stage version,' it was announced that 'Mr. George Meredith is preparing a stage version of "The Egoist"'—a most likely occupation for a man of seventy, who, save for occasional verse, had quite ceased from literary activity. But the newspaper paragraph was a good enough excuse for Mr. F. Anstey to begin in *Punch* of January 18, 1899, 'Mr. Punch's Dramatised Novels,' the first of which was the 'Egoist.' I am afraid it cannot be reckoned among the many successful pieces of this celebrated comic writer. Little or no attempt is made to imitate the Meredith manner; the purpose is rather to provide a comic criticism of the novel by means of dialogue between the chief characters portrayed in it, and so considered it is worthy of notice here, for, indeed, Mr. Anstey could scarcely produce anything that did not stimulate our interest or yield artistic pleasure. The scene of the third act is the laboratory at Patterne, in the evening, where Sir Willoughby, fumbling with his chemicals, soliloquises:

Sir W. 'At last I am to be allowed to speak. For two whole acts I have been forced to keep silence. Now to soliloquise. Why does Clara fly me? I have my points. Mrs. Mountstuart said I had a leg! How *does* that woman discover these things? But here is Lætitia. I must keep up my reputation for obscurity. (Enter *Lætitia.*) Lætitia, the fair besiege us, sweep to the assault, plead impassioned. Why, when the breach is carried, when they sweep and swim ebullient to the capture, call a halt, parley, fall back refluent? Or, to vary the metaphor, suppose a mansion strong, firm set, very rock. To it they strive pendulous, crepitant as dancers toe to heel advancing, swaying one foot up, t'other come down. Suppose——'

Lætitia. 'Sir Willoughby!'

Sir W. (aside). 'Interrupted, by Jove!'

Lætitia (anxiously). 'Are you quite well?'

Sir W. 'Of course. Why?'

Lætitia. 'Those involved sentences, those tortuous expressions. Should you not see a doctor?'

Sir W. 'Was ever a man so misunderstood! I was making you an offer of marriage.'

Lætitia. 'But you are engaged to Clara.'

Sir W. 'Clara asked me to release her after lunch. It's true I refused, but what of that? Lætitia, *you* are ever faithful. *You* shall marry me.'

Lætitia. 'Thank you; I'd rather not.'

Sir W. 'Lætitia, you amaze me. I ask you to marry me, marry *me*.' (He brandishes a test-tube.)

Lætitia. 'Do be careful. I am sure something will explode. Please put that nasty thing down.'

Sir W. 'Not unless you promise to be mine.'

Lætitia. 'Never.'

Sir W. 'Ah!'

(In his emotion he drops the test-tube, which blows up with a loud report. Sir W. falls prone.)

Lætitia. 'Clumsy man! I knew he would. Thank goodness that settles *him*. How pleased Clara will be. Now she will be able to marry Mr. Whitford. It's a poor explosion that blows nobody any good.' (Exit. Curtain.)

Mr. Owen Seaman's parodies of Mr. Meredith's prose style, in the form of single paragraphs instead of a complete story, which appear in his 'Borrowed Plumes' were also first published in *Punch*. A few of the happiest of Mr. Seaman's hits may here be quoted:

In the vestibule of Adolescence, the Boy stands at plastic pause, clay-soft to the imposed Idea. This is the Propagandist's hour; then, or never, the Vegetarian has his chance.

A woman more nosingly fastidious of essentials, you might waste a season of Church Parades and never come up with. Yet she married her husband for his gift of digesting Welsh Rabbit.

Present, you could swear to her for a glowingly constant; absent, she wrote 'Will wire,' and telegraphed 'Will write'—to the chilling of assurance.

A next-weeker for procrastination, there was Æcus in his eye for the delays of others. Chatham-and-Dover with himself, he was Time-and-Tide for the rest.

Bachelor by habit and a graceful seat by force of application, he had the manner of riding straight after hounds or women; but tempered by an instinct for country and a taste for the durable. He would choose the open gate at the fallow's corner, in contempt of incredulous eye-lifts thrown over shrug of shoulders leaning back for the rise, rather than risk his stable's best blood over a low hedge, flushing young Spring, with heavy drop at fourteen stone on macadam flints, shrieking menace of a wrung fetlock for the ten miles home. In the other kind of chase he had cried off on suspicion that the lady's mother had died fat.

It will be noticed that so far not a single example of poetical parody has been mentioned. I know of no parodies in verse except the two short pieces by Mr. Seaman in 'Borrowed Plumes,'—one with the refrain 'My Bismarck, O my Bismarck,' after 'The Nuptials of Attila,' the other a Meredithese description of the return of Mr. Joseph Chamberlain from a Mediterranean excursion,—and the longer parody which the same gifted writer contributed to the *Morning Post* in 1899, 'At the Sign of the Cock: Being an Ode in further "Contribution to the Song of French History," dedicated, without malice or permission, to Mr. George Meredith.' This, of course, had been inspired by the 'Odes' contributed to *Cosmopolis* for March, 1898, and reprinted by Constable in book-form that year. The poet's later habit of jerks and jumps is more pronounced in these 'Odes' than in any of his other poems, so that the parodist had fair game. Like so much of Mr. Seaman's brilliant verse, 'At the Sign of the Cock' suffers from having a number of allusions to politics of the moment, the recollection of which soon fades and leaves the reader of a later day somewhat befogged with certain points of the author's wit. It will suffice if I quote the first of the five verses comprising the parody, as it illustrates how effectively the tuneless and staccato movement of Meredith's later verse has been imitated with comic effect:

Rooster her sign,
Rooster her pugnant note, she struts
Evocative, amazon spurs aprick at heel;
Nid-nod the authentic stump
Of the once ensanguined comb vermeil as wine;
With conspuent doodle-doo
Hails breach o' the hectic dawn of yon New Year,
Last issue up to date
Of quiverful Fate
Evolved spontaneous; hails with tonant trump

The spiriting prime o' the clashed carillon-peal;
Ruffling her caudal plumes derisive of scuts;
Inconscient how she stalks an immarcessibly absurd
Bird.

With this the parody of Meredith ends. It will be observed that with the exception of the two pieces first appearing in the *Saturday Review* and the *Morning Post*, only the writers in *Punch* have given him the flattery of comic imitation. Perhaps his advanced years and austerity of life, his earnestness, may have restrained the hand of the comic writers more recently, though a study of comic literature does not leave us with the feeling that anything in life or literature is sacred to the parodist. Nor does our knowledge of Meredith himself raise the slightest feeling that he would have resented the widest liberty being taken with him or his works in this respect. Himself the greatest of modern humorists, and by that token sound of heart and head, tolerant of all criticism, rejoicing in ridicule of himself as he was wont in his lustier days to rejoice in the buffeting breezes of the Surrey Downs, he would surely have looked with a kindly eye on the work of any one who showed sufficient acquaintance with his own writings and the comic muse to make 'laughter of the mind' over the medium which he himself had invented chiefly for that purpose.

IX

THE NOVELS IN CONTEMPORARY CRITICISM

In the present chapter I do not purpose addressing myself to the formidable task of tracing from first to last the verdicts of the critics on the novels as a whole. A volume, and scarcely of the most profitable nature, would be required for that. My immediate purpose may be effected by less exigeant research: simply to gather together some of the most noteworthy criticisms of the novels in chronological order. Nor do I purpose devoting any considerable attention to the books which have been written on Meredith's prose: surely the most remarkable library of criticism about himself which any great author has ever had the opportunity of reading. Mr. Le Gallienne's admirable work, though penetrating and lacking in no point of intelligent appreciation, was, like one of the very latest—Mr. Richard H. P. Curle's—devoted to 'aspects' of the great writer rather than to an orderly and progressive study of the novels. So, too, was the late Miss Lynch's brilliant monograph, which had the feminine note and something of the Irish eloquence we associate with the Blarney Stone—'fruits of his colossal intellect,' 'masterpiece after masterpiece,' 'mighty genius,' 'had it been written in blood it could not be redder with life,' these are typical of her phrases, the last of 'Richard Feverel.' Mrs. Sturge Henderson, who has not the flowing pen of Miss Lynch, but is a thought more temperate, is concerned chiefly with Meredith's philosophy, and only in a minor degree with the æsthetics of his prose, in her able work, 'George Meredith; Novelist—Poet—Reformer.' Her point of view is briefly conveyed in her own words: 'Intermittently, Meredith is a great artist; primarily and consistently, he is a moralist—a teacher.' Mrs. Henderson would find it difficult, I fancy, to name any great artist who lacks these other attributes. It is not the function of art to moralise or teach, but all great art does both; as the greater includes the less. The moralising and teaching of a great artist in the intervals when he fails to be 'great' are not of much account! The single work in which a critic has confined himself exclusively to the study of Meredith's prose fiction is 'The Novels of George Meredith,' by Mr. E. J. Bailey, an American *littérateur*. Mr. Bailey writes with insight and knowledge of his subject; but he does not help us appreciably to a more intimate understanding of the novelist by his arbitrary division of Meredith's work into the three periods of 'apprentice,' 'journeyman,' 'master-workman.' 'Richard Feverel' ended the first period! 'Vittoria' the second, during which the novelist was working under 'assimilated influences,' which is true as regards 'Evan Harrington' only; and the third period, during which the novelist passes through two distinct phases of 'free invention' and 'concentrated interest,' opens with 'Harry Richmond.' Thus, you see, 'Richard Feverel' shows the 'prentice hand, 'Rhoda Fleming' the skilled journeyman's, and 'The Tragic Comedians' that of the master-workman! This won't do; so, adapting a phrase of Meredith the journalist, 'we dub Mr. Bailey theorist and pass on.'

Of course, as a glance at the other chapters in this work will indicate, the present is not the only one in which we are concerned with the novels. It is not in any sense an effort to dispose at one stroke of the criticism of Meredith's fiction, though its heading might give that impression. Chiefly, it is a bringing together of critical opinions, likely, thus assembled, to be suggestive and helpful to the student, but which did not conveniently fall into the ranks when other chapters were being mustered. We shall first take the novels in chronological order, noting how they have impressed their critics, and then endeavour to detach from the tuneless chorus some notes that harmonise.

Singularly little has been written concerning 'The Shaving of Shagpat,' although it had the distinction of being twice reviewed by George Eliot in terms with which we are already familiar. One seldom reads an essay on Meredith in which 'Shagpat' is not mentioned, and seldom more than mentioned. The late George Parsons Lathrop, in the *Atlantic Monthly*, February, 1888, writes thus of Meredith's first essay in prose fiction:

'The Shaving of Shagpat' is, in a measure, an imitation of 'The Arabian Nights,' half burlesque and half serious; with a moral concerning illusions in life and government tucked away in the end of the story like a gold piece sewn into the lining of a coat. The garment itself, however,—that is, the substance of the tale,—is so richly bedizened, and so marvellous a mixture of splendours and tatters, that by the time we have pulled it to pieces, for the sake of the treasure it contains, the hidden coin seems of little worth. In this story there are picturesqueness and spendthrift imagery to excess. It abounds in fantastic imagination, some of which is startling and impressive; but more often the effect is so extravagant as to excite an unpleasant mental vertigo. Especially is this so in the last part, with its colossal conflict of lightnings, vultures, scorpions, and the bird Khoorook, having wings a league long. And all this gigantic spectacle centres upon the rich and hairy clothier, Shagpat, whose false power resides in a single hair of his head, called 'The Identical,' which finally rises up, and burns for three days and nights; then turns into a fiery serpent, and emits a stream of other fiery serpents. There is a wide difference between even the wildest flights of sane imagination and the fantasies of mania. It is hard to conceive how Mr. Meredith could have conjured up these half-delirious phantoms without losing the best part of his head amongst them. Possibly they were applied with deliberation, by himself, as a test of his own steadiness; a discipline, a temptation, such as the anchorites and ascetics of earlier times considered indispensable to their equipment for final victory. Meredith appears to have passed through this particular temptation with colours flying forward. He has not since exposed himself to the sorcery of unbridled fancies. But no one could have predicted, from Shagpat, the future novelist.

'Farina; a Legend of Cologne,' has also been coldly neglected of the critics, and George Eliot's is the only noteworthy review of it. Parsons Lathrop considers that 'Farina' is not worthy of notice, except for giving token of Teutonic influence, 'traceable elsewhere through his writings, in an evident familiarity with German localities, a fondness for alliteration, tortured compound words, and an inverted order of construction.' He then goes on to say:

Whether this came from direct contact with German literature, or was derived from the impress of Carlyle, whose grandiose manner of manipulating little things is frequently echoed in Meredith, it is impossible to judge. But the spurious Orientalism of 'Shagpat' and the somewhat tawdry Germanism of Farina are interspersed with bits of verse little better than sublimated doggerel or the delusive Eastern poems of Mirza Schaffy; and Meredith has never quite shaken off his fondness for introducing this kind of sham pasteboard verse, which assumes the appearance of real golden goblets on the stage, into his serious novels. I have a suspicion, although I may be wrong, that in these two early compositions he had been emboldened by the example of Thackeray's success in semi-extravaganza. Natural gifts and power of expression they undoubtedly show; but the writer was trifling with his powers and gifts, and had not yet found his field. It was not until 1859, when

By permission of Messrs. Bradbury, Agnew & Co.]

[*From the drawing by Charles Keene in 'Once a Week.'*

TOM AND ANDREW COGGLESBY AT THE 'AURORA.'

Like sunshine after smart rain, the Port shone on these brothers.—*Evan Harrington.* Chapter VIII.

[*To face p.* 200.

he had reached the age of thirty-two, that he produced 'The Ordeal of Richard Feverel,' his first mature novel, charged to the brim with earnestness, wit, strength of conception.

'The Ordeal of Richard Feverel,' with the possible exception of 'The Egoist,' has been the most widely discussed of all the novels. The work of his 'prentice hand, forsooth, remains after half-a-century one of its author's most characteristic achievements. To Mr. Justin McCarthy belongs the credit of having been the first critic of note to attempt a serious exposition of the book; this, in the *Westminster Review* of July, 1864, under the theme of 'Novels with a Purpose,' reprinted later in the author's 'Con Amore.' I quote from the article in question as follows:

'The Ordeal of Richard Feverel' is a novel of the thoughtful, deep, half-cynical, wholly earnest kind which has so often striven, perhaps not with single success, to arrest the attention of a public only craving for easy entertainment. It is somewhat in the style of Sterne; a good deal in the style of one who, acknowledging himself a follower of Sterne, had a warmer heart, a purer soul, and a richer, quainter fancy than the British sentimentalist, I mean Jean Paul Richter. Mr. Meredith is often strikingly like Richter in style, with, almost as a matter of necessity, a considerable dash of Carlylese phraseology. Here and there, indeed, something of unmistakable and pure Carlyle flashes in.

'The Ordeal of Richard Feverel' is full of passages which are rich in quaint poetic beauty; full of keen, pungent, epigrammatic sayings; of sharp, shrewd reflections revealing much insight into the realities of human nature; of the warm glow of an ardent, manly heart, and of a tender, graceful, genial blending of love and pity. Utterly unlike in its plan and its personages, the book somehow reminds one frequently of Richter's 'Flegeljahre'; only that with George Meredith the ways and weaknesses and virtues of the two brothers seem fused into the form of Richard Feverel. It is essentially a book with a purpose.

It is not a very pleasant book. The mere quaintnesses and fantastic eccentricities of the style, though modest and sober when compared with those in which Richter revels, are quite enough to warn the commonplace novel reader at the very beginning that these paths are rather thorny and tangled for his easy lounging walk. But apart from merely superficial objections, the story, with all its beauty, tenderness, and boldness, leaves a melancholy, and what is perhaps worse, an unsatisfactory impression behind it.

People in general do not now, I think, read Rousseau's 'Emile'; but those who are familiar with that masterpiece of a dead philosophy will probably agree with me as to the profoundly unsatisfactory and disheartening impression which its catastrophe leaves on the mind. Was it for this, the reader is inclined to ask, that science and love did their utmost to make one path smooth, one human existence bright, and noble, and happy? Was Emile from his birth upward trained to the suppression of every selfish thought, to the scorn of all ignoble purpose, to an absolute devotion for truth, courage, purity, and benevolence, only that he might be deceived in his dearest affections, and that the crowning act of his existence might be an abnegation of self which we can scarcely even regard with admiration? The author had a right to shape his moral and deal with his creations as he would, yet we feel pained and shocked that he should have deemed it right to act thus harshly towards the beloved offspring of his system.

Something of this surprise and disappointment fills the mind when we have reached the close of Richard Feverel's ordeal, and find that he has left his brightest hopes and dearest affections dead and buried behind him. The book closes with a snap or crash; we feel as if something were suddenly wrenched away with pain and surprise; a darkness falls down upon the mind. Artistically I cannot help regarding this as a defect, although, of course, it is strictly in keeping with a recognition of the possibilities and even the daily chances of life. The course of the story does not lead us to expect anything of the kind, while its whole construction does lead us to expect a harmonious and dramatic conclusion. If Lady Castlewood in 'Esmond' were to die suddenly of an unexpected fever; if Romola were to be killed off, like the wicked personage in one of Massinger's plays, by a flash of lightning, no one could say that either of these catastrophes was out of the common range of human probabilities. But a work of fiction, whether novel or drama, requires harmony, coherence, or sequence; and, although talent can assert its powers over us in defiance of this law, yet it assuredly forfeits some of its legitimate influence when it fails to acknowledge it. One cannot see why poor little Lucy, Richard Feverel's gentle, innocent, loving wife, should be sacrificed in order that the ordeal of her husband should be made the more severe. In human nature, is such an ordeal really purifying and strengthening? Is heavy, unexpected, and, it must be added, really unmerited, calamity calculated to make the sufferer brave, and strong, and faithful? Truly, I doubt it. And I doubt still more whether the ardent, impulsive, fitful sort of being Mr. Meredith has painted as his hero, would become any the better for having so fantastic and remorseless a penalty attached by fate to his father's system and his own single transgression.

The late Allan Monkhouse, in his temperate and painstaking study of the novels, written for the *Manchester Quarterly*, October, 1890, and reprinted in his 'Books and Plays,' deals thus with

Meredith's first novel, which he describes as 'perhaps the most widely admired of his works':

Whether 'Richard Feverel' is the best of his novels or not, it contains much of his finest quality. . . . Richard and Lucy are our modern Ferdinand and Miranda, whose fortunes are wrecked by a blind and infatuated Prospero. A Prospero whom the winds and waves do not obey, whose belief in his spells is unshaken, and whose attitude of command is unreleased till the peremptory awakening of calamity is at once a comic and a tragic spectacle. . . . But Sir Austin is essentially a tragic character, and if there is some justice in the objection that the story's strange and pitiful ending is not inevitable as a tragic issue should be, it is, I think, because his position is not sufficiently enforced. He is a man of high intelligence and noble aims, whose fatal pedantry brings ruin and misery upon the son he loves. Of Richard's own contribution to the calamitous tangle in his neglectful absence from his wife, it is not easy to speak. It is inexplicable to the gross and literal sense of the dogged school of criticism, but we may take comfort in remembering that other inconsequent writer who taught us that 'cause and will and strength and means' may be a prelude with no succeeding act, and who has left unanswered and unanswerable the portentous question:

> Will you, I pray, demand that demi-devil
> Why he hath thus ensnared my soul and body?

The humour of 'Richard Feverel' is constant in operation and eminent in quality. It is sometimes snatched from the very jaws of tragedy, as in those daring and delightful episodes, the historical readings of the infatuated and bewildered Lord Mountfalcon. It gives us a wretched dyspeptic engaged on a history of Fairy Mythology and a 'wise youth,' himself a humorist, whose philosophy is cunningly undermined by his contemptuous author. Of its pathos I will only say that the last chapter is one of the most moving things in our literature.

But Mr. W. C. Brownell insists on the artificial character of the novel as a whole. He uses it to illustrate that perversity which he esteems the chief characteristic of Meredith's fiction.

The most noteworthy example of this perversity (says Mr. Brownell) is his one great tragedy, 'The Ordeal of Richard Feverel,' his first and, in the view of his most thoroughgoing admirers, his greatest book. It is a marvel of artificiality imposed upon the reader as exactly the converse. It assumes to record the remorseless working of relentless fate, and is in reality a remarkable piece of imaginative ingenuity as little convincing as a tract. Its framework and premises are ingeniously unnatural and it contains hardly a natural person, save the victims of the unnatural conduct of the others. The book is thus addressed directly to the nerves rather than to the mind or the heart, and in this respect is no more a book *de bonne foy* than the most painful of Maupassant's. The principle against which it offends is perfectly plain. The element of fate in tragedy to be legitimate must be fatalistic. In 'Feverel' one feels that it is absolutely facultative. Richard's ordeal would dissolve into the simplest of idyls at several stages in the development of the story, if it were not for the author's wilful ingenuity, exercised to the end of making the reader writhe. Being so quintessentially artificial, it is extremely typical of the succession of novels which thus ominously it introduced. It contains some of the best writing, some of the most winning scenes, some of the truest poetry to be found in Mr. Meredith's writings. But a tragedy of which the reader resents the obviously voluntary pre-determination of the author to exact the utmost possible tribute of distress from him is not so much tragedy as melodrama, and melodrama thoroughly sophisticated. Its psychology places it on a high plane for melodrama, but cannot disguise its character. And it is not difficult to see in the author's attitude toward his needlessly suffering characters the spirit which reveals Parrhasius, studying the contortions of his captive, as less a genuine artist than a dilettante *à outrance*.

On the other hand, while Mr. James Oliphant, in his 'Victorian Novelists,' seems to feel, though in a less degree than Mr. Brownell, the arbitrariness of the novelist's manner in dealing out doom to his personages, he is prepared to defend the death of Lucy as artistically inevitable. Moreover, we might ask, is it not true that in actual life Providence may often be accused of melodrama?

Who can read the final scene between Richard and Lucy (says Mr. Oliphant) before he goes to fight his duel, and the letter of Lady Blandish to Austen Wentworth telling how it all ended, without being stirred to a pang of sympathy that is almost too deep and painful for tears? It is little wonder if, in self-defence, we passionately refuse to believe that Lucy really had to die before she could even understand that she was on the threshold of a new chastened happiness that gave promise of a lifelong endurance. But the author was right. Lucy must have died, and it is a proof of Meredith's courage as an artist that he told the truth boldly as he saw it, when every consideration of mercy towards himself and his readers would have prompted him to stay his hand.

As we pursue our study of Meredith criticism we become impressed by the fact that, immense and inexhaustible though the

By permission of Messrs. Bradbury, Agnew & Co.]

[*From the drawing by Charles Keene in 'Once a Week.'*

TOM COGGLESBY'S ARRIVAL AT BECKLEY COURT.

The donkey-cart, in which old Tom Cogglesby sat alone, bunchy in figure, bunched in face, his shrewd grey eyes twinkling under the bush of his eyebrows.
—*Evan Harrington*. Chapter XXVIII.

[*To face p.* 204.

mass of these writings be, they seem to centre round certain of the novels in detail, while others are curiously passed over with the merest references to certain of their characters and to some of the more outstanding episodes in them. 'The Egoist' is a sort of Aaron's rod that has swallowed up all the rest from the critic's point of view, though 'Richard Feverel' and 'Beauchamp's Career' have certainly had their share of consideration. But it is surprising that so rich and fascinating a book as 'Evan Harrington' has not had a greater share of critical attention. As regards our immediate purpose, however, there is no reason to complain, for two such scholarly critics as George Parsons Lathrop, in America, and Mr. Arthur Symons, in England, have written about Meredith's second great novel with concentration of interest. Thus Parsons Lathrop:

The story unfolds a large picture of English life in certain of its phases, which is both amusing and instructive; but the author's quick discernment and lifelike delineation are set in a doughy mass of words. . . . The vicissitudes of young Evan Harrington are sketched with great gusto and, at times, with a most entertaining effect. Nothing could be better than the portrait of old Tom Cogglesby, and the account of a meeting between him and his brother Andrew at the Aurora tavern. The human nature is exact; the drawing is broad, yet nice; the tints are mellow; a delicious humour pervades the whole episode. But Evan's vagabond comrade, Jack Raikes, is a total failure. In him we discern the temporary sway of the Dickens star; but none other than Dickens himself could have done justice to this irregular personage. Meredith, in attempting to portray him, is ready enough with words to put into his mouth; but the mimetic or impersonating faculty does not answer at his call, and Mr. Raikes is all shell and no meat.

The Countess de Saldar—a scheming, insincere woman, affecting the airs of foreign nobility, even to her accent in speaking—is very much better rendered; but the recital of her wiles and the extracts from her letters are given at too great length. We know the character when the half has been told, and the added illustration of it becomes a dead weight. At last the bad tendencies in her are pushed to an extreme in her sudden amorous advances towards her sister's husband, Andrew. This is done abruptly; so that, while her action may be a logical enough outcome of her character, it appears precipitate, and makes an impression of purely superfluous coarseness.

In this pushing of his characters to an extreme, and his remorseless amplification of their attributes, he also betrays his overmastering impulse to make them absolute types. Obeying it, he makes of

'Mrs. Mel' Harrington, Evan's mother, an iron female, repulsive in her hard constancy to her humble position as the widow of the defunct tailor. . . . Mrs. Mel in reality would be a pathetic figure; but Meredith admits no hint of that likelihood. In his hands, she is purely an embodiment of harsh duty and fatefulness. Distinct and tangible she certainly is, in this aspect, as much so as the contact with cold metal. But it may be doubted whether she is humanly true. . . .

In spite of all its defects, 'Evan Harrington' contains more ingenuity of plot and is better constructed than most of its author's novels. A robust, rollicking humour pervades portions of it; and the chapter in which 'Old Mel's' daughters have to 'digest their father at dinner'—plainly speaking, suffer an exposure of their plebeian origin at a brilliant dinner-party—is not only fine, spirited and strong, but is also rendered tonic by a dash of searching satire. In this mixture of the bluff, sportive tone with wholesome castigation of shams, and with the intermittent moralising or discourse about his personages, which Meredith allows himself, we may, I think, accurately detect the occult control of Dickens and Thackeray, side by side. Not that the more recent writer is imitative of either; but he seems to have incorporated with his own singular and independent genius elements from the same sources on which those great but unlike masters drew.

I now quote the opinion of Mr. Arthur Symons from a review in *Time*, November, 1885, when 'Evan Harrington' came out in the first collected edition of the novels:

'Evan Harrington' is a story of modern society; not so philosophical, witty, profound, nor so deeply and pathetically tragic as 'Richard Feverel'—not so wildly adventurous, nor so romantic and fantastic as 'Harry Richmond,' but occupying a place midway between the two. Without being the greatest of Mr. Meredith's novels, it is the most evenly interesting, I think, the most easy, pleasant, absorbing, and ought to be one of the most widely popular. I have seen those who read 'Richard Feverel' with effort read 'Evan Harrington' with delight. . . . There are plots and counterplots, very Machiavellian, but never vulgar, and all in the very best society, where the touching a nerve is the blood-spilling of uncivilised battles, and the heroes triumph in tone of the voice. In the midst of it all, Evan, a fine figure of genuine manliness, a gentleman of heart and breeding, if not of birth, acts unconscious of the toils which are being woven for his benefit and against it, until at length he is caught in them, and appears for a time to be a disgraced hero, and finally triumphs, as heroes do.

Following Parsons Lathrop's very able analysis of 'Evan Harrington' and Mr. Symons's hearty recommendation of the novel as a piece of 'pure comedy, at once pleasant and bracing and inexhaustibly entertaining,' we are met by such a personal confession as this from Allan Monkhouse, who was no capricious admirer, but a sound critic:

I must confess that to me 'Evan Harrington' is the least worthy of Mr. Meredith's novels. The Countess de Saldar is not of the race of those great comic characters that justify themselves under any conditions. Never elsewhere has her author concerned himself so far with the presentation of a person essentially vulgar. She is an ordinary person in an extraordinary position, and 'Evan Harrington' is a comedy of circumstance rather than of character. The tenacity of an adventuress is not the most fruitful of themes for the creator of Richmond Roy and Sir Willoughby Patterne. She is a great success, but a success of a lower order. Rose and Evan are a delightful pair of lovers, Lady Jocelyn is excellent, and Mrs. Harrington, possibly the very best of minor woman characters, one of Mr. Meredith's strongest points. Mr. Raikes is, perhaps, dangerously near the line which separates the fantastical from the preposterous, but with old Tom Cogglesby, who seems to have strayed from Dickens' collection, he contributes some very curious and characteristic humour.

Thus the critics differ, though as a comparison of the foregoing opinions will prove, they are largely in agreement on the details of character, sources of influence, and the esthetics of the novel. By the same roads they seem to arrive at different conclusions.

When we come to 'Sandra Belloni' (first published as 'Emilia in England') we have also to reckon with 'Vittoria,' to which the former stands as no more than the first half of an extremely long and somewhat turgid tale. 'Rhoda Fleming' comes between the two parts of the history of Emilia. Here we shall choose to consider the two novels as one, since they do not bear even the ordinary relationship of a story and its sequel.

In many respects (writes Parsons Lathrop) they are very characteristic of Meredith; yet it must be confessed that they present a substance almost impossible to analyze. How any one ever came to conceive these tales, to what purpose they were directed in his own mind, why he should be at the pains to gather in one group so heterogeneous a lot of characters, and how he commanded the patience to pursue the threads of their actions and emotions, I am at a loss to guess. . . .

The idea which the writer wished to convey was, I suppose, that a woman so entirely given up to the liberation of her native land as Emilia, or Vittoria, is conceived to have been must forego the happiness of a genuine and complete union with any man. She destroyed the careers of her two English devotees, for the sake of Italy; but when she married Count Carlo she also sacrificed herself, because it turned out that her husband and herself were not wholly in unison, and that he did not trust her even in conspiracies for Italian freedom. Because he did not trust her, he lost his life in a futile revolt, and she was left to mourn him inconsolably. The lesson seems to be: For freedom and country everything must be sacrificed, even the love and the hopes of all individual patriots.

But if this be the meaning of these two novels, it surely might have been conveyed in much less space than Mr. Meredith has used. And he has filled the space, to the very horizon, with such a cloud of characters and so bewildering a mist of universal talkativeness that it is hard work to extract even this much of meaning from the thousand pages which are appropriated to the chosen theme. The best piece of portraiture discoverable in this two-part tragedy is the delineation of Barto Rizzi, the powerful, restless, mysterious Italian conspirator, of noble birth, relentless towards the treacherous, and suspecting everybody. This figure is worthy of Balzac; but, unhappily, it is not fully developed.

Still, when one looks back at these novels, and gives them the benefit of a liberal perspective, the character of Emilia (or Sandra, or Vittoria) comes out strongly in a large coherence and atones for many minor inconsistencies and, it may be added, for capital faults. It is under circumstances like these, when he is wrestling with the adversity of his own mistakes, that Meredith's great power of representing types comes to his rescue.

So Parsons Lathrop, obviously struggling to be just to the novelist, whom he admires, while he is endeavouring to square his personal likings with his critical instincts. But now observe Mr. Arthur Symons—I quote from his review in *Time*, March, 1886—without the least embarrassment on the subject of Emilia:

The book forms the first volume of the history of Emilia Alessandra Belloni, than which it is doubtful whether its author has ever done better and more satisfactory work. Those less admirable qualities of Mr. Meredith, which some people find so objectionable—his excess of wit and overdose of humour, his too conspicuous cleverness, and the most fantastically fanciful flourishes of his style—are here controlled, in great measure, by a profound seriousness of aim, noticeable even in the brilliant social satire which forms one element of the book, and especially prominent in the character and development of Emilia. . . .

The book is full of practical wisdom, of healthy human sympathy, expressed often enough in terms of gentle satire; it is instinct with passion and poetry, weighted with intellectual seriousness, and

By permission of Messrs. Bradbury, Agnew & Co.] [*From the drawing by Charles Keene in 'Once a Week.'*

EVAN'S MEETING WITH SUSAN WHEEDLE.

Striving to rouse the desolate creature, he shook her slightly. She now raised her head with a slow, gradual motion, like that of a wax-work, showing a white, young face, tearless,—dreadfully drawn at the lips.

—*Evan Harrington*. Chapter X.

[*To face p.* 208

balanced by artistic symmetry; a book that lives, and that will live, being ' of imagination all compact,' when the novels of the day or the hour, merry dancers on the yet green graves of their fellows of yesterday, have danced, they, too, the dusty dance of death to extinction.

Again, let us turn for a moment to Mr. Ernest Newman's study of the novels, from which I have had occasion to quote in an earlier chapter:

By one set of critics, not too robust in themselves (writes Mr. Newman) he is lauded as the exposer of sentimentalism, against which modern vice he has raised the banner in ' Sandra Belloni ' and in the preface to ' Diana.' It is hardly profitable to follow him into his analysis of sentimentalism; all the more so as the very books in which he wars against it are those in which he has inflicted upon us something almost worse than sentimentalism. One asks, after reading ' Sandra Belloni,' wherein the sentimental ladies, Arabella, Adela, and Cornelia, and the sentimental gentlemen, Barrett and Wilfrid, are worse than the heroic Merthyr and the heroinic Georgiana. Certainly it would be hard to find two more insufferable incarnations of the prig than these. Mr. Meredith's complacent declaration that he is on the side of the angels creates in us, when we see the company he keeps, an insatiable longing to be on the side of the other immortals.

Truly when the critics are so discordant what is the plain man to do? So far as ' Sandra Belloni ' and ' Vittoria ' are concerned, I suspect the plain man of leaving them unread, whereby he misses some rare delights, but also saves himself the yawns of a tedious tale. It is not the least of the drawbacks of the long history of Emilia that the first half of it is well-nigh stagnant, devoted to subtleties of character analysis, yet a reading of it is essential to the proper appreciation of the second, which moves to the throb of revolution and burning patriotism, amid scenes that glow like summer landscapes in the memory. Moreover, ' Vittoria ' has no Mrs. Chump to disfigure it. Perhaps the truth about these two books—if there can be such a thing as truth where the personal equation modifies so much—is midway between the opinions of Parsons Lathrop and Mr. Symons. It seems to me that one could illustrate all Meredith's great qualities from these two books, and some of his defects also, though curiously little could be quoted against his style, which is here, but especially in ' Vittoria,' at its supplest. Neither is a masterpiece in the sober sense of the word, and let them sneer at George Eliot who will, ' Romola ' is safer for immortality than 'Sandra Belloni.' That the novelist has made one of his supremest efforts in the character of Sandra is obvious, but all else has been subordinated to that, and despite so many beauties of description, thought, and action, there is the fatal lack of cohesion. What no critic has pointed out, to my knowledge, has always been present in my mind as a grave defect of 'Vittoria'—the failure to image the whole picture of Milan and Lombardy in revolt. We have a series of detached 'episodes,' told with much spirit, but the opportunity for an immense and thrilling spectacle of the whole, such as Zola could have realised, is frittered away in sketchy incidents, and no more than a spoonful of the boiling passions of the revolt bubbles in Meredith's pages.

If in the criticism of the novels we may be surprised at the lack of attention which 'Sandra Belloni' and 'Vittoria' have elicited, we shall be much more surprised to discover how little 'Rhoda Fleming' has attracted the critics. Surely it is in this great tragedy that Meredith is for the first time absolute master of his art. Why 'Richard Feverel' should have moved more brethren of the pen to ecstasies of admiration is one of the many inexplicable things in literary criticism. Perhaps it is because the first novel is a more 'pleasant' story. But that should not weigh with those whose function it is to seek out what is good in art and give it greeting. With the public, yes. One cannot understand why 'Rhoda Fleming' has never caught the patrons of the circulating library as 'Diana of the Crossways' and 'Richard Feverel' have caught them. Can there be something in titles after all? Certainly there is nothing in the simple title of 'Rhoda Fleming' to awaken any notion of the tremendous power of the story, its grim tragedy, its human passion, and profound interest for all who think squarely about the issues of this our life. But all these things, not patent to the general skimmer of current fiction, should be clear as noonday to those who practise criticism, and yet I could mention many an able study of Meredith's prose in which the name of Rhoda Fleming has only a passing nod from the writer. No other work of the same hand could better be advanced as a reply to the criticism that Meredith does not know how to 'jine his flats.' The intensity of his problem has fused its whole exposition in a way that was hardly to be expected in 'Richard Feverel,' where a theory of life furnishes the motive of the plot, and not a very present and heart-searching reality, such as we have here to consider. The result is a work of admirable balance, just proportions, and an ineluctable tragic fitness.

Somewhat against the scheme of this chapter, I have been tempted to expression of personal opinion, to refrain from which is almost Spartan austerity in one whose vocation is to write of books, but I must make way for the opinions of two critics of eminent authority, who differ widely in their conclusions. It was twenty years after its first unsuccessful publication that the late W. E. Henley reviewed the novel in the *Athenæum*, on its re-issue in the first collected edition, and his review is reprinted in 'Views and Reviews.' His theory of the failure of the novel with the public was based on the disagreeable nature of the problem it presents and its 'scathing attack upon the superstitions of respectability,' for the public 'cares for no passion that is not decent in itself, and whose expression is not restrained.' That the public, moreover, is not attracted by problems 'capable of none save a tragic solution' is also a just observation, and there, no doubt, we have the explanation. Of 'passion deeply felt and poignantly expressed,' Henley considers 'there is such a feast in "Rhoda Fleming" as no other English novelist alive has spread.' But he does not disguise the failures of the book, as, for instance, Anthony, the old bank porter—'such a failure as only a great novelist may perpetrate and survive'—Algernon the fool, 'of whom his author is so bitterly contemptuous that he is never once permitted to live and move and have any sort of being whatever,' and 'the chivalrous Percy, and the inscrutable Mrs. Lovell,' whom he describes as 'two gentle ghosts whose proper place is the shadow-land of the American novel.' Remove these, and a 'treasure of reality remains.' In a white heat of artistic joy in the work of his novelist the great critic then goes on:

> What an intensity of life it is that hurries and throbs and burns through the veins of the two sisters—Dahlia the victim, Rhoda the executioner! Where else in English fiction is such a 'human oak log' as their father, the Kentish yeoman, William Fleming? And where in English fiction is such a problem presented as that in the evolution of which these three—with a following so well selected and achieved as Robert Armstrong and Jonathan Eccles and the evil ruffian Sedgett, a type of the bumpkin gone wrong, and Master Gammon, that type of the bumpkin old and obstinate, a sort of human saurian—are dashed together, and ground against each other till the weakest and best of the three is broken to pieces?
>
> Mr. Meredith may, and does, fail conspicuously to interest you in Anthony Hackbut and Algernon Blancove and Percy Waring; but he knows every fibre of the rest, and he makes your knowledge as intimate and comprehensive as his own. With these he is never

at fault and never out of touch. They have the unity of effect, the vigorous simplicity, of life that belong to great creative art; and at their highest stress of emotion, the culmination of their passion, they appeal to, and affect, you with a force and a directness that suggest the highest achievement of Webster.

It has been objected to the climax of 'Rhoda Fleming' that it is unnecessarily inhumane, and that Dahlia dead were better art than Dahlia living and incapable of love and joy. But the book, as I have said, is a merciless impeachment of respectability; and as the spectacle of a ruined and broken life is infinitely more discomforting than that of a noble death, I take it that Mr. Meredith was right to prefer his present ending to the alternative, inasmuch as the painfulness of that impression he wished to produce and the potency of that moral he chose to draw are immensely heightened and strengthened thereby.

Oddly enough it is on 'Rhoda Fleming' that Mr. William Watson fastens in his famous article on 'Fiction—Plethoric and Anæmic' (*National Review*, October, 1889), to illustrate the chief defects of Meredith as he conceives them:

Like most of his books (says Mr. Watson) it is an ill-constructed and very unequally written story, having some fine scenes and clever, if equally unattractive, character studies. If only an author could live by virtue of sporadic good things! But a novelist, at all events, cannot. The nominal and official heroine is a farmer's daughter, beloved by Bob Eccles, *alias* Robert Armstrong, and eventually married to him. She does not give evidence of caring very much for him, and therein she certainly has our sympathies, since we do not care for him either. A more thoroughly uncompanionable and unmagnetic young man the writer does not remember to have met, even in real life. . . . The tragedy of the story is the fate of Rhoda's beautiful sister Dahlia, who has been led astray by a well-born young London lover, Edward Blancove. He is perhaps the most realisable person in the book, and as such its most satisfactory piece of portraiture. A young man of the world, not without ambition and some thin, hard intellectuality; entirely incapable of heroism, yet not deliberately a scoundrel, he wins Dahlia's trust, and betrays it. Circumstances, he subsequently explains, have been against him. For a while he seems to have deserted her utterly, but in the end he returns to her, truly penitent, and filled with an ardour of atonement. One does not see what motive impels him to this course, which might not be presumed to have been equally operative all along, but anyhow he turns up at the eleventh hour, for the purpose of righting Dahlia's wrongs, so far as he may. At this point Rhoda for the first time emerges into positive action. She has hitherto been pictured as a young woman

By permission of Messrs. Bradbury, Agnew & Co.] [*From the drawing by Charles Keene in 'Once a Week.'*

THE DEATH OF 'THE GREAT MEL.'

The curtains of the bed were drawn aside. The beams of evening fell soft through the blinds of the room, and cast a subdued light on the figure of the vanquished warrior. . . . Lady Roseley . . . had not looked long before she found covert employment for her handkerchief. The widow standing beside her did not weep, gazing down on his mortal length with a sort of benignant friendliness. At the feet of his master, Jocko, the monkey, had jumped up, and was there squatted, with his legs crossed, very like a tailor!

—*Evan Harrington.* **Chapter II.**

[*To face p.* 212.

of great and rather stubborn moral force, but playing a very passive part in the story. She now displays an amount of cruel wrong-headedness that goes far to place her outside the reader's sympathy. She thinks it her duty to frustrate the union of the lovers, from hatred and contempt of the man who has wronged her sister, but whose present conduct argues, if not heroism, at least reclamation. The scene where Dahlia discovers how Rhoda has blindly injured her, and barred the way against returning happiness, is very moving and powerful. It has a convulsive, paroxysmal kind of strength which recalls the fine things in some of the more spasmodic of our old dramatists. Unfortunately, like many another of Mr. Meredith's strong scenes, it is led up to by a sequence of moral incredibilities which admit of no intellectual defence. . . . In the way of story he has not very much to tell, and he is obscure simply because he has not an aptitude for telling it. There is literally no construction, but a certain not too great abundance of material lying loose about in various stages of disorder.

Here Mr. Watson's judgment is, to me at least, impossible of acceptance, though I realise the sincerity and masterliness of his critical method and find myself in sympathy with other opinions of his. Rather do I join with Mr. Symons in thinking that the book is Meredith's masterpiece in tragedy and that 'the plot is woven with singular closeness and deft intricacy; its exciting interest leading on the eye and mind at a gallop.'

When we turn to 'The Adventures of Harry Richmond' we approach a novel that has enjoyed both popular favour—it is one of the four 'best selling' works of Meredith, the others being 'The Egoist,' 'Diana' and 'Richard Feverel'—and ample attention from the critics. It does not rank with 'Rhoda Fleming' as a literary achievement, but it is largely inspired by the spirit of romance and that may account for the public liking it. A pure romance, of course, it is not, since there is analysis of character and study of emotions here as in all Meredith's fiction, if in a less degree, and both are foreign to romance. It might fairly be classed as romantic, but Mr. Symons proclaims it as 'that rare thing, a romance,' without modification, while Parsons Lathrop finds it fit in with his notion of the romantic until it is halfway through, when he considers that it breaks down utterly as a story, and Mr. W. L. Courtney seems never at all to have been caught by the romantic charm of the earlier chapters. I may here remark, what is perhaps already obvious, that I turn naturally to the writing of Mr. Arthur Symons and of the late George Parsons Lathrop for the purposes of this chapter, as they are among the few critics of note who have dealt with the chief novels individually, Lathrop, especially, affording us some cameo-like studies which help us to realise each book by itself rather than as part of an inorganic whole, and it is with the individual books, not with any effort to fix them into a purely fanciful relativeness, that we are for the moment concerned. Let me first quote from Mr. Arthur Symons's review in *Time*, August, 1886:

> Here in 'Harry Richmond' we have a romance of the very best sort; rousing, enthralling, exciting, full of poetry, and a serious and masterly study in character. On a first reading we are fairly swept away and carried along by the racing tide of the narrative; for bustle and movement, for breathless and almost exhausting speed of telling, I know but few stories to equal it. Brilliant and fantastically lighted pictures flit past, like the slides of a magic lantern. Almost before one is gone another follows. Only on a calm retrospect, or after a second reading, do we properly realise all the painstaking perfection and strenuous realism of the character drawing, and the superb intellectual quality of the book.

With all respect to Mr. Symons, a critic with whom to err were still better than to be correct with others one might name, he does not see quite clearly into this story of 'Harry Richmond,' though he is sound in his criticism of details. Romance and the romantic are by no means synonymous terms in serious criticism, the former is concerned with the spirit of place and the realm of pure imagination. 'La Belle Dame sans Merci' is about the last note of true romance in English. The romantic permits of character, and where character dominates all, as finally it does in 'Harry Richmond,' then even the romantic is abandoned for the novel of character. This, George Parsons Lathrop seems to feel quite clearly in his *aperçu* of the story, which here follows, for he speaks of the earlier adventures as 'seeming to have happened to ourselves'—their romantic spirit is thus implied.

> In 'Harry Richmond' the want of proportion is once more painfully felt (says Lathrop); yet there, too, we find magnificent studies of character, massive—monolithic, if the term be allowable—as though they had been hewn out of solid rock. Such are Harry himself; his father, Richmond Roy, the motive of whose life is his claim to bastard royal descent; choleric old Squire Beltham; his niece Janet; and that woman of ideal grandeur and sweetness, Princess Ottilia. All the earlier part of the book, which relates to Harry's boyhood, schooldays, and boyish loves as described by

himself, is fascinating beyond description. Everything that occurs seems to have happened to ourselves. For the time being we live in his world, and there seems to be no other world at all in our experience. But this illusion does not last.

The story breaks down utterly, in the middle. Continual hammering on one line of effect dulls the edge. The length of the narrative, too, the multitude of persons introduced, and their all but endless involvements tax the attention beyond endurance. Yet the unabated energy with which old Roy, gradually developing into insanity in his schemes for recognition by the royal family, is kept before us, stimulates even a tired brain; and Harry's slow evolution from blind love and worship of his father to a perception of his real worthless, erratic and scoundrelly character shoots through the whole an intensely vivid and pathetic ray of light. A sort of indirect advocacy of republicanism is perhaps discernible in the book. The pretence of royalty caricatured in the representative of a bastard line; the disgrace and humiliation which it brought upon Harry; and his final reconciliation with Janet, as the true union between equals, seem to point in this direction.

But, on the other side, we have Ottilia, the German princess, sincerely loving and appreciating the hero, and representing in her own person the genuine royalty, which is of the heart and soul, while conventional royalty is a mere mask or husk. But this forms only a minor interest; hardly felt, as the book stands, until the very end. The main interest lies in the great, turbulent human drama which is exhibited: and of this the din and tumult swell to such a degree that, towards the close, one feels as if his brain were assailed by the harmonic din of one of Wagner's stupendous operas.

If Mr. Symons were right about 'Harry Richmond' then, indeed, would Mr. W. L. Courtney be curiously wrong, for he finds it cold, lacking in tenderness and 'heart,' and the voice of middle age speaking through it. Judge ye how immeasurably distant these characteristics are removed from the enchanting realm of romance! Thus Mr. Courtney in the *Fortnightly* of June, 1886:

Perhaps in no novel do we find the absence of joy more conspicuous than in 'Harry Richmond.' Here is a young man who goes through a series of surprising adventures quite removed from the sphere of probability. He is fallen in love with by a German princess, and finds a lost father attitudinising as a bronze image on the top of a hill. The only literary excuse for such extravagances would be the rollicking character of the hero, such a one, for instance, as was endeared to our childhood by Captain Marryat or Kingston. But Harry Richmond does not rollick; he is never young, but talks about himself with the *maladie de la pensée* of a modern age.

The problem of harmonising the views of these three critics is one which I shall discreetly shun, but I may admit that my vote would most likely go to support Lathrop's opinion of 'Harry Richmond.' Mr. Arthur Symons's appreciation of 'Beauchamp's Career,' however, will almost certainly be applauded by most students of Meredith, though that is a novel on which there might reasonably be considerable divergence of opinion without any suspicion of injustice to the author. I quote from the note by Mr. Symons in *Time*, October, 1886:

Not one of Mr. Meredith's works impresses one with so keen a sense of absolute faithfulness to fact, to life, to human nature, and worldly circumstance. It cannot be called a political novel, in the sense of the term as applied to 'Coningsby,' for instance; but the political element is naturally very strong in a novel whose hero is a Radical candidate. Nevil Beauchamp, whose career, political and domestic, the story treats of, is one of the most admirably drawn of Mr. Meredith's heroes, and I think intrinsically the noblest in nature of them all. His strange, attractive character, with its fiery sincerity, its dashing and determined impulsiveness, its tenacity of will and temerity of purpose, is represented with spirit, but always sympathetic impartiality. The story of his career is saddening, in the contrast of so splendid a nature, and so small an appreciable result; such gifts for happiness and so troubled a life, so tragic a death. Yet the book is by no means a cheerless one; it has the comedy with the tragedy, the pleasantness with the sadness, of real life. . . . The greatness of the book lies in its effect as a whole, its breadth and fulness of outline, its vivid breadth of reality, its strength and grasp of the life around and the life within us.

Where Mr. Symons might possibly find some excellent critics to differ from him would be applying the epithet 'tragic' to the death of Beauchamp. Tragedy implies inevitableness, and many critics, like most ordinary readers, are inclined to think that the end of Beauchamp at the hands of his creator is more suggestive of the heartless gods, whose cold laughter is heard in the background, than of the doom which would be meted out by tragic art. Mr. W. C. Brownell, the brilliant American critic, as we might expect from what we already know of his point of view, is very emphatic as to Meredith keeping his personages in arbitrary control, and actually chooses Beauchamp as an example of how the author prevents us from 'warming to his personages.'

You are not allowed to (says Mr. Brownell). He banters you

out of it generally; even when such favourites of his own as Nevil Beauchamp are concerned, he is almost timorous lest your tenderness should be unintelligent. This is carried so far that one rarely cares much what becomes of these personages. You know in advance that they will never be the sport of any spontaneity. Their fate is sealed. They are the slaves of their creator's will, counters in his game. And this is why, in playing it, though he constantly challenges our admiration, he does not hold our interest. The air of free agency that he throws round them does not deceive us. We don't at all know what is to befall them, how they are going to act, but we have an ever-present sense that he does, and this sense is only sharpened by the knowledge, born of experience in reading his books, that he is going to make them surprise us. The induction he would have us make is, no doubt, that they are unaccountable, like human nature itself; but the one we make is that he it is who is unaccountable.

Perhaps the critic a little overstates his case here, for assuredly most of us have 'warmed' to Nevil Beauchamp, though we may be disposed to agree with Mr. Brownell that in the death of that true hero the novelist is 'unaccountable.' It is obviously meant to illustrate the slaps in the face which Fate loves to deal out to idealists, and it could be supported with any amount of evidence from real life. But so could any melodrama that ever ramped its hour upon the Surrey stage.

Whatever we may think of the end of Beauchamp, there can be no two opinions as to the eminence of the novel. Following the chronology of Meredith's works, 'Beauchamp's Career' shows the novelist unquestionably at the height of his power, 'Rhoda Fleming' alone among its predecessors ranking with it in the intense humanness and majestic sweep of the emotions. Lathrop is whole-hearted in his admiration for this genuine masterpiece. He says:

The story is consummately real, and the conclusion, succinct though it be, is deeply touching. It is a thoroughly manly book, but the women in it are as remarkable and commendable for truth as the central man is. One must search a long time in the masterpieces of fiction for a woman so complex, so natural, so wonderfully portrayed, as Rosamund Culling, who loves Nevil Beauchamp with a mingling of mother's and sister's love, and watches over him constantly.

Mr. T. P. O'Connor has several times described 'Beauchamp's Career' as his favourite among the works of Meredith, and Mr. Justin McCarthy in his 'Reminiscences' makes a similar confession, when he writes:

I think that for my own part I admire 'Beauchamp's Career' more thoroughly from first to last than any other of Meredith's novels, although I do not want my readers to suppose for a moment that I have grown in any sense cold to the merits of 'Richard Feverel' and 'Evan Harrington'—I have a friend, himself distinguished in letters and in politics, who insists that 'Evan Harrington' contains the finest picture of a certain kind of woman yet given in fiction, and I only feel inclined to qualify his opinion by expressing a reluctance to go in too absolutely for the use of superlatives. But I find much in 'Beauchamp's Career' which seems to lift me higher in thought and in soul and in hope than any other of Meredith's novels has done; and I do not know where, in fiction, one can find love scenes more beautiful than those which are pictured in what I may call the Venetian pages of the story. For the full enjoyment of these pages they should be read in Venice, as George Sand's story 'La Dernière Aldini' ought to be, and as Nathaniel Hawthorne's 'Transformation' ought to be read in Rome.

Intervening between the great achievement of his mid-career and the writing of 'The Egoist,' are the shorter stories 'The House on the Beach,' 'The Case of General Ople and Lady Camper,' and 'The Tale of Chloe,' the last especially ranking, in some respects, among his finest work in prose. These short stories have been but little criticised, and well-nigh twenty years had elapsed from their first appearance in the *New Quarterly Magazine* before they were reprinted in one volume together. In the *Scots Observer*, November 24, 1888, Mr. J. M. Barrie, in his own charming way, wrote, under the title of 'The Lost Works of George Meredith,' a plea for their republication, asking 'Are a hundred thousand words of a master's writings to perish of neglect? Although the magazine is dead, why should all its trophies be buried with it?' Well, they have now been available for fifteen years to all who care to read them, and it is to the credit of Mr. Barrie that when no other critic seemed to be troubling his head about these stories he at least urged the need to give them permanent form. He did not overstate the case when he said that 'these three stories have almost as much title to represent him as his longer tales.' Mr. Barrie then proceeded at some length to review the stories, and in his article there are certain passages which should be recorded here. Concerning 'The Case of General Ople and Lady Camper,' he writes:

Of these two delightfully contrasted characters it may be said, as Mr. Meredith has himself written of Miss Austen's Emma and her lover, that they 'might walk straight into a comedy, were the plot arranged for them'; indeed there is scene after scene in the story which leaves the vivid impression of an acted play. Cut out the author's comments, and a comedy for the stage remains, though not probably a comedy with sufficient guffaw in it to command success.

Of 'The House on the Beach' Mr. Barrie remarks:

It contains one striking figure, a former shopkeeper who, like the immortal 'old Mel,' wants to be a gentleman. But, unlike the tailor, he would be a gentleman on the cheap. The closing scene is great. This hero has been 'presented.' He loves to don his court dress in private, and he has it on when he is rescued from a flood that ruins him. The contrast between the costume and the wearer's condition haunts the memory: otherwise this is the least important story of the three.

Mr. Barrie then describes in detail the plot of 'The Tale of Chloe,' remarking that the story presents 'a picture of the Wells as vivid as the pump-room scene in "Harry Richmond,"' and that in the death of Chloe 'the author strikes a real tragic note,' while 'Beau Beamish is a memorable comedy figure.' Meredith, he is persuaded, 'could not have treated Chloe had he not dug down to the very roots of human nature.'

We pass now to the most discussed of all Meredith's books, though certainly not his greatest, if judged strictly as a novel, which would be to judge it by a false standard. The author describes it as 'a comedy in narrative,' and Henley advises those who are not familiar with the function of comedy to study Molière's comedies before taking up 'The Egoist.' Meredith himself had thoughtfully published his illuminating lecture 'On the Idea of Comedy and the Uses of the Comic Spirit' while he was at work on 'The Egoist.' As this is now available in the complete edition a reading of it might profitably precede the study of 'The Egoist.'

Henley did more than any one man to awaken the public to the unique greatness of 'The Egoist.' Immediately on the appearance of the book in 1879 he wrote at least three characteristic reviews of it, the first in the *Athenæum*, November 1, another in the *Pall Mall Gazette*, November 3, and a third in the *Academy*, November 22. After which that tireless enthusiast for great literature, who praised as valiantly as he blamed, might feel he had not neglected his duty by 'The Egoist'! He saw with noon-day clearness what Meredith's critics as a whole have perceived somewhat foggily: that 'The Egoist' must not be judged by the ordinary standard of prose fiction, since it is one of those rare creations of literature in which a great artist has performed the feat of expressing in terms of one art the spirit and purpose of another. Pure comedy is here embodied as a novel, through which the author 'pursues things unattempted yet in prose or rhyme.' Henley in his various studies of the book displays his truly remarkable critical perceptiveness, by the notable freshness with which, in each essay, he deals with the same subject. He, naturally, has comparisons and likenesses to institute with the master of comedy, showing that while Meredith has achieved, in Sir Willoughby Patterne, a universal type that might almost rank with Tartuffe and Alceste, Meredith's style is at the opposite pole from that 'union of ease and strength, of purity and sufficiency, of austerity and charm' which we recognise as Molière's. In the first of the above-mentioned studies we find him writing:

In 'The Egoist' Mr. Meredith is even more artificial and affected than his wont: he bristles with allusions, he teems with hints and side-hits and false alarms, he glitters with phrases, he riots in intellectual points and philosophical fancies; and though his style does nowhere else become him so well, his cleverness is yet so reckless and indomitable as to be almost as fatiguing here as everywhere. But in their matter the great Frenchman and he have not much to envy each other. Sir Willoughby Patterne is a 'document on humanity' of the highest value; and to him that would know of egoism and the egoïst the study of Sir Willoughby is indispensable. There is something in him of us all. He is a compendium of the Personal in man; and if in him the abstract Egoïst have not taken on his final shape and become classic and typical it is not that Mr. Meredith has forgotten anything in his composition but rather that there are certain defects of form, certain structural faults and weaknesses, which prevent you from accepting as conclusive the aspect of the mass of him. But the Molière of the future (if the future be that fortunate) has but to pick and choose with discretion here to find the stuff of a companion figure to Arnolphe and Alceste and Célimène.

There is a passage in the third of Henley's essays on 'The Egoist,' written for the *Academy*, which I wish to quote on account of its personal note, though it will be seen that with a writer like Henley, in whom the critical faculty was so eminently developed, the expression of a merely 'personal' opinion was hardly possible and his last word was, as usual with him, a lament for those defects of literary form which he deemed the result of an abnormal cleverness:

> Speaking for myself, I have read 'The Egoist' with great and ever-increasing interest and admiration. To me it is certainly one of the ablest books of modern years. It is full of passion and insight, of wit and force, of truth and eloquence and nature. Its characters, from Sir Willoughby downwards, are brilliantly right and sound; it has throughout the perfect good-breeding of high comedy; there is not a sentence in it, whether of dialogue or analysis, or reflection, but is in some sort matter for applause. All the same, I cannot but believe that its peculiarities of form are such as must stand inevitably in the way of its success. I cannot but believe that, with all its astonishing merits, it will present itself to its warmest admirers as a failure in art, as art has hitherto been understood and practised. Mr. Meredith has written for himself, and it is odds but the multitude will decline to listen to him. Nor, so far as I can see, is the multitude alone to blame.

If Henley was liable to find the critic in him subjecting the man in all expressions of artistic enjoyment, with R. L. Stevenson it was the reverse, for there at times we see the tastes and affections of the man prevailing over the instincts of the critic. His opinions of 'The Egoist' certainly are purely personal and informed with none of that critical discretion which is everywhere present in the judgments of Henley, to whom he addressed this oft-quoted letter in April, 1882:

> My dear Henley, . . . Talking of Meredith, I have just re-read for the third and fourth time 'The Egoist.' When I shall have read it the six or seventh, I begin to see I shall know about it. You will be astonished when you come to re-read it; I had no idea of the matter—human red matter—he has contrived to plug and pack into that strange and admirable book. Willoughby is, of course, a pure discovery; a complete set of nerves, not heretofore examined, and yet running all over the human body—a suit of nerves. Clara is the best girl I ever saw anywhere. Vernon is almost as good. The manner and faults of the book greatly justify themselves on further study. Only Dr. Middleton does not hang together; and Ladies Busshe and Culmer *sont des monstruosités*. Vernon's conduct makes a wonderful odd contrast with Daniel Deronda's. I see more and more that Meredith is built for immortality. . . .
>
> I am yours loquaciously,
>
> R. L. S.

Five years later Stevenson wrote in the *British Weekly*, May 13,

1887, an article on 'Books which have Influenced Me,' now reprinted in 'The Art of Writing,' wherein occurs this memorable passage on 'The Egoist':

> I should never forgive myself if I forgot 'The Egoist.' It is art, if you like, but it belongs purely to didactic art, and from all the novels I have read (and I have read thousands) stands in a place by itself. Here is a Nathan for the modern David; here is a book to send the blood into men's faces. Satire, the angry picture of human faults, is not great art; we can all be angry with our neighbour; what we want is to be shown, not his defects, of which we are too conscious, but his merits, to which we are too blind. And 'The Egoist' is a satire; so much must be allowed; but it is a satire of a singular quality, which tells you nothing of that obvious mote, which is engaged from first to last with that invisible beam. It is yourself that is hunted down; these are your faults that are dragged into the day and numbered, with lingering relish, with cruel cunning and precision. A young friend of Mr. Meredith's (as I have the story) came to him in an agony. 'This is too bad of you,' he cried. 'Willoughby is me!' 'No, my dear fellow,' said the author; 'he is all of us.' I have read 'The Egoist' five or six times myself, and I mean to read it again; for I am like the young friend of the anecdote—I think Willoughby an unmanly but a very serviceable exposure of myself.

The critics have not greatly concerned themselves with 'The Tragic Comedians,' being here at one with the reading public. Little has been written of this short and little-read novel. And that little is chiefly by way of adverse criticism. Even Henley had here to confess himself out of touch with the master who sought to give a fictive setting to the fantastic love-story of Lassalle and Helena von Doënniges, for he writes thus in 'Views and Reviews':

> Opinions differ, and there are those, I believe, to whom Alvan and Clotilde von Rüdiger—'acrobats of the affections' they have been called—are pleasant companions, and the story of those feats in the gymnastics of sentimentalism in which they lived to shine is the prettiest reading imaginable. But others not so fortunate, or, to be plain, more honestly obtuse, persist in finding that story tedious, and the bewildering appearances it deals with, not human beings—not of the stock of Rose Jocelyn and Sir Everard Romfrey, of Dahlia Fleming and Lucy Feverel and Richmond Roy—but creatures of gossamer and rainbow, phantasms of spiritual romance, abstractions of remote, dispiriting points in sexual philosophy.

Mr. W. L. Courtney, in the *Fortnightly*, was even more emphatic; but it is curious to note how a book that leaves one critic

DR. ALVAN.

(FERDINAND LASSALLE.)

The unhappy love story of the famous Jewish leader of German Liberalism and Helena von Doënniges, is the theme of 'The Tragic Comedians,' where Lassalle figures as 'Dr. Alvan.'

[To face p. 222.

utterly untouched may capture another and send him breathless to the reading of all the works from the same pen. So much did 'The Tragic Comedians' for Professor MacCallum of Sydney, as we gather from his admirable lecture on Meredith published in 1892:

About nine years ago some old college friends were discussing the relation of the will to the passions and the reason, when one of them quoted a phrase about 'that wandering ship of the drunken pilot, the mutinous crew and the angry captain, called Human Nature.' That was my first introduction to George Meredith; before then I only knew his name as the butt of reviewing wit, and had held myself exempt from the need of closer acquaintance with him as with any other luckless novelist of the hour. But the words quoted were unlike those of a third-rate novel; they suggested a writer who would at least be worth looking into. It was not easy, however, to do even this much, the only one of his works that could readily be got was 'The Tragic Comedians,' from which the quotation came, and I well remember the feeling of bewilderment as I read the opening chapters. No other novelist wrote like that, no characters in fiction talked like that, the story seemed the most wild and absurd extravaganza, yet with bright rifts in it through which the sun of genius flashed. Meanwhile a sketch of Lassalle's career, which was not then, as now, prefixed to the volume [This refers to Ward Lock's edition of 1892, in which Mr. Clement Shorter wrote a note on Lassalle], fell into my hands, and my astonishment was increased by the discovery that the story was almost literally true, the most extraordinary remarks had actually been made. I went back to the novel to find the style not tumid and stilted, as it seemed on the first unintelligent perusal, but aglow with passion and thought, the action set forth, the characters interpreted with a grand poetic power; from that reading I emerged a student of Meredith for life, resolved to make the rest of his works my own.

There has certainly been no lack of commentary on 'Diana of the Crossways,' but, chiefly, it is to be noted, relative to the character of the heroine, and not to the novel as a whole. The first noteworthy review of the book appeared in the *Academy*, February 28, 1885, and was from the pen of the late James Ashcroft Noble. In the course of his critique he wrote:

The author of 'Diana of the Crossways' has always seemed to us not so much a novel-writer as a singularly brilliant social essayist, who has wilfully chosen to cut up his essays into fragments of fictitious description and conversation. His books are always interesting, and yet, paradoxical as the saying may seem, we are interested neither in the personages themselves nor in what happens to them. We read simply that we may know what Mr. Meredith has to say, and that we may enjoy his manner of saying it. . . . There is nothing better in 'Diana of the Crossways' than the almost dazzlingly brilliant introductory chapter; and here Mr. Meredith is what we contend he ought always to be, an essayist undisguised in the fancy dress of a novel-writer. . . . The situations in the book are not inevitable. They have no imaginative necessity, but only an intellectual necessity. They are simply pegs on which to hang clever comments. We do not, we cannot, really care for Diana Warwick and her various entanglements with her lovers and would-be lovers; but it is interesting to see what Mr. Meredith can make of them. Once, indeed, Diana does become vividly human—in the scene where Percy Dacier casts her off because she has betrayed his great political secret to the London editor; but the chapter comes as a surprise, and it is a surprise that does not recur.

On the other hand, W. E. Henley, who wrote a long criticism of the book in the *Athenæum*, March 14, 1885, formed a very different opinion of the novel, beginning by saying that 'in "Diana of the Crossways" Mr. Meredith has atoned for the faults of "The Tragic Comedians."'

To our thinking (he declares), 'Diana of the Crossways' is one of the best of all Mr. Meredith's books. It has no touch of the tremendous spiritual tragedy which forms the subject of 'Rhoda Fleming'—in some ways the greatest of its author's achievements; nor, on the other hand, is its essence so peculiar and rare as that spirit of comedy whose expression in Sir Willoughby Patterne sets 'The Egoist' on a pinnacle apart among novels, and marks the writer for one of the breed of Shakespeare and Molière. It keeps a mean between the two extremes, it has affinities with both, and copies neither. It is a study of character, and it is also a study of emotion; it is a picture of fact and the world, and it is touched with generous romance; it is rich in kindly comedy, and it abounds in natural passion; it sets forth a selection of many human elements, and is joyful and sorrowful, wholesome with laughter and fruitful of tears, as life itself. In one word, it is a common novel, as 'Amelia' is, and 'Vanity Fair.' It ends as happily as the feeblest and flimsiest of visions in three volumes, and is only distinguished from the ruck of its contemporaries in being the work of a man of genius and a great artist.

Parsons Lathrop, who was also eloquent in praise of the novel, found in it qualities which, had they been present in other works of the same master-hand, would have made for popularity. He writes thus in the *Atlantic Monthly*, February, 1888:

In 'Diana of the Crossways' he has attempted, with partial success, to do something different from his usual line. He has, in fact, attempted to make himself popular. As a consequence, the book has, I believe, made better headway with the public than any of its predecessors; and yet there could hardly be a more convincing proof of the futility of the effort made by the author to render himself popular than that which is supplied by this production. He has chosen a pure, beautiful, gifted, and dazzlingly brilliant woman as his heroine; he has put her through a severe matrimonial, amatory, and emotional experience, and matched her at last with a strong, patient, sturdy, yet sensitive type of man who is quite worthy of her. He titillates the impure appetite of readers by introducing scandal and divorce proceedings. It may be that these elements have served to give the novel an impetus; but they do not make it genuinely popular. His way of telling the story is, in the main, as excellent as he knows how to fashion it—direct, dramatic, vivacious.

'And now a wonder comes to light, to show'—well, we'll let it go at that, but if one cared to press the case for criticism, it could be amply proved by the way in which the three remaining novels were received, and the lines from Goldsmith might be completed not without reason. I shall content myself by affirming that 'Shagpat,' 'Feverel' and all the intervening novels, with the possible exception of 'Rhoda Fleming,' were more enthusiastically received by the critics than 'One of Our Conquerors,' 'Lord Ormont and his Aminta' and 'The Amazing Marriage.' Yet we are told that only within the last twenty years of his life were Meredith's works adequately criticised. There can be few who have studied the criticism of Meredith so closely as I have, and I take off my hat to the critics, known and unknown, who handled his books before 1880: some of the soundest criticism ever written on contemporary fiction was enjoyed by Meredith long before that date. Let it be urged, if you will, that his last three novels were not sufficiently trumpeted; but that is the fault of those who are so prone to chide the critics of an earlier day for lack of perception.

We owe to Miss Harriet Waters Preston, the charming American essayist, the credit of a unique thing in Meredith criticism: the discovery that the last three novels are a 'great trilogy.' On the whole, I think, she makes out an excellent case, and her closely reasoned study of Meredith, under the title of 'A Knightly Pen,' contributed to the *Atlantic Monthly*, October, 1902, is a most valuable addition to the criticism of the novels. Her contention is that in these three works the novelist has said his last word in the rôle of 'a gallant champion of what are, *to him*, the sacred and inviolable Rights of Woman.' It will be said at once that in this sense all his novels are in harmony, and one will ask: What of 'Diana'? What of 'Rhoda Fleming'? But Miss Preston is no doubt right in her view that while the theme 'would seem to have haunted the novelist at intervals from youth up,' the searching and sustained discussion of it in the last three gives it and them a special significance. After sketching out the plot of 'One of our Conquerors' very vividly, Miss Preston goes on to say:

'Here's a sermon, Harry!' as the old Baroness Bernstein said to her Virginian kinsman, when he failed to recognise her own resplendent portrait as a girl. But there are subsidiary themes and incidental homilies in this extremely serious book which are hardly less impressive. There is the flaw, detected and exposed, of lurking vulgarity in the ideal of life accepted by every man who will be first and foremost a money king. There is the quaint idyl of Victor Radnor's confidential clerk, the converted pugilist, who consecrates his formidable fist to God and the intrepid Salvation lass whom he had rescued from the violence of a drunken brute. Above all, there is the effect of the long tragedy, they have seen so near, upon those fair-minded men of the world who have the run of Victor's house. Theoretically, of course, and in the face of that world, they stand by their own order and its Mohammedan traditions. But the 'pity and terror' of it all purify their feeling both for mother and daughter in degrees that vary exactly with the native nobility of each man's mind. The titled fiancée, so needful to the success of Victor's political plans, whom Nesta had dutifully accepted at her father's eager instance, but to her mother's unspoken distress, draws back naturally enough from the revelation that the mother is impelled to make, and half accepts the release which the girl instantly offers him when she herself is told the truth. Afterwards he repents, and would risk and condone all, but it is too late. In the forcing fire of that sharp crisis, the virginal soul of his bride that might have been has risen above and passed far away from him. If ever young woman 'grew upon the sunny side of the wall,' it was Nesta up to the time when she learned the truth about her parentage. And yet—*paratum est cor suum*—the divine preparation of the heart had been surely going on. And when the maiden of nineteen springs to mortal maturity in one fierce hour, we know not which to admire more—her arrowy rectitude, or her ample charity. Love answereth all things. She loves, encourages, and supports her mother. She loves, compassionates, and nerves her father. She never judges either. She seems not even to know how firmly she holds in her slender hand the balance between these two beloved beings of whose error she was born. In her large, fresh, and thoroughly illuminated inner being there is no room even for righteous scorn. And no more is there any hesitation or fear. Henceforth hers is a steady and undaunted championship of all women under a social cloud; both the actually 'fallen' and those like to fall; a championship whose Christ-like frankness comes near to appalling, at times, even the most generous of her own devoted followers among men. The author's divination of the probable workings of a brave, blameless, and clairvoyant woman's heart seems at this point little less than dæmonic.

Following her admirable appreciation of the story of 'One of Our Conquerors,' the style of which she criticises severely, Miss Preston turns to the second work of her trilogy:

The story of 'Lord Ormont and his Aminta' is briefer, and much more plainly, not to say bluntly told. . . . Upon the rebels, in this instance, Mr. Meredith pronounces no formal sentence. By implication he may almost be regarded as justifying them, for it is Lord Ormont and his kind against whom he trains the tremendous artillery of his moral. That valiant old soldier had, after all, so sound a heart, and so keen a faculty of discernment, except when swayed by petty personal spite! He thoroughly appreciated, nay, doted on the infinite possibilities of the rare young creature whom, still, the selfish custom of his sex and the indurated cruelty of his caste permitted him to abuse, as toy or instrument, until he had fairly driven her to insurrection and constructive crime. He had intended to right her so magnificently when it should be his own good time and royal pleasure to do so! He would deck her with the world-renowned family diamonds, and trample upon the whole impudent and ungrateful peerage in drawing her to his side. But when he finally turned and signified his gracious willingness to adjust her coronet, the youthful countess was gone.

Miss Preston is particularly keen in her praise of the Lady Charlotte, and doubts if any one except Shakespeare has ever so portrayed, 'to the inmost palpitating life, the rude, imperious, and at the same time intensely human and convincing character' which Meredith has drawn in Lady Charlotte Eglett. She next goes on to describe 'The Amazing Marriage' as a retelling of 'Lord Ormont and his Aminta' with altered characters and conditions, suggesting that this was done by the novelist to vindicate absolutely and conclusively his heroine. But to say that 'The Amazing Marriage' is only another version of the story of Lord and Lady Ormont is not, however, to suggest, for one moment, that the author repeats himself. Quite otherwise. He is indeed so affluent a creator of human types and combinations that the identity of the twice-told parable is not immediately apparent to the reader.

On the whole Miss Preston makes out a fairly convincing case for the relationship of the last three novels, in which Meredith advances the flag of Femininism even more vigorously and with greater *élan* than in any of his earlier works. But this we must consider further in the next chapter. Here we may profitably note another characteristic of his work which has seldom attracted the attention of his expositors, and, so far as I am aware, has been dwelt upon only by an able writer ('G.-Y.') in the *Bookman* of August, 1894, who contributed a study of 'Lord Ormont and his Aminta' from which I select the following:

> 'Lord Ormont and his Aminta' compels an inquiry into the nationality of Mr. Meredith's mind—though it gives no very definite answer. Read in one light, the book is a glorification of English boys, English school-boy honour, English pluck and daring, an eloquent tolerance of, an artistic esteem for, English defects. This kind of sentiment used to be embodied in stories by Mr. Thomas Hughes. Now-a-days an excellent interpreter of the Anglo-Saxon temper in its tougher moods has been found in Mr. Rudyard Kipling. (Was Mr. Meredith ever brought into such incongruous company?—but the incongruity is just the point.) They take English superiority for granted calmly, or hoist the flag aggressively, ignore the faults they do not wish to see, or berate their country soundly for others, and mainly for not being English enough. Mr. Meredith's lyrical enthusiasm for his country, and his intellectual enjoyment of her limitations, are something entirely different. With his cosmopolitan sympathies, his personal freedom from insular prejudices, he is exactly the type of man you expect to look on John Bull as a barbarian, and hold all Philistines in horror as unclean, or not conversible with fellow-citizens. But he does nothing of the kind. In the first place, perhaps, he has too much humour, but, secondly, he comes with such fresh, untired eyes to look at the Philistines that he finds them most amusing fellows, and thereupon sits down, not to laugh at them, but to describe their points of view till you are persuaded he is bringing you into a company of distinction. He is like a foreigner turned Anglophile, and there is nothing sincerer and heartier than the admiration of such. Just as the descendants of the English of the pale became more Irish than the Irish, so Mr. Meredith, with a mind that one does not at all recognise as native, is in certain moods more British than the British. I am not going to try and put a label on the nationality of his mind; perhaps there is no nationality ready to admit it on the score of very near kinship. But it is something swifter than English, and not only more agile, but more delighting

in agility; not more emotional or imaginative, but with a keener intellectual sense of the value of emotions and of the part imagination plays in ordinary life.

In the correspondence of York Powell, that ardent Meredithian, Professor Oliver Elton, quotes a letter, dated February 10, 1896, addressed to him, wherein Powell is hot in praise of the master's last novel, saying: 'I am sure this "A.M." will be one of the solid bases of M.'s fame. He has given time to it, I know, as well as inspiration. It is not "difficult." It is profoundly interesting.'

If one might now venture to give a general impression of the criticisms we have been discussing, that would shape itself broadly in these terms: The novels of Meredith, though lacking in construction, often crudely fashioned and at times tending to the melodramatic, are so rich in the variety, truth and freshness of their characters, that where they fail as stories they triumph abundantly as revelations of human life. That the art of the story-teller is at the command of the novelist, when he has chosen to curb his 'overmastering cleverness,' such a masterpiece of tragic drama as 'Rhoda Fleming' proves as completely as 'Sandra Belloni' illustrates his proneness to prolixity and the inconsequent.

While there is no feature of our social life into which the novelist has not looked with seeing eyes and studied profoundly, his sympathies are ever with the intellectuals; he moves uneasily among the lowly and the humble, where Dickens was at home, and seldom attempts the interpretation of common folk, whose hearts are more fruitful of study than their brains, without leaving the impression that he has tried to follow Dickens and failed.

That his characters talk as none we have known in life have ever talked—unless, indeed, it be Meredith himself—is a common and a thoughtless complaint; since their language is not that of ordinary fiction any more than the blank verse of Shakespeare's plays is that of ordinary speech, and is not to be criticised by common standards. This is original with him and germane to his method, which, failing sometimes, succeeds brilliantly and so often that all its failures are discounted. Here emphatically he has created the taste by which he must be judged and comparative criticism cannot be applied.

His attitude to life and to the personages of his novels is that of a keen-witted observer, seldom that of an emotionally warm and sympathetic friend; hence the feeling of aloofness which, barring the way to close intimacy of the heart, leaves open the road to intellectual admiration and communion.

An epic largeness of design is noted in most of his great novels without an equal largeness of achievement; but the mark being high and the aim likewise, the falling short still leaves the achievement immensely greater than the successful efforts of lesser and often more widely read contemporaries.

Above all is the remarkable allegiance to femininism, leaving the impression that in the novelist's own character there is a feminine strain, of which he is conscious and proudly so, as when he makes Alvan say: 'You meet now and then men who have the woman in them without being womanised; they are the pick of men. And the choicest women are those who yield not a feather of their womanliness for some amount of manlike strength.' The attributing of this sentiment to the author rather than to his personage, irregular as criticism in ordinary, is here legitimate, as it illustrates a further characteristic of this novelist: often his characters are uttering not their own thoughts, but their author's; too often to admit of his possessing 'absolute dramatic vision.'

Finally, his long series of novels is unique in our literature, and with all their faults of construction and style these works contain such a harvest of philosophy and humour as no other novelist of the Victorian era has garnered.

[*From the original drawing by Cyrus Cuneo*

MEREDITH AND SOME OF HIS FAMOUS CREATIONS.

The characters in this picture from left to right are (above) Emilia in 'Sandra Belloni'; (below) Rhoda Fleming and her father; Evan Harrington and Rose Jocelyn; (above) Aminta in 'Lord Ormont and his Aminta'; (below) Lucy in 'Richard Feverel'; Diana of the Crossways; and below on the extreme right Clara Middleton, 'the dainty rogue in porcelain' of 'The Egoist.'

[*To face page* 230

X

HIS HEROINES AND WOMEN-FOLK

'YOUR knowledge of women is almost indecent,' a celebrated lady novelist—of whose novels the same is partly true—once remarked to George Meredith. It was a flash of that Dianaësque wit which Meredith has done not a little to encourage, with results not always of the happiest. But it states a truism with the legitimate exaggeration of epigram. Since the little printer of Salisbury Square enchained the whole feminine world of his time with his 'Pamela' and his 'Clarissa,' no other novelist has rivalled Meredith in the appeal to femininity, though there is no striking likeness between them. Richardson most faithfully interpreted the contemporary feminine character; Meredith has sought to breathe into woman a larger life; to claim for her qualities that are not typical; to prove, above all, that she is not dominated by sex, but is as individual as man. Hence his women-folk are unique in literature, and perhaps in life. To him in particular is due the claim so strenuously urged by the modern 'advanced' woman, to be considered not as an atom of woman, but as an individual. The woman suffrage movement became in some sort his Frankenstein; and he had to condemn that propaganda of sex—which proves with ludicrous perversity the opposite of his contention—as unwise and disastrous. Unwomanly we cannot call it; since, with the uprising of the feminine 'individual,' the virtues once dubbed 'womanly' must now receive some other definition. That Meredith's ideal of womanhood carries us millenniumward is by no means the general opinion, though his insight into the mind of women—rather than of woman—is unexampled. In March, 1905, he wrote as follows to Mr. Hugh W. Strong, of Newcastle-on-Tyne:

Since I began to reflect I have been impressed by the injustice done to women, the constraint put upon their natural aptitudes and faculties, generally much to the degradation of the race. I have not studied them more closely than I have men, but with more affection, a deeper interest in their enfranchisement and development, being assured that women of the independent mind are needed for any sensible degree of progress. They will so educate their daughters that these will not be instructed at the start to feel themselves naturally inferior to men because less muscular, and need not have recourse to practise arts, feline chiefly, to make their way in the world.

In the same letter the novelist stated that he had no special choice among the women of his books, saying ' perhaps I gave more colour to Diana of the Crossways and Clara Middleton of "The Egoist," and this on account of their position.'

A French lady-writer, Mademoiselle Henriette Cordelet, whose study of ' La Femme dans l'Œuvre de Meredith ' will call for mention later, observes that of all the problems in life that interest the novelist the chief is ' the battle of the sexes.' This is true, and because of its truth we shall find that even the male characters of his novels are interesting largely on account of the sex relationship. It is man in relation to woman, and seldom man to man with which Meredith engages us. Sir Willoughby Patterne is negatively a study of feminism, so too Sir Austin Feverel—take Lucy away and what would be left of his ' system '? She was conceived at the moment of its birth, to condition everything. Beauchamp, also, though containing possibilities of existence apart from the influence of woman, is in the end dominated by the eternally feminine, and Victor Radnor most of all. Take all the novels that bear a masculine name; woman is as eminent in them as she is in those to which the names of the heroines are given. Assuredly his countrywomen ought to be his warmest partisans, for no other novelist has sought with such meticulous care to avoid presenting in all his legion of women characters a conventional figure based upon the ' veiled virginal doll ' of the writers of popular fiction. In his resolution to give to every feminine figure an individuality, he has, perhaps, endowed some of them more richly than nature warrants. The general result is to produce that impression of tense femininity to which reference has already been made.

Is it possible that a novelist who sees more in womar than she can see in herself fails of that widest reading public for fiction simply because he is to her—as his own Mrs. Berry puts it—' like somethin' out o' nature '? That is a question involving a long and debatable answer, which can scarcely be attempted here. In his ' Life ' of Browning, the late William Sharp has a reference to

Meredith's insight into feminine character that is worthy of note. He writes:

Only two writers of our age have depicted women with that imaginative insight which is at once more comprehensive and more illuminative than women's own invision of themselves—Robert Browning and George Meredith, but not even the latter, most subtle and delicate of all analysts of the tragi-comedy of human life, has surpassed 'Pompilia.' The meeting and the swift uprising of love between Lucy and Richard, in 'The Ordeal of Richard Feverel,' is, it is true, within the highest reach of prose romance: but between even the loftiest height of prose romance and the altitudes of poetry there is an impassable gulf.

Professor Oliver Elton, too, writes wisely on this aspect of Meredith's fiction, but argues that man is the better painter of woman, without suggesting the possibility of man himself having something of the feminine in him, which, plus his manhood, enables him to see with clearer vision—to wed instinct with reason, so to say—into the dimmer recesses of women's nature. In his brilliant study of Meredith, appearing in 'Modern Studies,' Professor Elton writes:

He seems to have 'reversed the order of Paradise,' and to have created his woman first, and so to have had less clay at disposal for fashioning their mates. Renée, Emilia, Carinthia, Lucy, with their musical names—in their talk, and his talk about them, his style is at its purest and clearest, and the colours of the portraits are unfading. Women are nearer to nature than men, and the power to paint them can only come straight from the breast of nature—from experience lived through and transmuted into artistic form. Indeed, the business of 'reading the female heart' has not often been practised in English prose without a dispiriting effect. The tradition of unreality is old and obstinate. It runs far back to the Renaissance romance, like Sidney's 'Arcadia'—where, indeed, there is one tragic feminine figure, the queen Gynecia; and to the long-winded books in French and English consumed by our seventeenth-century ancestresses. But those old romances were apt to be made by courtly, artificial men or by spinsters without any profitable experience of humanity. One of these, Samuel Richardson, succeeded once, despite his fussy morals and clammy rhetoric. The laborious knife of George Eliot sometimes bites deep. But a man, if only he is great enough and can rise above the natural barrier ('La haine entre les deux sexes,' says Joubert, 'ne s'éteint guère'), is the best and kindest painter of women and of their ailments of the soul, and the best describer of them. Or so the event seems to have proved. This is not a reflection upon women; for, after all, it is better to belong to the class that is pictured than to the class that paints pictures.

Balzac and Mr. Meredith, diverse in almost all ways, have both left behind them a portrait gallery of actual and living women. Balzac exceeds with older, harder, and stranger natures. The Englishman, more of a poet at the heart, prefers to celebrate youth and beauty that are victorious after long inward and outward trial.

Mr. W. C. Brownell goes much deeper in his examination of this same subject. He points out what most writers are apt to ignore, if indeed they have noticed it: the paradoxical result of Meredith's treatment of women. And he explains the paradox very satisfactorily. While the whole force of the novelist's propaganda is to individualise women with men, yet he fights for 'the sex,' which implies the ancient attitude of those who have not yet doubled Cape Turk! Mr. Brownell's views are thus set forth in his 'Victorian Prose Masters':

A considerable part of Mr. Meredith's vogue is probably due to his treatment of women, which is very special, and for that reason, no doubt, has especially won the suffrages of 'the sex,' as he is fond of calling it. The approbativeness of 'the sex' at its present stage of evolution is perhaps manifested quite as much with reference to evaluation and appreciation as a sex as it is individually. It can hardly have escaped observers of such phenomena that it is as a sex that, currently, women particularly appreciate being treated as individuals. The more marked such treatment is, the more justice they feel is done to the sex. Mr. Meredith's treatment of them is in this respect very marked—so much so, in fact, that he obliterates very often the broad distinction usually made between the young girl and the married woman. Diana, for example, leaves —in some respects—a maidenly, and some of his maidens produce a matronly, impression. With his women readers he has accordingly been, perhaps, particularly successful. He makes it unmistakably clear that women are psychologically worth while, complex, intricate, and multifarious in mind as well as complicated in nature. He makes a point of this, and underscores it in a way that produces a certain effect of novelty by the stress he lays on it. The justice so fully rendered is given the fillip of seeming tardy justice, and therefore an element of Mr. Meredith's originality among writers of fiction. This is a good deal, but I think it is witness of a still greater originality in him that he goes still further. He lays even greater stress upon the fact that the being thus intricately interesting and worthy of scrutiny from the constitution of her individual personality is also that most interesting of all personalities, a feminine one. He adds the requisite touch of chivalry. He is, after

By permission of Messrs. Bradbury, Agnew & Co.] [*From the drawing by Charles Keene in 'Once a Week.'*

THE COUNTESS DE SALDAR.

Idleness was fashionable: exquisite languors were a sign of breeding; and she always had an idea that she looked more interesting at dinner after reclining on a couch the whole of the afternoon.

—*Evan Harrington.* Chapter XIX.

[*To face p.* **234.**

all, a true *aficionado* of 'the sex.' He can be trusted to understand, not to be too literal, not to forget that the singularisation implied in apotheosis is a very different thing from that involved in limitation. Women are to be discriminated as individuals, like men, but the fact that they possess in common and as women a certain distinctive quality is, above all, not to be lost sight of. This is the permanent, the *ewig*, fact about them. Only it is to be taken as a crown, not as a mere label.

So far we have listened to judgments of men in a matter where woman have surely a right to be heard, and before proceeding to look at certain of Meredith's female characters in some detail we cannot do better than discover what his women critics have had to say on the subject of his heroines and women-folk. Here one turns naturally to the first lady-writer of note who has dealt with Meredith's work as a whole; George Eliot having reviewed only his two earliest prose fictions. Miss Flora L. Shaw (Lady Lugard), in her noteworthy study (*New Princeton Review*, March, 1887) gave less attention than one might have expected to the femininism of Meredith, deeming it a subject whose consideration would have led her beyond the scope of a single review article. But what she did write was suggestive and to the point. She said:

The most striking feature of his presentation of women is the frankness with which he takes them on their merits. He surrounds them with no halo, he wraps them in no mystery, but, approaching them as simply as he approaches man, he lays the strength and the weakness open before us.

The embryonic condition of their reasoning powers, the reliance on the senses, which long process of evolution has made almost instinctive to them, are facts which he very honestly calls on them to recognise and remedy. He entirely refuses the doubtful form of homage which consists in putting them on a plane other than that of the understanding, but no living writer of English has done higher honour to the qualities which they possess. The friendship of Emma and Tony, in 'Diana of the Crossways,' is one among many instances. His gallery of heroines speak for themselves. Lucy, Emilia, Rose, Jenny, Diana, Emma, imperfect every one, still send us seeking for comparison to Shakespeare. And Renée, graceful Renée, cannot, for all her faultiness, be omitted. . . .

Humanity is not passing as an ironic procession before eyes which have rested comprehendingly on these bright figures. The difficult task of their creator has been to show that feeling, however sweet and good, is insufficient. If immeasurable love were perfect wisdom, one human being might almost impersonate Providence to another. Alas! love, divine as it is, can do no more than lighten the house it inhabits—must take its shape, sometimes intensify its narrowness; can spiritualise, but not expel, old life-long lodgers above stairs and below.

The late Miss Adeline Sergeant who, in her time, had some vogue as a novelist, essentially of the conventional school, contributed anonymously to *Temple Bar*, June, 1889, an article on 'George Meredith's Views of Women,' which proved her a sound thinker and independent of mind, though her conclusions differed widely from Meredith's. Her right to speak for the women of her time gives some value to her opinions, which might be profitably circulated in these days of feminine agitation. Miss Sergeant entirely applauded Meredith's interpretation of woman's character and his opinion of woman's present position in society, but she dissented as strongly from his ideal of the future woman and his views of her functions.

He aims high, but not high enough. He does, indeed, set before us the hope that we may in time arrive at a true conception of the right heroical woman to be worshipped; and, if you prove to be of some spiritual stature, he says, you may reach to an ideal of the heroical feminine type for the worship of mankind; an image as yet in poetic outline only on our upper skies. But what, on analysis, is this heroical feminine type? Its progenitor seems to hold the view that the natures of women have been differentiated from those of men simply through man's agency, by man's tyranny and oppression acting on woman's physical weakness; that woman's highest aim is to reinstate herself by his side, to become his equal —'the mate of man, and the mother of a nobler race'; and that she may some day attain to this proud position of likeness and equality, but only by man's aid and man's consent. If this be Meredith's theory, it seems to me to be founded on a wrong view of the physical nature, the mental weaknesses, and the moral capacities of both women and men.

There is scarcely a woman in his books who is not, righteously and grandly, in revolt, at war with herself, or with society; at war with the ignorance, the cowardice, the want of candour, want of judgment, want of sense, which a bad education, rather than a bad disposition, has made characteristic of woman; at war with society for its narrowness, its harshness, its want of humour and tolerance, and its impenetrable stupidity. With these the best among us are constantly at war; and we owe thanks to George Meredith for his pictures of women nobly at odds with themselves and with the world.

The gist of the whole matter, as regards these objections to Meredith's views of women, lies in his failure to discern the ever-

By permission of Messrs. Bradbury, Agnew & Co.] [*From the drawing by Charles Keene in 'Once a Week.'*

EVAN AND ROSE ON BOARD THE 'JOCASTA.'

One, a young lady, very young in manner, wore a black felt hat, with a floating scarlet feather, and was clad about the shoulders in a mantle of foreign style and pattern. The other you might have taken for a wandering Don, were such an object ever known; so simply he assumed the dusky sombrero and little dangling cloak, of which one fold was flung across his breast and drooped behind him.

—*Evan Harrington.* Chapter IV.

[*To face p.* 236.

lasting differences between the natures of women and men. A careful examination of his books, and particularly of 'Diana of the Crossways' and 'The Egoist,' tends to convince me that he thinks of woman as of a lesser man, unfairly treated because she is not judged according to the standard applied to man, nor allowed his liberty of action and thought. I grant the unfairness of this kind of treatment, but not the reason given for it. Under no circumstances will women ever be the mates of men in the sense which Meredith attaches to the words. A woman's physical constitution alone disables her from becoming what is usually called 'the equal' of man. But the words 'equal,' 'superior,' or 'inferior,' are utterly out of place when used of creatures so different in capacity and temperament. The same laws and the same moralities will never fit the two. George Meredith forgets that where there are root-differences of physical constitution there are also sure to be root-differences of mind and temper. To grant the first and deny the second is to involve ourselves in endless difficulties; no amount of intellectual training will obliterate these distinctions of sex; and as, by the operations of unchanging law, higher organisation tends towards the differentiation of species, we shall more closely follow nature's lead if we emphasise rather than seek to lessen the differences between women and men.

Miss Harriet Waters Preston stresses his demand for courage in women with many an apt illustration, but she finds his ideal of womanhood, instead of being a new conception and in advance of his age, to be taken from the thirteenth century and the age of chivalry. 'The oddest feature of Mr. Meredith's crusade,' she writes, 'is this':

> The emancipation which he invokes for the suffering fair is in no sense an intellectual one. It is anything and everything rather than an affair of sciences, languages, courses, and careers. And still less is it what is quaintly called by a certain class of agitators 'economic.' It is purely moral, and can be achieved only through the moral regeneration of woman's natural master. A champion of Woman's Rights—even with capitals—Mr. Meredith stands confessed; yet with the clearly defined proviso that a woman has no rights, under the present dispensation, save such as may accrue to her through the righteousness of man. No other author ever gauged so accurately all that a high-spirited woman feels, as none, surely, ever exposed so relentlessly the dastard quality that may shelter itself within the clanging armour of your imposing masculine bravo. Nevertheless Mr. Meredith takes his text quite frankly from 'Paradise Lost,' 'He for God only, she for God in him.' The first and by far the most difficult part of this antiquated ideal once realised, the second would be found to comprehend the way

of all blessing for man and woman alike. The woman's office ir creation is to be magnified, her ways, in so far as she has beer made 'subject to vanity, not willingly,' are to be justified, her more than Augustinian 'love of love' is to be satisfied; but all and strictly within the adamantine limits established, from the beginning in the order of nature, by the Author of Life. . . .

In short Mr. Meredith's ideal is that of the thirteenth century rescued from disrepute and ridicule, and shaped, so far as may be to the uses of the third millennium.

Yet it is but natural that most writers on Meredith's heroines should expend their criticisms on the intellectual qualities of these fair women. Their individuality is so insistent that one is apt to overlook their physical attractions. We have noticed that not a fev critics accuse the novelist of failing to visualise or realise his personages for us. The truth seems to be, as regards his heroines at least, that he does not so fail, but by overwhelming the mind o the reader with a veritable avalanche of character analysis, he i apt to blot out the picture of the personage which, at first and witl the most intimate detail, he had been at pains to create. If we bu read him carefully we shall find that his heroines and women-foll are all described with so much loving care that we cannot fail t see them with the mind's eye. The pity is in some cases that w might retain a clearer vision of them did we not bear them compan to the end of the last chapter! Miss Elizabeth Luther Cary, a American writer in the New York *Critic*, October, 1905, has give more attention to the physical charms of his heroines than any o his other lady critics, and her observations are not without point:

> Their aspect is never conventionally described, and occasionally as in the case of Carinthia, it is of a type too rugged and large t be widely appreciated, but for the most part their author's stud of graceful gesture and delicate surface and line result in unmis takable combinations of beauty. The way of turning the head, th carriage and poise, the walk, are all acutely observed and recorded We may forget the psychological features presented to us, but w are bound to remember the expressive faces, the slim spirite figures, the invariable grace and plasticity. In these portraits c women it is impossible, indeed, to get away from the suggestion c the painter's craft, such a passionate zest for the interpretation c colour and form is displayed. We are even haunted by intimation of particular masters with their individual ways of renderin technical problems. What student of English art, for exampl can read of Lucy Desborough's fresh and tranquil comeliness with

out seeing her lean from a canvas by Romney, the light of the English painter's ideal on her fairness and youth.

In the portraits of the later books there is sometimes less fluency, less felicity of touch, but always there are both distinction and life-likeness. The detailed description of Clara Middleton with 'the mouth that smiles in repose,' the eyelids lifted slightly at the outer corners, the equable shut mouth, and so on, is too categorical to charm, but there is the style of Botticelli in the other sketch of her walking 'insufferably fair' on the highway to Sir Willoughby's displeasure, in a dress 'cunning to embrace the shape and flutter loose about it like the spirit of a summer's day,' trailing her garlands and moving as if she were 'driving the clouds before her,' a sight 'to set the woodland dancing.' Another enchanting picture is that of Diana kneeling by the fire at The Crossways, 'a Madonna on an old black Spanish canvas,' to the eyes of her faithful champion; and still another is the vision of Vittoria singing her great song in the presence of the enemies of Italy, dressed 'like a noble damsel from the hands of Titian,' a figure in amber and pale blue silk, 'such as the great Venetian might have sketched from his windows on a day when the Doge went forth to wed the Adriatic: a superb Italian head, with dark banded hair-braid, and dark strong eyes under unabashed soft eyelids.' In the same gallery with these we must put the happy study of the child princess Ottilia on her pony, against the background of a German forest, and the swift sketch in outline of Rose Jocelyn in her black hat with its scarlet feather, on the deck of the homeward-bound *Jocasta.* It is difficult to conceive what Mr. Meredith's work would be for us without its pictorial side. No English writer so fills our mind with decorative figures and poetic landscape.

Readers of different tastes will naturally single out different types of female character as their favourites, and this is a matter in which individual taste may, to some extent, take the place of criticism, which strictly can have no 'favourites.' It is not criticism that decrees Diana Warwick the favourite of Meredith's heroines; but she would seem to have won the suffrages of most readers, and she is, perhaps, the most characteristic of his women. It is not criticism again that makes Sandra Belloni a wearisome bore to many readers of good sense. She is a finer creation of art than Diana, and yet even the critic, admiring the artistry, may find himself drawn more to Diana. Perhaps Diana may owe just a suspicion of her popularity to the impression that she was studied from life and was not without a scandal attaching to her name. And this raises a point that calls for some notice. In 'Diana of the Crossways,' as in other works of his, the novelist deals to some extent with personalities of recent history. There is, of course, no comparison between the treatment of the historical characters in 'The Tragic Comedians,' which is avowedly 'a study in a well-known story,' and the extent to which a popular story concerning that celebrated woman of wit and beauty, the Hon. Mrs. Caroline E. S. Norton, is made use of in 'Diana.' A great deal of confusion still seems to prevail over this matter. While, on the one hand, we still find writers guilty of stating that 'Diana' is the story of 'the Mrs. Norton who betrayed Peel's decision to repeal the Corn Laws to the *Times* for——' (fill up the blank with any silly thousands); on the other, we have writers, scarcely better informed, at pains to assure us that the character of 'Diana' is in no sense studied from Mrs. Norton and must be read as pure fiction, pointing triumphantly to the note with which the novelist has prefaced the book since its third edition in 1897:

> A lady of high distinction for wit and beauty, the daughter of an illustrious Irish house, came under the shadow of a calumny.
>
> It has latterly been examined and exposed as baseless. The story of 'Diana of the Crossways' is to be read as fiction.

So; but Meredith made use of the calumny in all good faith, believing the story to be true. There can be little doubt to any one who is familiar with the career of the charming and unfortunate lady of history that the Diana of fiction is largely modelled from her, and is credited in earnest with a baseness of which Mrs. Norton was never guilty. The slanderous nature of the story, which was an invention of some malicious gossip, had been repeatedly exposed even before 'Diana of the Crossways' was written, but evidently Meredith was not aware of this until the novel had been published and the old scandal revived. Mrs. Norton was one of the three beautiful granddaughters of Brinsley Sheridan and her eldest sister became Lady Dufferin, hence the efforts of the late Lord Dufferin, when, in 1894, the hoary scandal raised its head again in the autobiography of Sir William Gregory, to have the story authoritatively denied. He wrote to the late Henry Reeves, editor of the *Edinburgh Review*, to help him in the matter, and in the issue of that periodical for January, 1895, Reeves referred to the incident in 'Diana of the Crossways' as 'suggested not by facts, but by calumnies which were exposed and refuted, though for a time they obtained circulation and a certain credence.' He also added the following note:

> We observe with regret that the late Sir William Gregory in

[*After the picture by Hayter.*

THE HON. MRS. CAROLINE NORTON.

Although we are rightly instructed that the story of 'Diana of the Crossways' is to be treated as fiction, it was admittedly based to some extent on the career and personality of this gifted and much wronged lady.

[*To face p.* 240.

his interesting autobiography has revived a calumnious and unfounded anecdote, to which Mr. Meredith had previously given circulation in this novel. We are enabled to state, and we do state, from our personal knowledge, that the story is absolutely false in every particular, and that the persons thus offensively referred to had nothing to do with the matter. The intention of the Government to propose the repeal of the Corn Laws was communicated openly by Lord Aberdeen to Mr. Delane, the editor of the *Times;* there was no sort of intrigue or bribery in the transaction.

There is the true account of the affair, and as 'Diana of the Crossways' had done not a little to give credence to the slander, the next edition of the novel bore the note which has been quoted above, and appears in all subsequent issues. But it will be seen from this that to assert that Meredith had in no sense studied his Diana from the celebrated Mrs. Norton is quite as wrong as to believe to-day that Mrs. Norton took money from the *Times* for disclosing a secret of State. Sheridan's gifted granddaughter, poetess and novelist, who lived apart from her husband for some fifty years, having been the innocent respondent to his groundless action for divorce when only twenty-eight—Lord Melbourne being cited as co-respondent—a woman of great beauty and brilliant intellectual gifts, the intimate of the most notable people of her day, but ever under the chill shadow of her unhappy marriage, was clearly the original of Diana.

The late Miss Hannah Lynch in her monograph on George Meredith gives us an uncommon view of Diana, and her comment on the episode of the betrayal of the State secret is eminently just. She writes:

As Sir Willoughby is Meredith's typical analysis of the male's character, so is Diana Warwick his chief type of woman, and just so ruthlessly as he is drawn is she drawn mercifully—too mercifully, perhaps, for she is painted in all the glowing colours of love. Mr. Meredith is not the analyser of Diana; he is her ardent lover. He adores her unscrutinisingly, as it behoves the true lover to adore his lady. He paints her very faults upon worshipping knees, and does not think it necessary to apologise for her or urge one word of excuse or depreciation when, following fact, she stoops to a shabby breach of confidence worthy the lowest new journalist. She is Diana to him in all her moods, a bewildering and adorable creature, and as such he expects the reader to swallow her thankfully, rejoicing in her as he does, wondering at the stupidity and evilness of the world that condemns her, censuring the meanness of the recreant lover who deserts her upon discovery of her unexplainable betrayal of his confidences. If his lady chooses to start out at midnight, fresh from a love-scene in which she has learnt from her lover a great political secret, to sell it for a very substantial sum to a London editor, Mr. Meredith simply follows her as an admiring recorder, and finds it sufficient explanation to tell us pityingly that she was a child in this world's affairs, that she was as ignorant as a child in business matters, and has no idea of the gravity of her action. This last plea we accept willingly, for impulsive women like Diana rarely have any notion of the weight of actions, and never can measure their consequences; but for a simpleton in worldly affairs she shows a pretty accurate knowledge of the value of her secret and of its market price, and for a lady to sell secret information learnt in a love-scene seems to us an unmistakable fall which, however much we may deplore, we hold ourselves exempt from admiring, or even condoning, as Diana's apologist desires us to do.

Henley, in his brilliant critique of 'Diana' in the *Athenæum* of March 14, 1885, accepts the likeness between Diana and Mrs. Norton, but considers that while 'she suggests Mrs. Norton . . . she suggests George Meredith still more, and Rosalind most of all.'

The comparison is, no doubt, startling (writes Henley), but, we take it, it is legitimate. For such a union as she presents of capacity of heart and capacity of brain, of generous nature and fine intelligence, of natural womanhood and more than womanly wit and apprehensiveness, we know not where to look save among Shakespeare's ladies, nor with whom to equal her save the genius of Arden. Like Rosalind, she is pure woman; and like Rosalind (and her sisters) she has in her enough of her spiritual sire to proclaim her birthright and affirm the illustrious kinship. Mr. Meredith has wrought from within, and behind his Diana you feel the presence of her maker, as you are aware of Shakespeare when you consort with Rosalind and Hermione. Now and then her wit is, like Rosalind's, her father's own, her intelligence and expression are touched with a familiar attribute—when her empire totters, and her influence is for a second in peril of wavering. But this is only now and then. Throughout, as with Rosalind, her royal origin is patent otherwise; like Orlando's mistress, she betrays her parentage in a hundred gallant and inspiring qualities—the quickness and brilliance of her blood, her exquisite and abounding spirit, her delicate vigour of temperament, her swiftness of perception, her generous intensity of emotion. In love, in war, in friendship, in ambition and sorrow, in thought and deed and feeling, she is ever her noble self. She is admirable even in her delusions; you visit her errors with unfailing respect. She is a woman, she has a woman's needs; and she betrays them in turns so quick and warm, yet so chaste and sweet, they make the reader think a certain episode in 'The Mill on the Floss' as grosser and more offensive than perhaps it really is. And the fate of Percy Dacier—'mated with a devious, filmy sentimentalist, likely "to fiddle harmonics on the sensual strings" for him at a mad rate in the years to come'—appears, albeit thoroughly deserved on his part, and on hers the earnest of salvation, a punishment almost savagely inhumane.

Henley was very obviously a whole-hearted admirer of Diana, the glamour of the woman had caught him, and, keen-witted critic though he was, we see him so fascinated by the woman whom the genius of Meredith had evoked that he does not even demur to the State secret episode which Miss Lynch, with all her Celtic enthusiasm, refused to accept. The late Cosmos Monkhouse, on the other hand, in his criticism of the novel in the *Saturday Review*, March 21, 1885, is prepared to believe Mrs. Norton guilty of that baseness, but Diana—no! His views are thus expressed:

It is to be doubted whether even a poet is a more difficult character for fiction than a witty woman of the world; and amongst all his intellectual and literary feats, Mr. Meredith has, perhaps, never accomplished one more striking than in making us feel that his Diana justified her reputation. He has made her move and speak before us as a living woman, dowered with exceptional gifts of 'blood and brains.' Of the two the brains 'have it' decidedly. She is too much like Charles II in the contrast between her sayings and doings. The latter are almost invariably foolish. Though not without precedent, she is none the less difficult to credit or to sympathise with in this particular. Her first folly, her marriage with a fool and a brute, is explained, but scarcely justified, by circumstances; the 'queenly comrade,' with 'a spirit leaping and shining like a mountain water,' should not have been at a loss for a nobler mate. To be 'the crystal spring of wisdom' to a potent old Minister was more worthy of her, and palliates much indiscretion, but to take up with and fall fatally in love with his inelastic and commonplace prig of a nephew, even though he also were a politician of some mark, was almost as silly as her marriage. She was young and impulsive, and love is blind, and the rest of it, no doubt, and that might be an excuse for her in real life, but in fiction the heroine has no right to go so very near wrecking herself on a character for whom the reader has not an atom of regard or admiration. Allowing, also, as historic the fact that a lady sold her friend's political secret to the *Times*, it yet seems incredible that Diana should do so; and it is still more improbable that this woman, so full of knowledge of the political world, should plead that she 'had not a suspicion of mischief' in doing so. But of the reality of her brains there is no doubt; she is intellectually the same woman throughout. If she cannot manage her conduct wisely, she can reason about it. The reviews of her various situations of difficulty, her analysis of her own motives, her arguments for and against herself and the world, are at once clear and subtle, and stirring with vitality. Joyful or joyless, sweet or bitter, they are animated by the same rich intellect, the same noble and passionate soul.

Truly Diana is the heroine of all Meredith's heroines, not only in popular but in critical estimation, and one could go on at any length quoting from the tributes of the critics, for even Mr. W. L. Courtney describes her as 'a real living and breathing woman, gracious in all her divine impulse and her mortal errors;' but there are many others that claim our attention in the galaxy of Meredithian women. Perhaps Emilia Alessandra Belloni is the one whose name and image leap to the mind as readily as Diana's, though we have seen that the novelist himself seems to favour Clara Middleton in company with Diana. Sandra, whose story needs two long novels to do it justice, is certainly the most minutely studied of all the heroines, and consequently her character has been the subject of an immense amount of critical analysis. So long ago as 1864 Mr. Justin McCarthy wrote of her thus in the *Westminster Review*, ere yet she had taken the name of Vittoria:

Emilia's own character is the life and beauty of the story. She is genius without culture; goodness without rule; love without worldly restraint. Her passion for music, for Italy, and for Wilfrid is blended with consummate skill. I remember no character in modern literature that so faithfully pictures the nature which is filled with a genius for music. Not even Consuelo, in George Sand's novel, is so perfect an impersonation. The musical and the poetic are not represented in life by the same sort of human nature; but in books there is hardly any distinction ever drawn. The novelist commonly acts as if there were but one kind of artist nature, and as if the sole difference between painter, poet, and musician were contained in the different modes wherein the genius of each expresses itself. In life every one must be to some degree conscious how entirely unreal is this assumption. The most gifted musician often disappoints in intellectual companionship all but musicians. Intellect, and strangely enough the more poetic phase of intellect, seems often wanting in the singer whose whole soul is filled with music. Mr. Meredith has expressed his sense of this peculiarity in the admirably drawn character of Emilia. In everything, save that which regards song alone, her intellectual nature is commonplace and prosaic. Passion lifts her to heights which are in themselves essentially poetic and dramatic; and a pure, truthful simplicity keeps her always above the vulgarities of existence. That which would vulgarise others is dignified by her; but still she has nothing whatever in her honest childlike heart which reminds one of the Sappho or the Corinna; or even of the stage singer whom ordinary romancists have sometimes painted.

Mr. Arthur Symons would seem to place Emilia at the head of all her fair sisterhood, and one cannot but admire his courage in contrasting her with a heroine of William Black's! The late Allan Monkhouse, too, was all for Sandra, rightly observing that the story of her early life cannot be excelled as an example of Meredith's power in simple, passionate narrative. He quotes the familiar passage beginning: 'Such a touch on the violin as my father has, you never heard.' And after remarking that this is an instance in which, to use a famous phrase, 'Nature takes the pen from him and writes,' he proceeds:

She is a natural young woman, a living refutation of the doctrine of original sin, and an assurance of her author's belief and hope in human nature. She does not comprehend evil, but instinctively abhors it. Without superficial cleverness, she penetrates to essentials. She has something of the primal gratitude and devotion of an animal. Among the highly-organised ladies of Brookfield she moves like a young panther among domestic cats. These civilised young persons who are, if less amusing, on a higher plane of comedy than the Countess de Saldar, have some reason to complain of the fate that confronts them with nature in the phenomenal forms of Emilia and Mrs. Chump, by whom their distinctions, their reserves, their ideals, are roughly broken down and inexorably scattered.

Perhaps the less said about Mrs. Chump the better. Mrs. Berry most people consider a success, Mr. Le Gallienne saying she is a character that would have been a feather in the cap of Dickens. 'Doubtless,' retorts Miss Hannah Lynch, 'but that is not a compliment to Mr. Meredith, for what would do honour to Dickens cannot be said to be worthy of him.' After such a piece of 'criticism' I may be asked why I proceed to quote from the writer. Well, hers is the voice of a woman—and an extremely able woman—and she leads us through Mrs. Berry to Lucy with some sound sense to boot, so that we may forgive the injustice to Dickens. Miss Lynch writes:

Mrs. Berry is witty and original to an alarming degree. She

is a sort of compromise between Mrs. Quickly and Juliet's nurse; not quite so coarse as either, perhaps, but more exhaustively garrulous and obtrusive. In the fifteenth century she might have been possible and pleasant, but not so in ours. She is an anachronism that we resent. The fault may be with us, but the fact remains, that we could not tolerate a Mrs. Berry in the flesh. . . .

A gentleman who loved his Lamb and relished his Dickens would put up with her for the sake of her wit and originality, accepting her as a possible character, which I am not disposed to do. But no young girl, with even less of Lucy's refinement, could submit to her gross indelicacy in that scene between them in the Isle of Wight. We know how reticent and shy young girls have become since Juliet's day; still more so young brides with the most intimate of their sex—their mothers and their sisters; how easily affronted are their susceptibilities by the slightest trending towards ground they so savagely regard as sacred. It is as much as one's life is worth almost to speak to a very young bride about her married life; above all, if she be deeply enamoured of her husband, and for her mother to seek to unveil it would be sacrilege. . . . This reproach I make to Lucy is not only in the case of her tolerance of Mrs. Berry's coarse talk, but in the occupation it enters her mind to allot her undeclared lover, Lord Montfalcon. I reproach, in fact, Mr. Meredith, with the entire creation, all the more so as she is the only girl he has drawn upon the old wearisome lines of masculine taste, of the eternal old-fashioned ivy-type, common-place, loving and pretty, without character or interest apart from her second in the immortal duet with his breathless love. She is charming, as all creatures lovely to look upon and purely natural must be charming; but the freshness of youth and the pleasant daisy-and-buttercup flavour vanished with the years and increasing domestic cares, what would there have remained in her to interest us and satisfy a soaring nature like Richard's?

This is, on the whole, a very reasonable estimate of Lucy and is in tune with criticism generally. It has the additional value of being a woman's estimate. Men and women are alike in thinking that Lucy is Meredith's most conventional heroine; but perhaps Miss Lynch, when she goes on to speak of Clara Middleton, is more of the woman than the critic. She writes:

In all fiction there is not another girl so enchanting and healthily intelligent as Clara Middleton—none described like her. In addition to the attractions of birth, breeding, and beauty which the writer thoroughly relishes, are those of sensibilities that can be delicate without affectation, a delightful wit untainted by smartness, singular good taste and tact, and honesty of soul. Here is a sparkling

Photograph by courtesy of 'The Bystander.'] [*From the minature by Mr. Herbert Bedford.*

CLARA MIDDLETON.

'Just the whiff of an idea of a daughter of a peccadillo-Goddess.'

[*To face p.* 246.

young woman as clear as daylight, as fresh as the morning dew, beautiful to look upon, as Meredith's women always are, sweet and bewitching without any shabby tricks of mind or habit, who at the same time thinks for herself, a rare virtue in the male novelist's heroines. She is all warm blood and variable moods, as befits her age and sex, but never once untrue to the finest instincts of maidenhood, and unerring in her judgment. She is not perfect, her accomplishments are not enumerated, we never find her playing Beethoven or reading the stars, and somehow without one word having been said upon the subject, we get the impression that she is a young woman of intellectual resources, and qualified to pronounce upon the subjects that engage the minds of sages and artists, while the music of youth runs blithely through her veins, and her feet are nimble in a race with a school-boy.

Perhaps the most comprehensive survey of 'The Women of Meredith' yet attempted was Mr. Garnet Smith's long and closely written essay with that title in the *Fortnightly* of May, 1896. It is indeed so finely spun in warp and woof that it is not easy to make quotation from it; and none too easy to gather the drift of it, as the writer has packed too much criticism and study into too little space. Of Clara he writes:

Clara Middleton is a Cecilia, but capable of some strength; English, but enlivened by Irish blood. She has pledged herself to Sir Willoughby, the Egoist, the spoiled favourite of society, in ignorance, before her character is formed. The Egoist is rather the Paternal Despot, the Autolater; chiefly, the Sentimental Egoist, therefore womanish, and requiring that his betrothed shall be weakly womanish, adorned with sentimental attributes, characterless. Clara, outwearied by the monotonous sentimentality of his love-speeches, grows critical, detects in him the sentimental egoist. Hungering for liberty, she must make account of restraining honour and cowardice, and comes to more or less clear recognition that to be honourable, dutiful, is to outrage and deform her nature. Learning that the Egoist had been already detected, that a previous betrothed had taken courageous flight with a courageous comrade, she looks about for such a comrade. Vernon Whitford, no sentimentalist, only proffers reasonable advice, bids her know her own mind, rely on decisive courage. . . . Mr. Meredith, condemning the Egoist to self-punishment, passes a favourable verdict on Clara and Vernon, takes them under his protection. Clara, if, like Cecilia, she dallies with the ideal of the disengaged mind, if she reveals herself weak and sentimental and womanish, and such as man has made of her sex, has not fluttered all too cowardly. Like Sandra, Rhoda, and Diana, she has educated herself to the perception that if most men are weak and tyrannous, some few are unselfish, serviceable, and strong, able to be helpmates; that woman, as she is constituted at present, is incapable of self-reliant freedom, needs a sustaining helpmate. Vernon bears the due stamp; Vernon, at least, has reason enough for two, and the pair between them may possibly compass some measure of serviceable strength.

Of Rhoda Fleming Mr. Garnet Smith says:

Rhoda Fleming, like Sandra, is a child of nature, strong, very natural. Not of 'the comfortable classes,' a farmer's daughter, she has thus escaped, even as Sandra, the deformation of training to cowardice. Rhoda is proffered passionate love by strong Robert; but Rhoda is a savage, freedom-loving virgin. She has some idea, indeed, that the love of a dainty 'gentleman' would be preferable to that of a rough Robert, but her passion and pride are fixed on her weak sister Dahlia; and Dahlia is betrayed by a 'gentleman.' 'It is ignorance that leads to the unhappiness of girls. How can girls know what men are?' she cries. She will right her sister at all hazards. Stern, bitterly strong, she achieves that which she judges to be just, rights her sister most wrongly, thwarts the repentance of her sister's lover and beloved. . . . There is tragedy in Rhoda's strenuousness in well-meaning error. . . . Mr. Meredith—ardent match-maker on philosophic principles—is desirous that men and women shall be strong and passionate in love, that so they may be helpful to each other and the world; and as condition of helpfulness he posits that first they shall understand each other. The women of the comfortable classes do not understand men, he is sure, because they are educated to be ignorant; Rhoda, not of these, does not understand Robert because, wholly untutored for good or ill, she is ignorant that the strong man can help her. Robert knows that she can help him, can reclaim his passionate strength from vicious waste; Rhoda comes to know that without his help her strength runs out to error. Let them mate, and either is helpmate to the other, and their joint sagacities will hit right action in the white; the pair are serviceable to the world. Add two wasteful strengths together, and you get due economy, it would seem. Or rather, perhaps, their added strengths will be mutually corrective.

It is in the treatment of such a character as Dahlia Fleming that we are reminded of what the unsentimental Meredith may be said to owe to the sentimental Richardson. Clarissa Harlowe made Diana and Sandra possible, and Richardson on the moral issue was as much ahead of his age as Meredith was of his on the intellectual. As an able but anonymous writer in *Macmillan's Magazine* of March, 1902, shows very persuasively, Richardson and Meredith come together in their treatment of the unmated woman with a sympathy

Photograph by courtesy of 'The Bystander.'] [*From the miniature by Mr. Herbert Bedford.*

RHODA FLEMING.

'She has a steadfast look in her face. She doesn't look as if she trifled.'

[*To face p.* 248.

we look for, with little hope of finding, in early Victorian fiction, and with none at all in eighteenth-century fiction outside of Richardson. In the days of Richardson and later, pursuit and conquest, with 'the rapture of pursuing' as the prize and not the conquest, represented the relationship of the sexes, rather than that state of 'duel' which Meredith takes as typical of his own time, and a great advance on the age preceding. A consequence was that the unpursued female was an object of scorn: she who was betrayed by the male hunter, run to earth, and then abandoned, had at least the dismal satisfaction of having been pursued! Thus the 'old maid' grew into a stock figure of fiction, represented as a pitiful, ogling creature, manœuvring blatantly for the attention of the males and corroded with jealousy of her female friends: in brief, an object of heartless contempt. So we find her in Fielding and only less so in Dickens, both novelists representing faithfully the norm of their age. As the writer in *Macmillan's* aptly observes:

We can easily imagine what either of them would have made of Lætitia Dale in 'The Egoist.' Lætitia is a spinster, decidedly faded, who has cared, and allowed it to be known that she cared, for a man who has flirted with her and thrown her over. When that man brings a younger and brighter rival on the scene, we might expect some reminiscence of the convention of Fielding and Dickens. But Mr. Meredith never for a moment allows Lætitia to appear ridiculous. In her explanation of her position to Clara there is an accent of real dignity. 'Ten years back, I thought of conquering the world with a pen. The result is that I am glad of a fireside, and not sure of always having one, and that is my achievement. Last year's sheddings from the tree do not form an attractive garland. Their merit is that they have not the ambition. I am like them.'

Another point is suggested by the relations of Lætitia with her rival, and other groupings of women which will occur to any reader of Mr. Meredith's work. That two women can be in love with the same man, and be loyal, just, and forbearing to each other; that the loss of youth and charm, and the empire that they give, may be accepted with temper and dignity, are conceptions quite as familiar in modern novels as they are to the observer of ordinary life. But that they are so, is surely due, in some measure at least, to the influence of Richardson. . . .

Again and again in Mr. Meredith's books there is the perception of what a woman may owe to a woman. We remember how that blunt Englishwoman, Janet Ilchester, met the Princess Ottilia, and 'her first radiant perception of an ideal in her sex.' We remember the patriotic comradeship of Vittoria and Laura Piaveni, and that episode when Sandra, an innocent outcast on the London streets, craves pitifully for a woman's arms about her and a woman's tenderness.

Although there is much that might be written and more that might be quoted, of such wonderfully different female characters as the Countess de Saldar and Lady Charlotte—which latter Mr. Garnet Smith likens to the heroines of George Sand—of Georgiana Powys and the Pole sisters, of 'Mrs. Mel' and Laura Piaveni, of Janet Ilchester, the Princess Ottilia, Cecilia Halkett, Jenny Denham, Renée de Croisnel, Nataly, Nesta, Mrs. Lovell, Aminta, Carinthia Jane, Chloe—'one of Mr. Meredith's chosen ladies, very loving, much enduring, smiling for all wounds, gentle, decorous, distinguished,' says Mrs. Meynell—and the many other strongly individualised women of Meredith's fiction, it is impossible here to pursue the subject, interesting and alluring though it be, into the detail of these characters, which, of course, have already been under discussion in other chapters of this work. The mere mention of their names is enough to remind the reader already acquainted with them—if such reminder were ever necessary—how marvellously rich, fresh and unconventional is the gallery in which the portraits of Meredith's women characters are assembled. His portraiture of womenkind is certainly unique in modern fiction.

But before leaving the subject there is one character, concerning whom something further may be noted—Clotilde von Rüdiger. Like Diana, like the tragic Chloe also, Clotilde is studied from life, 'only more so.' 'The Tragic Comedians' is a human document; the remarkable woman whose character is so remorselessly analysed in it, and against whom the novelist pronounces formal judgment while showing her in a light that warms her humanly to us, is still alive, or was living at a very recent date. In the story the novelist has adhered closely to the facts as they are known, and as Mr. James Huneker, the brilliant American critic, proves in his article on 'A Half-Forgotten Romance' (New York *Bookman*, October, 1907), though he declares that Meredith has not been as faithful to the 'well-known story' as he might have been. Mr. Huneker's paper, which is one of great interest to all Meredithians, opens with a description of a scene in a German restaurant in New York some twenty years ago, where he saw for the first time 'the Red Countess,' a striking and admirable figure of a woman. 'She must have been in the forties, and the contour of her finely moulded head, her aristocratic bearing and the air of one accustomed to command' attracted his attention. She was none other than the Countess Shevitch, formerly the Princess Racowitza, originally Helena von Doënniges, the original of Clotilde. Her husband for political reasons was self-exiled in New York, where both were then supporting themselves by their pens—the Countess had written a book entitled 'Rags,' depicting the seamy side of New York life—but soon after this time they returned to Europe on the Count regaining possession of his estates, and their home at Munich, according to Mr. Huneker, 'is a magnet for the literary, musical and artistic elements of that delightful city on the green river Isar.'

Quickly to summarise the facts that mainly concern us: Helena von Doënniges was the daughter of a General of that name, Bavarian Ambassador to Switzerland, and both her parents were extreme Protestant types. She was 'educated in a Hebrew-hating house,' as Mr. Huneker—whom one suspects of Hebrew origin—puts it. At this time Ferdinand Lassalle (Dr. Alvan of 'The Tragic Comedians') was 'the fine flower of the Jewish-German; a thinker, a born leader, and one of the handsomest men of his day.' Bismarck feared and respected him, and, though leader of the German Democratic party, he had many friends among the eminent public men of the day. His father, moreover, was rich, and Ferdinand himself was one of the most brilliant men at the bar. There were rumours that he was dissolute, and though Mr. Huneker shows how unfounded and slanderous such stories must have been, this was doubtless the cause of Helena's parents opposing with every device and force the union of their daughter with this man. The facts of Lassalle's relationship with the Countess Hatzfeldt (the Baroness Lucie of the novel) are set forth as follows by Mr. Huneker:

A few years later he became immersed in the legal affairs of Countess Hatzfeldt, who, desiring to sever her marriage with a gay husband, employed the young lawyer with the eloquent tongue. If Helena von Doënniges was his fate, so was this Hatzfeldt woman, who stood by him in all his troubles, always playing the friend—some deny she was anything else—and giving him an annuity of 7,000 thalers for winning the case against her husband, that gave her a share in large landed estates. But there was a disagreeable occurrence during the progress of the trial. Count Hatzfeldt presented a certain feminine acquaintance of his with an annuity bond of £1,000 value. Lassalle, they say, instigated the pursuit of both bond and lady and secured the former for the

Countess. His companions in the undertaking were arrested, indicted, condemned to prison. Ferdinand escaped only after a trial in Cologne, in 1848, and because of his irresistible address in the court-room. Nevertheless, the story of the stolen *casette* stuck to him, and coupled with the fact that he had been imprisoned six months for participation in the socialist riots at Düsseldorf in 1846, his reputation was too much for the Von Doënniges. Wagner disliked him; some say he was jealous of his personal success. Von Bülow, the pianoforte virtuoso, admired him, though Lassalle offended him when he declared that Cosima von Bülow was a blue-stocking. 'Citizen of the world,' as he delighted to call himself, Lassalle was at the height of his powers, intellectual and physical, when he was introduced to Helena von Doënniges.

This fateful meeting was some time in January, 1862, the lovers having first heard of each other's attractions—her 'gold-crested' beauty, his wit and eloquence—from mutual friends. Mr. Huneker goes on to explain why Helena was attracted to Ferdinand, in these terms:

Just because Lassalle was abused at home for a Jew, a demagogue and a man who was said to live on the bounty of a titled woman—the latter was a false assertion—just because of these well-nigh inscrutable barriers, the capricious young person fell in love with him; while he, desirous of settling in life and not blandly indifferent to the social flesh-pots of the proud Munich family, assumed the attitude of the accepted conqueror. Mr. Meredith gives an electric presentment of the first meeting; but for a more sober, more truthful rendering of the same incident, it is better to go to Helena von Doënniges-Shevitch herself. She published in Breslau, 1879, a little volume entitled *Meine Beziehungen zu Ferdinand Lassalle* (My Relations with Ferdinand Lassalle). . . . There are many *lacunæ* in this confession of an unhappy woman, yet the impression of sincerity is unmistakable; too much so for Mr. Meredith, who was in search of a human document over which he could play his staccato wit and the sheet-lightnings of his irony.

It will be noticed that the American critic is no admirer of Meredith, and it must be his prejudice against the novelist that makes him declare the latter has distorted facts while he presents the 'facts' himself precisely as they are to be read in 'The Tragic Comedians.' But it is interesting thus to notice how the actual story of the two chief personages in this historic love-drama runs with Meredith's fiction. Mr. Huneker proceeds to summarise from Helena's published confessions, and judge ye if the results are not precisely an epitome of the same episodes in 'The Tragic Comedians':

[*After the painting of Franz von Lenbach.*

CLOTHILDE OF 'THE TRAGIC COMEDIANS.'

Helena von Doënniges, who married the Prince Racowitza after he had encountered her lover Lassalle in a duel which ended fatally for the latter, and who afterwards became the Countess Shevitch.

[*To face p.* 252.

We learn from Helena that she was no novice at flirtation, and that, like many girls of high spirit, she refused to be auctioned off to the highest bidder by her worldly parents. She resolved to marry Lassalle. There were cries of indignation. She was sent to Switzerland, but at the Righi she contrived to meet Lassalle. Contemporaneous with her passion for him, she permitted the amiable attentions of a young Wallachian prince, Von Racowitza, 'a Danube osier with Indian-idol eyes,' as Meredith calls him. This prince, affectionate, good-hearted, rich, was the choice of Helena's parents. She told him that she loved Lassalle and that she intended to marry him. The prince concurred in her plans. He was a nice youth and as pliant as a reed. Finally, at Geneva, in the summer of 1864, seeing that she would be sequestrated by her father, she left his roof and went to Lassalle's hotel, accompanied by her faithful servant, Marie-Thérèse—a venal wretch, as she found out later.

Then Lassalle assumed his most operatic attitude. Elopement? Never! Either you come to me, a gift from your father's hands——! You may guess the pose of the fiery orator. Bewildered, the girl could not understand that the man feared the loss of political prestige if he carried off the daughter of a prominent government official. So he procrastinated—those whom the gods hate they make put off the things of to-day until to-morrow. Proudly—for Lassalle's pride was veritably satanic—he returned Helena to a family friend—she refused to go home—and her parents were summoned. There was a painful interview between the mother and Lassalle—Helena in the background—one that would make a magnificent fourth act for an ambitious dramatist.

What follows in Mr. Huneker's words is equally fact for fact with the sequence of the novelist's story, with the added detail as to the venal Thérèse:

Lassalle kept his temper and went away decidedly the hero of the occasion. Alas! he also left Helena to the tender mercies of two enraged parents. The General entered cursing and actually dragged his daughter by the hair through the dark avenues to her home. Locked up, without the slightest hope of reaching Lassalle—she was told that he had immediately left the city—threatened with severe personal abuse, for General von Doënniges was an old-style Teutonic father, the wretched girl lost all hope. Daily was she upbraided by her parents, by her sister and brother. The entire family battery was trained on her, and as she despaired of Lassalle—she was assured by forged proofs that he was glad to get rid of her—and was sick in body as well as soul, she capitulated. She promised not to see him. What she didn't know was that Lassalle was raising heaven and earth to get at her; that he had appealed to Church, State, to the Court itself; that he had recruited an army of friends, and, finally, that he had bribed the unspeakable Thérèse, Helena's maid, with 180 francs to carry a letter, planning an escape, to her mistress. Thérèse took the letter to the General and was given 20 francs, thus selling the poor girl for £8. Police guarded the house. Negotiations were forced on Von Doënniges by the now aroused Lassalle, who realised what a mistake he made when he had juggled with fortune, no matter what his exalted motives.

So to the end the novelist is faithful to the 'well-known story': the challenge from Lassalle to General von Doënniges, the acceptance of the same by Helena's princely lover, the 'Indian Bacchus,' and the death of Lassalle on August 31, 1864, in the agonies of peritonitis caused by the bullet of the timid, inexperienced prince. Mr. Huneker, referring to Helena's own confession, now carries the story to its conclusion, and throws a side-light on the character of the woman and the circumstances in which she was placed, that is distinctly valuable by way of corrective criticism as to the novelist's own reading of Clotilde's mind and heart:

And now our credulity must be strained. Six months after Lassalle's interment, Helena von Doënniges, hating her parents, at war with the world and herself, turned to the only friend she had in all Germany—Yanko von Racowitza. He was half dying. The shock of events had been too much for his frail, sensitive nature. In pity and as a terrible penance, Helena outraged the world by marrying the slayer of her lover. Five months later she buried him. . . . Meredith depicts Clotilde as 'the imperishable type of that feminine cowardice' to which he says all women are trained. This may be true of the characters in the book, not of Helena. Young women who are imprisoned and stuffed with lies about their lover are not cowardly if they weaken, especially after the shocking experience Helena had undergone with Lassalle. She had, brave as she was, put all to the test and had lost. Is it any wonder that her nerves played her false when the man—as she thought—had deserted her? At least she cannot be compared with the lady in Browning's 'Statue and the Bust.' Helena greatly dared.

And behind all this really tragic romance (not a tragic comedy) was something the English novelist forgot—the mating of a young man with a young woman; which is, whether we subscribe to Schopenhauer's view or not, the most significant fact in the life of our planet. The world was well lost for love by Lassalle; for Helena von Doënniges nothing remained but the mastication of Dead Sea fruit. When we understand, we sympathise.

While Meredith is in some sort an unsympathetic optimist, Mr. Huneker would appear to be a sympathetic pessimist, but as regards

Clotilde he does the novelist the injustice of taking him at his word. Here Meredith suffers at times, womanlike. The American critic is right in quoting the novelist as to the 'imperishable type of feminine cowardice'—woman's cardinal sin, as courage is her greatest virtue, according to Meredith—but while the illustration of this is the obvious aim of the novel, the author has contrived to give so large a view to the character of Clotilde, to light it from so many sides, that the lasting impression is not the mere memory of another lesson in 'feminine cowardice,' but of a strong, passionate, impulsive woman, foredoomed to tragic life, capable of great love and great sacrifice. Indeed, a curious feature of Clotilde is that she is often beyond the control of the novelist, who allows her to do and say the things that win our sympathies, while condemning her when he plays the part of chorus. Surely the sympathy of every reader is with Clotilde when, warm with love for Dr. Alvan and ready for any sacrifice, the hero is true to his theatrical star and returns her to her parents, that he may give later an exhibition of his giant power in winning her from them by legitimate methods. Emphatically, after that Clotilde has every honestly human heart on her side, and Meredith makes us feel this, while still theorising on the 'cowardice' theme: in a word, the novelist is here stronger than the philosopher, though the latter had hoped for the ascendency!

The last word on Meredith's womenkind may be given to Mr. Garnet Smith, who thus sums up his long and intimate study already quoted:

> Mr. Meredith has conceived a great distaste for what he takes to be the Hanoverian or early Victorian type of woman; and, accordingly, since individuality, character, rests in divergence from type, presents his heroines as having at least the instinct and desire to be wholly divergent from this type of his abomination. We were told long ago that there is a constant feud between the philosopher and the poet, the moralist and the artist. If the moralist were to have his way; if all men and women were what he would have them be; monotony would ensue, the artist's occupation would be gone. Happily for Mr. Meredith, the artist, his heroines range freely between the extremes he poses, have their varying moods of submission and revolt, of relapse to the detested and aspiration to the desired type—are so vivid, indeed, in their seasons of aspiration and revolt that the men they meet seem but as dull foils. And, alas! if Mr. Meredith, the novelist, were to have his way! For would not the artist then have to set about presenting heroines individually, characteristically divergent from his desired type? To escape the dilemma, one might perchance take refuge in the theory

that women are 'of mixed essences shading off the divine to the considerably lower,' as Mr. Meredith somewhere writes; that there are different spiritual species of the genus woman, recurrent in each and every age under changeful disguises. But if the moralist is to have his way, then he must constrain the artist to win the ear of young men and maidens, that so the Meredithian woman may be demanded and supplied. Youth, however, as Mr. Meredith knows, requires simple, decisive directness; and Mr. Meredith is complex and indecisive just because he takes careful philosophic account of truth and life. Is it, or is it not, a paradox that he is less likely to win the ear of young England in proportion to his wisdom? True wisdom, at least, is always complex and given to self-contradiction; and Mr. Meredith at some time or other reconsiders and attenuates all the more trenchant of his statements. Whereby he further renders nugatory such critical restatements as are all too simple and decisive.

By permission of Messrs. Smith, Elder & Co.] OTTILIA. *[From the drawing by George du Maurier in the 'Cornhill.'*

I saw her standing with a silver lamp raised in her right hand to the level of her head, as if she expected to meet obscurity. She was like a statue of twilight.
—*Harry Richmond.* Chapter XXV.

[The artist has made a mistake as to the hand in which Ottilia carried the light; a not uncommon error when drawing on wood, the picture having to be drawn reversed.]

[To face p. 256.

To attempt a [illegible] a task that no one [illegible] that is most wh[illegible] octave volume. [illegible] One may doubt [illegible] times drawn forth [illegible] on that of Meredith [illegible] by the critics that [illegible] literary interest.

There is something [illegible] were long neglected [illegible] steadily enhancing the few and [illegible] only here and there [illegible] critics discovered that [illegible] and in some way [illegible] switched their search [illegible] craft and, lo, his poetical [illegible] light! Truly, volumes might be collected [illegible] Meredith's verse and [illegible]

XI

HIS POETRY

Earth made herself a laureate, to bring
  The hearts of all her children to the light:
  She took a meteor in the tracks of flight
To be his brain—in jewels scattering.

So that with lovelier cadence he might sing
  She gave him of the voices of the night.
  And there was nothing hidden from his sight
In all the tale of man's imagining.

Earth's minstrel! You have chanted to and fro,
  The boon companion of the wandering wind,
For you have tarried where love's roses grow
  And soared where eagles would be stricken blind:
  From rapture to profundities of mind;
And there you found the wand of Prospero.

HENRY BAERLEIN in the *Daily Chronicle.*

To attempt a study of Meredith's poetry in a single chapter were a task that no one familiar with his subject would essay. Yet all that is most worthy of his poetry would fill a comparatively small octavo volume. Its importance is out of all proportion to its bulk. One may doubt if so small a body of poetical writing has in modern times drawn forth one half of the criticism which has been lavished on that of Meredith. Of late years it has been far more discussed by the critics than his prose, and bids fair to swamp the novels in literary interest.

There is something of the caprice of fashion in this. His poems were long neglected, and while his reputation as a novelist was steadily enhancing, the few and slender volumes of his verse had only here and there a discerning reader. Then one by one the critics discovered that this master of the art of fiction was not less, and in some ways more, a master of the art of poetry, so they switched their searchlights on to what had erstwhile been his darker craft and, lo, his poetical barques were now seen sailing in a blaze of light! Truly, volumes might be compiled from the criticism of Meredith's verse and of high merit, for the criticism of poetry is apt to bring out what is best in its writers. It has produced, for instance, so notable a work as Mr. G. M. Trevelyan's 'Poetry and Philosophy of George Meredith,' a piece of brilliant exposition which ranks with the best in its class; worthy of its subject and the splendid traditions its author has inherited.

Clearly, then, there can be no attempt in this present chapter at a deliberate and definite study of Meredith's poetry, especially as Mr. Trevelyan's work must be familiar to every student; but it is possible to present here, within the compass of a single chapter, a useful contribution to the criticism of the poet, by passing in review the opinions of all the noteworthy critics, and so to arrive at some general notion of the trend of that body of criticism. In order to achieve even this, it will be necessary, I find, to set limits to the chapter, which I imagine Mr. Trevelyan would approve, for he declares that 'poetical inspiration and intellectual power are developed each to the same degree,' in Meredith's poetry, whereas 'in most writers one is the handmaid of the other.' Nay, more than this, 'in Mr. Meredith they contend or unite on equal terms.' This means that poetical power and intellectual power are different forms of energy and may be considered apart. I am none too certain of the truth of this; it is a proposition capable of much discussion. But this, I think, will be allowed; the æsthetics, the literary technique of poetry, comprehended in the wider and nobler conception of 'poetical power,' is capable of treatment apart from the philosophy, the teaching, or the 'intellectual power,' if you will, of the poetry. To separate from the criticism of Meredith's poetry what concerns only its æsthetics and what its philosophy is not entirely practicable, so closely has criticism applied itself to the poetry as a unified expression of the philosopher's mind. But if in culling some flowers of literary criticism I gather also some sprigs of philosophical criticism, the chapter which is to follow on Meredith's philosophy can well stand the loss, so rich a store is ready for garnering there.

Criticism is very far indeed from being harmonious in the matter of the novelist's poetry; farther from harmony, if possible, than in respect to the poet's prose. Yet there is not one writer who is not prepared to concede to Meredith the occasional achievement of the highest. Indeed the sum-total of the criticism of the poetry is on a par with that of the prose: an artist capable of the best, achieving it sometimes, failing oftener than he succeeds, but wiping out all his failures in the greatness of his successes. As a consequence, criticism would make quite a small selection of Meredith's poetry which is assured of immortality; but it would still be sufficient to keep his name among England's true poets, though not among the greatest. As we proceed we shall note what are the poems, what the qualities of the poet, that justify this opinion.

That the author of 'The Ordeal of Richard Feverel' is a poet, is patent to any reader without the need to turn to his books of verse for proof. Indeed, some critics are tempted to declare him more of a poet in his novels than he is in his poems. 'He has the poet's concrete vision,' says Mr. Brownell, alluding to his prose; but his poetic faculty, though 'very clear and very distinguished,' as 'exhibited in his formal verse' is 'perhaps too surcharged with significance to have the plastic interest essential to verse.' In this judgment Mr. Brownell is by no means alone. One of the finest studies of the poetry was published in the *Times* on the celebration of the eightieth birthday, and there we find this point advanced with more precision, but with special reference to the poet's interpretation of Nature, or Earth:

He does, perhaps, teach and preach and argue about her a little too much, but no one can make the surrender to the spell of her beauty more completely than he. That may be known indeed through the novels to those who have never read a line of his verse. And, fiercely as he likes to declare his adhesion to the bare facts of her, he will take her beautiful things and give them back to us drenched with a dew of human emotion that might come from Keats himself. Who that has ever read of it has forgotten the stream that ran through Beckley Park, whose 'view was sweet and pleasant to Evan Harrington as winding in and out, to east, to north, it wound to embowered hopes in the lover's mind, to tender dreams.' Of the 'Golden lie the meadows: golden run the streams' of Richard Feverel there is no need to ask the question, nor of much else. It is true that there is nothing in the poems quite so perfect as these enchanted islands of the novels; and it is strange, as some of his admirers think, that his greatest handling of the human drama should be no novel but a set of sonnets, and his nearest approaches to that beauty which is the visible form of the harmony of Heaven and Earth and the Human Soul should not be poems at all but prose passages in the novels. Still, the poet of 'Love in the Valley,' 'The Lark Ascending,' 'The Woods of Westermain,' 'The Day of the Daughter of Hades,' 'Phœbus with Admetus,' 'Melampus,' 'The South-Wester,' 'The Thrush in February,' is a great poet; not only, in his own phrase, of the 'Joy of the Earth,' but also of her beauty. It is true that he never attains to the divine spontaneity with which the greatest men have handled Nature. Here, as everywhere in him, the intellect overweights not only the imagination but even the soul, so that he cannot attain to that melodious union of all the forces which supreme poetry demands. He seems too often to be giving us the fresh observation, the original thought, which had the making of a great poem or great passage in them; but it is not made.

This feeling of failure may be due chiefly and inevitably to the Celtic strain in the character of the poet, as I think I have endeavoured elsewhere to illustrate. The Celt stands for failure and derives his romantic interest from the falling short of supreme achievement. The late Grant Allen in his study of 'The Celt in English Art,'—*Fortnightly*, February, 1891,—remarked that:

> Our fairy lore is in large part Celtic, as is also the great mass of our ballad poetry: the touch of fancy, of beauty, of melancholy, of pathos, of the marvellous, the mysterious, the vague, the obscure in all our literary work descends to us as an heirloom from the elder and less successful race in these islands. From it we derive our Carlyles and our Merediths.

And towards the conclusion of the same article he wrote:

> One day this last summer, I came straight back from Bruges, and fresh from my Memlings, looked again at the Briar Rose. How exquisite, how sad, how tender, how soulful! The deep melancholy of the Celtic temper—so human, so humanising—the rich dower of a conquered race, long oppressed and ground down, speaks forth with mute eloquence from every storied line of it. Our sweetest songs are those that tell of saddest thought. From Ossian and Llywarch Hln to Burne-Jones and George Meredith, Celtic art in all forms has struck that note most consistently.

Naturally most of the critics have instituted comparisons or likenesses between the poetry and the prose, so that the poet has probably suffered here from having furnished in his prose fiction certain standards by which he may be judged. Thus we find W. E. Henley writing in 'Views and Reviews':

> His verse has all the faults and only some of the merits of his prose. Thus he will rhyme you off a ballad, and to break the secret of that ballad you have to take to yourself a dark lantern and a case of jemmies. I like him best in 'The Nuptials of Attila.' If he always wrote as here, and were always as here sustained in inspiration, rapid of march, nervous of phrase, apt of metaphor, and moving in effect, he would be delightful to the general, and

[From the drawing by Sir John Millais in 'Once a Week.'

THE HEAD OF BRAN.

Princes seven, enchaining hands,
  Bear the live head homeward.
Lo! it speaks, and still commands;
  Gazing far out foamward.
—*George Meredith.*

[*To face p.* 260.

that without sacrificing on the vile and filthy altar of popularity. Here he is successfully himself, and what more is there to say? You clap for Harlequin, and you kneel to Apollo. Mr. Meredith doubles the parts, and is irresistible in both. Such fire, such vision, such energy on the one hand and on the other such agility and athletic grace are not often found in combination.

This is the merit and distinction of art: to be more real than reality, to be not nature but nature's essence. It is the artist's function not to copy but to synthesise; to eliminate from that gross confusion of actuality which is his raw material whatever is accidental, idle, irrelevant and select for perpetuation that only which is appropriate and immortal. Always artistic, Mr. Meredith's work is often great art.

While Henley's remark as to the obscurity of the ballad form, where directness and simplicity are the first essentials, is true on the whole, and as intended by the critic, it does not apply generally, and indeed no criticism applies generally, to Meredith. Swinburne, for instance, in his 'Essays and Studies,' declares that Rossetti's 'Sister Helen' is, 'out of all sight or thought of comparison the greatest ballad in modern English,' and adds that 'perhaps not very far below it, and certainly in a high place among the attempts in that way of living Englishmen, we might class George Meredith's pathetic and splendid poem of "Margaret's Bridal Eve."' Put this with Henley's reference to Meredith's capacity for failure in the ballad form and you have as near an approach as possible to a judgment on almost any aspect of his art.

Just as it would be difficult to convey to one who had not already read the poems for himself any real notion of their beauty by means of quotation, so is it difficult to set down in any general terms a criticism of the poetry. There are about half-a-dozen passages from 'The Woods of Westermain,' 'Love in the Valley,' 'Modern Love,' and 'Melampus' that are certain to be quoted in every article that deals with the poetry. I could prove this literally, if necessary. This does not so much suggest the sheepishness of the critics in following a lead, as the difficulty of illustrating the poetry by quotation. Equally, criticism is apt to diffuse itself in the treatment of certain poems and not of the poetry as a whole. Notable among those who have attempted to present a view of Meredith the poet in terms of general criticism is the veteran of the art, Professor Edward Dowden, who writes as follows in his study of 'Mr. Meredith in his Poems' in the *Fortnightly*, March, 1892 (reprinted in 'New Studies in Literature'):

When we have learnt how to straighten out his twisted phrases, to leap his aëry chasms of remote associations, to catch a prospect through his eyelet holes of intelligence to practise a certain legerdemain and keep five balls of meaning a-dance together in the brain—when we have learnt these various things and several others, then the total significance of Mr. Meredith as a poet is found to be good: is found to be sound and sweet and sane, seed for a hopeful sowing and clean wheat for our quern.

Of course, it may be said that the demands which Mr. Meredith makes of his readers are exorbitant, and that a difficult style is necessarily a bad style. A student of the history of literature, however, knows that the charge of obscurity, which is one of the charges most confidently brought by contemporaries, can be finally adjudicated on only by time. It may be sustained, or it may be refuted. To many of his contemporaries Gray was a tangle of difficulties; for critics of authority in a later period Wordsworth and Shelley and Coleridge wrote unintelligible nonsense; and in our own day we have seen the poetry of Robert Browning slowly but surely expounding itself to a generation. Even caviare, it seems, may become a little fly-blown. Perhaps Mr. Meredith's style is difficult; but difficulty is a relative term, and experience should have taught us that this is a point on which it is wise to reserve an absolute judgment. Sword-practice is difficult to those who have not exercised the muscles of the wrist; and some dancers who foot it merrily in the waltz stand grim against the wall looking condemnation at the lifted leg and pointed toe of the *pas de quatre*. If Mr. Meredith can teach young folk to dance to his music, the most reluctant of us will be forced to admit by and by that he has achieved what is the essential thing. . . .

In a dozen volumes of prose the eager student of human nature has told us of his discoveries. Prose is proved by the achievement of his forty years of authorship to be the main stream; verse is no more than a slender affluent. But both are *Dichtung*, and both, it may be added, are *Wahrheit*. Or, to vary our metaphor, the *Dichtung* written in prose is the lake, broad-bosomed, with countless coves and creeks; the *Dichtung* written in verse is a lakelet higher among the hills, less easy of access, but open to the skies and to the passage of the stars, though at times involved in wreathing mists; and a stream runs down from lakelet to lake, connecting the two—for Mr. Meredith's prose is at times such prose as a poet writes, and the thought and feeling expressed in his novels are fed from the contemplations of a poet. His subtlety and his analytic power have in the novels a wider range for play; his faith and hope are more directly expressed in his verse. In both prose and verse his felicities are found in infelicity—or what for the present seems such; his infelicities are found amid felicity; he is at once a most alluring and a most provoking writer.

Mr. Richard Le Gallienne in his well-known monograph describes most happily these provoking and alluring qualities of Meredith's prose, when he says:

He has more than one resemblance to Browning, but he undeniably has one, and that is at once the power and the disregard of form. That he has such power no one can doubt who has read his 'Modern Love,' 'The Meeting,' 'Phœbus with Admetus,' 'Melampus,' or 'Love in the Valley,' but that he no less often exhibits that disregard is unhappily equally certain. At the same time, that less perfect part of Mr. Meredith's poetry is not so as Wordsworth's barren patches are, it is far from barren indeed, it is full of song and flowers, though wild as wild; it is like a mass of rich yarn that awaits the weaver, full of threads of wondrous colour, but still yarn. And so it comes about that we cannot speak of Mr. Meredith's poetry as a whole, as we can of Wordsworth's, wherein division of unmistakable sheep and unmistakable goats is comparatively easy. To select the perfect and abide by that would not only be to leave out a good half of his work, which, whatever its imperfections, is yet full of beauty and power, but would also mean missing a certain peculiarity of flavour which these very poems alone possess. All Mr. Meredith's verse has imagination, music and colour, such as the great among the poets alone bring us, but not all has that orbed completeness which can only come of form. Thus he may be said to give us more poetry than poems, and excepting 'Phœbus with Admetus,' 'Melampus' and one or two more, it would not, I think, be unjust, for the purpose of a broad division, to include all his nature-poetry under the former head. For they read too often like the first drafts of poems, loose in texture, and full of dropped stitches—here a line of masterly compression, there an inorganic stretch of twelve. It is poetry in the ore, all aglitter with gold, but the refiner has been lazy or indifferent. Yet gold it is, gold of Ophir.

The late James Ashcroft Noble was never a critic given to enthusiasms, so we need not be surprised to find him somewhat coldly critical of Meredith's poetry, but his observations are of real importance, and several passages from his essay which appeared in the first edition of Mr. A. H. Miles's admirable work 'The Poets and the Poetry of the Century,' are worthy of consideration:

In speaking of Mr. Meredith's poetry (he writes) the first thing needing to be said is that his prose achievement is a natural growth, while his work in verse is a product of deliberate choice. His speaking voice is an affair of organisation; his singing voice is the result of careful training. Some fervid devotees have had the temerity to place him at the head of living novelists; no admirer, howsoever indiscriminating, would dare to place him even in the front rank of living poets; and yet the qualities which give to his work permanent interest and value are more clearly visible here and there in his verse than in any of his novels, save perhaps in one or two passages, such as the description of the early meetings of Richard Feverel and Lucy Desborough, where the form only is that of prose, while the emotional pitch and imaginative plane are the pitch and plane of poetry. Such a chapter as that entitled 'Ferdinand and Miranda' has the Miltonic essentials of poetry; it is simple, sensuous, passionate; and even a person of very moderate sensibility will be aware in reading it that he is in the presence of a writer with the poet's capacity of feeling and rendering, and possibly or probably, therefore, the poet's command of that medium of utterance in which such capacity naturally expresses itself. If, however, he turns from such a passage to one of Mr. Meredith's slim volumes of verse, his disappointment will probably be great and bitter, unless some rare guidance of happy fortune leads him to the small group of poems of which later on something must be said. Simplicity will reveal itself only too seldom, and though he will discern that sensuousness and passion are less scantily represented, he will often feel that they are so strenuously intellectualised, so tricked out in complexities of elaborated metaphor, as to be deprived of their essential character. . . .

There is much in Mr. Meredith's poetry that is strained, artificial, obscure; there is much that is strong, picturesque, penetrating, but his true individuality is made manifest most clearly and delightfully in those poems in which he deals with the sensuous side of Nature and the homelier conditions of unsophisticated human life. . . . He will never be a popular poet, and yet he has written poems which deserve the best kind of popularity.

Though this is criticism that rings hard and clear, like steel, and not soft and sweet as gold, it is quite true of its kind, and Ashcroft Noble indicates correctly wherein the true poetic Meredith reveals himself. He does not, however, as Mr. Le Gallienne very rightly does, lay stress on the unique character of all Meredith's nature-poetry. Says Mr. Le Gallienne:

The wonderful natural descriptions scattered broadcast over his novels are sufficient earnest of a power in the quality of which he is especially alone. For, his nature-poetry is indeed quite different from any other before known in English literature. And the difference lies in the fact that, while most other poets have sung of Nature in the abstract, have moralised, sentimentalised, transcendentalised her, Mr. Meredith has cared more to sing her as she is in the concrete. His predecessors have, in the main, sung the

[*From the drawing by Sir John Millais in 'Once a Week.'*

THE CROWN OF LOVE.

Unhalting he must bear her on,
  Nor pause a space to gather breath,
And on the height she would be won ;—
  And she was won in death !
  —*George Meredith.*

[*To face p.* **264.**

spirit of Nature; he sings her body, which is the earth, as well—'this Earth of the beautiful breasts.' . . . He sings of Nature, not because he worships her in some vague way afar off, as one might the abstract Woman, but because he has loved and worshipped her as a man his wife, lying in her arms, eye to eye, breath to breath. He has lived with her day by day for many years, he knows all her moods, moods of summer and winter, of joy and travail, strange moods of contradiction hard to bear, and yet alike in one as in another he has never lost his faith that her heart is love—'love, the great volcano.'

It will not be denied that Mr. Le Gallienne here utters sober criticism though its terms are those of frank appreciation. Ashcroft Noble is perhaps too timid of praise though he is never unjust. 'Whenever Mr. Meredith is content to feel Nature rather than to analyse her, he reveals himself as a seer whose every glance is unerring, a singer whose every note is clear and true.' So he thinks, and most critics will endorse his judgment. In the following passage it will be seen that Noble is really at one with Mr. Le Gallienne in the strict letter of criticism, but just escapes being warmed by contact with the poet:

Such poems, or portions of such poems, as 'The Woods of Westermain,' 'The Lark Ascending,' 'Hard Weather,' 'Autumn Even-Song,' to name only four out of many, stand almost alone in modern poetry. Various English poets, for example, have sung of the skylark, but in all of them—with, perhaps, the solitary exception of Hogg—the bird has been more or less spiritualised or moralised: the actual theme has been charged with, and sometimes almost overlaid by, a burden of ethical or intellectual significance supplied by the mind of the human singer rather than inevitably suggested by the mounting minstrel of the sky. Towards the close of the poem just named, Mr. Meredith, like Shelley and Wordsworth, uses the lark as a text for a discourse not less true and beautiful than theirs; but in the earlier verses, he sees, hears, feels the object as in itself it really is, and renders it with an opulence of sensuous and emotional realisation which his predecessors with all their magic fail to achieve. Their poems are lovely; each of them is, indeed, in its own way perfect; but if a man who had never heard the skylark longed to know all the words that could tell him of the rippling rapture of the marvellous music of the air, his lack of one of the most exquisite of all the joys of sense would be supplied more inadequately—or perhaps one ought to say less inadequately—by Mr. Meredith than by either Wordsworth or Shelley. Hogg comes nearer to the bird, but his bounding lyric, fine as it is, might have been written of rumour rather than of the close-loving knowledge, the very absorption of intimacy, which makes itself manifest in every phrase of a song which is itself lark-like.

One of the most charming pieces ever written about Meredith is from the pen of Mr. A. T. Quiller-Couch, and appears in that unique and delightful book 'From a Cornish Window.' It is there given in the form of a racy dialogue between the author and a literary friend, and if, in selecting a brief page or two, I may have sought to preserve its value as criticism at the expense of its charm as witty colloquy, Mr. Quiller-Couch will doubtless forgive me for the end I have in view:

Meredith, if a true poet, is also and undeniably a hard one: and a poet must not only preach but persuade. 'He dooth not only show the way,' says Sidney, 'but giveth so sweet a prospect into the way as will entice any man to enter into it.' . . .

Is Mr. Meredith a persuasive poet? . . . He can be—let us grant—a plaguily forbidding one. His philosophy is not easy; yet it seems to me a deal easier than many of his single verses. I hope humbly, for instance, one of these days, to discover what is meant by such a verse as this:

Thou animatest ancient tales,
To prove our world of linear seed;
Thy very virtue now assails
A tempter to mislead.

Faint, yet pursuing, I hope; but I must admit that such writing does not obviously allure, that it rather dejects the student by the difficulty of finding a stool to sit down and be stoical on. 'Nay,' to parody Sidney, 'he dooth as if your journey should lye through a fayre Vineyard, at the first give you a handful of nuts, forgetting the nut-crackers.' He is, in short, half his time forbiddingly difficult, and at times to all appearances so deliberately and yet so wantonly difficult, that you wonder what on earth you came out to pursue and why you should be tearing your flesh in these thickets.

And then you remember the swinging cadences of 'Love in the Valley'—the loveliest love-song of its century . . . And you swear that no thickets can be so dense but you will wrestle through them in the hope of hearing that voice again, or even an echo of it.

'Melampus,' 'The Nuptials of Attila,' 'The Day of the Daughter of Hades,' 'The Empty Purse,' 'Jump-to-Glory Jane,' and the splendid 'Phœbus with Admetus,'—you come back to each again and again, compelled by the wizardry of single lines and by a certain separate glamour which hangs about each of them. Each of them is remembered by you as in its own way a superb performance; lines here and there so haunt you with their beauty that you must go back and read the whole poem over for the sake of them. Other lines you boggle over, and yet cannot forget them; you hope to like them better at the next reading; you re-read, and wish them away, yet find them, liked or disliked, so embedded in your memory that you cannot do without them. Take, for instance, the last stanza of 'Phœbus with Admetus':

> You with shelly horns, rams! and promontory goats,
>   You whose browsing beards dip in coldest dew!
> Bulls that walk the pasture in kingly-flashing coats!
>   Laurel, ivy, vine, wreathed for feasts not few!
> You that build the shade-roof, and you that court the rays,
>   You that leap besprinkling the rock stream-rent;
> He has been our fellow, the morning of our days;
>   Us he chose for house-mates, and this way went.

The first thing that made this stanza unforgettable was the glorious third line: almost as soon 'promontory goats' fastened itself on memory; and almost as soon the last two lines were perceived to be excellent, and the fourth also. These enforced you, for the pleasure of recalling them, to recall the whole, and so of necessity to be hospitably minded towards the fifth and sixth lines, which at first repelled as being too obscurely and almost fantastically expressed. Having once passed in, I find 'You that leap besprinkling the rock stream-rent,' with its delicate labial pause and its delicate consonantal chime, one of the most fascinating lines in the stanza. And since, after being the hardest of all to admit, it has become one of the best liked, I am forced in fairness to ask myself if hundreds of lines of Mr. Meredith's which now seem crabbed or fantastic may not justify themselves after many readings.

Mr. Quiller-Couch here writes in the true spirit about Meredith's 'obscurity.' Let us always remember that the critics who are most conscious of the poet's defects are those most alive to his merits.

Mr. Macaulay Trevelyan's ingenious description (in 'The Poetry and Philosophy of George Meredith') of how the taste for Meredith's poetry grows on one, is no doubt a record of personal experience, and it is an experience probably general to all the discerning students of the poet. Devoid of all appeals to the popular taste, there is no way else in which his poetry could possibly reach its mark, but for this very reason, once the mark is reached, the work of no other poet can so intimately touch the soul of the reader, none so haunt his ear with fresh, strange melody, in which 'the incommunicable' is by the subtle magic of words conveyed to the receptive mind. Perhaps enough has been said in general in respect to the poet's witchery of words. The criticism of his prose style is, with no great modifications, applicable to his poetry. His use of metaphor is no whit more pronounced, unless it be that the compression of poetry brings one metaphor on the heels of another more quickly than in prose. Mr. Trevelyan characterises very neatly the danger of trying to follow the Meredithian metaphor, in terms which are Meredithian, when he says: 'You are meant to catch the first light that flies off the metaphor as it passes; but if you seize and cling to it, as though it were a post, you will be drowned in the flood of fresh metaphor that follows.' There is no sequence of imagery in the poetry, and he who attempts to read it as an orderly progression is doomed to disappointment and happily so, for its magistral power is derived in large part from the white heat of the words and phrases in which the poet beats out his meaning with splendid swinging hammer-strokes and none too mindful of the sparks that fly off in the process. What Mr. Trevelyan calls 'foreshortening' of phrase, whereby the effect is achieved by a minimum of words, is illustrated in these lines from 'The Young Princess':

> All cloaked and masked, with naked blades,
>   That flashed of a judgment done,
> The lords of the Court, from the palace-door,
> Came issuing silently, bearers four,
>   And flat on their shoulders one.

It is thus that the other lords have fulfilled the lady's word.—'Flat on their shoulders one' (says Mr. Trevelyan) is a memorable instance of Mr. Meredith's foreshortening method. The unessential has been most emphatically banished from the line, and yet it leaves nothing more to be asked or explained. Like the blow of the Matadore, it makes an end.

Our attention will now turn from the general to the particular, that we may see in the criticism of his most characteristic poems what are those qualities it has been found so difficult to express in general terms, chiefly for lack of standards of comparison.

We are already familiar with Kingsley's and Mr. W. M. Rossetti's reviews of the 'Poems' of 1851, to which some attention has been devoted in an earlier chapter. Perhaps it is surprising that in all the later criticism of Meredith's poetry so little has been written about his earliest verse. 'Modern Love' is the favourite starting-point. The tendency has been to dismiss the first collection as mere juvenilia, and this was induced perhaps by the work being so long unobtainable: more than forty years elapsed before its contents were reprinted in the collected edition of the works, issued in 1896–98. The poet's later revision of 'Love in the

Valley '—misnamed in scores of books and reviews 'Love in *a* Valley '—has frequently been regretted, and some day the first version may be restored. It is of that, most probably, that one of Leslie Stephen's daughters is speaking in this note from Maitland's 'Life and Letters' of her father:

> He loved, too, and knew by heart since he had first read it, George Meredith's 'Love in the Valley,' and he made us remark—and this was a rare instance of its kind—the beauty of Mr. Meredith's metres and his mastery over them. As a rule he disliked criticism of technical qualities, and, indeed, disliked being drawn into criticisms of any kind.

York Powell may not have been referring to the first version when he wrote in a letter to Professor Oliver Elton, his biographer, touching an essay of the latter on Meredith:

> You must specially praise 'Love in a Valley,' the most gorgeous piece of rhythmical work and passion. You have left it out. Meredith is a great metrist, but Browning writes poorly as regards musical verse. Meredith has *invented* his great metres.

Stevenson, likewise, would probably be more familiar with the later form of 'Love in the Valley,' of which he wrote from Vailima to Mr. W. B. Yeats, in April, 1894:

> Long since when I was a boy I remember the emotions with which I repeated Swinburne's poems and ballads. Some ten years ago a similar spell was cast upon me by Meredith's 'Love in the Valley'; the stanzas beginning 'When her mother tends her' haunted me and made me drunk like wine, and I remember waking with them all the echoes of the hills about Hyères.

But Turner Palgrave in his personal recollections of Tennyson, contributed to the present Lord Tennyson's 'Life' of his father, leaves us in no doubt that it was the 1851 text of the poem that delighted Tennyson, and evidently disapproves of the altered form of thirty years later. Beyond the notable criticisms quoted in the chapter on 'Early Appreciations' little of importance has been written on the 1851 volume, and when we arrive at later criticism of 'Love in the Valley' we shall find it is always the version appearing in 'Poems and Lyrics of the Joy of Earth' that is in question.

Of 'Modern Love' there is abundance of excellent criticisms. Mr. Swinburne's famous letter to the *Spectator* has been given earlier in the present work. It is from it that Professor Dowden quotes in the following note which I take from his study of 'Mr. Meredith in his Poems':

The most important document in the study of the human heart which Mr. Meredith has given us in verse is doubtless 'Modern Love.' 'Praise or blame,' wrote Mr. Swinburne, 'should be thoughtful, serious, careful, when applied to a work of such subtle strength, such depth of delicate power, such passionate and various beauty' as this. Praise or blame seems each equally needless now; the poem has taken its place; there it is, and there it will remain. The critic's complaint that 'Modern Love' deals with a deep and painful subject on which Mr. Meredith has no conviction to express, was a natural outbreak of human infirmity; we all like to have the issues of a difficult case made clear; we all like to have a problem worked out to its solution. But in art, as in life, it is not always good policy to snatch at a near advantage:

Oh! if we draw a circle premature,
  Heedless of far gain,
Greedy for quick returns of profit, sure,
  Bad is our bargain!

Sometimes it is more for our good that art should put a question courageously than that it should propose some petty answer to the question. In 'Modern Love,' if Mr. Meredith does not prescribe a remedy for the disease of marriage perverted from its true ends—unless that remedy be the general one of more brain, and so more spirit, more righteousness, more beneficence—he at least makes a careful diagnosis of the case. It is something to describe the phases of the malady, and to issue no advertisement of a quack nostrum. And in that silence which precedes one last low cry—'Now kiss me, dear! it may be, now!' does not Mr. Meredith make us feel, with a sense too deep for tears, how Pity pleads for Sin? and is not this something as helpful to us as if he had expressed 'a conviction on a painful subject'?

The earliest study of Meredith's poetry as a whole dates back only some twenty years, and was from the skilled and sympathetic pen of Mr. Arthur Symons, the medium of its publication being, appropriately enough, the *Westminster Review*, of September, 1887. In this Mr. Symons writes as follows concerning 'Modern Love':

Mr. Meredith's longest poem is also, beyond a shadow of doubt (so it seems to us), by far his best work in verse. . . . We have never been able to tell quite what it is that gives to these sonnet-like stanzas (with all their obscurities of allusion and their occasional faults in versification) a certain charm and power which fascinate and fasten upon mind and memory at once. Mr. Meredith has

[*From the drawing by Hablot K. Browne ('Phiz') in 'Once a Week*

THE LAST WORDS OF JUGGLING JERRY.

'Lean me more up on the mound; now I feel it:
  All the old heath-smells! Ain't it strange?
There's the world laughing, as if to conceal it,
  But He is by us, juggling the change.'—*George Meredith.*

[*To face p.* 270.

never done anything else like it; this wonderful style, acid, stinging, bitter-sweet, poignant, as if fashioned of the very moods of these 'modern loves,' reappears in no other poem (except faintly in the 'Ballad of Fair Ladies in Revolt'). The poem stands alone, not merely in Mr. Meredith's work, but in all antecedent literature. It is altogether a new thing; we venture to call it the most 'modern' poem we have.

'Modern Love' is a poem of the drawing-rooms; it is tinged throughout with irony; it moves by 'tragic hints.' In the same volume we have a group of 'Poems of the English Roadside,' studies, as they are also termed, of 'Roadside Philosophers.' Here we are in a new atmosphere altogether, an atmosphere in which we can breathe more freely, under the open sky, upon the road and the heath. This little group of homely poems, to which should be added 'Martin's Puzzle,' a poem of the same period, seems to us, after 'Modern Love,' perhaps the most original and satisfying contribution made by Mr. Meredith to the poetry of his time. One poem, at least, is an absolute masterpiece, and of its kind it is almost without a rival. There is a sly and kindly humour in 'The Beggar's Soliloquy,' a quaint wit in 'The Old Chartist,' a humorous wisdom tinged with pathos in 'Martin's Puzzle'; each of these poems is a greater or less success in a line of work which is much more difficult than it looks; but 'Juggling Jerry,' notwithstanding a flaw here and there in the rhythm, quickens our blood and strikes straight from the heart to the heart as only a few poems here and there can do. We said that of its kind it is almost without a rival; we may say, indeed, quite without a rival, outside Burns.

Personally, it is a pleasure to me to find so subtle a critic of poetry as Mr. Arthur Symons enthusiastic for 'Juggling Jerry' when I remember Mr. Le Gallienne's somewhat slighting references to the simple, guileless folk who can admire Meredith in such a vein and think him by that token great. Mr. Le Gallienne is so good a critic himself, discounting always his tendency to let enthusiasm sway his pen at times, that it may seem ungracious to say he is apt to admire the uncommon more because it is uncommon than because it is good. I mean that anything unconventional would receive a welcome from him before he had inquired into its other merits. Admirers of 'Juggling Jerry' need not be disappointed that he is cold to them; and they may approve what he has to say of 'Modern Love' none the less because they would expect it to make peculiar appeal to his tastes. He writes of it in these terms:

'Modern Love' is the one poem of closest kin to Shakespeare's sonnets. The kinship is hardly in the form, which is, without exception, composed of four Petrarchian quatrains, each independent in respect of rhymes; nor is it merely in the 'Shakespearian ring' of the verse. That is a trick soon learnt, and may mean something or nothing. It is simply in 'the fundamental brainwork,' which one feels alive through every line and word of the poem, the spaciousness and strength of the imagination revealed to us by that greatness of metaphor, and that compression of phrase, which marks all great literary art. . . . The last quatrain of the poem alone, if nought else were left, should witness a master. Whether or not the kinship to Shakespeare's sonnets seems a real one to others, or whether it is but an eccentricity of my own judgment, is of little moment; it is only important that 'Modern Love' should be recognised as a great poem of 'tragic life.'

Mr. Le Gallienne's is the voice of the enthusiast; but the late Ashcroft Noble, who had none of the younger man's poetic fervour, or at least never let that flush his criticism, formed a very different opinion of 'Modern Love.' After giving a clear and concise summary of the theme of the poem he declared that 'the dramatic motive is far fetched and fantastic, with no recognisable hold upon the actualities of human nature.' He continues:

The poem as a whole is a morbid conception embodied by a huddling together of strangulated metaphors and hints for epigrams. It is all strain, there is no repose; it lacks the satisfying quality of adequate final expression. When not incompetent critics speak of 'Modern Love' as its author's masterpiece, they deliver themselves of a judgment which is not only fantastic but injurious, because it tends to divert attention from other work which has the very charms of healthy emotion, clear vision, and simple rendering which are here so conspicuously deficient.

Ashcroft Noble has here in mind the aforesaid strictures of Mr. Le Gallienne on those who venture to admire 'Juggling Jerry' and some other of the 'Poems of the English Roadside,' in which unquestionably 'both the matter and the manner are of universal interest,' and so make the universal appeal.

Such universality (says Noble) can be predicated of 'Juggling Jerry,' as it cannot be predicated of 'Modern Love,' and in virtue of it the former poem stands upon a higher plane. The old juggler represents a type so broadly human that it has been, is, and will be familiar to every country and to every age; he may, indeed, without exaggeration be called Homeric, for he is a homely Odysseus who has had his life of wandering, has looked upon the world with shrewd, open eyes, and has acquired the simple wisdom of such an experience. . . .

[From the drawing by Frederic Sandys in 'Once a Week.'

THE OLD CHARTIST.

Now, what is yon brown water rat about,
Who washes his old poll with busy paws?
What does he mean by't?
It's like defying all our natural laws,
For him to hope he'll get clean by't.
* * * * * *
I never found so true a democrat.
Base occupation
Can't rob you of your own esteem, old rat!
I'll preach you to the British nation.
—*George Meredith.*

To face p. 272.

Yonder came smells of the gorse, [illegible]
Golden-tongued [illegible]; it's the [illegible]
Better than [illegible] and pretty,
Is God's [illegible] sharing [illegible]
Lend [illegible] the second [illegible]
All the [illegible]
There [illegible] as if [illegible]
But [illegible] the [illegible]

Whether it [illegible] or not [illegible] such a stanza [illegible] a [illegible] ecstasy of simple [illegible] which [illegible] that we would [illegible] all the recondite [illegible] possession.

Touching the [illegible] Powell, in a [illegible] poetry, says: [illegible] nets." The Elizabethan [illegible] are not Petrarchan [illegible] glory of the [illegible] 'Modern Love' [illegible] the Joy of Earth [illegible] had published [illegible] splendid reception [illegible] Mr. Theodore [illegible] Pattison, and Mr. [illegible] 1883, Mr. Watts-[illegible] balanced enthusiasm of [illegible] quote his article [illegible] wise exposition [illegible] writes of any [illegible] of discovery [illegible] knowledge. But [illegible] of Meredith, whose [illegible] 'It is a comfort [illegible] Earth."' After showing how [illegible] merely to voice their own emotions, never [illegible] the elemental, while others, and even of the [illegible] in the orchestra of [illegible] 'soaring away into cloudy regions instead of [illegible] where' and giving to abstractions a concrete [illegible] Watts-Dunton goes on to say:

Yonder came smells of the gorse, so nutty,
  Goldlike and warm: it's the prime of May.
Better than mortar, brick, and putty,
  Is God's house on a blowing day.
Lean me more up the mound; now I feel it:
  All the old heath-smells! Ain't it strange?
There's the world laughing as if to conceal it,
  But He is by us, juggling the change.

Whether it be 'incommunicable' or not there is something in such a stanza as this—a fulness of life, a keenness of sensation, and ecstasy of simple human enjoyment—which makes some of us feel that we would rather have written it than we would have written all the recondite verses which the coteries hug as their peculiar possession.

Touching the verse form of 'Modern Love,' the late York Powell, in a letter to Professor Oliver Elton, discussing Meredith's poetry, says: 'Don't say (of "Modern Love") "misnamed sonnets." The Elizabethans would have called them "sonnets." They are not Petrarchian sonnets, but that doesn't matter. "There is a glory of the sun, and another glory of the moon."'

'Modern Love' appeared in 1862 and 'Poems and Lyrics of the Joy of Earth' in 1883: a gap of twenty years in which the poet had published no collection of his verse. The new book had a splendid reception, and among the notable critics who hailed it were Mr. Theodore Watts-Dunton, Mrs. Alice Meynell, the late Mark Pattison, and Mr. W. L. Courtney. In the *Athenæum*, July 23, 1883, Mr. Watts-Dunton reviewed the new book with the finely balanced enthusiasm of the clear-minded critic. One could wish to quote his article at some length, so rich is it in allusiveness and wise exposition of the poetic art, for Mr. Watts-Dunton never writes of any particular book without taking his reader on a voyage of discovery whence he returns laden with new treasures of literary knowledge. But here we must confine our attention to his opinion of Meredith, whose 'Poems and Lyrics' he hails with the words: 'It is a comfort to find at last a poet who can sing "The Joy of Earth."' After showing how so many try to sing its misery or merely to voice their own emotions, never coming within sight of the elemental, while others, and even of the great, tune their lyres in the orchestra of 'Nowhere,' imitating Shelley's example of 'soaring away into cloudy regions' instead of singing from 'Somewhere' and giving to abstractions a concrete poetic form, Mr. Watts-Dunton goes on to say:

All that the poet has to do with abstractions, though he had always much better leave them alone, is to do as Shakespeare does—take them and turn them into concretions; for the artist is simply the man who by instinct embodies in concrete forms that which is essential and elemental in nature and in man, the poetic artist being he who by instinct chooses for his concrete forms musical language. And the questions to be asked concerning any work of art are simply these: Is that which is embodied really elemental? and is the concrete form embodying it really beautiful? Any other question is an impertinence. 'Somewhere' being the poet's home, the most awkward results naturally follow if the poet wanders, as so many of our contemporary poets do wander, into 'Nowhere,' the most unpleasant of these results being that when he comes to address us he can sing about nothing and nobody but himself; whereas his highest duty as a singer, to say nothing of his duty as a gentleman, is to keep himself modestly in the background and sing about other people. Mr. Meredith recognises this fact in the most beautiful poem of his volume—'The Lark Ascending.'

Still, Mr. Meredith should bear in mind that he who would sing to us of the joy of earth should first make sure that he has a good voice for singing. Throughout the entire animal kingdom there is, it seems, no subject upon which a vocalist is so apt to deceive himself as upon the quality of his voice. 'It is given to the very frogs,' says Pascal, 'to find music in their own croaking'; and no doubt the looks of self-satisfaction on the face of a croaking frog is scarcely to be matched in nature. Nor, we may rest assured, is there one among the countless verse-mongers of our time who does not find a music in his own lines delightful to himself, though perhaps undiscoverable to other and shorter ears than his own. But the singer of the 'joy of earth' requires a voice of such exceptional power and sweetness that partial failure in such a song should be called partial success.

The descriptions in the first poem in the volume, 'The Woods of Westermain,' are exceedingly vivid and beautiful. . . .

On the whole, the most important poem in the volume is 'The Day of the Daughter of Hades.' Mr. Meredith seems to have an ear for iambic rather than for anapæstic movements, though, for some reason or another, he seems fond of writing in anapæsts. There is no more clear and sharp distinction between poets than that which divides them between poets who have the iambic ear and poets who have the anapæstic. While writers like Keats and Wordsworth in passing from the iambic to the anapæstic movement pass at once into doggerel, writers like Shelley and Mr. Swinburne are so entirely at home in anapæstic movements that even their iambic lines seem always on the verge of leaping into the anapæstic dance.

If verse were simply quintessential prose, then assuredly Mr. Meredith would be one of the most effective poets living. In the art of 'packing a line' he is almost without living equal. Take the following stanzas from the poem called 'Earth and Man':

> He may entreat, aspire,
> He may despair, and she has never heed
> She drinking his warm sweat will soothe his need,
> Not his desire.
>
> *She prompts him to rejoice,*
> *Yet scares him on the threshold with the shroud.*
> He deems her cherishing of her best—endowed
> A wanton's choice.

The two lines italicised are much more than quintessential prose, they are poetry worthy of almost any writer in the English language. But the line which follows them is metrically bad, and bad in the worst way, for it shows that he whose natural instinct, judging from the sonnets in the volume, is to avoid elision and to spread out the syllables of his lines after Keats's fashion, attempts an elision here without having the slightest notion of what is the true nature and function of elision in poetry. And throughout the book there are lines which strike upon the ear like flints:

> She fancied; armed beyond beauty, and thence grew.
> In mind only, and the perils that ensue.
> Hear, then, my friend, madam! Tongue-restrained he stands.

Still, notwithstanding all the rugged lines in this volume, such a poem as 'The Lark Ascending' is enough to show that Mr. Meredith has a true call to express himself in metre. And this is no faint praise, for among those who express, or endeavour to express, themselves in metre, how many have really a call to do so?

Mr. Watts-Dunton concludes his brilliant study by quoting 'The Orchard and the Heath,' of which he says: 'Here the picture is brilliant, the suggested lesson of life healthy, manly, and bracing, and the metrical music as good, perhaps, as Mr. Meredith has achieved.' And his final verdict on 'Poems and Lyrics' is: 'Manliness and intellectual vigour combined with a remarkable picturesqueness are the most noticeable qualities of his volume.'

Mark Pattison, who reviewed the volume of 1883 with even greater intentness on Meredith, bore a name that will be long remembered in the world of scholars, and a criticism from his pen is to-day of the utmost value. To the *Academy*, July 21, 1883, he contributed a most careful review of considerable length, and from this I take several passages with which students of the poetry should be familiar:

What is true of a whole poetic career is also true of any volume of collected pieces composed at long intervals. No one, not even a critic, is always at his best. But in poetry we may go further, and say that the best of any poet is so rare and costly that it is indeed *paucorum horarum*. . . .

It is, therefore, no disparagement to say of the poems in the present volume that they are unequal in poetic merit. They all have the Meredithian quality, but in varying degrees of perfection. They are all out of the same vineyard, but of different vintages. To come to details. 'Love in the Valley,' *e. g.* does not rise in general conception and design above the average level of the 'minor poet' as we know him. For this reason it will probably be one of the most popular. It has also the ordinary fault of the modern English poetry—diffuseness, the beating out of a small particle of metal into too thin foil. Yet 'Love in the Valley' is redeemed from commonness by single strokes which are not within the reach of everyday, as well as by a vigour of language which is Mr. Meredith's own property among all his competitors. Take this stanza, descriptive of morning light:

> Happy, happy time, when the white star hovers
> Low over dim fields fresh with bloomy dew,
> Near the face of dawn, that shows athwart the darkness,
> Threading it with colour, like yewberries the yew.
> Thicker crowd the shades as the grave East deepens
> Glowing, and with crimson a long cloud swells.
> Maiden still the morn is; and strange she is, and secret;
> Strange her eyes; her cheeks are cold as cold sea-shells.

I do not defend 'bloomy' here said of dew. Mr. Meredith might have learned the meaning of 'bloomy' from Milton, who uses it properly of the spray bursting into leaf in an English April. To apply 'bloomy' to dew is too like that displacement of epithet which is one of the tricks by which the modern school of poets seeks to supply a spurious originality.

'The Day of the Daughter of Hades' is also liable to the charge of diffuseness. And it has the more serious fault of being a versified treatment of a legend provided by the Greek mythology. . . . The nineteenth-century poetical reader knows nothing of Grecian Sicily. It is superadding another difficulty, which is superfluous, to one which is inherent in the nature of the case. We have to make a separate effort to get together the Greek imagery, in addition to the effort which all poetry demands of passing beyond the stereotype forms of everyday life to the spirit within them.

The piece which gives its character to the volume, and raises the whole above the average of the reproductions of Rossetti with which we are familiar, is the first, which is entitled 'The Woods of Westermain.' This piece seizes the imagination with a power which the vague and rather featureless 'Daughter of Hades' does not possess. Many poets have signalled the romance that lies in forest depths, the 'calling shapes and beckoning shadows.' No poetical forest has surpassed in wealth of suggestion 'the woods of Westermain.' In these woods is no wizardry; no supernatural agents are at work. But if you enter them with a poet's eye and a poet's sensibility you may see and hear that natural magic which surpasses all the fictitious tales of sorcerers, witches, wood gods, of Fauns and Dryads. The poem teaches, not didactically—for nothing is farther from its form or its thought than the inculcation of doctrine—how what we see depends upon what we are. . . . The doctrine is old enough; the psychology of religion and that of poetry agree in it. . . . It is wholly in your power what you shall make of earth. As you choose to look, she is either a dust-filled tomb or radiant with the blush of morning. Gaze under, and the soul is rich past computing. You must not only look, you must put off yourself, sink your individuality, you must let her 'two-sexed meanings melt through you, wed the thought.' Your rich reward will not only be in the power of understanding, but in a quickening joy, the 'joy of earth' showered upon you without a stint. In contrast with the pessimistic tone and despairing notes of the modern school, Mr. Meredith offers 'a song of gladness,' and smiles with Shakespeare at a generation 'ranked in gloomy noddings over life.'

Mrs. Alice Meynell, the foremost woman poet of our time, and a rare critic of poetry, does not agree with Pattison in his opinion of 'The Day of the Daughter of Hades'; and while no less an admirer of Meredith's poetry, she has a charge against it of a graver nature than inelegance of compound words, which Pattison, in common with many other critics, has esteemed one of the poet's besetting sins. Mrs. Meynell reviewed 'Poems and Lyrics' in *Merry England*, August, 1883, and though her observations were brief they stand high in the criticism of Meredith's poetry.

There are no disheartening shortcomings or boundaries in these large and vigorous poems (writes Mrs. Meynell). If every poet must have one of two demerits—faults or limitations—Mr. Meredith is to be congratulated on having faults, and not limitations. To our mind the possession of faults is preferable to that of limitations. At times he frees his reader's thought, sets him above the poverties of time and place, and asks him, as Virgil asked Dante in an eternal world, '*Che pensi?*' 'What thinkest thou?'

We have said that this is one of the more fortunate poets who have faults. The principal of these in his case is obscurity, seldom if ever unconquerable by a little application, but sometimes profound at the first glance. Again, Mr. Meredith has a way, which many must find distasteful, of overworking a simile too precisely and insistently. This is an instance:

'Spiral,' the memorable lady terms
Our minds' ascent: our world's advance presents
That figure on a flat; the way of worms.

By the way, who is the lady quoted, Will any of our readers tell us? The saying sounds like one of George Eliot's, though we do not remember it in her writings. With regard to metrical form, it is to be noted that Mr. Meredith uses quantity in a manner unusual in English or any modern verse. Those of his poems in which this peculiarity occurs should be read in time as music is sung. Negroes would recite them to perfection. He evidently doubts his white readers' comprehension of rhythm intended, for he gives a guide to the scansion. This is a specimen of lines in which quantity plays this important part:

Lovely are the curves of the white owl sweeping
Wavy in the dusk lit by one large star.

This is indeed *tempo marcato;* and we cannot but think the insistent rhythm is undignified. To thresh to, to march to, to rock or dance a baby to, quantitative verse is all very well; but accent is sufficient for poetry which is read in repose.

The fourth of the noteworthy criticisms of 'Poems and Lyrics' mentioned above was from the pen of Mr. W. L. Courtney, and occurred in the course of his article on 'Poets of To-day' in the *Fortnightly*, November, 1883. Mr. Courtney is one of our most scholarly writers on literature, little given to the personal in the expression of his opinion, but a scholar of a different range, of course, from so remarkable a man as Pattison. Yet we have to note that from the detached and austere standpoint of impersonal criticism the one singles out for praise the very poem which the other stigmatises as the work of the average 'minor poet' and 'for this reason it will probably be the most popular.' Mr. Courtney writes as follows:

Mr. Meredith describes the main theme of his 'Poems and Lyrics of the Joy of Earth' in one of his sonnets.

I say but that this love of Earth reveals
A soul beside our own, to quicken, quell,
Irradiate, and through ruinous floods uplift.

This soul of Nature he tries to find with an ardour almost as great as that of Wordsworth, but with a totally different result. For '*Natura non nisi parendo vincitur*,' and the soul of Mr. Meredith, which reflects the soul of things outside, is a *speculum inæquale*, too full of artificiality, of poetic conceits, of far-fetched circumlocutions and periphrases, to mirror with perfect fidelity the difficult simplicity of Nature. 'O good gigantic smile o' the brown old earth!'—Mr. Browning is not especially a poet of Nature, but no one could better give us that attitude of patient receptivity of natural influence, in the absence of which Mr. Meredith will never make us feel the reality of his Nature-worship. In every way these poems are worthy of the author of 'The Egoist' and 'The Tragic Comedians'—that is to say, they give the same impression of cold brilliancy, of epigram and antithesis, and absence of native simplicity and warmth. Few readers will peruse with pleasure the more difficult poems in this book, 'The Woods of Westermain' and 'Earth and Man'; while the sonnets at the end of the volume, though often ingenious, are rarely musical, and sometimes the lines are more than difficult to scan. On the other hand, nothing but praise should be accorded to the beautiful pastoral 'Love in the Valley,' with its racy, exhilarating metre; and there are parts of 'The Lark Ascending' which breathe the true spirit of poetic rapture. If only Mr. Meredith would make an effort to acquire what he describes in the lark's music, 'a song seraphically free of taint of personality,' he would be a better artist and a sweeter singer.

In the face of Mrs. Meynell's complaint as to the technical quality of 'Love in the Valley,' Pattison's dismissal of it as 'minor poetry,' Mr. Swinburne's description of it as 'the finest love-song of the century,' and Mr. Courtney's opinion above quoted, one may ask again, What is the plain man to think? The plain man will most probably come under the spell of its strangely sweet and swinging cadences, and prefer it to anything else in the volume, saving 'The Lark Ascending.' He will have Tennyson, Stevenson, Leslie Stephen, and many another famous name to quote in defence of his admiring the simple and unrestrained beauty of that pastoral, and in the lapse of time plain man and critic alike will be reading 'Love in the Valley' and 'Juggling Jerry' when the dilettante may have forgotten Meredith altogether in the discovery of some new genius whom the common herd have not had the sense to understand, for your true dilettante loses interest in his idol the moment he sees the handful of devotees swell into a throng.

'Ballads and Poems of Tragic Life,' in 1887, does not seem to have aroused so much interest among the critics as the collection of four years earlier. But Henley wrote at least two reviews of the new volume: one in the *Athenæum* and another in the *Saturday Review*, both of June 11, 1887, in which he said the same things in ingeniously different phrases. Nor can 'A Reading of Earth,' which appeared the year after 'Ballads and Poems,' be said to have produced any commotion in criticdom. The only criticism of real note devoted to this book of verse was that by the late William Sharp in the *Scottish Art Review*, February 4, 1889. Sharp begins with a very reasonable denunciation of that criticism of Meredith's poetry which seeks to establish such distinctions as 'a writer of poetry, who has never written a poem,' or 'a great poet without music,' and with the other sort that strives to establish likeness or contrast between this or that poet and Meredith. He has no difficulty, of course, in illustrating how gloriously musical Meredith may be—quoting 'that most exquisite couplet':

> Maiden still the morn is; and strange she is, and secret;
> Strange her eyes; her cheeks are cold as cold sea-shells—

nor in showing that he can write a poem as well as poetry, that he has concrete beauty not less than visions of the abstract, and equally how foolish it is to compare him with others instead of judging him by his own standards, the only true way of criticism. Applying himself to the poems of 1888 in particular, William Sharp sets forth his views in these words:

In 'A Reading of Earth' there is, it would seem to be necessary to say, ample proof that the quality of music is in no abeyance. It must of course be remembered that Mr. Meredith is not content to make a sweet sound about nothing; if he did so desire, it would probably be of little avail, for it is undeniable that his poetic work does not in the main possess a certain charm, that of rhythmic spontaneity. He is not a singer for the sake of singing, so much as a poet for the sake of poetry. There are thoughts and aspirations which he prefers to give forth in verse, concepts of abstract, renderings and interpretations of concrete beauty for which he cannot adequately or even aptly find expression in prose; but the passion of song, for song's sake, irrespective of its significance, does not seem to be his. It is difficult to say what is and what is not his dominant impulse; for, above all writers of the day, he has his falcon of poetry as much as his steed of prose in magic restraint—and we may be sure that so conscientious and so thorough an artist does not practise renunciation unless to some high end of art. . . . That Mr. Meredith would have attained as relatively high, or higher, a rank as a poet as he has done of a novelist, had he devoted himself absolutely to the art which he indubitably loves so well, and has, indeed, long so loyally served, I feel well assured. . . .

It will be safe to predict that few readers of this book will repeat the echo-cry about lack of music. Music of utterance, happy epithets, and felicities of selection where natural description is concerned, abound. 'The South-Western' is the finest of poems to the true lord of all the winds that blow. 'Mother to Babe,' 'Woodland Peace,' 'Outer and Inner,' with its sweet complexities of rhyme

By permission of Messrs. Bradbury, Agnew & Co.]

[*From the drawing by Charles Keene in 'Once a Week.'*

THE PATRIOT ENGINEER.

Loud rang our laughter, and the shout
Hills round the Meuse-boat echoed about.

'—Ay, no offence: laugh on,
    Young gentlemen: I'll join.
  Had you to exile gone,
    Where free speech is base coin,
 You'd sigh to see the jolly nose
 Where Freedom's native liquor flows!'

Fair flash'd the foreign landscape while
We breath'd again our native Isle.

—*George Meredith.*

[*To face p.* 280.

and metre, and the 'Dirge in Woods,' are among the most delightful of the shorter poems. The last-named was written, and in an extended form published, some nineteen years ago; and it was, as Rossetti himself told me, the direct progenitor of his lyric, 'Cloud Confines.' 'The Thrush in February' is a poem of forty octosyllabic quatrains, and is worthy of the haunting fascination of its title. In 'The Appeasement of Demeter' a novel and suggestive phrase is given to an old theme, with an effect, upon the present writer, as of something definitely decorative, of an actual fresco, or heroic design in tapestry. Not that it lacks the vitality of a living thing; it might well be called the 'Joy of Life.' A remarkable poem follows it. Entitled 'Earth and a Wedded Woman,' it deals with the vague physical experience of a child of nature, as she lies on her bed and thinks dreamily of her long-absent lover while she listens to the pouring of the incessant rain. But the finest poem in the volume is the superb 'Hymn to Colour,' which, with 'Love in the Valley,' I should rank foremost among the sensuous poems of George Meredith. There is not a line that is not exquisite in beauty.

Save for a notice in the *Saturday Review*, 'Poems: The Empty Purse, with Odes to the Comic Spirit, to Youth in Memory, and Verses,' appeared in the winter of 1892 without awakening any interest, and 'Jump-to-Glory Jane,' included in this volume, also appeared separately in 1892, lavishly illustrated by Lawrence Housman, and 'edited and arranged' (whatever that may imply) by the late Harry Quilter, who had first given the poem to the world in the pages of his *Universal Review*, October, 1889. The *Times*, October 20, 1892, seems to have been the only journal that paid the least attention to this remarkable poem and the no less remarkable manner of its publication. But when the poem appeared in the *Universal* it would seem to have occasioned some considerable discussion, to which the editor refers in his interesting 'Word on the Birth, History, Illustrations and First Reception of "Jane."' Although this note is bibliographical rather than critical, its intrinsic interest, and the two letters of Meredith's to Quilter, fully justify its quotation here. It is as follows:

> When this poem first appeared, in the *Universal Review*, it shared the fate which has attended many of Mr. Meredith's novels; the critics were puzzled, the public doubtful. Demands for explanation flowed in upon me by every post; clergymen remonstrated: not very clear as to their grievance these last, but 'doubtful of the tendency,' a happy phrase which has in its time covered as many sins as charity. The very artist I wished to illustrate the poem not only began, but continued, to make excuse, and finally confessed

that he could not do justice to the verses, and would rather not undertake them. Somehow this got abroad, and certain journals made themselves merry over the artist's incapability to understand the text submitted to him. Then the journalistic word went forth that this poem was 'a satire on the Salvation Army,' and as such it was gravely characterised in several papers. 'Forced, feeble and vulgar,' was this 'tedious doggerel' according to one authority; 'silly and incomprehensible' growled a second; 'scarcely likely to add to the author's reputation' sighed a third, and so on throughout the list. If a kind word was spoken of 'Jane' here and there, it was not written; my very publisher asked me privately what it meant, and friends and relations looked grave; discreetly avoided the subject, as one which was undoubtedly painful.

And yet they were wrong—and will have to 'own up.' Friends and relations, critics and all, must one day confess that this is a good piece of work, and a not incomprehensible one. It is, however, no 'satire on the Salvation Army,' and has no connection with that estimable but unpleasant organisation; and if it be a satire at all, which must be left to the perception of the reader, the poem is also, as Meredith calls it, 'one of the pictures of our England.'

Quilter deems it a 'sly *reductio ad absurdum* to the doctrine which Kingsley set such store by: the connection between physical health and religious feeling.' Meredith himself, writing from Box Hill, August 15, 1889, with regard to illustrating the poem, says:

Whoever does it should be warned against giving burlesque outlines. It is a grave narration of events in English country (? life). Jane, though a jumping, is a thoughtful, woman. She has discovered that the circulation of the blood is best brought about by a continual exercise, and conduces to happy sensations, which are to her as the being of angels in her frame. She has wistful eyes in a touching, but bony face.

In a second letter, dated September 10, 1889, the poet declares Mary Ann Girling, the originator of the 'Shakers,' as a prototype of his 'Jane,' and there it may be said that to be true to life is to be satirical. He writes:

Yes, they are a satire, but one of the pictures of our England as well. Remember Mrs. Girling and her following, and the sensations of Jane, with her blood at the spin with activity, warranted her feeling of exaltation. An English middle-class Blavitzky maniac would also be instructive, though less pathetic than poor Jane.

Mr. G. M. Trevelyan considers 'The Empty Purse' one of the poems which had better been cast in prose.

Perhaps the finest criticism of the 'Odes in Contribution to the Song of French History,' which were reprinted from *Cosmopolis* and published in separate form in 1898, is Mr. Owen Seaman's delightful parody, 'At the Sign of the Cock,' quoted in another chapter of the present work. But there is a passage in an excellent review by 'A. M.' in the *Bookman*, December, 1898, which I take to be from the pen of Miss Alice Macdonell, that accurately touches the later affectation of the pretentious Meredithians, and does justice to the merits without turning a blind eye on the poetic demerits of these 'Odes.' This critic observes:

It is, indeed, a strange irony of fate that the lucid genius of France should be sung in such desperately tortured and turgid strain. True, one hears very little of the difficulty of the poems from the critics, but that is because Mr. Meredith and all his ways are now accepted. Every cultured person is expected to understand him as a matter of course. But I will make bold to say it is a very hard student of the 'Odes' who has come to an approximate comprehension of certain passages, and I am not convinced that the difficulty arises from anything worthier than the common source of such difficulties—a defective expression and a carelessness of beauty. The new affectation of understanding all is hardly less absurd than the old one of failing to understand anything. So we must in honesty speak not of the whole, but of parts.

There is one ode to which this criticism does not apply—that to France in 1870. It has been already published. Perhaps some will recall it for its memorable line—

By their great memories the gods are known,

It is a fine poem finely fashioned. No son of her womb has sung a higher song to her, nor one to make her wince more wholesomely in certain moments.

In the fine study, 'Mr. Meredith's Poetry,' in the *Times*, February 13, 1908, I find this reference to his political odes:

His magnificent political odes have recalled the great days of Shelley's 'Liberty,' Wordsworth's 'Sonnets,' and Coleridge's 'France.' They unite the youth's ardour and intense hold on the present with the seer's vision brooding over time and eternity. There has been nothing like them in the last hundred years. Tennyson was indeed the ideal voice of English political wisdom, but these issues did not greatly move him; and Mr. Kipling has kept in the main to an altogether lower level. But these glorious French odes seem to bear us up away from the dusky lights of earth, which are all the politician has to guide himself by, into the very splendour of the heavens. They quiver with sympathy, they burn with righteousness, they even have at times the stately motion of their own poet's 'army of unalterable law.' No poet has ever come more triumphantly out of the difficult field of contemporary politics. And there is another thing—the history the poets have given us has generally been more poetical than historical. That has not been the case with Mr. Meredith. There is no sketch of Napoleon in existence that contains so much of the essential truth about him as Mr. Meredith's ode. Everything that Napoleon was to France, and France to him, of curse and blessing, is there, nothing extenuated and nothing set down in malice, however sternly one-sided the balance ultimately falls. The only criticism to make on it is that it is perhaps a little too tumultuous; we are everywhere in the whirlwind and the storm; there is too little of the delightful ease of great poetry; but then it may be that that mighy ghost is not to be raised without the whirlwind's help.

Meredith's last book of verse, and his last work of all, 'A Reading of Earth,' published in the summer of 1901, had far less notice at the hands of the critics, and was not so warmly received in any quarter, as his first book, 'Poems,' published exactly half-a-century before it, yet Mr. Trevelyan makes more references to it in illustration of Meredith's philosophy than to almost any other of his works. It is essentially a book of philosophic poetry, and if at times the philosopher elbows out the poet altogether, it still contains in such fine poems as 'The Night Walk,' 'The Test of Manhood,' and many others, a firm and vigorous declaration of the poet's unswerving faith in the high destiny of Earth's children; the note sounds clear and true after fifty years of enunciation and three and seventy years of life.

Before quitting the subject of Meredith's poetry, there remain a few characteristics to be noted that have been passed untouched both in the general view with which this chapter opened and in the particular references to his various books. On the appearance of 'Ballads and Poems of Tragic Life,' for instance, the *Spectator*, October 15, 1887, printed a very able article on 'An Inarticulate Poet,' that dealt very justly with an aspect of Meredith's poetry which, once thoroughly appreciated, enables the reader, without surrendering any degree of his admiration for the poet, to understand him even in his so-called obscurities and to realise his greatness when he fails; to understand, in a word, that his partial failures have very often to be regarded as partial successes. I do not purpose following the *Spectator* writer in the detail of his

[*From the drawing by Charles Keene in 'Once a Week.'*

THE BEGGAR'S SOLILOQUY.

Now, this, to my notion, is pleasant cheer,
  To lie all alone on a ragged heath,
Where your nose isn't sniffing for bones or beer,
  But a peat-fire smells like a garden beneath,

The cottagers bustle about the door,
  And the girl at the window ties her strings.
She's a dish for a man who's a mind to be poor;
  Lord ! women are such expensive things.

—*George Meredith.*

[*To face p.* 285.

criticism, with which few would be inclined to cavil, but his general observations on the subject of articulateness in poetry are certainly worthy of consideration. He writes:

'The Song is to the singer, and comes back most to him,' says somewhere Walt Whitman; and who can doubt that this in reality is the characteristic of the true poet? His creations are, and must be, more to him than to the rest of the world, for they are the outcome of his own emotions and of his own sensations, though not necessarily of his own experience. But whoever yet could clothe in words the whole of what he felt,—did not leave perhaps the most essential and compelling sense within him unexpressed? But if this is the necessary characteristic of the poet, it is also his chief danger. Not seldom the song is so much to the singer, that he is indifferent what it may be to the world. His instinct very likely tells him truly that his poem is good, for it has sprung straight from some deep well of emotion. He knows, too, that the work in which he has laboured to enshrine it, is wrought with the fine gold of imagination and rhetoric. He forgets that to the world at large it expresses nothing. The emotion of which it was the outcome was either essentially inarticulate or only articulate on one side, and that side he has omitted to show. The judgment of the really great and successful singer is, then, as important as his power to feel and to sing. He must select as well as refine, and must for ever be stepping outside his own work and judging it as from the stranger's standpoint. Only by the use of this judgment which can choose between the expressible and unexpressible, can the poet be articulate, be the singer of songs that the world can understand. Without the power to be articulate no poet can win the highest praise.

But though this is so, it would be far too much to deny altogether the name of poet to a writer because of the frequent absence of articulateness in his verse. Indeed, were we to do so in the present generation, we should banish from the ranks of the poets more than one writer whose name is, in every sense, essentially poetic. It is of the verse of such a partially inarticulate poet that we desire to speak here. As a novelist Mr. George Meredith has won, and deservedly won, a very high reputation among, if not the largest, at least the most thoughtful class of readers. As a poet, however, he has received no adequate recognition. This may, we believe, be accounted for by the fact stated above—the greater part of his verse is inarticulate. It is in no sense meaningless; it is simply unable to say what it desires to say. Take as an example the last stanza from 'Bellerophon':

Lo, this is he in whom the surgent springs
Of recollections richer than our skies
To feed the flow of tuneful strings,
Show but a pool of scum for shooting flies.

> How few are those who could read this and not be repelled Yet what pleasure do they miss who are repelled, who never learn to know the other side of Mr. George Meredith's writings, and to love the noble chords of music he sometimes strikes! It is, then our intention here not to dwell upon what is harsh, crude, unintelligible and pedantic in Mr. Meredith's verse, but to show instead what a pure and lucid strain of lyric sweetness, what floods of passionate eloquence, are to be found side by side with his crudest and most repellent verse.

I do not follow the *Spectator's* critic further, for the simple reason that he says nothing else which has not already been said and is perfectly familiar to every reader.

It is, I hope I may say, a merit of the present work that no timidity has been shown in admitting every sincere opinion of its subject; 'both sides of the question' have ever been kept in view, with the result that no adverse criticism of the poetry or the prose of Meredith can disturb the equanimity of his convinced and fortified admirers, just as no extravagant laudation of his art can make them forget that he has his great faults as well as his great qualities.

Mr. Arthur Symons is one of the soundest critics of Meredith's poetry, a warm admirer, but a candid friend. For a general view of the poetry up to the year 1887, no better exposition could be wished than Mr. Symons's article in the *Westminster Review*, for September of that year. Mr. Symons, like many another, is puzzled by the joy of the poet's earth-worship and the sombreness of his poetry of human life. 'These two elements, Nature as a source of joy and healing, Life a tragic tangle, form between them the substance or the basis of Mr. Meredith's poetry,' he observes. But to explain this he does not attempt. We may find some sidelight from other minds that will help us to understand this when we come to examine the criticism of Meredith's philosophy. Here, of course, our main business has been with that aspect of his poetry which concerns the art of verse and neither philosophy nor psychology, except in a merely incidental way. The conclusion to which Mr. Symons's study of the poetry brings him is admirably expressed in the following passage, with which his charmingly written and closely reasoned article ends; it might stand for the last word on Meredith the poet:

> Uncertain we cannot but hold Mr. Meredith's art to be; and it is this, and this alone, that can at all render doubtful his claim to a very high place among contemporary poets. He has imagina-

tion, passion, real and rare harmony, varied gifts—gifts utterly wanting to several poets we might name, whose possession of just the one gift in which he is lacking has allowed them to far outstrip him in the popular estimation, and may do much to foist them permanently into a place above him. . . . Over too much of his harvest-field an enemy, an enemy within, has sowed tares. As in the parable, wheat and tares grow together; there is no plucking out the weeds without carrying the good corn with them; and we must leave it to Time the careful reaper, the reaper who never errs though he is long in reaping, to gather together first the tares and bind them in bundles to burn them; but to gather the wheat into his barn.

Mr. Laurie Magnus in his noteworthy article on 'The Succession of Mr. Meredith,' contributed to the *Fortnightly*, December, 1907, has some apt observations on the technique of the poetry, which may help the student to a nicer appreciation of Meredith's efforts to extract from the English language a greater service in suggestiveness than any other poet has attempted. Mr. Magnus writes:

He has been regarded too long as a poet apart from the poetic line, and something of this neglect has been due to the common confusion between thought and style. The progress of poetry is not marked by steps in the excellence of *technique*. Its true progress lies in its successive and successful powers of assimilating, interpreting, and representing to the age in which the poet lives the new experience of life which is gathered in his age, and which is added to the accumulating evidence of God to man. His instrument—a feeble one—is language, and, as the experience is more novel and the evidence more unexpected, so his instrument proves less serviceable and malleable. There are even occasions when the commonest currency of speech has to be called in to be re-coined, in order to remove its trite appearance, and to repair its expressiveness. The imperfection of language as a medium of truth is remedied in course of years. It repeats, in similar circumstances, differing only in degree, the history of its original development. All this is familiar enough, but, till recently, it has not been applied to the criticism of Mr. Meredith's poetry; and, thus applied, it explains his makeshift with an adjective where no substantive exists —'wing our green to wed our blue' is a typical example out of many; it explains his use of 'Earth,' and, partially, his disuse of 'God'; and it explains the cause, if not altogether the result, of the obscurity of such poems as his 'Hymn to Colour.' There he is adapting an old language to the requirements of a late philosophy; and, while we are certain that the instrument will ultimately be sharpened to its new use, we are grateful for the rough-hewn thoughts, which it has been forced meanwhile to shape by the invincible purpose of the poet's forward imagination. And often the purpose conquers; the instrument and the design are at one. Sometimes in a lonely line, sometimes, here and there, in a stanza, at other times in whole poems, the expression is equal to the thought, and truth flashes in our eyes. Take, for instance, the last magnificent revelation of 'Meditation under Stars':

> A wonder edges the familiar face:
> She wears no more that robe of printed hours:
> Half strange seems Earth, and sweeter than her flowers.

As to the veiled verdict of Time on the poetry of George Meredith, I find myself reverting to the most suggestive *Times* article, to which attention has been given above; for there the writer strikes the truth concerning the relative values of prose and poetry in their endurance of the test of Time:

> Every one knows his novels, but only the few who go to seek literature wherever they can find it have much acquaintance with his poetry. Yet poetry has, on the whole, proved so much the most lasting of the forms of creative human speech that it may well be that 'Love in the Valley' may be remembered at least as long as 'The Egoist.' 'Rasselas' had in its day many more readers than 'The Vanity of Human Wishes'; and Sidney was long thought of as the author of the 'Arcadia,' and not as the writer of the Sonnets to Stella; but in each case, for us to-day, the verse has a stronger life than the prose. The fact, perhaps, is more that the pleasurable excitement afforded by metre, and the higher mood in which poetry is usually written, carry us into an atmosphere in which we are less conscious of changed fashions in thought and expression than we inevitably are in prose. There is in poetry an element of strangeness which makes us ready to welcome a certain unlikeness to our ways of speech and our own point of view. But that is not so in prose. The fancies which are delightful in Elizabethan verse are only tolerable in the contemporary prose; the conceits which we endure in Donne or Cowley would not be endured in any writer who was not a poet. Perhaps the truth is that, with contemporaries, prose has a better chance than verse, other things being equal; with posterity, other things being equal, verse has a better chance than prose.

It may be idle to prophesy, but, with all its faults, there are in Meredith's poetry certain elements of vitality which will enable it to endure, and perhaps to find an infinitely wider range of life in the minds of men, when much of his prose will have been forgotten. He may be, in a certain sense, 'an inarticulate poet,' but only for the reason Mr. Laurie Magnus has explained in his apt allusion to 'the invincible purpose of the poet's forward imagination.' For this reason, apart from others, is he likely to prove articulate to following generations in an immensely greater degree than to his own, and chiefly through the medium of his poetry. We may let the last words on Meredith the poet be these favourite lines of his own:

> Full lasting is the song though he
>   The singer passes; lasting, too,
> For souls not lent in usury,
>   The rapture of the forward view.

XII

THE COMIC SPIRIT

THE Spirit of Comedy broods over Meredith in all his writings. He is ever conscious of her presence 'overhead.' The marvel is that, so inspired, he never attempted writing for the stage, which, as he assures us, 'would be a corrective of a too-encrusted scholarly style, into which some great ones fall at times.' Often in the course of his narrative we seem to detect a yearning after stage effect; the mind of the novelist is asking him how this or that scene he is depicting would 'go' in an acted comedy. He is fond, too, of theatrical similes; 'The Egoist' he calls 'a comedy in narrative,' and the stormy love-story of Lassalle and Fraulein von Doënniges he turns into fiction as 'The Tragic Comedians,' while his stories abound in passages cast in terms of the stage instead of those of ordinary prose narrative. It might be wrong, however, if we concluded from this that the real tragedy of Meredith's literary career was an unrealised ambition to transfer his personages to the stage. Dickens's passion for the theatre was something quite different. Most human beings go through a period of life during which they are fascinated by the glamour of the theatre; some never outlive it; and Dickens was in the latter category. But we have no reason for supposing that Meredith was ever in the first condition. He shows no inkling of love for the theatre in the sense of the 'stage-struck' Dickens. It is again an affair of the intellect; the Greek theatre, with its chorus and 'gods,' unlike those of the hearty gallery, are more to his mind. His notion of the stage is thus seldom, if ever, the concrete institution of our time, but rather an academic abstraction in some sort; a mirrored memory of the Athenian. If this be so, it is not surprising that he never seriously attempted writing for the stage; certainly his method is the antithesis of the purely dramatic, and we cannot imagine that success would have awaited him as a playwright. Yet he is an essential dramaturge in his attitude to his personages; he watches over them and directs them; he plays chorus to them with more gusto than he does anything else; but he does not steadily advance his drama in the spoken words of his characters; they may be quick with life, but it is not always, nor often, dramatic life. Withal, Molière is his greatest master, and if Meredith has never given a comedy to the stage, Comedy has given Meredith to literature. Nor is this to be regretted.

Mr. Humphrey Ward has a very just note on this in his 'Reign of Queen Victoria,' when he remarks:

> Nature designed George Meredith for a great writer of serious comedy, a compeer of Congreve. The incompatibility of literary merit with dramatic success in our day drove him to the novel, which he peopled with the characters of the stage. He paints and dresses for artificial light; hence the apparent want of nature, which disappears on a fair consideration of his aim. No modern novelist demands so much intellect from his readers or gives them so much of his own. What pith and sparkle are to him, an extraordinary delicacy of observation is to Thomas Hardy, who has made more of a few square miles of Dorsetshire than many other novelists have been able to make of the great metropolis.

How vital has been the influence of the comic spirit on the novelist we may judge, not merely by its abundant evidence in his works, or by his splendid ode 'To the Comic Spirit,' but by his only essay of importance being that 'On the Idea of Comedy and of the Uses of the Comic Spirit,' delivered at the London Institution, February 1, 1877. A few brief passages from the revised edition of the lecture, as published in book-form in 1897, will put us in possession of Meredith's main ideas of Comedy before we proceed to consider them in the light of criticism. Let us first note these distinctions and their personal applications:

> You may estimate your capacity for comic perception by being able to detect the ridicule of them you love, without loving them less: and more by being able to see yourself somewhat ridiculous in dear eyes, and accepting the correction their image of you proposes.
>
> If you detect the ridicule, and your kindliness is chilled by it, you are slipping into the grasp of Satire.
>
> If instead of falling foul of the ridiculous person with a satiric rod, to make him writhe and shriek aloud, you prefer to sting him under a semi-caress, by which he shall in his anguish be rendered dubious whether indeed anything has hurt him, you are an engine of Irony.
>
> If you laugh all round him, tumble him, roll him about, deal him a smack, and drop a tear on him, own his likeness to you and yours

to your neighbour, spare him as little as you shun, pity him as much as you expose, it is a spirit of Humour that is moving you.

The Comic, which is the perceptive, is the governing spirit, awakening and giving aim to these powers of laughter, but it is not to be confounded with them: it enfolds a thinner form of them, differing from satire, in not sharply driving into the quivering sensibilities, and from humour in not comforting them and tucking them up, or indicating a broader than the range of this bustling world to them.

In the following Meredith states his main contention as to the uses of the comic spirit:

Its common aspect is one of unsolicitous observation, as if surveying a full field and having leisure to dart on its chosen morsels, without any fluttering eagerness. Men's future upon earth does not attract it; their honesty and shapeliness in the present does; and whenever they wax out of proportion, overblown, affected, pretentious, bombastical, hypocritical, pedantic, fantastically delicate; whenever it sees them self-deceived or hoodwinked, given to run riot in idolatries, drifting into vanities, congregating in absurdities, planning shortsightedly, plotting dementedly; whenever they are at variance with their professions, and violate the unwritten but perceptible laws binding them in consideration one to another; whenever they offend sound reason, fair justice; are false in humility or mined with conceit, individually, or in the bulk—the Spirit overhead will look humanely malign and cast an oblique light on them, followed by volleys of silvery laughter. That is the Comic Spirit.

With these passages before us it is interesting to turn to the *Spectator's* comment on this lecture, in its issue of February 10, 1877. The writer declares that 'the aroma of the lecture almost entirely exhales,' and he seems unable to recapture it. The article is admirably written and closely reasoned. Though based evidently on an incomplete report of the lecture, the writer loses nothing essential of Meredith's meaning, which may be a point in favour of a condensed report, for the elaborated lecture, as it now stands, is none too easy to follow, and the first reading leaves one somewhat fogged. Thus the *Spectator:*

As we understand Mr. Meredith, he intended to insist that the capacity for 'thoughtful laughter,' as distinguished from broad laughter, and still more from vacuous laughter, is one of the most unerring as well as subtle tests of civilisation, and if our reading is true, we can most cordially agree with him. To be capable of thoughtful laughter, of enjoying, say, a comedy in which the follies of the day are ridiculed without bitterness and without gross exaggeration, and laughter is sought in provoking the sudden sense of surprise that a situation so familiar should be so ridiculous, a man must have most of the qualities which, when developed in a large aggregation of men, produce civilisation. He must be able to appreciate a kind of humour, in which the element of latent cruelty that goes to make broad humour, the humour of Western farce, is absent, as well as the grossness which performs the same function in the East; must be of perception quick enough to catch instantly the meaning of a situation; must have the habit of reflection, and must be, above all things, habitually tolerant, so tolerant that the laugh which strikes himself gives him a hint instead of creating irritation. A whole nation composed of such men would undoubtedly be in most respects in the mental condition to which civilisation is acceptable, and which, therefore, sooner or later produces it. We could not imagine an uncivilised nation cordially appreciating, say, merely to take an illustration of the hour, Mr. Robertson's 'Caste'; nor could we believe that a class capable of revelling in Miss Austen's novels, the whole merit of which is the sustained production of thoughtful laughter, was uncivilised. They were not boors, whatever their vices, who smiled over Molière. . . . A nation may be full of capacity for enjoying thoughtful laughter, and yet may from circumstances neither produce nor enjoy comedies of the highest kind. Mr. Meredith himself has mentioned the possibility of the capacity being restrained by mistaken religious feeling, but a people may be so situated that this special source of this special enjoyment is not encouraged sufficiently by the classes that support the theatre, and playwrights may be compelled to attract audiences by evoking a broader or more vacuous laughter. That must be the case more or less in every nation which is not, like the Athenian people, an aristocracy resting upon slave-labour, and in which there are violently differing grades of cultivation; and that is, we suspect, for other reasons, the case in England now. We are not about to discuss the causes of the situation, but as a fact, high comedy, comedy up to Mr. Meredith's ideal, does not 'draw.' Some exercise of the intellect is necessary to thoughtful laughter, and the classes who throng the theatres visit them in the main in the hope of being amused without intellectual exertion—wish for stimulus of a rougher kind, be it good or bad, strong situation or break-down dancing, and find their provocation to thoughtful laughter elsewhere than on the stage. It may be questioned if the theatres could be maintained by comedies of the kind which Mr. Meredith admires, and quite unquestionable that they are not produced in any numbers; that the Victorian Age, whatever its other merits—and they are great—will never be quoted as the age of an English Menander. It might be harsh to say that no play of our day will live except as a poem, but it may be taken as certain that no comedy will.

In spite of the fact that the theatre has outlived the Puritanical ban and that the nation is willing to be entertained by it, no one expects to see produced on the stage of our day, as described by Meredith, the ideal comedy, which will hold its place on the stage for centuries to come. But that is no proof, says the *Spectator,* that English civilisation has failed. The critique of the lecture concludes in these words:

The nation which in one generation has produced, recognised, and enjoyed Sydney Smith, Thackeray and George Eliot has no reason to defend its capacity either for producing or for enjoying thoughtful laughter. The love of the gently humorous and even of the subtly humorous has become a distinct characteristic, reaching farther down in society than many who habitually depreciate Englishmen are perhaps aware. Mr. Meredith must widen his test-question, to make it applicable to English society; but when it is widened it is, we admit, one of the most searching of all. The laughter that springs of thought is the prerogative, as it is perhaps the highest intellectual enjoyment, of the civilised alone.

When 'The Idea of Comedy' was published in 1897, after being for twenty years accessible only in the files of the *New Quarterly Magazine*, among the critics who were attracted by it were Mr. G. B. Shaw and Mr. William Archer, to both of whom, as profound students of the stage, there was here much for reflection. Mr. Bernard Shaw, in his article in the *Saturday Review*, March 27, 1897, described Meredith as 'perhaps the highest living English authority on its subject.' He considered that Meredith knew more about plays than playgoers, and demurred to the statement that 'the English public have the basis of the comic in them: an esteem for common sense,' even when qualified with 'taking them generally.' To this Mr. Shaw rejoined:

If it were to be my last word on earth I must tell Mr. Meredith to his face that whether you take them generally or particularly—whether in the lump, or sectionally as playgoers, churchgoers, voters, and what not—they are everywhere united and made strong by the bond of their common nonsense, their invincible determination to tell and be told lies about everything, and their power of dealing acquisitively and successfully with facts whilst keeping them, like disaffected slaves, rigidly in their proper place: that is, outside the moral consciousness. The Englishman is the most successful man in the world simply because he values success—meaning money and social precedence—more than anything else, especially more than fine art, his attitude towards which, culture-affectation apart, is one of half-diffident, half-contemptuous curiosity, and of course more than clear-headedness, spiritual insight, truth, justice and so forth. It is precisely this unscrupulousness and singleness of purpose that constitutes the Englishman's pre-eminent ' common sense '; and this sort of common sense, I submit to Mr. Meredith, is not only not ' the basis of the comic,' but actually makes comedy impossible, because it would not seem like common sense at all if it were not self-satisfiedly unconscious of its moral and intellectual bluntness, whereas the function of comedy is to dispel such unconsciousness by turning the search-light of the keenest moral and intellectual analysis right on to it. . . . Thus he (the Englishman) is a moralist, an ascetic, a Christian, a truth-teller, and a plain dealer by profession and by conviction; and it is wholly against this conviction that, judged by his own canons, he finds himself in practice a great rogue, a liar, an unconscionable pirate, a grinder of the face of the poor and a libertine. Mr. Meredith points out daintily that the cure for this self-treasonable confusion and darkness is Comedy, whose spirit overhead will ' look humanely malign and cast an oblique light on them, followed by volleys of silvery laughter.' Yes, Mr. Meredith; but suppose the patients have ' common sense ' enough not to want to be cured! Suppose they realise the immense commercial advantage of keeping their ideal life and their practical business life in two separate conscience-tight compartments, which nothing but ' the Comic Spirit ' can knock into one! Suppose, therefore, they dread the Comic Spirit more than anything else in the world, shrinking from its ' illumination ' and considering its ' silvery laughter ' in execrable taste! Surely in doing so they are only carrying out the common-sense view, in which an encouragement and enjoyment of comedy must appear as silly and suicidal and ' un-English ' as the conduct of the man who sets fire to his own house for the sake of seeing the flying sparks, the red glow in the sky, the fantastic shadows on the walls, the excitement of the crowd, the gleaming charge of the engines, and the dismay of the neighbours.

All this is very characteristic of Mr. Bernard Shaw, and there is his usual seriousness threading his lively wit. If Meredith has never spared the Englishman, what shall we say of Mr. Shaw? Meredith's severest trouncings of John Bull have been but gentle corrections compared with the whirling onslaughts of ' G. B. S.' Mr. Shaw even soundly asserts that the English playgoing public ' positively dislikes comedy '; but we must remember this was before his own comedies found fit audience in London as well as in New York and Berlin. Yet he makes a point when he says:

No: if this were an age for comedies Mr. Meredith would have been asked for one before this. How would a comedy from him be relished, I wonder, by the people who wanted to have the revisers of the Authorised Version of the Bible prosecuted for blasphemy because they corrected as many of its mistranslations as they dared, and who reviled Froude for not suppressing Carlyle's diary and writing a fictitious biography of him, instead of letting out the truth? Comedy, indeed! I drop the subject with a hollow laugh.

Mr. William Archer, in the *Westminster Gazette*, March 16, 1897, described the 'Essay on Comedy' as 'one of the subtlest, wittiest and most luminous pieces of criticism in the English language,' and declared that had he known it from its first magazine appearance it 'would have been a thing of light and leading' to him. He gives an excellent summary of its leading points rather than a running criticism of the same, and the most interesting paragraph of his article is that reprinted below:

One could wish that Mr. Meredith had said more of the relation between the comedy of types and the comedy of individual character. He has himself drawn the great type-figure of modern fiction—I mean, of course, 'the Egoist'—fusing, in that masterpiece, the two methods of art, and making of a colossal type a complete individual. Has it ever occurred to Mr. Meredith that the decline, not to say the impossibility, of pure comedy on the modern stage is due to the fact that the broad types are exhausted, and that individuals, if they live at all, touch our sympathies so nearly as to interfere with the free play of the Comic Spirit? It may be too much to say that the types are exhausted; but in any case the centring of all attention upon one vice or foible strikes us, in modern drama, as an expedient of farce. I am inclined, however, to foresee a revival of pure comedy (as distinct from farce on the one hand and the drama on the other) so soon as we shall have got over that itch for action and intrigue with which Scribe inoculated us. We are gradually expelling it from our blood; but it takes time. Fancy 'Le Misanthrope' or 'Les Femmes Savantes' produced for the first time before an audience of to-day! How the critics would cluster together in the *entr'actes* and buttonhole each other to explain that 'there's no action,' that 'nothing happens,' that 'we don't get any forr'ader,' that 'it's all talkee-talkee,' and so on through the whole litany! Which of us, I wonder, would pluck up heart to cry, like the legendary man in the pit, '*Courage, Molière! Voilà la bonne comédie!*'

Taking Meredith's own ideals of comedy and applying them to him as a novelist, 'F. Y. E.,' writing in the *Speaker*, October 31, 1903, on 'The Laughter of the Mind,' is led to this conclusion:

If we English have no such school of comedy, we have a literature

By arrangement with the 'Pall Mall Magazine.'] [*From a drawing by William Hyde.*

'THE WOODS OF WESTERMAIN,' NEAR WOOTON, SURREY.

[*To face p.* **296.**

steeped in the comic idea. We have Fielding, Goldsmith, Jane Austen—and another novelist's name must be added to these, their superior in the hierarchy of the imagination, their equal, at least, in the large sanity of his vision. The comic spirit is the spirit which has most constantly governed the attitude of Mr. Meredith towards his creatures. His appeal has been neither to the puritan nor to the hypergelasts, 'the excessive laughers, ever laughing, who are as clappers of a bell that may be rung by a breeze, a grimace, who are so loosely put together that a wink will shake them'; least of all to the sentimentalists who approve of satire because 'it smells of carrion, which they are not,' but dread comedy which 'cannot be used by any exalted variety as a scourge and a broom.' That in his vast and impressive work he transcends the comic goes without saying; but one great novel of his is entirely a comedy, and in that little masterpiece, 'The Case of General Ople and Lady Camper,' if the lady's treatment of the General is of the nature of irony, the author's treatment of both is purely comic. No Englishman writing fiction has aimed so directly at the head of his readers; none, seeing how thin is the drapery veiling our human passions, teaches us so clearly to respect it in the hope of something better; none, while showing men and women by unhappy chances justly or excusably rebellious against our state of society, has implicitly professed a more rooted belief that our state of society is founded in common sense, or so often provided the best correction of the bitterness that comes of dwelling upon contrasts, by arousing the Laughter of the Mind.

Mr. W. L. Courtney very happily chose for the title of his *Daily Telegraph* article on the eightieth birthday 'George Meredith and the Spirit of Comedy,' though only a few passages in the article justify its title. One of these passages, however, helps forward our present consideration of the subject. Mr. Courtney writes:

The finest flower of the Comic Spirit is to be found in Meredith's great novel 'The Egoist.' The earlier romances were more boyish, more boisterous. 'Evan Harrington,' for instance, is a kind of romantic farce, especially in the character of the Great Melchisedek, in which the author is supposed to have availed himself of some of his father's eccentricities, much as Dickens permitted his father to stand for part of the portrait of Mr. Micawber. 'Harry Richmond' was almost as youthfully hilarious. But when we get to the later work—for 'The Egoist' only appeared in 1879—we find a subtlety of analysis, an accuracy of perception, a mordaunt criticism, which the earlier work did not admit of. In many ways the portrait of Sir Willoughby Patterne in his relations with Clara Middleton is one of the most merciless pieces of dissection which was ever attempted. It is not altogether unkindly in tone, but it is perfectly deadly in effect. We see before us exposed in a capital instance that which Meredith was inclined to think the great fault of the time, the narrow self-absorption, the splendid selfishness, the genial belief that the world existed in and for the sole personality of the self-conscious hero. Here the comic spirit is at work with a vengeance. Take, for instance—and it is a most suggestive contrast—the love-making in 'Richard Feverel' and the love-making in 'The Egoist.' Our octogenarian novelist is a romantic in the true sense of the term, in that he has the most sovereign faith in love. But he knows the difference between the youthful, ingenuous ardour of two human beings upon whom the divine madness has descended for the first time, and the paler, more ineffectual, more calculated philandering of the middle-aged.

Mr. Courtney then goes on to quote the well-known love-scene from 'Feverel,' and sets side by side with it Sir Willoughby's insisting upon Clara to swear she will love him 'beyond death,' leaving us, perhaps, to infer that the one is informed by the spirit of romance and the other by that of comedy, though further than observing that 'the egoism of Sir Willoughby stands bare' he offers no comment. But surely the whole scheme of 'The Ordeal of Richard Feverel' is as deeply rooted in comedy as that of 'The Egoist,' and even the love passages are in perfect tune with the comic spirit, though apart from the whole they might pass for romantic. We do not look for romance or the romantic under such a title as 'A Diversion played on a penny whistle,' nor do we get it, if we regard this scene as of a piece with the whole tragi-comedy, which we are surely justified in doing.

On the whole the criticism of Meredith and the Comic Spirit is the least satisfactory reach of the veritable Mississippi of Meredith criticism. It is apt to run to shallows, as we shall see presently. Instead of viewing him squarely as, first and last, a writer depicting life by means of types born of the comic spirit or, where otherwise conceived, still made to play their parts in comedy, his critics have been apt to content themselves by naming some subsidiary endowment of the comic as one of his attributes: now it is wit, now humour, and again it is satire or irony. Each of these qualities is distinct from the other, and seldom are any two of them found together, yet we find them all loosely attributed to the same man and touched upon without the slightest understanding by many otherwise excellent critics. If Meredith's own definitions already quoted in this chapter be kept in mind, we shall run no risk of confusing wit with humour, or irony with satire; and testing some f the criticism by the aforesaid definitions, which are, beyond all avil, just, we shall be able to correct much that has been written bout him and is so near the truth that only the loose application f words keeps it from touching the mark. Broadly, Meredith is either a wit nor a humorist, an ironist nor a satirist; but he is great comic writer and as such 'he enfolds a thinner form' of ll these others, making use of them all, but humour least of all, etting them in perspective, governing and directing them under the omic. Mr. W. C. Brownell, I fancy, sees this clearly enough, hough he sees it entirely to Meredith's disadvantage, since in his Victorian Prose Masters' it leads him to this conclusion:

His devotion to the tricksy spirit of Comedy led him early to mulate her elusiveness; the interest in the game grew upon him, nd his latest books are marked by the very mania of indirection nd inuendo. It is not obscurity of style that makes it difficult to ollow the will-o'-the-wisp of his genius disporting itself over, it ust be confessed, the marshiest of territory often, but the actual *hevaux-de-frise* his ingenuity interposes between his reader and his eaning. The obscurity lies in his whole presentation of the ubject. He doles it out grudgingly, and endeavours to whip your terest by tantalising your perceptions. The elaborate exordium of Diana of the Crossways' should be read after reading the book. he prelude of 'The Egoist' can be understood at all only as a ostlude. The beginning of 'Beauchamp's Career' is essentially a eroration, and in reading it how long is it before you discover that is about the Crimean War you are reading? If an incident is mminent he defers it; if it is far in the future he puzzles you with dumbrative hints of it; if it is likely he masks its likelihood by esenting it fancifully; if it is improbable he exhausts ingenuity rendering it probable. It is impossible not to conceive the notion at he is enjoying himself at your expense, at least that he is the st having a good time at his own party. It is not an occasional it a frequent experience to find the key to, say, three pages of ddle on the fourth page. And this would not be so disconcerting it is, were it not for the fact that the riddle of the first three is refully dissembled under that deceitful aspect of something lpably preliminary; so that until you come to the key you are t conscious of the existence of the riddle and only wonder why u don't comprehend. The interest of the dilettante is universal d no doubt includes the pleasure of mystification. The effect oduced is, however, not suspense, which has been a reliance of ss original novelists, but disquiet. His motive is to keep you essing. He only explains when you have given it up. In the d even the reader who enjoys guessing must lose interest. For ner readers the dullness of long stretches of his books must be appalling. A great part of the art of fiction consists in making the filling of the grand construction interesting and significant. But this demands temperament, and Mr. Meredith has to depend upon artifice. And his artifice is mainly mystification. It is the coquetry of comedy, not its substance.

This is an extreme criticism, for while it embodies certain strictures which are just and called for, it overstates Mr. Brownell's case—a good one in the main—and needs only one comic figure—one of so many—to be advanced against it to crumble it down; Mr. Brownell says 'it is the coquetry of comedy,' and we have but to take Sir Willoughby and retort, 'Behold the substance!' Henley, in his appreciation of 'The Egoist' quoted in a preceding chapter, has done full justice to Sir Willoughby; but at this point I should like to introduce a passage from M. Le Gallienne's well-known work on the characteristics of Meredith, which provides a good counterblast to Mr. Brownell:

Mr. Meredith names 'The Egoist' 'a comedy in narrative,' but in doing so he uses the word comedy with a significance rarely respected . . . mere satire, humour, or any species of fun-making are all very distinct from, however related to, that significance These but result from the working of the comic spirit which in itsel is only a detective force; they are, of course, included in this presen comedy, but they are far from all. When one comes to conside Sir Willoughby one realises how far. He is Mr. Meredith's grea study in that Comic Muse which he invokes in his first chapter and yet he hardly keeps the table on a roar. At least, laughter i not the only emotion he excites; tears and terror rainbowed b laughter might figure our complicated impression. A tragic figur discovered for us through the eye of comedy. It is certainly comic in the customary sense, to see that great-mannered sublimity, tha ultra-refined sentimentalism reduced to paradox by the exposur of its springs; but the laugh is only at the inconsistency, it ca hardly face the fact. And to see Sir Willoughby on his knee vainly imploring that Lætitia, who has all through served but as a 'old-lace' foil for Clara, and with utter difficulty at last winning he not for her sake either, but for fear of the world, the east win of the world, and no longer the worshipful Juggernaut Lætitia o old, but Lætitia enlightened and unloving—all this is comic, o course; to see tables turned is always comic, but we must no forget that life is before them, and, as Hazlitt says, 'When th curtain next goes up it will be tragedy'—if the situation on whic it falls can be called anything else. Sir Willoughby indeed inspire that greatest laughter which has its springs in the warmth and th richness of tears. If he is Mr. Meredith's greatest comic study he is, at the same time, his most pathetic figure. Of course, his pathos is not of the drawing-room ballad order, any more, indeed, than his comedy would 'select' for a 'library of humour'—those fields are fuller, Mr. Meredith rarely strives there, possibly for the same reason that Landor strove not. But those for whom he has any appeal must feel with his creator that 'he who would desire to clothe himself at everybody's expense, and is of that desire condemned to strip himself stark naked, he, if pathos ever had a form, might be taken for the living person. Only he is not allowed to run at you, roll you over and squeeze your body for the briny drops. There is the innovation.' The pathos, as everything else in the book, is *essential.* That is, of course, why 'The Egoist' is so pre-eminently Mr. Meredith's typical book, and Sir Willoughby his typical characterisation; and there could hardly be a more victorious justification of a method.

That is as good as anything that has been written about Meredith and the Comic Spirit, and one cannot help feeling that even so fine a critic and devoted a Meredithian as the late James Thomson ('B. V.') does not quite hit the mark when he writes ('Cope's Smoke-room Booklets,' 1889):

George Meredith is distinctly rather a man's than a woman's writer. He has the broad, jolly humour, full-blooded with beef and beer, of great Fielding, as well as his swift, keen insight; he has the quaint, fantastic, ironical humour of the poet and scholar and thinker—freakish touches of Sterne and Jean Paul and Carlyle and his own father-in-law (Peacock, of 'Nightmare Abbey,' 'Gryll Grange,' 'Headlong Hall,' and other enjoyable sojourning places, who had Shelley for a friend). In brief, he is humoristic and ironical; and women in general care for no humour save of the nursery, distrust and dislike all irony except in talking with and about one another. But men will savour in that dialogue of Tinker and Ploughman the fine open-air wayside relish in which our robust old plays and novels are so rich, in which most of our modern are so poor. George Borrow, George Eliot, George Meredith, can reproduce for us this pithy, vulgar talk, succulent with honest nature and bookless mother wit; but how many else can furnish it unadulterated? I have named our most popular—and justly popular—great novelist along with him who is one of the least popular; and to my mind he is throned not less eminent than she; and if certain jewels in her crown are lacking in his, he has others not less precious that are wanting in hers.

Thomson in the foregoing has failed of the larger view, and the best that Henry Holbeach (William Brighty Rands) could say was that Meredith was 'above all things capable of being a humorist of the Shandean school.' The fact is that we should have had less difference of opinion as to the Comic Spirit and Meredith if he had been more of a humorist and less a wit. But then he had not been George Meredith. A humorist could never have set out to war on sentimentalists, as he must be something of a sentimentalist himself. Note his own analysis of the humorist, and we shall see how seldom it applies to himself. We do not find him often 'laugh all round him (the ridiculous person), tumble him, deal him a smack, and drop a tear on him,' and the rest. The Comic is his inspirer, and, true to his muse, he is rarely to be found 'comforting and tucking up' the objects of his attention, as the humorist, out of his kindly, sympathetic heart, is for ever doing. Mr. J. M. Barrie, surely one of our greatest humorists, writes of Meredith with real insight when he says, in the *Contemporary*, October, 1888:

> It is Mr. Meredith's wit that wearies many of his readers. He is, I think, the greatest wit this country has produced. Sheridan is not visible beside him, and Pope has only the advantage of polish. Mr. Meredith is far more than a wit, but wit is his most obvious faculty, and he seldom keeps it in subordination. Wit does not proceed from the heart, and so in many of Mr. Meredith's books there is little heart. They compare badly in this respect with Thackeray's novels; indeed, his characters are often puppets, as Thackeray's were not, and the famous ending to 'Vanity Fair' would be in its proper place at the end of 'The Egoist.' This want of heart is a part of the price Mr. Meredith pays for his wit, but he also suffers in another way, that damages his books as comedies not less than as novels. He puts his wit into the mouths of nearly every one of his characters. They are all there to sparkle, and in the act to destroy their individuality. They are introduced in lines so wise and pointed that at once they stand out as sharply defined human beings; then they talk as the persons we had conceived could never talk, and so we lose grip of them. It is this that makes so many readers unable to follow the story; they never know when they have the characters.

Of course, even in this Mr. Barrie is dealing only with one aspect of the subject, and that is concerned more with the medium than with the matter. No criticism of Meredith that treats largely or in detail of his literary style is going deep enough. We are still among the shallows when we have said all that can be said about his witty presentment of his themes. We have to take his novels as a whole, ignoring all verbal eccentricities, all that may run counter to established notions of literary art, and ask ourselves what is the driving force that gave them being. So regarded, the Comic Spirit is seen over and in them all, dictating 'The Shaving of Shagpat' and presiding forty years later over the writing of 'The Amazing Marriage.' The 'sword of common sense' gleams through each one of the splendid series.

Sword of Common Sense!—
Our surest gift: the sacred chain
Of man to man: firm earth for trust
In structures vowed to permanence:—
Thou guardian issue of the harvest brain.

XIII

HIS PHILOSOPHY OF LIFE

Deepest and keenest of our time who pace
The variant by-paths of the uncertain heart,
In undiscerned mysterious ways apart,
Thou huntest on the Assyrian monster's trace:
That sweeping-pinioned Thing-with-human-face—
  Poor Man—with wings hoof-weighted lest they start
  To try the breeze above this human mart,
In heights pre-occupied of a god-like race.

Among the stammering sophists of the age
  Thy words are absolute, thy vision true;
No hand but thine is found to fit the gage
  The Titan, Shakespeare, to a whole world threw.
Till thou hast boldly to his challenge sprung,
No rival had he in our English tongue.

W. MORTON FULLERTON, in *The Yellow Book.*

'HE, too, like all the larger spirits of this age of inward trouble and perplexity, whether with or against his will, must needs be a preacher,' says Dr. Dowden in his study of Meredith's poetry. Some would have it that he is a preacher before all else, that his philosophy will outlast his art. But as to what that philosophy is, he has left us in no doubt, it is enunciated with sufficient clearness and consistency in his prose and poetry. In the poems it is, of course, expressed with a concentration, a compression of words, which makes many a ringing phrase memorable, unforgettable, and so leads one to the erroneous conclusion that it is more ingrained in his poetry than in his prose. The observant student knows it is not so. Yet examine the writings of the critics who have sought to express Meredith's philosophy, and you will find the rarest brief mentions of the novels. I have read every article of the kind, every incidental reference, and I declare one might conclude from them that Meredith's novels had scant concern with philosophy. The fact is that, had he never written a line of verse, every feature and detail of his philosophy had been obvious in his prose fiction, but, having given us the essence of his philosophy in his poetry, his expositors naturally and wisely choose that for their exegeses. It is

By arrangement with the 'Pall Mall Magazine.'] [*From the drawing by William Hyde.*

IN MEREDITH'S COUNTRY: 'SUNLIT SLOPES, LOOKING TOWARDS LEITH HILL.'

[*To face p.* 304.

not a case of the one medium amplifying or correcting the ethical teaching of the other, but of both setting forth the same reading of life and earth.

A probable consequence of this would lead us to thought of Meredith's ultimate place, a subject reserved for consideration in a later chapter. But here one is tempted to observe that if it is his teaching that singles him out from the writers of his time, and if that teaching is given with more intensity and directness in his poetry, the chances are that his fame as a poet will outgrow and finally obscure his reputation as a novelist. Furthermore, if it is philosophy men will seek for in his poetry, in turn the æsthetic consideration of that may give place to the ethical, and the teaching of the poetry, hardening into a quickly-defined creed, even the poetry, which is not always most pleasing where it is most philosophic, may cease to attract, and the poet become a force in the abstraction of thought rather than a companion singer of the thoughtful reader.

Half-a-dozen lines of his verse might be chosen as a sort of tabloid of his teaching. It is capable of the utmost compression and the utmost expansion. Join 'The Egoist' to 'Richard Feverel,' 'Vittoria,' 'One of Our Conquerors,' and 'Lord Ormont'—a mighty mass of exposition—and it is by no means complete. Take 'Modern Love' and the whole is there; every phase and facet of it there! And in the sixty lines of 'Earth and a Wedded Woman' the whole immutable ethic of nature, as he conceives it, is epitomised. But of this later; we have to note many features of his teaching before we arrive at his 'reading of earth.' His point of view, his mental approach, must first engage us, and this was put in a striking way by Mr. J. A. Newton-Robinson in 'A Study of Mr. George Meredith' in *Murray's Magazine*, December, 1891, where he wrote:

Life to Mr. Meredith is a game, though it is true he watches the moves of the pieces with keen and serious interest. His characters are machines which he expounds to us. He is a psychological showman.

'Ladies and gentlemen, walk this way! Here is an interesting model never before placed under the microscope. Observe the dull blood running through the heart, how slow and pulseless! Note that subtle manifestation of egoism, that burst of emotion! This exhibit, on the contrary, is morally well put together, and shows the action of a noble unselfishness. This interesting creature has gleams of poetry and grace'—and so on, and so on, till the brain grows wearied and confused with hearkening to the whirr of the wheels of our mental clockwork. This dissection of the human soul is, however, done with marvellous dramatic skill, and an exquisitely handled knife. The exposition is not *doctrinaire* or dogmatic, but rather empirical and living, proceeding by examples rather than by theory, and bears the impress of a mind of high quality and rarest insight, being in fact, after all deductions, the work of true genius.

There is no manner of doubt that intellect counts for more with Meredith than with any other novelist or poet we can name. He looks at everything with the mind, never with the feelings, and even when he touches us emotionally,—as he does magnificently in such an episode as the swimming Aminta, calling 'Matey' to Weyburn in the sea, and freeing herself for ever from Lord Ormont by her heart-cry to her first lover,—look close and we shall find that the whole effect is intellectually considered from the author's side. Miss Flora L. Shaw (Lady Lugard), in her valuable study of Meredith, contributed to the *New Princeton Review* of March, 1887, gives the gist of a talk with him in which he had been advancing the banner of intellect. She writes:

Mr. Meredith held intellect to be the chief endowment of man, and that in him which it is most worth while to develop. 'By intellectual courage,' he said, 'we make progress. Intellect is the guide of the spiritual man. Feeling and conduct are to be thought of as subordinate to it. Intellect should be our aim. It can be developed by training. The morbid and sentimental tendencies in the ordinary healthy individual can be corrected by it. Starting wrongly, a man can be brought right by it. The failure of many eminent men in old age is to be attributed to the habit of looking at life sentimentally rather than intellectually. Truth seeks truth! And we find truth by the understanding. Let the understanding be only fervid enough, and conduct will follow naturally. When we consider what the earth is and what we are, whither we tend, and why, we perceive that reason is, and must be, the supreme guide of man. Perceive things intellectually. Keep the mind open and supple. Then, as new circumstances arise, man is fit to deal with them, and to discern right and wrong.'

'But Socrates'—and I ventured here to quote Professor Clifford's 'Virtue is habit.'

'Unquestionably that applies to the moral truths already conquered. Virtue is the habit of conforming our actions to truth, once perceived. But in the life of every man and nation unforeseen circumstances arise, circumstances which are outside the ordinary, already decided laws. It is by the intellect, by the exercise of reason, that we can alone rightly deal with these. The man whose intellect is awake will conquer new domain in the moral world. It is our only means of spiritual progress. Habits of conduct, though excellent, are insufficient. They guide us in the beaten track; when new matter presents itself they are evidently unable to deal with it.'

I wish I could recall the vivacity, the keen vigour, the wealth of wit and illustration with which he sustained his theme. As we walked along a stretch of turf on the summit of Box Hill, with the southern landscape lying pearly beneath us, and a south-east wind boisterously singing through the reddening woods upon the hill, he seemed to raise our spirits to corresponding heights, rough, pure and keen, where footing was not easy, but invigorating, and every breath was sharp and good to draw. We spoke of death. He said, 'It should be disregarded. Live in the spirit. Project your mind toward the minds of those whose presence you desire, and you will then live with them in absence and in death. Training ourselves to live in the universal, we rise above the individual.'

This leaves us in no degree of doubt as to the controlling force of Meredith's life: the force that finds expression in all his works. It also explains many things affecting the public appeal of his fiction —'Narrative is nothing,' he said to Miss Shaw; 'it is the mere vehicle of philosophy'—but that is not our immediate concern. The extraordinary feature of his worship of intellect, his belief that intellect can furnish all the moral and spiritual needs of man, is that he retains both 'sweetness and light.' Yet he has often been accused by the thoughtless of cynicism, touching which Miss Shaw observes:

It has been said, on the one hand, that he is a cynic; on the other, that he writes over the heads of the public, and is unreadable. With regard to the first accusation, it is the lot of every one who wars against sentimentalism, especially where the strokes are delivered with the Homeric vigour of Mr. Meredith's; but it is altogether unfounded. He says of himself: 'I never despair of humanity. I am an ardent lover of nature. It is therefore impossible that I should be a cynic.' The business of the novelist who aims at truth is to illustrate the variability of the human species. He must take men and women as they are, not by any means all commonplace, but with human liability to error, which heroism does not necessarily eradicate. The best men are still imperfect. To recognise this is not cynicism, while we perceive that the imperfect may also be the best.

Assuredly there is no abstraction Meredith has warred against more valiantly than 'sentiment' or 'sentimentality.' But it is a moot question whether author and reader are ever quite clear as between them on the exact shade of meaning that is to be given to the word 'sentiment.' For this the author is perhaps as much to blame as his reader, and the very competent critic who took his text from Miss Flora Shaw's article to deliver in the *Atlantic Monthly* of June, 1887, 'A Word with Mr. George Meredith,' shows that the philosopher is tempted to push his campaign too far, while also venturing to discount somewhat Meredith's estimate of intellect as the spiritual treasure-house of man. The *Atlantic* critic puts his case in this way:

> What the novelist means is plain enough, and undeniably it is true doctrine; but I would except against his using the word 'sentiment,' where what he really descrics is sentimentality. Sentiment is not passion, it does not imply any deep or strong feeling, but it is something so far as it goes; its tendency may be to run into sentimentality, still it ought to be distinguished from the latter. . . .
>
> Mr. Meredith's remedy for the cure of 'sentiment' is development of the reasoning powers, and the raising of the intellect into lordship over sensation and fancy. Here, it strikes me, he preaches a half truth only. It is indeed hard to say too much for the value of rationality in all the concerns and relations of life. Irrationality is the huge, lumbering giant against whose strength we have to contend daily, and who is overthrown now only to rise in renewed force in some other shape to-morrow. It is true that what looks like heartlessness in people is sometimes simple stupidity; yet this is not the sole root of difficulty, and Mr. Meredith, if he could invent some clever process for the sharpening of men's wits and proceed to apply it universally, might be surprised to learn that, though he had possibly destroyed false sentiment, true feeling was not invariably found to take its place. The sad fact is that many people have very little feeling at all, and it is not the most enlightened intellects that go together with the warmest and sincerest hearts. Different capacities of feeling exist in men and women, and these natural capacities are so unevenly developed! The problem is a far harder one than Mr. Meredith supposes. . . . What we want in place of false sentiment is genuine, deep, warm feeling. But where it is not, there to plant and make it grow,—tell us how to do this, O ye wise!

This would certainly be a teasing task for many Merediths! 'It is not the most enlightened intellects that go together with the warmest and sincerest hearts,' says the critic, laying his finger on the weak spot of the Meredithian intellectualism. We must all recognise that it is here Meredith's philosophy of pure reason fails. Dickens may have been a mere dealer in sentiment, occasionally in sentimentality, but does he not gain humanwise because he is not afraid at times to be guided by his feelings, where Meredith would look for a lead to his brain only?

But it is easy to make too much of Meredith's intellectuality; the tendency is to over-emphasise it. Mr. G. M. Trevelyan coins an excellent phrase for it when he describes him as 'the inspired prophet of sanity.' Professor Oliver Elton has a fine chapter on Meredith in his 'Modern Studies.' In the course of his study he writes with real discernment on Meredith's philosophy, and I must find space here for this instructive passage:

Mr. Meredith has never struck home to them (the bigger reading public) as Dickens struck home with his splendid humanity, his uncertain art and modern education, and his true wealth of genial and farcical type. Some, too, of those devoted to Thackeray's vast and populous canvas, to his occasional classic sureness and constant elegance of speech (amidst much that is merely journalistic fiction), and to his half-dozen scenes of vehement human drama, may have shivered at the refreshing east wind and shrunk from the mountain sickness that the reader of Meredith must face. To read him is like climbing, and calls for training and eyesight; but there is always the view at the top, there are the sunrise and the upper air. Nor is such a tax always paid him willingly by the better-trained serious public of escaped and enlightened puritans, the dwindled public of George Eliot. Nor has he much in common with the novelists, English and other, of a later day.

For he, like Goethe, 'bids you hope,' while 'Tess of the D'Urbevilles' and 'The Wings of the Dove' do not. The movement of later fiction is toward pessimism, and its best makers, Guy de Maupassant, Gorky, D'Annunzio, agree in their want of hopefulness if in nothing else. They have been catching up and expressing in fiction ideas that found a nobler expression, philosophical or lyrical, nearly a century ago, in Schopenhauer and Leopardi. The same discouragement lay at the base of Tolstoy's thought, before he found his peculiar salvation, and it still tinges his fiction when he forgets his creed and remembers he is an artist. The history of this pessimistic movement in fiction is still unwritten, and the movement itself is unexhausted.

But the groundwork of Mr. Meredith, with his forward look, his belief in love and courage, is different. It is stoical rather than pessimistic; and in that he resembles Zola, whose method—laborious, serried, humourless—is the opposite of his. Mr. Meredith grew up on the high hopes fed by the revolution of the mid-century, and the most heroic figure in his books is Mazzini, the 'Chief' in 'Vittoria.' He has a moral and spiritual afflatus of the nobler order, peculiarly and traditionally English, in that line of the great

English prophets which come down from Langland and Sir Thomas More to Carlyle. His creed does not depend, visibly, on formal doctrine for its force, but neither does it rest on any pre-occupying enmity towards doctrine. His inspiration plays in various moods —strenuous, ethereal, ironical—rarely serene, over his vision of 'certain nobler races, now dimly imagined'; and casts a new interpreting light, above all, on the rarer forms of love and patriotism and friendship. Yet there are none of the airs of the prophet, for the media preferred by Mr. Meredith in his prose are wit and aphorism, situation and portraiture, and to these the lyrical didactic elements are subordinate.

One might fancy that the foregoing are among the passages referred to by the late York Powell in a very breezy and characteristic letter to Professor Elton printed in his 'life' of Powell, whence I quote the following; but Dr. Elton informs me that they refer to an earlier essay of his :

Balzac if you like; a thinker, an historian, an artist, a mighty labourer; but Tolstoy does not deserve comparison with Meredith. Don't laugh, think it over, without remembering it is 'prejudiced' I that write this.

Well and finely done, too, the last paragraph. You might enlarge on the Earth-spirit. Try and smite out the man's creed in one or two sentences, for he *is* a prophet as well as an artist. He has something to tell us : 'we bid you to hope.' Tolstoy, good God ! a miserable nonconformist set of silly preachments. Meredith is sound like Shakespeare. Do bring in Balzac. . . . Cut out Tolstoy. Away with these half-baked potatoes. Balzac and Meredith will represent their century. Do not mention such a person as George Eliot, let her lie. She did some good work and much bad. She meant well, and she and Mrs. Grundy quarrelled, and made it up over filthy Ghetto piety. . . . I am boiling because I can't sit opposite you to argue with. You have done a fine bit of work. I am glad you praised Henley. He is the only man who has really tried to judge G. M. W. Morris says, 'A clever man, not an artist.' *He* can't rise above the naïve melodic.

Professor Elton was evidently not inclined to 'away with the half-baked potatoes,' as we have seen there is a reference to Tolstoy in his later study, as well as in the earlier one which had been submitted to Powell for criticism. But this conjunction of the names of Tolstoy and Meredith—concerning which most Meredithians will echo Powell's lusty veto—does help to an understanding of the greater man by contrasting the feebler Russian with the magnificently energetic Briton. Meredith himself supplies us with a picture of Tolstoy, for in a talk with Mr. G. H. Perris (*Westminster Gazette*, February 9, 1905) he delivered himself in good set terms as to the Tolstoian precept of 'non-resistance':

'I am perfectly persuaded,' he said with emphasis, 'that submission to evil is a distinct evil in itself. But I am not prepared to say that a bloody resistance is required, unless, as in this case, when a nation may be compared to a man with another holding a knife at his throat. In such a case, not to resist is grave error; and I imagine that, in the revolution of time, what the English call unmanliness proves to be a dangerous thing for men even to witness, let alone to practise. Tolstoy's is a too-easily saddened mind. Of course I recognise his power; it is a reminder to us that if a man devotes himself to one particular object he becomes a force whenever that object comes prominently before the mind of the world. But no! I don't go with him so far in his Christian precepts, though I can well understand that a brave man may feel himself under the dominion of Christ, and therefore that he would follow the lead of his Lord to the end. Tolstoy is a noble fellow, but he is *tant soit peu fanatique.* I listen to him with great reverence, sure of his sincerity, but not always agreeing with his conclusions.'

In the course of the same interview Meredith touched upon his own stoical interpretation of Nature in these words:

We are all hunted more or less. Yet Nature is very kind to all her offspring. If you are a fine runner and your blood is up, you don't, in point of fact, feel a half of what you do when lying in bed or sitting in a chair thinking about it. A man in battle array facing his enemy with his blood up is ready to give and take. If these humanitarians would only study Nature more!

We must all bear our burden in the world. True, it is a kind of world Nietzsche and other preachers of Nirvana—and our dear Tolstoy comes near them sometimes—don't approve, and even proclaim better ended. I imagine such people must have been begotten in melancholy mood—by a man in a fury with his natural appetites, and a woman reluctantly wishing for a child. Hence this singular issue, that they look upon extinction as a saving grace. It is those who are the foes of Nature. Probably many of them are of a delicate constitution, unable to rough it with the rough. So they look upon the shocks of life as though ferocious demons had been sent to work among them; the truth being that we have all come from the beasts, and the evil they talk about is nothing but the perpetual recurrence of beast-like tendencies. Those we may hope to exercise; but we cannot depart from the founts of our origin, our links with the world of Nature.

As to Death, any one who understands Nature at all thinks nothing of it. Her whole concern is perpetually to produce nourishment for all her offspring. We go that others may come—and better, if we rear them in the right way. In talking of these deep things, men too often make the error of imagining that the world was made for themselves.

In an interview with Mr. H. W. Nevinson (*Daily Chronicle*, July 5, 1904), eight months earlier than that quoted above, Meredith had also touched upon the attitude of mankind towards death, saying that 'fearlessness of death is a necessary quality,' and that it is 'essential for manliness.'

'Doctors and parsons are doing a lot of harm' (he went on) 'by increasing the fear of death and making the English less manly. No one should consider death or think of it as worse than going from one room into another. The greatest of political writers has said, "Despise your life, and you are master of the lives of others." Philosophy would say, "Conquer the fear of death, and you are put into possession of your life." I was a very timid and sensitive boy. I was frightened of everything; I could not endure to be left alone. But when I came to be eighteen, I looked round the world (as far as a youth of eighteen can look) and determined not to be afraid again. Since then I have had no fear of death. Every night when I go to bed I know I may not rise from it. That is nothing to me. I hope I shall die with a good laugh, like the old French woman. The curé came wailing to her about her salvation and things like that, and she told him her best improper story, and died. The God of Nature and human nature does not dislike humour, you may be sure, and would rather hear it in extremity than the formless official drone. Let us believe in a hearty God—one to love more than to fear.'

His tone then changed a little, and, rather as if in soliloquy, he passed into regions more remote.

'There is Pan,' he said. 'You know something about Pan, too. He has always been very close to me. He is everywhere—so is the devil, who was framed on the model of him by our mediæval instructors. Just now the devil is more thought of in England than the Christian God. He is more popular. The time will come for the mind of man to see the veritable God. Nature goes on her way, unfolding, improving, always pushing us higher; and I do not believe that this great process continues without some spiritual purpose, some spiritual force that drives it on. Change is full of hope. A friend of mine was lamenting over the sadness of autumn. "Are you sad when you change your coat?" I asked him.'

By permission of Mrs. Harry Quilter.]

ONE OF MR. LAWRENCE HOUSMAN'S ILLUSTRATIONS FOR 'JUMP-TO-GLORY JANE.'

Her first was Winny Earnes, a kind
Of woman not to dance inclined.

[*To face p.* 312.

All this, though it may be described as merely the obiter dicta of an aged philosopher, deserves to be recorded, since it is in tune with the philosophy expounded in the prose and poetry, that 'stoic ecstasy' expressed in his familiar lines:

> Oh, green and bounteous earth,
> Into the breast that gives the rose
> Shall I with shuddering fall?

And now the need arises for devoting particular attention to Meredith's interpretation of Nature, whose almost pagan worship shared with Intellect the whole passion of his being. There is much here to engage us, and as a prelude to the study of this aspect of his philosophy it is interesting to quote a passage from a long-forgotten article by the late Moncure D. Conway, contributed by him to the *Glasgow Herald*, August 14, 1883, and descriptive of his voyage round the world. Conway read 'Poems and Lyrics of the Joy of Earth' on a 'soft July day in mid-Atlantic,' and he speaks of the book as a call to come back to old England, where are all the joys of earth, and where the wanderer may find all that he has gone in search of in his far journeyings. So Conway is led to moralise in this strain:

It may also be needful that one should circumnavigate the Earth to win what another finds by circumnavigating a dewdrop. He must have lived long and voyaged far who can explore this little book, and even understood the Joy of Earth it sings. Therefore it is too much to hope that the millions will pause to listen to this poet who, did they know it, might set their myriad footfalls to music. In these songs, fresh from the soul of this summer, George Meredith appears to me one of the few poets who greet with joy a dawn which more famous morning-stars of song meet with threnodies of fear and pain. With the unbelief revealed alike in pessimism, philosophy and panic he has simply nothing to do. Take all that belongs to you, gentlemen—so he meets the sceptic and the scientist—and I will even add all you may suspect belongs to you, myself included! What then? That skylark will sing all the vanished angels sang, heaven will smile through that child's eyes bright as through the olden stars, and the heart of the universe will not cease to beat so long as I love. There are things that live in undiminished strength when opinions of them have passed away; nay, which are even enhanced by knowledge—like that rosy cloud on which Columbus and his mariners gazed, but which proved to be the New World. Most of our opinions will be fossil remains after a time, and it would appear that experience has gradually trained the heart of man to love and seek a satisfaction in the realm which poetry and art can actually build out of that heart's emotions and aspirations. The task of George Meredith is different from that assigned the poet by the Wordsworthian or any other school. It is not interpretation of nature as a pantheistic phenomenon; it is not to deal with nature as symbolism of another and invisible, though equally material, nature. Rather it is to detach the roses of nature from their thorns, to anticipate the evolutionary work of ages and show the far final outcome of things as if present in the joy of their vision. There is no awe, no worship of hugeness and force, but of beauty, loveliness, sweetness, and in the rapture of this worship the vileness and agonies of the earth are abolished and forgotten. Let who will deal with the evil side of nature, the inhuman side, this poet will, imaginatively, create for us a world in which all evil shall be fabulous as dragons, and teach us a secret of spiritual selection by which we may surround ourselves with a harmonious order crystallised out of common quarries, like the diamond. Is not this better than to turn our May-Day evil with ravings against our age, especially as the age doesn't in the least care for our ravings? Is it not the better poetic art to show what peace, hope, joy may be gathered as wayside blooms, and show every petal of them tinted with glow of the ancient heavens?

A very full and minutely considered estimate of Meredith's philosophy of nature was that contributed by Miss F. Melian Stawell to the *International Journal of Ethics*, April, 1902, entitled 'The Conception of Nature in the Poems of Meredith.' The writer begins by disposing of the false notions which have been attached to the word 'Nature' in our time, restating the chief meaning of it still current. What she chiefly aims at is the exclusion of that interpretation of nature which would have every impulse 'natural' and so make ethical chaos come again. She sets herself also to the identification of certain dimly realised impulses springing from nature and inquires why 'natural' could have become synonymous for 'good.' While reminding us that even lovers of nature are not blind to the fact that all is not beautiful in nature, she sums up by saying that 'if nature is not moral in herself, she is yet on the side of morality.' Indeed, it would not be misrepresenting Miss Stawell's roughly thrown out definitions of nature to say that it is something closely resembling Matthew Arnold's description of God: 'the enduring power, not ourselves, which makes for righteousness.' How far, if at all, this squares with the Meredithian notion of nature, we shall see. Miss Stawell thus sets forth the latter, by no means confining her inquiries to the poems, though the title of her article would give that impression:

The external world, apart from the wills of men, Meredith holds to be the manifestation of one Power, 'Nature,' a power distinct from Man and yet akin to him, akin to the best he has it in him to be. And the urge in each of us towards physical life and enjoyment springs from the same source, and shows in a similar way a real connection with the Best.

Nature in us is, primarily, the force that makes for individual life, and these impulses are therefore 'natural' in the prime sense of the word. But they make for something more, and therefore they are to be called 'good' also, not good, that is, just because they are natural, but because the natural holds in it the seed of good. But the seed is, so to speak, dormant, and can only be developed by our struggle, a struggle that is not ignorant of pain and failure.

Though Meredith 'does not attempt to define with philosophical accuracy the precise relationship between these impulses and what we may call their fulfilment,' he makes it clear that these impulses 'do prompt to something beyond themselves, something that our reason could recognise as absolutely good.' One of the 'gates of life' is the physical joy or 'bodily exaltation' which lifts one towards 'the footstool of the Highest.' 'Through Nature only can we ascend,' is one of the maxims from 'The Pilgrim's Scrip':

It is in such a spirit as this (says Miss Stawell) that Whitman can celebrate 'the life of my senses and flesh, transcending my senses and flesh,' and that Wordsworth can sing of

> Spontaneous wisdom breathed by health,
> Truth breathed by cheerfulness.

Half understood, often misunderstood, again and again this belief in Nature and health comes back upon man. The Bacchanal madness may have meant little else. Such a wild guess at truth is Meredith's theme in the daring impressive grotesque he calls 'Jump-to-Glory Jane.' To Jane, the peasant founder of a Shaker Sect, jumping has become the very way of life. She has been visited with sensations of bodily health and vigour that open spiritual vistas, sensations that 'are to her as the beings of angels in her frame,' and through all the whimsical absurdity Mr. Meredith never lets us forget that

> It is a lily-light she bears
> For England up the ladder-stairs.

It is not that the indulgence of the senses is a kind of pleasurable sauce to be supped now and then in a holiday mood: the senses are rather the raw material of the satisfying life: they are even more, for they are no alien matter on which a form has to be imposed from without: of themselves they demand from their own peace a higher use: the body, as Meredith puts it, is the bride calling for the spirit who is to be the bridegroom; it is 'by her own live warmth' alone that Nature can 'be lifted out of slime.' Reason is the child of the great mother, the child who is to interpret her inarticulate cries. There is no ultimate discord in the elements of which we are made. Here on this earth we can come in sight of what Browning calls

> The ultimate angel's law,
> There where life, law, joy, impulse, are one thing.

But to achieve this starry harmony man must toil; the forward reach, the upward struggle alone can realise the ideal of 'Three Singers to Young Blood,' when, from having been jarred and discordant, 'chimed they in one.' Nature alone and independent of Man is not moving towards a great ideal. Meredith has remembered what Browning said of

> . . . . . . how the devil spends
> A fire God gave for other ends.

when he himself sings in 'The Empty Purse':

> How the God of old time will act Satan of New,
> If we keep him not straight at the higher God aimed.

And the business of life when life is 'thoroughly lived' is just this interpretation of Nature, this 'reading of Earth.' This is what it means to 'keep faith with Nature'—we are not 'wise of her prompting,' we have not understood the rose of her in our blood, if it gives no birth to the 'rose in brain,' if the human Good does not blossom out of the natural. Nor does Meredith leave that Good a mere abstraction, though it is not his task to give an inventory of its contents. Sympathy and courage are for him true flowers of that immortal garland whose roots are 'in good gross earth.' Our problems must all be solved in 'the soul of brotherhood.' 'Not until we are driven back upon an inviolated Nature, do we call to the intellect to think radically: and then we begin to think of our fellows.' Thus it is idle to dream of mere self-indulgence. The man who has been deceiving himself under the pretext that he is 'made of flesh and blood' finds no answer to soothe him after he is started into a searching doubt of his 'clamorous appeals to Nature.' 'Are we, in fact, harmonious with the great Mother when we yield to the pressure of our nature for indulgence? Is she, when translated into us, solely the imperious appetite?'

Clearly no, for Meredith's plea is that, in order to correspond in the widest sense to our environment (if I may use Spencer's phraseology here) we have, as Miss Stawell puts it, 'to refuse the demands of our narrow self in the name of the wider.' This ceaseless struggle with our own appetites, even against 'natural instincts,' means the winning of wisdom, but the struggle must go on, and man's conquest is the fact that he takes part in it, he is victorious in the mere wage of the battle and beaten only should he cease to fight. 'The fact that character can be and is developed by the clash with circumstances is to Meredith warrant for infinite hope.' Again I quote from Miss Stawell:

But just as the urge to life within us holds, wrapped up in it, much more than mere living, so the union with Nature means much more than this. To be in contact with natural things is to touch a source of righteousness as well as of strength. All poets, perhaps, have felt something of this faith, but Meredith makes it a corner-stone of his thinking. Wordsworth and Whitman offer the nearest parallels to his work in this as in many other points. Whitman will create his poems in the open air and test them 'by trees, stars, rivers'; he knows that system 'may prove well in lecture-rooms, yet not prove at all under the spacious clouds and along the landscape and flowing currents.' True religion is taught to Wordsworth's 'wanderer' as much by 'his habitual wanderings out of doors' as by his 'goodness and kind works.' Meredith makes a Diana who has lost her way feel that 'one morning on the Salvatore heights, would wash her clear of the webs defacing and entangling her.' In one of his most striking poems ('Earth and a Wedded Woman') a 'lone-laid wife,' tempted to weakness and inconstancy, lies awake all night after a season of drought 'to hear the rain descend,' and the mere sound and smell of the rain, the breathings from Earth's 'heaved breast of sacred common mould' of themselves bring to her strengthening that she needs. So special and marked, indeed, is the virtue that goes out of Nature that these three poets are agreed in placing it, in a sense, above what can be got from Man. Why is this? Is it just because Nature is the expression of something *other*, though akin, of an aspect of the whole that could not be resolved into human consciousness? The poets do not answer, but they hold unmistakably that there is something to be got from Nature which cannot be supplied elsewhere. It is doing Wordsworth wrong to explain away his outburst (in 'The Tables Turned'):

One impulse from a vernal wood
  May teach you more of man,
Of moral evil and of good
  Than all the sages can.

Meredith's 'South-West Wind in the Woodlands' echoes the thought, almost the very words:

The voice of Nature is abroad
This night; it fills the air with balm;
Her mystery is o'er the land;
And he who hears her now, and yields
His being to her yearning tones,
And seats his soul upon her wings,
And broadens o'er this wind-swept wold
With her, will gather in the flight
More knowledge of her secret, more
Delight in her beneficence,
Than hours of musing, or the love
That lives with men could ever give!

In this same spirit Whitman speaks of the impression from the starlit sky as beyond anything from art, books, sermons, or from science old or new.

But what we have to know of man in his intercourse with nature is that something more than the heroic temper is required of him. 'Faith,' Meredith frankly tells him, is needed; as if he were an orthodox preacher pleading with them 'of little faith.' His own faith in a something in Nature for transcending all phenomena is made intensely real to every reader of his poetry. 'Nature he believes not only sends us after a good which is our good, but she whispers that we can reach it,' and so we are led to the belief that 'Nature is another partial expression of the same ultimate Power working for good that stirs in us, a Power which is greater than either of its manifestations, which in the end is ruler of all.'

But Meredith is reticent on the matter (says Miss Stawell), and it is hard to be sure of his precise view. Whatever it is, however, there can be no doubt of his hope. We shall gain, if we are valiant, what will content the valiant. Nothing can stand in the way of that, not death itself. The impulse, fortified by communion with Nature, to face everything that can befall us whether from within or from without, in the faith that it can be stamped with heroism, is a sign that the soul of man can conquer in the battle: in the words of his Diana, it is 'a little boat to sail us past despondency of life and the fear of extinction. . . . *There is nothing the body suffers that the soul may not profit by.* . . . With that I sail into the dark; it is my promise of the immortal: teaches me to *see* immortality for us.' The real worth of life lies in the effort to attain the ideal, and the sense of the reality of that ideal coupled with recognition that the force at the back of Nature is in harmony with it, can show us life beyond the death that ends this life of sense.

But here arises a question of great importance and difficulty. In what precise sense does Meredith mean that life outlasts death? Does he mean to imply personal immortality, or is he only thinking of the effect on other lives springing from the work done and the life lived by the worker who himself passes utterly away? Passages might be quoted to support either view, but on the whole it seems impossible to explain the triumphant confidence in Nature with which he faces Death on the supposition that it is the end of the individual life:

> And O, green bounteous earth!
> Bacchante Mother! stern to those
> Who live not in the heart of mirth;
> Death shall I shrink from, loving thee?
> Into the breast that gives the rose
> Shall I with shuddering fall?

Making all allowance for a poet's metaphors, how can the earth be to him such a mother if she is after all only 'the place of graves'? And in the wonderful poem called 'Earth and Man,' he recognises expressly that the desire for permanence and joy, the shrinking from dust as the end, springs from the heart of Nature as much as the impulse to heroic effort.

But no doubt Meredith holds that the veil is not fully lifted. He sees 'the dawn glow through,' but that is all. The faith that he is really concerned to hold to is that it is worth while to go on: that there is 'a heart of eternal goodness to receive' the dead, 'whatever the nature of the eternal secret may be.' How much is involved in that 'eternal goodness' he does not care to inquire. What the heroic man has a right to claim for his satisfaction will be granted to him, but he is not yet told what that will be. To refuse to continue the struggle unless a detailed answer can be found means, Meredith thinks, a lack of spiritual vigour. The great mother teaches a patient trust:

> And 'If thou hast good faith, it can repose,'
> She tells her son.

We have simply to do our work,

> Leaving her the future task,
> Loving her too well to ask.

It is not the proof of immortality that can make us feel that life is worth living: it is the sense of its worth that assures us of immortality. Nature whispers to the valiant heart that nothing of real value can perish:

> Near is he to great Nature in the thought
> Each changing season intimately saith,
> That nought save apparition knows the death;
> To the God-lighted mind of man 'tis nought.
> Close on the heart of Earth his bosom beats,
> When he the mandate lodged in it obeys,
> Content to breast a future clothed in haze,
> Strike camp and onward, like the wind's cloud-fleets.

Such an attitude explains the sternness with which Meredith

speaks of 'the questions.' If they could all be answered, which they cannot be, what ultimate good should we gain? Scientific proof, if it was to be had, of life after death could not give us the inner significance of life itself.

'Strike camp and onward' is really the last word, and sums up Meredith's whole doctrine of purifying toil, while for earnest of immortality he declares—

> That from flesh unto spirit man grows
> Even here on the sod under sun.

Where Meredith's teaching fails to satisfy the more orthodox among the thinkers of our time is in its avoidance of personal immortality. No craven avoidance truly; but a cold ignoring of the question as though it did not matter, and indeed, in face of the grander issues of his life's philosophy, it does not matter. The Positivist position might perhaps be likened to Meredith's, were it not that he can glow with a spiritual passion we do not discover in Comte or his followers. Concerning man's aspiration after God he is clear and unequivocal, as in this, an example of many ringing evidences of his faith:

> The Great Unseen, nowise the Dark Unknown,
> To whom unwittingly did he aspire
> In wilderness, where bitter was his need:
> To whom in blindness, as an earthly seed
> For light and air, he struck through crimson mire.

But the mind of man so long schooled to dream dreams of a personal immortality, and naturally loth to lose its vision of a happy state in which the individual will continue to exist, purged of the grossness of this earth, is still some way from accepting the Meredithian creed with its light valuation of personality, its splendid enthusiasm for the race. Whether it implies a higher plane of spiritual development to be anxious only for 'man's future as part of the cosmic process,' or for one's own future; ready to make self-sacrifice for the race or merely to assure oneself a happy hereafter, does not seem to be a question capable of much discussion. This, however, the Rev. James Moffat, D.D., makes the point of his criticism of 'Mr. Meredith on Religion' in the *Hibbert Journal*, July, 1905. Dr. Moffat is a sincere and competent critic, and from his point of view his case is admirably stated in the subjoined passage:

While Meredith has no place for the idea of probation which Browning found so fruitful in the argument for immortality, he resembles that poet in the sturdy front which he inculcates as the

By permission of Mrs. Harry Quilter.]

ONE OF MR. LAWRENCE HOUSMAN'S ILLUSTRATIONS FOR 'JUMP-TO-GLORY JANE.'

Those flies of boys disturbed them sore

. . .

With withies cut from hedge or copse,
They treated them as whipping tops,

. . . . .

Yet all the flock jumped on the same.

[*To face p.* 320.

one duty of man towards death. . . . His [illegible] just reproach, to the insurgent hope of [illegible] swells out, e. g. in Mr. Fairbrook [illegible] Promise of Immortality. [illegible] example:

Oh dreadful strength! [illegible]
Are but foundations of a [illegible]
Stones which [illegible] and [illegible]
A white [illegible] Parthenon.
And thither, [illegible] hereafter, youth and maid
Seek with glad [illegible] the unbarred shade
And in procession [illegible] bent
Still [illegible] words [illegible]
Not [illegible] that [illegible] columns [illegible]
Each on [illegible]
That to [illegible]
Across the [illegible] and souls

To Meredith this does not seem a [illegible] is, I grant, in the [illegible] of "Attrition" [illegible] slight advance upon some of his earlier [illegible] sionate assertion of [illegible] as part of the [illegible] never supplemented by [illegible] heart [illegible] lessness of personality, [illegible] and [illegible] can hardly bear with patience [illegible] I imagine, he is swayed by the [illegible] disparagement of the human personality, as if [illegible] some taint or alloy of individualism. So, [illegible] Lesson of Grief" and "The Question Whither," [illegible] the lurking selfishness of man, a selfishness [illegible] way into the holiest phases of his being, [illegible] he is apt to take too [illegible] of self [illegible] he fails now and then to do any sort of justice [illegible] personal immortality which is as far above [illegible] of reward or fame as it lies remote from any [illegible] senses. It is a longing which [illegible] human personality which, on Meredith's own showing [illegible] and supreme an expression of Nature's being [illegible] of her spirit, can be treated as mere material [illegible] up for greater issues—issues that involve a [illegible] sonality and a decline from the level of its [illegible] general heart will be up in protest. And some will [illegible] Meredith against himself. They will venture to [illegible] the far future by the ruddy faith of the lines [illegible] modern France—daring to hope their mankind [illegible]

Like a brave vessel under press of steam
Abreast the winds and tides in angry seas
Plucked by the [illegible] of present [illegible]
Will drive through darkness and with faith
Have sight of haven and the crowded [illegible]

one duty of man towards death. . . . His theory lies open to one just reproach, to the insurgent heave of human passion, which swells out, *e. g.* in Mr. Frederick Myers's poem on 'The Implicit Promise of Immortality.' Take this arresting, august protest, for example:

> Oh dreadful thought! if all our sires and we
> Are but foundations of a race to be,—
> Stones which one thrusts in earth, and builds thereon
> A white delight, a Parian Parthenon.
> And thither, long hereafter, youth and maid
> Seek with glad brows the alabaster shade,
> And in procession's pomp together bent
> Still interchange their sweet words innocent—
> Not caring that those mighty columns rest
> Each on the ruin of a human breast—
> That to the shrine the victor's chariot rolls
> Across the anguish of ten thousand souls.

To Meredith this does not seem a dreadful thought at all. There is, I grant, in the closing words of 'Vittoria' and elsewhere, a slight advance upon some of his earlier utterances, but the passionate assertion of man's future as part of the cosmic progress is never supplemented by any positive or hearty word upon the deathlessness of personality. Such outcries and yearnings, indeed, he can hardly bear with patience or treat as reasonable. Insensibly, I imagine, he is swayed by the semi-pantheistic temper into an undue disparagement of the human personality, as if it necessarily involved some taint or alloy of individualism. So eager is he, as in 'The Lesson of Grief' and 'The Question Whither,' to thwart and erase the lurking selfishness of man, a selfishness which can worm its way into the holiest phases of his being, into love and grief, that he is apt to take too stunted a view of self; with the result that he fails now and then to do any sort of justice to that longing for personal immortality which is as far above any thirsty expectation of reward or fame as it lies remote from any nervous revolt of the senses. It is a longing which tenaciously refuses to admit that human personality which, on Meredith's own showing, forms so vital and supreme an expression of Nature's being, so perfect an organ of her spirit, can be treated as mere material to be eventually used up for greater issues—issues that involve a disintegration of personality and a decline from the level of its consciousness. The general heart will be up in protest. And some will prefer to quote Meredith against himself. They will venture to read humanity in the far future by the ruddy faith of the lines which he devotes to modern France—daring to hope that mankind too,

> Like a brave vessel under press of steam,
> Abreast the winds and tides, on angry seas,
> Plucked by the heavens forlorn of present sun,
> Will drive through darkness, and with faith supreme
> Have sight of haven and the crowded quays.

Read 'heaven' for 'haven,' they will plead; take the vessel as the purified soul or ego; and then the voyage will satisfy the just, keen intuitions of the human soul. Not otherwise. No lesser freight than personality is worth the passage. When Meredith invites them to launch out with 'the rapture of the forward view,' that is, with an ardent hope for the ultimate, collective welfare of the race; when he exults, in lines of chiselled strength and grace,

> With *that* I bear my senses fraught
> Till what I am fast shoreward drives.
> They are the vessel of the Thought,
> The vessel splits, the Thought survives,

then they will be dimly conscious that, while it is wise for them to understand, and well for them to assimilate, much else in this great writer's teaching, here he is putting them off with a mist of coloured, gleaming words. For beyond the bar which he summons the soul thus cheerily to cross, it is doubtful if any Pilot is to be met face to face, and more than doubtful if any haven lies for what men learn upon these shores of time and space to prize above all price.

Dr. Moffat's is, of course, the orthodox view, and Meredith is an essential heretic. Yet nothing that the poet-philosopher has written need rob the soul that longs for continuity of that Godward urge, for surely the conduct which he has outlined for man implies as much austerity and self-abnegation as any ever demanded of him by all the prophets of a heaven of many mansions and celestial bliss for the elect. If we think over his 'reading of earth' as outlined above we shall never be conscious that it runs counter to Christ's teaching, no matter how strangely different it be phrased. Saying Meredith is a heretic, one means, of course, that his attitude is utterly independent of orthodoxy, and that orthodoxy does not imply the teaching of Christ, but the schoolmen's conventionalised interpretation of that teaching. No poet-philosopher of the nineteenth century offers the larger spirits of to-day who are breaking away the lingering trammels of mediævalism from religion such 'driving force of thought' as Meredith has dowered them with in his noble and beautiful philosophy of Nature.

Far from chilling the hopes of the heaven-aspiring soul, Meredith is the rarest tonic that soul can conceive, and simply because he has come to optimism not by shutting his eyes to the misery of the world, not by ignoring the tragedy of life—a greater tragedy than death—but by seeing all and being not afraid. Though it is no doubt true that we should not label Meredith 'optimist' or 'pessimist,' or any other 'ist,' since his view of life is so comprehensive, still when Mr. Le Gallienne calls him the only living optimist whose faith carries any conviction he conveys a notion of his outlook which is true so far as a small word can express the general sweep of a great mind facing boldly great problems. Professor M. W. MacCallum does not overstate the sustained 'uplift' of Meredith's philosophy, its consistent note of triumph, its flying banners of conquest, when he writes:

> Meredith is terribly in earnest and unflinchingly severe, and every one of his chief persons is measured by the spiritual standard, not by any code of the conventional man, or of the natural man. Yet his books have not the melancholy undertone that we note, say, in the positivist George Eliot; there is no discord audible in them, but a full-toned harmony that subdues the jarring notes, that solemnises, but inspirits and delights. Where George Eliot sees only the irremediable in our acts, their linkage in an iron chain of cause and effect, the infinite generation of evil in a world that, after all, is not spiritual; George Meredith has trust in a power that makes even the wrath and the folly of man to praise it, and so when our misdeeds have been visited with their just reward, he can say over the grave of the erring, 'Earth makes all sweet,' and look for a harvest, not of corruption, but of life. Talking of Shakespeare's profundity of knowledge he says:
>
> Thence came the honeyed corner at his lips,
> The conquering smile wherein his spirit sails.
>
> I should like to apply the words to himself. Like Shakespeare of 'the bitter taste' to those who are at odds with nature, he is also like Shakespeare the 'blind and mild' to those whose spirits are in tune.

Mr. G. K. Chesterton in his paper on 'Some Aspects of George Meredith' (*Great Thoughts*, October, 1904) is, as we might expect from so vigorous a thinker and lusty knight of the pen, impressed particularly by his robust naturalness, and he makes a most interesting comparison between Meredith and Thomas Hardy in his characteristic style, when he writes:

> The best example of the basic attitude on philosophy of Meredith, regarding things in general, can be found in his way of dealing with such elements in our civilisation as he conceives to be archaic or cruel, such, for instance, as the benevolent enslavement of women. And the easiest way of bringing this out is to compare him in this matter with another very great man, also a novelist, also an Englishman, and also a man in revolt against many conventions and laws. Thomas Hardy is like Meredith, that thing for

which the words Liberal and Radical are very inadequate synonyms. He is, like Meredith, particularly impressed with the tragedy of the feminine nature under existing conditions. They are both in some sense diagnosing the same problem; they both in some sense trace it to the same disease. And yet their cures are so startlingly opposite that they might be dealing, one with apoplexy, and the other with anæmia. And their two methods, large, distinct, unmistakable, are the two methods which two large, distinct, and unmistakable schools of reformers have from the beginning of the world taken towards what needed reform. When the first shaggy tribesmen differed about how to improve a wicker boat, one was Hardy and the other Meredith.

Let us suppose there is something that is in great need of improvement. Let us suppose it is the primeval wicker boat above mentioned. There is one primeval reformer whose method of reform is this. He stands and points to the boat and says, 'There is a miserable thing for you. Clumsy, unmanageable, a disgrace. I took it out this morning and it leaked in five places. I would as soon go to sea in a sieve. Let us make it better.' And there is another primeval reformer whose method of reform is to stand over the boat and speak strangely thus, 'There is a glorious thing for you; a thing that can drift and swing on the terrible waters that have no end. I took it out this morning and I felt like a god, floating in space. It would be splendid to move on the face of the waters, even in a sieve. This magical invention opens a vista before us; to what lands may we not go? with what swiftness may we not move? What strange fishes may not be in our nets; what strange winds in our sails? Let us make it better.' One says a thing is so bad that it must be improved. The other says it is so good that it must be improved. One is Hardy and the other Meredith.

Continuing his comparison, Mr. Chesterton illustrates it further by showing that while the one reformer would free the slave because his condition is hopeless and degraded, the other would give him liberty because, withal, 'he is a jolly fellow,' worthy of freedom, 'a man like you and me.' Equally the one would emancipate woman because she is downtrodden and kept in ignorance of her potentialities for greatness, and the other because 'even in captivity she is felt to be a queen.' The one argues from her failure, the other from her success. 'The first reformer created Tess, and the second Rose Jocelyn.' Hence in Mr. Chesterton's opinion Meredith is 'a great and powerful paradox; he is an optimistic reformer.'

For a direct pronouncement on religion I turn to Mr. W. T. Stead's character sketch in the *Review of Reviews*, March, 1904, in the course of which he records various conversations he had been privileged to have with Meredith. What follows is most worth noting here:

Like all serious-minded natures, Mr. Meredith is profoundly religious, although his method of phrasing his convictions would jar somewhat upon the orthodox. One of his grievances is that religion has to suffer a heavy handicap in being saddled with the burden of a multitude of beliefs and myths, which are essentially material. To him the need of presenting a more scientific aspect of religion is just as great as the importance of presenting the Christian ideal was to the Apostles who went forth to combat against the materialised conception of the anthropomorphic paganism. The idols of the market-place, the idols of the temples, have become to his thinking materialised obstacles in the way of a realisation of religion. From the Roman Catholic Church little could be expected in the way of this new reformation, but he thought Protestant ministers ought to set about the task, and especially in drawing a much broader line between the teachings of the Old Testament and the higher and more spiritual revelation of Christ.

'I see,' he said to me, 'the revelation of God to man in the history of the world, and in the individual experience of each of us in the progressive triumph of God, and the working of the law by which wrong works out its own destruction. I cannot resist the conviction that there is something more in the world than Nature. Nature is blind. Her law works without regard to individuals. She cares only for the type. To her, life and death are the same. Ceaselessly she works, pressing ever for the improvement of the type. If man should fail her, she will create some other being; but that she has failed with man I am loath to admit, nor do I see any evidence of it. It would be good for us,' he added thoughtfully, 'if we were to take a lesson from Nature in this respect, and cease to be so wrapped up in individuals, to allow our interests to go out to the race. We should all attain more happiness, especially if we ceased to care so exclusively for the individual I. Happiness is usually a negative thing. Happiness is the absence of unhappiness.'

Apart from religion and ethics, much might be written of Meredith's political faith, though of course that is of a piece with his whole philosophy. Mr. Chesterton has studied him as a reformer, and Mrs. M. Sturge Henderson, as we all know, has even written a book which deals with him chiefly as a reformer. In Mrs. Henderson's article on 'The Forward View' (*Westminster Gazette*, February 12, 1908), she gives the pith of her able and painstaking work. A few brief passages from the article in question will help to give completeness to the present chapter in which I hope no vital feature of Meredith's teaching has been passed untouched. Mrs. Henderson writes:

Of the nature and growth of Mr. Meredith's political creed after generations, it may be ventured, will be at more pains than our own to inquire. When the history of our latest political development comes to be written, he may be discovered to have predicted and inaugurated it. . . . The story of Mr. Meredith's Radicalism is written in 'Beauchamp's Career.' 'Beauty,' he says of his hero, 'plucked the heart from his breast. But he had taken up arms, he had drunk of the *questioning* cup, that which denieth peace to us, and which projects us on the missionary search of the How, the Wherefore, and the Why not, ever afterward. He questioned his justification and yours, for gratifying tastes in an ill-regulated world of wrong-doing, suffering, sin, and bounties unrighteously dispensed —not sufficiently dispersed. He said by and by to pleasure, battle to-day.' And the object of battle is to bring beauty to the many instead of the few. . . . A new tide has been setting, new ideals are at work. Society has not, as yet, control of its limbs; but at least it knows itself as an organism, and can never again feel that the full possibilities of life have been realised in it,

Until from warmth of many breasts, that beat
A temperate common music, sunlike heat
The happiness not predatory sheds.

Its watchword henceforth is Community, and the future is in the hands of those who voluntarily unite with the forces that are at work in that direction. . . . The flood of democracy cannot be stayed; but if those with social advantages will but take their place in the fray and not continue to cling to obsolete privileges, the good they will get in exchange for those privileges will more than outweigh the loss of them; so much more than outweigh, Mr. Meredith thinks, that, as soon as the wealthy and powerful can be induced to see the facts, no doubt will remain in their minds as to the relative values:

'By my faith,' he declares, 'there is feasting to come,
Revelations, delights! . . .
. . . I can hear a faint crow
Of the cock of fresh mornings, far, far, yet distinct.'

And this declaration of faith, this assurance of the sound, sweet heart of things, is offered to an age unburdened with consciousness of its capacity for thinking and feeling by a man of incomparable sensitiveness, a man who has faced the thickets of thought and traced impalpable horrors of nerve and sensation down to their lair.

XIV

JUDGED BY HIS FELLOW-NOVELISTS

PERHAPS this title is not quite the most accurate, as it suggests a packed jury summoned to pronounce on one of their fellows; and that is no proper description of this chapter. For the most part the 'judgments'—this jury has many voices and no foreman—were not intended by their utterers to have the finality of a verdict. The jury is not so much 'packed' as it is pressed, and I stand guilty of the pressing. It has, however, seemed to me worth while to examine the critical writings and ephemeræ of Meredith's fellow-novelists with a view to bringing together a selection of opinions which might be held to be interesting as much on account of those who subscribe to them as for their own intrinsic merits; more, perhaps. The unhappy condition of English letters, which forces men, against their inclinations often, to specialise in one particular branch of literary production, has banished that universality which the French, for instance, reasonably account one of their glories. It pays to write novels when once you have caught your public; it pays to write only that particular brand of novel with which you have fluked into popularity; and so we have the melancholy spectacle of many able English writers continually straining to produce new books on the lines of their lucky ones. The English novelists who can or do write decent criticism are singularly few; there are some who, before they won fame with fiction, did write good criticism, and others, again, who have deserted criticism and *belles lettres* to chase the elusive sprite of Fiction none too successfully. The consequence is that, having set myself the theme indifferently expressed by the title of this chapter, diligent research has left me with no great matter to furnish it forth; but even so there is enough of interest to justify its inclusion in the present work.

Where the word 'judged' is scarcely appropriate is in such a case as R. L. Stevenson's perhaps loosely-delivered opinion recorded by a correspondent of the *San Francisco Examiner* in July, 1888, who had a conversation with the novelist on his setting-out for the South Seas. But what Stevenson then said has often been quoted; and he spoke to this effect:

> I am a true blue Meredith person. I think George Meredith out and away the greatest force in English letters, and I don't know whether it can be considered a very encouraging thing that he has now become popular or whether we should think it a very discouraging thing that he should have written so long without any encouragement whatever. It is enough, for instance, to disgust a man with the whole trade of letters that such a book as 'Rhoda Fleming' should have fallen flat; it is the strongest thing in English letters since Shakespeare died, and if Shakespeare could have read it he would have jumped and cried, 'Here's a fellow!' No other living writer of English fiction can be compared to Meredith. He is the first, and the others—are not he. There is Hardy, of course. I would give my hand to write like Hardy. I have seen sentences of his that I don't think could be bettered in any writer or in any language. Still, I serve under Meredith's colours always.

Stevenson was an enthusiast; he did nothing by halves, but had he been writing a studied criticism instead of entertaining an 'interviewer' he might have given a touch of sobriety to certain of the foregoing phrases. Yet they are warm and hearty, and were no doubt spoken in all sincerity. They are a noble tribute from one great man of letters to another still greater.

Of his fellow-novelists who have passed away and who have written of Meredith, I think few had more potentialities of greatness than David Christie Murray. There was a born story-teller, a man who might have won a real niche of fame, who came within sight of the highest at times and went out a failure. Murray had a splendid forthright style which gave distinction to his somewhat egotistical work, 'My Contemporaries in Fiction,' from which I quote the following characteristic passage:

> It is not likely that in the broad sense he will ever become a popular writer, for the mass of novel-readers are an idle and pleasure-loving folk, and no mere idler and pleasure-seeker will read Meredith often or read him long at a time. The little book which the angel gave to John of Patmos, commanding that he should eat it, was like honey in the mouth, but in the belly it was bitter. To the reader who first approaches him, a book of Meredith's offers an accurate contrast to the roll presented by the angel. It is tough chewing, but in digestion most suave and fortifying. The people who instantly enjoy him, who relish him at a first bite, are rare.

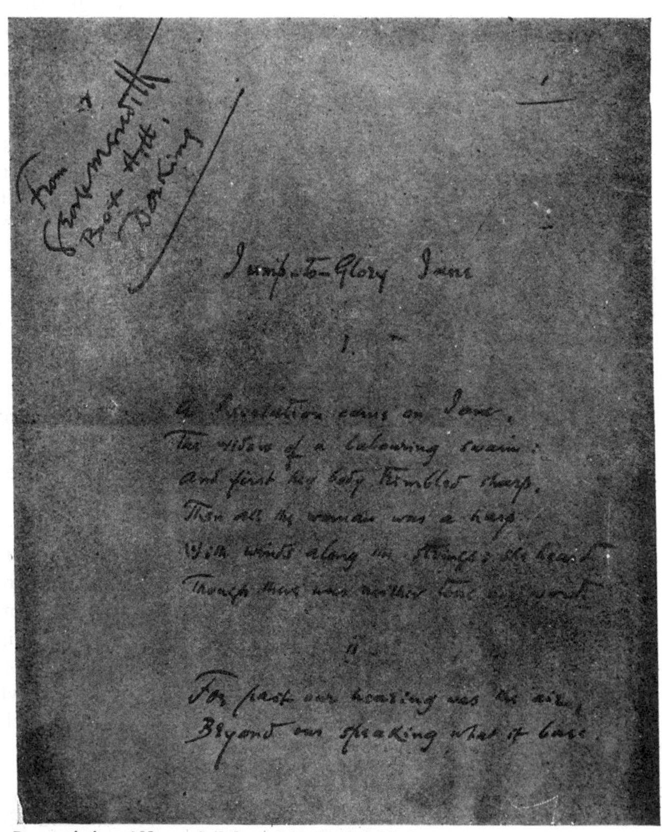

1

From George Meredith, Box Hill, Dorking

Jump-to-Glory Jane

I.

A Revelation came on Jane,
The widow of a labouring swain:
And first her body trembled sharp,
Then all the woman was a harp
With winds along the strings; she heard,
Though there was neither tone nor word.

II

For past our hearing was the air,
Beyond our speaking what it bare.

By permission of Messrs. Sotheby and Mr F. T. Sabin.]

FACSIMILE OF MEREDITH'S MANUSCRIPT.

[To face page 328.

Personally, I am not one of the happy few. I am at my third reading of any one of Meredith's later books before I am wholly at my ease with it. I can find a most satisfying simile (to myself). A new book of Meredith's comes to me like a hamper of noble wines. I know the vintages, and I rejoice. I set to work to open the hamper. It is corded and wired in the most exasperating way, but at last I get it open. That is my first reading. Then I range my bottles in the cellar—port, burgundy, hock, champagne, imperial tokay; subtle and inspiring beverages, not grown in common vineyards, and demanding to be labelled. That is my second reading. Then I sit down to my wine, and that is my third; and in any book of Meredith's I have a cellarful for a lifetime. . . .

Modern science can put the nutritive properties of a whole ox into a very modest canister. Meredith's best sentences have gone through just such a digestive process. He is not for everybody's table, but he is a pride and a delight to the pick of English epicures.

The late James MacLaren Cobban was a novelist of lesser mould than Murray, but a critic of distinction, as those familiar with his work under Henley's banner in the old *Scots Observer* will recall. There he wrote (September 28, 1889) the study of Meredith in the series of 'Modern Men,' and from this I select what follows:

What excellences give George Meredith his peculiar position among his admirers? To speak of them, to examine them is to contend with a great *embarras de richesses*. There are plenty nowa-days to vote the literature of the Rowdy Boy immortal in itself and the wine of life, the only true elixir for every one in mental health. But, the Babel of them notwithstanding, the constant value in fiction is the manifestation of human nature—human nature sounded from the lowest even to the very top of its register. What is commonly called 'character'—character in action—is the perennially interesting thing, and when to character is added right emotion, then the novel may be great. Viewed from this point of vantage the work of Meredith stands fair and full above that of all but the best. What shapes arise as you recall it! Not puppets stuffed and stiff-jointed, not vague and floating shadows, but full-bodied, full-blooded creations, moving in a living world without exaggeration, yet with all the free action of life and instinct with the fire and breath of life! . . .

When George Meredith fails—as in Shrapnel, Old Antony, Mr. Raikes, and the like—he fails prodigiously: not trailing clouds of glory, but running into avalanches of sawdust. But the best of his characters reveal an amazing insight into human nature, and a knowledge wide and deep of the springs of human action. . . . His passion ravishes, and his pathos melts; you would like his good men for friends and neighbours, and the successes among his women for sweethearts and wives: he is not pre-eminently a humorist, but he sometimes makes you laugh; and if he hath a devil of wit, and would liefer die than submit to exorcism, his wisdom (which is neither of the ascetic nor of the worldling, but of the man who commands the secret of both) instructs, enlightens, even fortifies. As for genius, it is recorded of Thackeray that as he sat writing that immortal scene of Becky and the Marquis and the avenging Rawdon, at a certain instant of creation he slapped his hand upon the table, and said he, 'By —— that genius!' Well, such instants are broadcast in Meredith, and when a man can have all these differences in an author, what more can he want for his amusement and delight, what more for his reproof and instruction?

The author of 'Lorna Doone' was very far from being prone to pass judgment on his fellows of the pen, with whom he held less converse than any author of his time, so that the passage from a letter of his quoted by Mr. James Baker in 'Literary and Biographical Sketches' is the more interesting for that reason. Touching the election of Meredith as President of the Authors' Society Blackmore wrote:

I think Meredith was the right man for President, failing Ruskin and Mr. Besant. I should have voted for Meredith. Not that I care for his books, the style is too jerky and tangled, and structure involved, and tone too dictatorial for my liking. Still, he is emphatically an author's author, and the best men admire him beyond all others, and so I conclude that my judgment is wrong.

We have already ascertained Mr. Justin McCarthy's views on certain aspects of Meredith's art, but here I have reserved for quotation a general estimate of the novelist, in which, while we can plainly see a warm admirer of Meredith, Mr. McCarthy steadily refuses to allow his personal pleasure to modify his criticism. We have to remember that what I am about to quote was written in Mr. McCarthy's *Westminster Review* article of July, 1864, and revised for his 'Con Amore' in 1868, thus being a judgment that preceded the writing of 'Harry Richmond,' 'Beauchamp,' 'Diana,' 'Lord Ormont,' and other important works of Meredith's essential to a final verdict. On the other hand Mr. McCarthy was probably familiar with 'Rhoda Fleming,' and as that is unquestionably Meredith's masterpiece *quâ* 'story' he would possibly find little to revise in the following, even after forty years:

His works, as a whole, reveal undoubtedly the operations of a mind endowed with great and genuine power; of a quick, sensitive, feeling nature; of a rich and sometimes a prodigal fancy; of an intellect highly cultured, and matured by much observation. Still, the books are hardly to be called successful in themselves. They exhibit a combination of faculties entirely above the ordinary range, they are distinguished by a freedom from the commonplace rare indeed in our days; and they have the power to set the reader thinking more often and more deeply than even the productions of greater intellects can always do. But the intellectual man predominates in them; and therefore they are no great works of fiction. The fusing heat of emotion which melts the substances of a novel into one harmonious and fluent whole is wanting. The glow of absolute genius is never felt. The moment of projection never arrives; the several substances never combine into the golden mass; they remain cold, solid and individual to the last. The reader is never carried away by the story; he never loses sight of the narrator, he never for a moment feels as if he were moving among the people of the novel, sharing their trials and their joys. Mr. Meredith falls into the common error of intellectual men who go about to construct a story upon purely intellectual principles. It is not enough to draw men and women with vigorous and life-like touches. Mr. Meredith has done this in many instances with entire success. Emilia is a character wholly new to literature, and painted with consummate skill. Adrian, the Wise Youth of 'Richard Feverel,' is such a picture as Bulwer in his brightest days might have been proud to own. It is not enough to have a keen observance of the shades of human feeling; it is not enough to write eloquently, epigrammatically and pathetically; to have a racy faculty of humour; even to have deep feelings of the capacity to express it in words and scenes. All these faculties, or most of them, are essential to the entire success of a novelist. But besides all these, there is something else needed. These are the ingredients; but there must likewise be the capacity to combine and fuse them into one harmonious whole. There must be, in fact, the story-teller's essential faculty—the capacity to tell a story.

Mr. Meredith always seems to write with a purpose. He is always apparently meditating on some phase of human life, some tendency of human nature, some melancholy confusion or misdirection of human effort; and his whole soul is not in the work itself but in something behind it, and of which it only faintly shadows out the reality and the meaning. He is too much of a thinking man; he needs the spirit which abandons itself wholly to the work, becomes lost in it, and has for the time no *arrière-pensée*, indeed no individual existence apart from it. The critical faculty is too strong in him, and therefore, even when he begins to grow earnest, he forthwith sets about to analyse this very earnestness, and it naturally vanishes in the effort. 'I have never thought about thinking,' says Goethe. Mr. Meredith seems almost always to think about thinking.

Mr. Hall Caine is another novelist who began his career of letters as a critic and speedily deserted criticism for creative literature, as it is called—though why any more 'creative' than the best class of criticism it would baffle some novelists to explain—when 'The Shadow of a Crime' very honestly won for him a footing in fiction. Since 1885 he has written little by way of criticism, but in 'The New Watchwords of Fiction,' in the *Contemporary* of April, 1890, he makes an incidental reference to Meredith that may justify the inclusion of the paragraph here:

We are asked to say how fiction can live against such conditions of the circulating libraries as degrade a serious art to the level of the nursery tale. The answer is very simple: English fiction has lived against them, and produced meantime the finest examples of its art that the literature of the world has yet seen. Unlike the writers who pronounce so positively on the inferiority of fiction in England, I cannot claim to know from 'back to end' the great literatures of Europe; but I will not hesitate to say that not only would the whole body of English fiction bear the palm in a comparison with the whole body of the fiction of any other country, but the fiction of England during the past thirty years (when its degeneracy, according to its critics, has been most marked) has been more than a match for the fiction of the rest of the world. Indeed, I will be so bold as to name six English novels of that period, and ask if any other such bulk of work, great in all the qualities that make fiction eminent—imagination, knowledge of life, passion and power of thought—can be found among the literatures of France, Russia, or America. The six novels are 'Daniel Deronda,' 'The Cloister and the Hearth,' 'Lorna Doone,' 'The Woman in White,' 'The Ordeal of Richard Feverel,' and 'Far from the Madding Crowd.' All these novels are products of romanticism, and the circumstance that they were written amid the hampering difficulties that are said to beset the feet of fiction is proof enough that where power is not lacking in the artist there is no crying need for licence in the art.

In January of the same year as Mr. Hall Caine's article was published, Dr. Conan Doyle (as we then knew him) contributed a carefully studied paper to the *National Review* on 'Mr. Stevenson's Methods in Fiction,' in the course of which he incidentally throws out a judgment on Meredith when examining how far the elder novelist has influenced the younger, his avowed disciple. He writes as follows:

Meredith was made to be imitated. His mission is not so much to tell stories himself, as to initiate a completely new method in the art of fiction, to infuse fresh spirit into a branch of literature which was in much need of regeneration. His impatient and audacious genius has refused to be fettered by conventionalities. He has turned away from the beaten and well-trod track, and has cleared a path for himself through thorny and doubtful ways. Such a pioneer would have worked in vain were there not younger men who were ready to follow closely in his steps, to hold what he has gained, and to strike off from it to right and to left. It is a safe prophecy to say that for many generations to come his influence will be strongly felt in fiction. His works might be compared to one of those vast inchoate pyramids out of which new-comers have found materials wherewith to build many a dainty little temple or symmetrical portico. To say that Stevenson was under the influence of Meredith is no more than to say that he wrote in the last quarter of the nineteenth century, and was familiar with the literature of his day.

Mr. J. M. Barrie wrote many admirable essays in criticism before the novel claimed his energies, as the stage has later ousted the novel. I have already had occasion to refer to his study of Meredith's novels in the *Contemporary* of October, 1888, and although it is difficult to detach from that any critical summing-up on Meredith's art in general, it is interesting to discover what is Mr. Barrie's opinion of the highest attainment of the novelist in the creation of character. This, concerning Roy Richmond, will serve to show us pretty clearly where Mr. Barrie would place Meredith:

To me Harry Richmond's father is Mr. Meredith's most brilliant creation. What novelist has not worked the 'adventurer'? In Dickens he is a low comedian or a heavy villain, coloured as only the most richly endowed imagination ever novelist had could put on colour, always warranted to draw laughter or a shudder. Thackeray's Barry Lyndon is a more enduring study, one of the author's greatest triumphs, yet Roy Richmond is, I think, a greater. They are in different worlds, and to compare them would be folly. Barry, with all his exaggeration, is the more true to life; he is the adventurer vulgarised till he is human; while Richmond, the fantastic, in fiction the 'greatest, meanest of mankind,' a dreamer of magnificent dreams, one who cannot bring his mind back to the present, is a comedy figure. This dweller in the future is a strangely romantic conception from beginning to end of his wonderful life, and his death is not to be forgotten. The most tenderly pathetic scene in fiction is probably Colonel Newcome's death, but the most impressive is the death of Roy Richmond. Tragedy rings down the curtain. . . . Thackeray admitted that when he had written a certain great scene in 'Vanity Fair' he felt that it was genius. We are as far as ever from a definition of genius, a word not to be lightly used, but there are some unmistakable instances of it, and I cannot think that Roy Richmond is not one of them.

Mr. George Moore, the author of 'Esther Waters,' in his 'Confessions of a Young Man,' published in 1888, tells us that he had been an admirer of Meredith's poetry, but when he turned to his prose and took up 'The Tragic Comedians,' expecting for the poet's novels one of his 'old passionate delights,' he was 'painfully disappointed.' He conditions his criticism, however, by observing that 'emotionally' he does not understand Meredith and 'all except an emotional understanding is worthless in art.' He seems dimly to recognise him as a personality, but the reading of his prose makes him feel so hopelessly out of sympathy with the author that he doubts if he can criticise him in the true sense. Clearly it is the Meredithian 'style' that is to blame, in the first place, as Mr. Moore goes on to say:

In Balzac, which I know by heart, in Shakespeare, which I have just begun to love, I find words deeply impregnated with the savour of life; but in George Meredith there is nothing but crackjaw sentences, empty and unpleasant in the mouth as sterile nuts. I could select hundreds of phrases which Mr. Meredith would probably call epigrams, and I would defy any one to say they were wise, graceful or witty. I do not know any book more tedious than 'Tragic Comedians,' more pretentious, more blatant; it struts and screams, stupid in all its gaud and absurdity as a cockatoo. More than fifty pages I could not read. . . .

I took up 'Rhoda Fleming.' I found some exquisite bits of description in it, but I heartily wished them in verse, they were motives for poems; and there was some wit. I remember a passage very racy indeed, of middle-class England. Antony, I think is the man's name, describes how he is interrupted at his tea; a paragraph of seven or ten lines with 'I am having my tea, I am at my tea,' running through it for refrain. Then a description of a lodging-house dinner: 'a block of bread on a lonely plate, and potatoes that looked as if they had committed suicide in their own steam.' A little ponderous and stilted, but undoubtedly witty. I read on until I came to a young man who fell from his horse, or had been thrown from his horse, I never knew which, nor did I feel enough interest in the matter to make research; the young man was put to bed by his mother, and once in bed he began to talk! . . . four, five, six, ten pages of talk, and such talk! I can offer no opinion why Mr. George Meredith committed them to paper; it is not narrative, it is not witty, nor is it sentimental, nor is it profound. I read it once; my mind astonished at receiving no sensation cried out like a child at a milkless breast. I read the pages again . . . did I understand? Yes, I understood every sentence, but they conveyed no idea, they awoke no emotion in me; it was like sand, arid and uncomfortable. The story is surprisingly commonplace—the people in it are as lacking in subtlety as those of a Drury Lane melodrama.

'Diana of the Crossways' Mr. Moore liked better, and, had he been absolutely idle, might have read it through; but judged by the final test of all fiction, 'the creation of a human being,' he found it a failure. 'Into what shadow has not Diana floated?' he exclaims. He does not state how far he bore her company, but perhaps the suggestion is that if she could not induce him to follow her to the end she was indeed a phantom. He could find nothing in the work to be mentioned with Balzac; an opinion to which many sincere admirers of Meredith might be willing to subscribe. And he thus pronounces on the novelist's failure—as he considers it—to realise the character of Diana:

With tiresome repetition we are told that she is beautiful, divine; but I see her not at all, I don't know if she is dark, tall, or fair; with tiresome reiteration we are told that she is brilliant, that her conversation is like a display of fireworks, that the company is dazzled and overcome; but when she speaks the utterances are grotesque, and I say that if any one spoke to me in real life as she does in the novel, I should not doubt for an instant that I was in the company of a lunatic.

There is a certain charm of style about Mr. Moore's very frank expression of his dislike for Meredith, and modified as it all is by his avowed lack of sympathy with, and his emotional distance from, the object of his criticism—a premise difficult of admission—it might still pass for an attempt at criticism; but when he roundly declares that 'Mr. Meredith's conception of life is crooked, ill-balanced, and out of tune,' even the most lukewarm Meredithian will protest that Mr. Moore might at least have read several of the novels to the bitter end—so to say—before venturing on a generalisation so sweeping and unsupportable. Yet withal, after suggesting that Mr. Meredith resembles a man who does a lot of shouting and gesticulating but utters little worthy of notice, he can find it in his heart to call him an artist. 'His habit is not slatternly,' he writes, 'like those of such literary hodmen as Mr. David Christie Murray, Mr. Besant, Mr. Buchanan. There is no trace of the crowd about him. I do not question his right of place. I am out of sympathy with him, that is all; and I regret that it should be so, for he is one whose love of art is pure and untainted with commercialism, and if I may praise it for nought else, I can praise it for this.'

There is some very sound criticism in 'Letters to Living Authors,' which Mr. John A. Steuart wrote eighteen years ago, ere he, too, deserted the art of criticism for that of fiction. Mr. Steuart addresses seventeen English and American authors then living, of whom ten have now passed away, and the place of honour is given to Meredith. In Mr. Steuart's views of Meredith there is nothing particularly fresh to any one who has followed the whole stream of criticism so closely as we have in this work; but he writes so engagingly, putting certain long-accepted opinions in a new and effective way, that I venture on the following quotation from his 'letter':

You have been quixotical enough to remain steadfastly true to your early ideals. You have given the world, not what it wanted, but what you thought was good for it. You have put intellect into every sentence you have written, reckless of consequences, therein departing very far indeed from the glorious traditions of English fiction. To say the truth, I think you have been too lofty in your contempt of the rights and prerogatives of that well-meaning and not ill-deserving, in not very intelligent, individual, the habitual novel-reader. Other novelists may occasionally take the bit between their teeth, as it were, and indulge in a gallop to please themselves, but they quickly slacken down to the conventional ambling pace, and make everything comfortable for the party in the saddle. To change the metaphor, they mostly dilute their draught of thought to suit the taste of consumers; but you stubbornly persist in for ever giving yours over-proof, perfectly indifferent if people turn away gasping. That is not the way to be popular, and indeed you are at opposite poles from one's ideal of a popular writer.

Your only commodity is thought, which is not in any great demand in the present era. You made a mistake at the beginning, and, less discriminating than many who are your inferiors, you have never seen it. All along you have gone on the assumption that the world is craving for more light, whereas it is rather obscuration and forgetfulness it is seeking. You fancied that on certain weighty and perplexing problems, which lay very near your heart, mankind was pining for enlightenment, and, with the noble audacity of a generous and gifted soul, you undertook to make things clear; and you have succeeded but too well. That is, you have led the reading public to understand that you are a moral and social reformer, and not a story-teller. But for the ample proof to the contrary contained

By permission of Messrs. Bradbury, Agnew & Co.]

[*From the drawing by Charles Keene in 'Once a Week.'*

EVAN AND ROSE IN THE CONSERVATORY.

She plucked both a white and red rose, saying: 'There! choose your colour by-and-by, and ask Juley to sew the one you choose in your button-hole.'—*Evan Harrington*. Chapter XVI.

[*To face p.* 336.

in your works, your policy might lead one to [illegible] little or nothing of human [illegible] has been the [illegible] of [illegible] a twentieth part [illegible] aloft into fortune [illegible] remained toiling [illegible] for appreciation [illegible] pendence, of [illegible] Happily there are signs that the long delay [illegible] last, that you are [illegible] criticism, that [illegible]

In Mr. Cou[illegible] Dead Man's Diary [illegible]

I do not know whether [illegible] any part—pretend [illegible] thought, but I remember [illegible] morning preceding [illegible] poetry. I recollect [illegible] the fact that he [illegible] his own poems. Not that [illegible] wonder, for I can recall [illegible] one even in heaven. [illegible]

Those of my readers who fail to appreciate [illegible] ing of 'Diana of the Crossways' [illegible] souls meet their fellows [illegible] is an incommunicable [illegible] multitude,'—may [illegible] of the 'multitude,' [illegible] stand how the souls [illegible] language of Shakespeare, [illegible] a whirlwind by a [illegible] witchery of a couplet by Keats [illegible] the tender grace of a line [illegible] with an exquisite [illegible] the diamond-pointed prose of George Meredith [illegible] crystal-clear and luminous as the scintillations [illegible] their judicial poise and calmness emitted like [illegible] at a white heat, which affect me in a similar [illegible] other writers of whom I could affirm this [illegible] but Meredith's thoughts have crystallised into [illegible] prose—every sentence of which is a satisfying [illegible] lectual hunger—which is sometimes pure poetry.

Mr. Neil Munro, the author of 'John Splendid,' [illegible] in the course of a study of Meredith in *Britannia* [illegible] in your works, your policy might lead one to think that you know little or nothing of human nature. Your course, in a worldly sense, has been the height of inexpediency. . . . When writers, without a twentieth part of your gifts or your culture, have been shooting aloft into fortune, and what is temporarily taken for fame, you have remained toiling in comparative obscurity, no doubt eagerly panting for appreciation, yet determined to bate not one jot of your independence, or in the smallest particular prove a traitor to your ideal. Happily there are signs that the long-delayed victory is coming at last, that you are gaining recognition, or, to use a cant phrase of criticism, that you 'are swimming into the ken of culture.'

In Mr. Coulson Kernahan's remarkable and beautiful book, 'A Dead Man's Diary,' I find the following noteworthy passage:

I do not know whether the literary associations of the room had any part—probably they had—in determining the current of my thought, but I remember that, during the first few hours of the morning preceding my death, I found my mind running on poets and poetry. I recollect that I was thinking chiefly of Rossetti, and of the fact that he was haunted, as he lay a-dying, by passages from his own poems. Not that I saw or see any cause in that fact for wonder, for I can recall lines of his which I can believe would haunt one even in heaven.

Those of my readers who fail to appreciate in its fulness the saying of 'Diana of the Crossways,' that in poetry 'those that have souls meet their fellows,' or that of the *Saturday Review*, that 'there is an incommunicable magic in poetry which is foolishness to the multitude,'—may think this an exaggeration. Ah well, they are of the 'multitude,'—the more pity for them!—and can never understand how the soul is stirred by a simple sentence in the godlike language of Shakespeare, or is as irresistibly swayed as are trees in a whirlwind by a single stanza from Swinburne; how the magic witchery of a couplet by Keats can bring tears to the eyes; or how the tender grace of a line from Herrick can set the senses vibrating with an exquisite thrill of joy. Nay, I could indicate sentences in the diamond-pointed prose of George Meredith, pellucid sentences, crystal-clear and luminous as the scintillations of Sirius (and for all their judicial poise and calmness emitted like the Sirius scintillations at a white heat), which affect me in a similar way. There are few other writers of whom I could affirm this with the like confidence; but Meredith's thoughts have crystallised into a brain-stimulating prose—every sentence of which is a satisfying mouthful to our intellectual hunger—which is sometimes pure poetry.

Mr. Neil Munro, the author of 'John Splendid,' writes as follows in the course of a study of Meredith in *Britannia*, July, 1904:

The hour of perfect harmony, when inspiration, argument, and style were in the happiest accord, seems to have come to Mr. Meredith, when—that amazing corybantic Eastern performance, 'The Shaving of Shagpat,' accomplished, doubtless to the artistic joy and profit of himself, if not very much to the edification of the early fifties—he tamed his heart of fire and produced 'Richard Feverel.' The world, which, given an adequate period for reflection, is always right in its estimates of art, has, in half a century, grown to love 'Richard Feverel' above all others of Mr. Meredith's books, and I think it will remain obstinately in that preference, despite the hectorings and the lecturings of the professional critic. We listen patiently to the protestations of the elect that the later Meredith is obscure only for indolent and unable intellects, and that his early work was tentative; we confess the marvellous nature of his analysis of a complex Society, the mordant wit of his dialogues, the truth of his observations of the mind of man and woman, and the uniqueness of his imagination, all as displayed in the noble array of books that stand to his credit, but it does not alter our conviction that his golden hour was the hour of 'Richard Feverel,' when he wrote of love from a full young heart, and cherished his feelings more than his phrases.

In 'Richard Feverel' we have the essence of all the author's gifts as a novelist. It is a story flowing with spring winds, odorous with flowers, touched with Pagan delight in earth and rude elemental things, abounding, despite its tragic conclusion, in that grave optimism which is not wanting in his very latest work. . . . 'Richard Feverel' also indicated the danger into which its creator was apt to fall. The lucidity of its telling was sometimes marred—as we must humbly think—by a device of concealing the most ordinary information in fantastical language.

Withal he remains the most brilliant and ingenious novelist of his age. . . . In the work of no other novelist is conversation so consistently pitched on a high key and so limited to the essentials. The right instinct for a dramatic situation is ever his, and there is rich arterial blood in all his characters.

Another of the younger generation of novelists, Mr. H. B. Marriott Watson, thus sums up a brief study of Meredith published in the *Daily Mail*, November 2, 1907:

Our conceptions of fiction have sensibly altered during the last sixty years, yet we do not judge the pioneers of the Grand Manner by our later canons. We keep Dickens and Thackeray upon their pedestals, as we do Scott and Fielding. George Meredith is in the same category. In the face of his construction, or his mannerisms, or his volubility, for instance, we are mute. All that matters is the light and life that leap from his pages. It is an affair of genius only, where animadversion of mere manner or style fails. We judge him by his galleries, the great dramaturgist of our times. And never was there so vast and varied an assemblage since Shakespeare. Do you remember the Miss Poles? And do you remember Lucy? And do you remember Rhoda? . . . A great range of diverging womanhood lies between these extremes. And in the last resort one must judge a novelist by his women. Their creation is his greatest task.

With the foregoing opinions of his fellow-novelists before us, it is more than ever evident how completely Meredith had won his fellows of the pen to his side. As Shelley was called the poets' poet, so may Meredith be named the novelists' novelist.

XV

HIS PLACE IN LITERATURE

We can hope to define this only so far as criticism may be prophetic, no more. This is not a great way, it will be said; but it is as far as erring man may go, reasoning from premises which he establishes too often to suit the end he aims at. Yet criticism as a whole is by no means so futile in its forecasts as the critic in his bilious moods would have us believe, excepting always himself—and perhaps St. Beuve!—as papal in his infallibility. Nor is English criticism in a bad way just now, any more than it was when Meredith first assaulted its exponents with his new creed and his newer expression thereof. There are times when I am tempted—as one who has read not a little in modern criticism—to think that the standard of English critical writing in our country has been equal to that of the creative literature during the last half century. To-day, indeed, it is not too much to say that the criticism of prose fiction is on the whole superior to the literature it examines. Take a review of the latest novel in the *Times*, or the *Westminster Gazette*, or in almost any of the better-class dailies, and you will probably find it is written with more literary grace, a finer savour of style, a wider acquaintance with letters, than you will discover in the book it criticises, perhaps appreciatively. There is a notion gaining ground that if a man can 'spin a yarn' he is a better fellow than the ablest critic, even though he does not know the rudiments of grammar and could not save his neck, were he put to it, by composing a paragraph of decent English. To this pass has the amazing popularity of the novel brought us, so that a word for criticism would be in season.

But to return to the subject in hand, it may be said that whatever failures in prophecy can be laid at the door of literary criticism, out of the glowing mass of opinions we can always strike shape into something that will stand for the essence of these opinions and provide ourselves with an approximation to truth, or at least to wisdom, which itself only approximates to truth. That is what I purpose attempting here; but in an effort of this kind the reader must co-operate by forming for himself some general opinion from the views it is my task to bring together. If, at the end, the reader finds an idea disengage itself from the whole that refuses to join hands with the main idea I have taken from the same source, I shall say no more than that the 'personal equation,' which makes it impossible for two men to give precisely the same report of the same occurrence half-an-hour after it happened, operates here, as it does throughout the whole field of critical opinion.

Swinburne is a good judge to start with. In 'A Note on Charlotte Brontë,' published in 1877, he wrote:

> Perhaps we may reasonably divide all imaginative work into three classes: the lowest, which leaves us in a complacent mood of acquiescence with the graceful or natural inventions and fancies of an honest and ingenious workman, and in no mind to question or dispute the accuracy of his transcript from life or the fidelity of his design to the modesty and the likelihood of nature; the second, of high enough quality to engage our judgment in its service, and make direct demand on our grave attention for deliberate assent or dissent. . . . Of the second order our literature has no more apt and brilliant examples than George Eliot and George Meredith.

Oscar Wilde, in one of his subtlest essays, that on 'The Soul of Man under Socialism' (*Fortnightly,* February, 1891), in a few deft and telling touches gives the verdict of one man of genius on another thus:

> One incomparable novelist we have now in England, Mr. George Meredith. There are better artists in France, but France has no one whose view of life is so large, so varied, so imaginatively true. There are tellers of stories in Russia who have a more vivid sense of what pain in fiction may be. But to him belongs philosophy in fiction. His people not merely live, but they live in thought. One can see them from myriad points of view. They are suggestive. There is soul in them and around them. They are interpretative and symbolic. And he who made them, those wonderful quickly-moving figures, made them for his own pleasure, and has never asked the public what they wanted, has never cared to know what they wanted, has never allowed the public to dictate to him or influence him in any way, but has gone on intensifying his own personality, and producing his own individual work. At first none came to him. That did not matter. Then the few came to him. That did not change him. The many have come now. He is still the same. He is an incomparable novelist.

Two years earlier the same critic had written of the same novelist in a colloquy which is famous as one of the most brilliant examples of his style and went far to establish his fame as a writer of paradox. I refer, of course, to 'The Decay of Lying,' contributed by Oscar Wilde to the *Nineteenth Century*, January, 1889, and reprinted in 'Intentions.' Subjoined are the paragraphs of immediate import:

Cyril. . . . I also cannot help expressing my surprise that you have said nothing about the two novelists whom you are always reading, Balzac and George Meredith. Surely they are realists, both of them?

Vivian. Ah! Meredith! Who can define him? His style is chaos illumined by flashes of lightning. As a writer he has mastered everything except language: as a novelist he can do everything, except tell a story: as an artist he is everything, except articulate. Somebody in Shakespeare—Touchstone, I think—talks about a man who is always breaking his shins over his own wit, and it seems to me that this might serve as the basis for a criticism of Meredith's method. But whatever he is, he is not a realist. Or rather I would say that he is a child of realism who is not on speaking terms with his father. By deliberate choice he has made himself a romanticist. He has refused to bow the knee to Baal, and after all, even if the man's fine spirit did not revolt against the noisy assertions of realism, his style would be quite sufficient of itself to keep life at a respectful distance. By its means he has planted round his garden a hedge full of thorns, and red with wonderful roses.

Again, in 'The Critic as Artist,' in the same volume, occurs this most characteristic deliverance of Wilde's, though he places it in the mouth of a lay figure:

Yes, Browning was great. And as what will he be remembered? As a poet? Ah, not as a poet! He will be remembered as a writer of fiction, as the most supreme writer of fiction, it may be, that we have ever had. His sense of dramatic situation was unrivalled, and, if he could not answer his own problems, he could at least put problems forth, and what more should an artist do? Considered from the point of view of a creator of character he ranks next to him who made Hamlet. Had he been articulate, he might have sat beside him. The only man who can touch the hem of his garment is George Meredith. Meredith is a prose Browning, and so is Browning. He used poetry as a medium for writing in prose.

Turn we now for a moment from the dazzle of Wilde's paradox, his wise and allowable affectations, his studied cleverness enclosing genuine criticism, to a forthright critic of the old-fashioned 'plain-

Jane-and-no-nonsense' school—the late H. D. Traill. So long ago as 1875—when 'Beauchamp's Career' was appearing in the *Fortnightly*—he wrote as follows, in the *Nineteenth Century* of October, on 'The Novel of Manners':

The novel of modern life and society, in so far as it does not rely for its attractions on mere sensational incident, is generally a study of male and female character—mostly, indeed, of one male and one female character—with a few elaborate sketches of scenery for a background, and a clumsy caricature of some two or three well-known contemporary personages thrown in to give it an air of actuality. The close objective study of social *types*—not of their superficial peculiarities only, but of their inner being—appears to be becoming a lost art. Where, indeed, are we to look for the observation, the humour, to say nothing of the *wisdom*, which was brought to bear upon this branch of the art of fiction by its great masters in the past? We have but one living novelist with the adequate intellectual equipment; but Mr. George Meredith is poet, philosopher and politician, as well as novelist, and we must be satisfied, I suppose, that brilliant studies of manners form an element, and an element only, in his varied and stimulating work. For the rest, we have 'pretty' writers in abundance, and a few of genuine power in the creation of individual character. But the generalising eye, the penetrative humour, and the genial breadth of sympathy, which is needed to portray the social pageant as a whole, appear to be gifts which are becoming rarer and rarer among us every day.

The comparison with Browning which Oscar Wilde made so neatly is perhaps the commonest of the commonplaces of Meredith criticism. The late James Thomson ('B. V.') in an essay on the occasion of the one volume issue of 'Richard Feverel' advanced it thus, in *Cope's Tobacco Plant*, May, 1879:

He may be termed, accurately enough, for a brief indication, the Robert Browning of our novelists; and his day is bound to come, as Browning's at length has come. The flaccid and feeble folk, who want literature and art that can be inhaled as idly as the perfume of a flower, must naturally shrink from two such earnestly strenuous spirits, swifter than eagles, stronger than lions, in whom, to use the magnificent and true language of Coleridge concerning Shakespeare, 'The intellectual power and the creative energy wrestle as in a war-embrace.' But men who have lived and observed and pondered, who love intellect and genius and genuine passion, who have eyes and ears ever open to the mysterious miracles of nature and art, who flinch not from keenest insight into the world and life, who are wont to probe and analyse with patient subtlety the intricate social and personal problems of our complex quasi-civilisation, who look not to mere plot as the be-all and end-all of a novel reflecting human character and life, who willingly dispense with the childish sugar-plums of so-called poetical justice which they never find dispensed in the grown-up work-o'-day world, who can with thought to thought, and passion to passion, and imagination to imagination; and, lastly, who can appreciate a style vital and plastic as the ever-evolving living world it depicts, equal to all the emergencies, which can revel with clowns and fence with fine ladies and gentlemen, yet rise to all grandeurs of Nature and Destiny and the human soul in fieriest passion and action: such men, who cannot abound anywhere, but who should be less rare among meditative smokers than in the rest of the community, will find a royal treasure-house of delight and instruction and suggestion in the works of George Meredith.

Whereas Browning is esteemed a prosateur struggling with poetry for his medium, Mr. Arthur Symons would have it that Meredith is a poet trammelled by prose, if I correctly interpret the concluding paragraph of his 'Note on George Meredith' in the *Fortnightly*, November, 1897. And observe the recurrence of the Browning comparison in Mr. Justin McCarthy's estimate of Meredith in 'A History of Our Times,' from which I quote below the general reference only and not the finely condensed appreciation of 'Beauchamp's Career':

Distinct, peculiar, and lonely is the place in fiction held by Mr. George Meredith, the author of 'The Ordeal of Richard Feverel,' 'Beauchamp's Career,' 'The Egoist,' and other novels. Mr. Meredith has been more than once described as a prose Browning. He has indeed much of Mr. Browning's obscurity of a style, not caused by any obscurity of thought, but rather by a certain perverse indifference on the part of the artist to the business of making his meaning as clear to others as it is to himself. He has a good deal of Mr. Browning's peculiar kind of grim Saturnine humour, not the humour that bubbles and sparkles—the humour that makes men laugh even while it sometimes draws tears to the eyes. He lacks the novelist's first charm, the power of telling a story well. But, despite these defects, he is unquestionably one of the most remarkable of all the modern novelists, short of the very greatest.

Mr. Herbert Paul has naturally a good deal to say of Meredith in 'The Apotheosis of the Novel under Queen Victoria,' contributed to the *Nineteenth Century*, May, 1897, but his generalisations rather than the detail of his criticism are here in point and as a contribution to the subject in hand I quote the following:

[*From the drawing by Sir John Millais in 'Once a Week.'*

THE MEETING.

The girl for her babe made prayerful speech;
  The youth for his love did pray;
Each cast a wistful look on each,
  And either went their way.
—*George Meredith.*

[*To face p.* **344.**

Mr. George Meredith has long stood, as he deserves to stand, at the head of English fiction. . . . His style is not a classical one. But it suits Mr. Meredith, as Carlyle's and Browning's suited them, because it harmonises with his thought. Nobody says that Mr. Meredith's strong point was the simple and perspicuous narrative of events. He is not in the least like Wilkie Collins. He is not like anybody, except perhaps Peacock. But he is a great master of humour, of fancy, of sentiment, of imagination, of everything that makes life worth having. He plays upon human nature like an old fiddle. He knows the heart of a woman as he knows the mind of a man. His novels are romances, and not 'documents.' They are often fantastic, but never prosy. He does not see life exactly as the wayfaring man sees it. The 'realist' cannot understand that that is a qualification and not a disability. A novel is not a newspaper. 'Mr. Turner,' said the critical lady, 'I can never see anything in nature like your pictures.' 'Don't you wish you could, ma'am?' growled the great artist. Mr. Meredith has the insight of genius and of poetical genius. But he pays the reader the compliment of requiring his assistance. Some slight intellectual capacity and a willingness to use it are required for the appreciation of his books. They are worth the trouble.

'How much of Mr. Meredith will our children read?' asks Mr. W. L. Courtney in the *Fortnightly* of June, 1886, and proceeds thus to answer his own question:

Perhaps two or three novels at most—'Evan Harrington,' 'Richard Feverel,' and 'Diana of the Crossways.' Even these we can hardly imagine entering into their life, as 'Romola' and 'Adam Bede' have into ours. For towards Mr. Meredith we always must have a certain reserve; he does not come into the heart, we are still out of doors. Yet his is a powerful mind, full of philosophic culture. Some of his sayings will not leave us, even though the total impression be forgotten. This is just what might be expected in the case of a clever student of life, whose analytic power has been fostered at the expense of constructive art.

But if we wish to discover where enthusiasm would place Meredith, we have only to turn to Mr. Richard Le Gallienne, of all his critics the most constant in his admiration. Writing in the *Novel Review*, May, 1892, he says:

The fundamental element of great work is passion. It is that which vitalises all the rest—the creative passion, whether it be poetic or humorous or what, the gusto with which an artist first dreams, and then translates his dream into his chosen material.

This passion still heaves like a bosom in great books. A man with a bounteous, enthusiastic temperament puts his life at its highest moments into them, and there it will go on beating so long as books exist—just as he himself had gone on had his body been but as durable a material as a book. . . . With this passion Mr. Meredith's books tingle from end to end.

The other fundamental quality of great work is what we call humanity. That is, man is presented in proper relationship to his environment, to the earth below and the heaven above; neither is forgotten, neither is exaggerated. No essential condition or characteristic is ignored.

Whatever subtleties of evolution may be the artist's theme, he must never forget that they have developed 'under the sun,' in the face of an infinite mystery, and from roots in earth. We must recognise the characters as beings, however different in developments from ourselves, as having the same origin, compounded of the same element, and as having the same destiny. We must be quite sure that they are flesh and blood, and not flesh and water. . . . Now Mr. Meredith's work fulfils this condition also. . . .

After passion and humanity, the common qualities of great work, of course, the other qualities depend on the individual. Whether his theme shall be the tragedy or comedy or mere beauty of existence, or all three, chances according to the gifts of the artist. The greater imitate life itself in combining all in their works, and certainly Mr. Meredith is of these. It is hard to say whether as a poet or a humorist he is most notable; indeed, it is unnecessary, for he is in no small degree both.

Mr. Meredith is indeed singularly complex.

He unites in a quite remarkable degree high powers as a poet, a humorist, a thinker, and a wit, all subserved, with the exception of five very small volumes of verse, to his work as a novelist. This complexity gives his novels their exceptional piquancy of appeal, for, as, perhaps, no other English novelist ever did, he sees a character or situation from every different point of view at once. His mind is, so to say, a prism which subdivides the primary aspect of such character and situation into all its subordinate aspects, though he is far too artistic not to respect the dominant impression. This, of course, is the true realism. Thus Mr. Meredith is always convincing.

It is clear from this where Mr. Le Gallienne would pinnacle his Meredith; the pedestal would be only a little lower than Shakespeare's, but lower, for he has said that he is one of those who 'could not love their Meredith so well loved they not Shakespeare more.' Mr. J. M. Barrie writes always, as we might expect, with a shade more reserve and yet we cannot suppose that his admiration for Meredith is a degree less warm than Mr. Le Gallienne's. The conclusion of his study of the novels in the *Contemporary*, October, 1888, is noteworthy. There Mr. Barrie writes:

> In this paper I have confined myself to Mr. Meredith's prose works, and I believe they will outlive his poetry. As to how many generations they will go down to, I shall make no predictions. Mr. Stevenson, with the audacity of a generous spirit chafing at the comparative neglect which has been the lot of his master, calls 'Rhoda Fleming' the 'strongest thing in English letters since Shakespeare died.' I shall only say that Mr. Meredith is one of the outstanding men of letters since the Elizabethan age, and that, without dethroning Scott, he is among the great English writers of fiction. We have a novelist of genius with us still. The others had their failings as he has, and, if the future will refuse to find room for so many works as he offers it, one may question whether it will accept theirs. To say that he is a wit is not to pronounce the last word. He is the greatest of the wits, because he is greater than his wit.

But if we want a finely-tempered judgment by way of counter-poise to Mr. Le Gallienne's—though I am by no means wishful to belittle the ardent appreciation of that most engaging writer, since one can admire enthusiasm even where differing from its opinions—one cannot do better than turn to Mr. W. C. Brownell, who sums up Meredith as follows in 'Victorian Prose Masters':

> He stands quite apart from and unsupported by the literary fellowship which is a powerful agent in commending any writer to the attention of either the studious or the desultory. He cannot be placed. He has no derivation and no tendency. His works inhere in no larger category. He gains nothing from ancestry or association. He fills no *lacunæ*, supplements no incompleteness, supplants no predecessor. He is so wholly *sui generis* that neglect of him involves neglect of nothing else, implies no deficiency of taste, no literary limitedness. Failure to appreciate him is no impeachment of one's catholicity. If he has a philosophy he is too original to let it be perceived; if he has even a point of view he is too original to preserve it long enough for the reader to catch. The whole current of the literature of his day has flowed by him without apparently awakening any impulse on his part to stem or accelerate it, without even attracting from him more than the interested glance of the spectator. . . . He is too large a figure to be obscured even by his own 'originality,' on the one hand, or, on the other, to be belittled by the extravagant admiration of 'the elect.' He has written many novels and not one that does not furnish brilliant evidence of remarkable powers. His poetry is a secondary affair altogether, whatever its value, and it is as a novelist

that he ranks in the literature of his time. And as a novelist it may be claimed and must be conceded that his position is not only unique, as I have said, but of very notable evidence. What other writer deserves to rank with Thackeray and George Eliot in the foremost files of Victorian fiction?—I do not mean for extraordinary genius, like Dickens's, or for dramatic psychology, such as Mr. Hardy's, but for his 'criticism of life.'

The foregoing is criticism of the best kind, which faces the defects of a great master boldly and discovers his greatness in spite of the prickly hedges he has himself set about it. It has this advantage over the praise of the enthusiast, that, being based upon a deliberate and dispassionate investigation, it is less liable to the slings and arrows of the adverse and antipathetic. It is rock-built, less beautiful than the illuminated shrine of the devotee, but weather-proof. Mr. Brownell's judgment runs, on the whole, pretty evenly with that of his fellow-countryman, the late George Parsons Lathrop, but the latter was perhaps a step or two farther on the way to be a 'true blue Meredith man.'

The judgments of certain of the younger critics now fall to be recorded, and perhaps none is more strikingly conveyed than that of Mr. G. K. Chesterton, who writes as follows in his essay, 'Aspects of Meredith,' from which quotation has already been made:

Amidst and yet above this vast general drift towards mere differentiation, towards mere moods and manners, towards a sort of psychological Barnum show, stand two or three great men out of the age of the giants. They have all the interest of the moderns in the fascinating divisions, in the beautiful incongruities between man and man. But they still retain, out of a greater time, a greater memory. They remember this, that however deep, however wild, however baffling and bizarre be the difference between man and man, still it is a difference between man and man, not a difference between centaur and hobgoblin, between a mermaid and a hippogriff, between a kelpie and a dragon. Of these great men, the links between all that was good in the old philosophy of man and all that is good in the new study of men, the greatest is George Meredith. . . . Meredith stands alone in combining with his minutiæ and insight that ancient sense of human fraternity which makes him like Scott and Dickens and Fielding, more a brother to his villains than the modern novelist can be to his hero.

Mr. James Douglas, one of the most brilliant of the younger

critics, with an unfortunate tendency to pursue a paradox careless of whither it will lure him, as may be noted in his study of Meredith in the *Morning Leader* on the occasion of the eightieth birthday, expresses in the following paragraph an opinion with which many critics concur:

The best in him comes out in his poetry, for there he breaks free from literary convention. 'Modern Love' is truer than many of his novels, for in those marvellous sonnets he faces the torture and torment of the human mind caught in the labyrinth of romance. But, like Disraeli, he is in his novels always on the side of the angels, and he seldom works out a situation to the bitter end. He has, like all the romancers, the cowardice of his convictions, and the convictions of his cowardice. He might have cut more deeply into the carcase of life if he had been writing in German or French or Russian or Norwegian, but he has never forgot the gaunt spectre of Philistian convention behind him, moderating and diluting and controlling his thought. He is, in spite of everything in him that makes for conformity, far in advance of his day, and he has a strong, resolute strain of dauntless Liberalism in his blood, which breaks out finely at intervals. His place as a novelist is not quite easy to fix. One feels that he is likely to become, like Browning, a bookshelf classic. But even that dusty immortality is not given to many mortals.

But in all the surge of criticism which burst upon us, flood-like, on February 12, 1908, I recall nothing that summarised with more point the distinguishing feature of Meredith, the tangible 'something' by which we can contrive to give him his 'place' in the great hierarchy of English letters, than a short letter, signed 'E. S. G.,' to the editor of the *Spectator*, in its issue of February 29. Who the writer may be I do not know, but his little note on 'Mr. Meredith's Modernism' distinctly calls for quotation here:

In your reference to Mr. Meredith's birthday (*Spectator*, February 15) you suggest one peculiarity in the work of our greatest living novelist which explains why recognition has come to him so tardily. 'His life spanned the whole Victorian age,' and yet he has never represented that age. In the nineteenth century he stood alone. His kindred will not be found in his great contemporaries—Dickens, Thackeray, George Eliot, Tennyson—but in Fielding, Smollett, and Sterne. He is their lineal descendant, and if we can find a parent for any work so distinctly original as his, we can find it in Fielding. Even his titles have an eighteenth-century ring—*e. g.* 'The Adventures of Harry Richmond,' 'Beauchamp's Career,'

'Lord Ormont and his Aminta.' His is not the actual eighteenth-century manner; it is an evolution of the eighteenth century, sublimated and impregnated with French charm and lightness. If the Fielding novel had continued on its own lines, and had not been diverted, partly through the influence of women writers, it would have evolved into something like the characteristic Meredithian novel—*i. e.* fictitious biography, chapters of a great *Comédie Humaine*. Yet Mr. Meredith has always been more 'modern' than the Victorians. He joins the eighteenth to the twentieth century as if there never had been a Victorian gap. From the date of his earliest novels he anticipated what we understand to-day by Modernism. The Victorian age was one of idealism and spirituality, of sentiment that at its best was exalted and noble, and at its worst was sentimentality. Heart was even more important than brain in the world of Dickens and George Eliot. There was a stronger sense of the seriousness than of the humour of life. Religion or religious philosophy was an important element. Mr. Meredith reacted against nearly every trait of his own times, and in reacting towards the past he produced a new type, a future, which has already become the present with us. The qualities he especially emphasises are strength with power, and, above all, brains. The head rules the heart; 'soul,' if such an obsolete term may pass, does not appear. The most distinctive feature of the style is polished, and yet genial, satire. Sentiment and emotion are drawn as weakness and follies; sentimentality is the cardinal sin. Instead of idealism he gives us almost scientific naturalism, and the love passion is frankly physical. Most of these traits are the common property of our twentieth-century writers. They, too, have reverted in many ways to the Fielding age, partly, no doubt, under Mr. Meredith's influence. Intensely modern he may be, but he has always been intensely un-Victorian.

I have kept for final quotation the judgment of a critic who might equally have been the first of our authorities, but whom I have designed to be the last because he is unexcelled among Meredith's critical exponents, the least prejudiced, the best admiring and the most unsparing. Thus Henley's words coming last will emphasise and underline much of what precedes them. Assuredly the true voice of criticism speaks in such a passage as this from 'Views and Reviews,' originally written for the *Athenæum*, November 1, 1879:

To read Mr. Meredith's novels with insight is to find them full of the rarest qualities in fiction. If their author has a great capacity for unsatisfactory writing, he has capacities not less great for writing that is satisfactory in the highest degree. He has the tragic instinct and endowment, and he has the comic as well; he is an ardent student of character and life; he has wit of the swiftest, the most comprehensive, the most luminous, an humour that can be fantastic or ironical or human at his pleasure; he had passion and he has imagination; he has considered sex—the great subject, the leaven of imaginative art—with notable audacity and insight. He is as capable of handling a vice or an emotion as he is of managing an affectation. He can be trivial, or grotesque, or satirical, or splendid; and whether his *milieu* be romantic or actual, whether his personages be heroic or sordid, he goes about his task with the same assurance and intelligence. In his best work he takes rank with the world's novelists. He is a companion for Balzac and Richardson, an intimate for Fielding and Cervantes. His figures fall into their places beside the greatest of their kind. . . . In the world of man's creation his people are citizens to match the noblest; they are of the aristocracy of the imagination, the peers in their own right of the society of romance. And for all that, their state is mostly desolate and lonely and forlorn.

Henley, again, in the same month as he wrote the foregoing, gives us a generalised verdict on Meredith in his review of 'The Egoist' in the *Pall Mall Gazette*, November 3, 1879, where he says:

At its best, his work is of the first order; at its worst, it is brilliant, but tedious. One of the very few moderns who have the double gift of tragedy and comedy, he is one of the wittiest men of his generation and an original humorist to boot; he has a poet's imagination, and he is a quick observer; he has studied human nature and human life and he is a master of his native tongue. But with all this he fails of acknowledged pre-eminence in his art. And the reason appears to be that he writes for himself alone. Extremely clever, he seems to prefer his cleverness to his genius. He is usually so bent on giving full play to his intellectual activity as to seem to ignore the novelist's main function, and to do his best to misuse the novelist's best gifts. He fatigues and bewilders where, if he so willed it, he could more easily attract and explain. You cannot see what he would do for the sparks he beats out in the doing. . . . It is no wonder that he should have been called 'a kind of Foppington-Fielding,' or that one should think of him as of a Molière who somehow prefers to be Marivaux. . . . Of course, it is a good thing to be the author of 'Rhoda Fleming,' and 'Beauchamp's Career,' of 'Richard Feverel' and 'Emilia,' for with all their faults those books are so many works of genius, and works of genius are not common. But it would have been a better thing so to have written them as to have made them intelligible to the world at large.

We have now examined a sufficient number of critical estimates to have gathered some general notion of where criticism would 'place' Meredith. While it may be thought at first glance that there is wide divergence of opinion—as when Oscar Wilde and Mr. Herbert Paul point out how he is in nowise a realist, whereas Mr. Le Gallienne is at pains to show how he is an example of the 'true realist'—there is really far more harmony than discord in these judgments of many minds.

We usually find the enthusiasm tempered, the admiration modified, by the recognition of certain grave faults which should not be present and cannot possibly inhere in the complete achievement of the highest. Henley and Mr. Brownell are the frankest in recognising these blemishes, and, despite the prejudiced opinion of the late York Powell, they are faults we do not find in George Eliot, who is in some ways Meredith's superior, though she falls behind him in the vivid creativeness of the imagination, and that splendid sense of power with which he confronts life as a whole.

It will be noted that his critics place him variously in the company of Balzac, Fielding, Scott, Browning, Dickens, and George Eliot—Mr. Chesterton alone drags in the feeble egoist Tolstoy—but this is seldom done with the idea that comparative criticism may be applied in his case, since most of them are agreed in the main that 'Meredith is Meredith.' It is rather an effort to express in a quick way some notion of his eminence in literature, not to suggest a likeness. He has done work which warrants the mention of his name with any of these, and he is, judged as a whole, utterly unlike each one of them. There is certainly no more likeness between him and Dickens than there is between Mont Blanc and the River Mississippi—both are great in different ways.

The resemblance to Browning—so much insisted upon, is no doubt more obvious, and yet at heart the two are strangers, for Browning is an essential Victorian and Meredith a 'modern,' in the sense so admirably explained above by 'E. S. G.'

His remoteness from his own age is due to his guiding star of comedy. He has written one of the finest tragic stories in the English language, and 'Rhoda Fleming' might well outlive most of his works, but comedy is the star to which he is ever true, and comedy was dead in the Victorian age, whereas it flourished in the Georgian, and has had re-birth in the twentieth century. Comedy can live only when men place themselves under the banner of Brain and determine to think rather than to feel, or at least to let their feelings be subject to their reason. As Oscar Wilde very happily expresses it, Meredith's creations are not merely 'alive' in the sense that we feel Dickens's personages to be alive, sensuously that is to say, but 'they live in thought,' hence as a novelist he is 'interpretative and symbolic,' which is of the essence of comedy.

What is truly surprising in all these opinions we have examined is the lack of insistence on this aspect of Meredith. It is not enough to say that he is a great psychologist, that he is a philosophical novelist; he is the master mind of comedy using the modern novel as his vehicle instead of the stage. He has no fellowship with his younger contemporary, Mr. Thomas Hardy, who is a greater artist regarded purely from the point of view of the novel; that is to say, Mr. Hardy's novels are better, *quâ* novels, than Meredith's, but Meredith's are greater books, and only suffer by comparison when we test them by standards of conventions to which they were never intended to conform.

Whatever may be found lacking under microscopic criticism in Meredith's books, there is the continual sense of a fearless attitude to life, a great and noble spirit moving forward serenely to its destiny, amused the while with what it finds in humanity to interest itself. But whether this implies immortality for these books is a very different question. We may not be so unhopeful of Meredith's fate at the hands of posterity as Mr. Courtney is, and yet venture very seriously to doubt whether his fame will stereotype into a dusty convention such as Richardson's, or flourish, a fact of vigorous life, such as Fielding's or Smollett's or Sterne's is to the thinking book readers of our day. For Meredith with a following such as that of Scott or Thackeray or Dickens we simply cannot conceive.

What further strikes one in the opinions above quoted is the steady ignoring of Meredith the poet. Mr. Brownell flatly dismisses his poetry as a 'secondary affair,' and all the rest of the critics, without a word about it, seem to be of opinion that his place in literature will be fixed by his novels. Well, after all, it is somewhat idle to speculate, and posterity has a knack of thwarting the earlier generation in its cherished wishes. Meredith the poet may outlive Meredith the novelist, and, again, he may not; and then, again, it does not matter! He is to us now, and to all who come after us with the perception necessary to enjoy a rare and great mind, an incomparable writer of fiction, concerning whom to all who understand it is enough to say, 'Meredith is Meredith.'

This may be added finally, that while Meredith does not typify an epoch, his name will at least remain for all time a landmark of English letters, but it will not mark the era in which his life was chiefly lived and all his work achieved, so much as that succeeding it. In brief, this 'last of the great Victorians' is more likely to be regarded in time to come as first of the prophets of 'Modernism.'

XVI

THE CONTINENTAL VIEW OF MEREDITH

THERE is not, of course, a critical estimate of Meredith generally established on the Continent, radically distinct from the general estimate of him in England and America. French critics have, on the whole, shown most interest in his work, and indeed some of the studies which have appeared in the Paris reviews exceed in length and thoroughness anything ever printed in England or America on the same subject. But whether he is more widely read in France than in Germany is not an easy question to answer. Up to 1904 there were certainly more translations of his works in French than in German, but in that year a collected edition of the novels was begun in Berlin and is still in progress: an undertaking which France has not yet faced. It has to be remembered, however, that a larger proportion of Germans than of French read English, and as copies of many of his books in the familiar Tauchnitz edition have been in circulation on the Continent since 1875, when 'Richard Feverel' first appeared in two volumes, we may assume among German readers an acquaintance with Meredith at least equal to that of French readers, apart from the purely critical class. Doubtless more Germans than French have read him or wrestled with him in his native tongue. We must not too readily conclude that translations of his works in a certain language imply on the part of those native to that language a greater knowledge of the English writer than is the case with others into whose tongue no translations have been made. I do not know, for instance, of a Dutch translation of any of Meredith's works, yet the following letter was printed in the *Nation*, February 22, 1908:

Sir,—Mr. G. M. Trevelyan in saying about Mr. Meredith, 'But the world that so honours him is the English world alone,' overlooks my country. Here, in Holland, Meredith is very well known and much admired, of course, not by the public in general—neither is he, I feel sure, in England—but there is a large circle here where his books are read and highly appreciated. And this is not only so in later years; for at least twenty years Meredith has been a familiar figure for our cultured people.—Yours, etc.,

A DUTCHMAN.

Rotterdam, February 17, 1908.

This would be news to many people, but what weight the letter may carry one cannot guess. The educated class of the Dutch, however, is noted for its linguistic attainments, and probably in no foreign country is there proportionately more English literature read by people of an alien tongue. Certainly Mr. Trevelyan was somewhat short of the mark in the phrase quoted by 'A Dutchman.' For, even when he was penning it, the *Revue des Deux Mondes* was printing one of the finest appreciations of Meredith ever written. Nothing so good as M. Firmin Roz's article was drawn from any English critic by the eightieth birthday celebrations. M. Roz remarks in a footnote to his first paragraph that 'the fame of George Meredith, established even here from his earliest days in literary and artistic circles, did not begin to spread until 1879, after the appearance of the "Egoist."' Clearly Meredith was long ago 'honoured' by French critics, but if his novels have never run as *feuilletons* in the dailies of the boulevards, like those of Sir Arthur Conan Doyle, and Mr. H. G. Wells, that need not cause us surprise. 'The Egoist' would probably have been rejected by the fiction editor of the *Daily Mail.*

Before I proceed to examine the French criticisms, it may be worth while to set down in a brief paragraph a note of the translations which have appeared. First of all, was the greatly abridged translation of 'Sandra Belloni' by M. E. D. Forgues, which appeared in the three numbers of the *Revue des Deux Mondes* for November 15, December 1 and 15, 1864, and was later republished in 1866 by Hachette as part of M. Forgues's volume of English adaptations. In the same review and again in three different issues—those of April 15, May 1 and 15, 1865—and likewise by the same translator, an abridgement of 'Feverel' was printed as 'L'Epreuve de Richard Feverel.' The French version of 'The Egoist,' by Maurice Strauss, published in 1904, is, I gather from M. Roz, extremely unsatisfactory, but a translation of 'Diana of the Crossways' was in hand at the time of his writing, from which he seemed to expect better things. The 'Essay on Comedy' had also been obtainable in French since 1898, when M. Henry D. Davray's excellent translation was published separately by the *Mercure de France*, which review also printed in its second February and both March issues of 1908, a translation of 'The Story of Chloe' by Marguerite Yersin. It will be seen from this that the amount of Meredith obtainable in French is small and unrepresentative, but there was never English author more difficult to convey into a foreign tongue with any approach to likeness.

Apart from the authorised German version of the novels, begun in Berlin in 1904, the only other German translation of which I have note is that of 'Harry Richmond,' published at Minden in 1904, in which year a Bohemian version of 'Feverel' was issued at Prague. In 1873 there was an Italian translation of 'Feverel,' published in a popular series at Milan. This is the entire tale of Meredith in foreign tongues and its poverty is no occasion for wonder, when we remember that so many of his countrymen find him addressing them in a speech so unusual that it seems as difficult to them as another language than their own.

Passing from bibliography to criticism, we find that the earliest notice of Meredith outside his own country occurs in a most competent study of 'Le Roman Anglais Contemporain' by M. E. D. Forgues in the *Revue des Deux Mondes*, June 15, 1867. Oddly enough the writers whom M. Forgues brings into juxtaposition, on account of their having followed the tracks of Byron and Shelley in the enchanted land of Italy, are Trollope, Mrs. Browning, Mr. Alfred Austin and Meredith. Mr. Austin has published a novel, now long forgotten, entitled 'Won by a Head'—it sounds more like Hawley Smart than the staid and heavy laureate of our day—in which all the characters are brought together in Florence, and by virtue of this he rubs shoulders with Meredith for the only time in criticism, so far as I know. It is 'Vittoria' that M. Forgues is concerned with, and that novel had a special interest to him and the readers of the review, as the sequel to the story M. Forgues had in part translated less than three years earlier. The French critic is evidently somewhat exhausted after his bout with 'Vittoria,' and his judgment of the work would hardly whet the appetite of the readers of the *Deux Mondes*, though he says nothing that has not been said many times since by English critics, when he writes to this effect:

It would be a hard task to describe in detail the happenings of a life in which the troubles of the artiste, the jealousies of behind the scenes, the rivalries in love-affairs, are complicated with ceaseless journeyings, intrigues, abductions, fightings, spyings, duels; all moving swiftly, huddled together, confused and obscure enough to baffle the quickest understanding, the most sustained interest. Imagination and wit are excellent gifts, so long as one does not misuse them. That is the conclusion to which one is inevitably led by the reading of this crowded work; where each chapter is a 'curtain'; where breathing space is lacking, so to say; where intelligence is accustomed to longing and to waiting; where the characters perform in a mist and seem as if they had become breathless and exhausted in their dizzying careers. Let us add, lest we be accused of injustice, that here and there is a glade, a vista if you prefer it, on the front of whose flowery confusion we catch a glimpse of the trail of the lion, sure signs of a power which, had it been but constant, would have become masterly.

Many years passed, so far as I can discover, before the name of Meredith engaged the readers of any French review again as a subject of criticism—thirty years almost! This one short note of M. Forgues was all that French criticism had to say for well nigh three decades, if we are to believe the most diligent of bibliographers; and yet the literary and artistic circles of Paris were familiar with Meredith 'from the earliest days' of his career! But when the French critics did engage themselves with the English novelist, it was to some purpose. Nothing could be more charming, for instance, than the way in which the late Marcel Schwob, who visited the novelist at Box Hill, presented Meredith to the French public in his rare and masterly 'Spicilège,' from which I have quoted at some length in an earlier chapter. He does not bear out M. Roz, when he begins by explaining the difficulty of his task at a time—1896—when Tolstoy and Ibsen were the vogue in Paris and thus easy to discuss, whereas of Meredith's works 'one knows nothing at all here.' He adds, perhaps excusingly, and none too correctly, that seven years earlier England was as ignorant of the novels. The reasons he gives for the long neglect are, of course, commonplaces of our criticism: the packed and overweighted sentences, staggering with their loads of meaning, the involved psychology of the characters, implying too arduous a task from readers accustomed to the simpler emotions touched in the novels of Dickens and George Eliot.

M. Schwob then goes on to discuss how Meredith ever came to be accepted of the public, and gives the credit chiefly to Swinburne, Henley and Stevenson, for their 'repeated articles' in his praise. This, of course, applies only to Henley, of whom M. Roz has truly said that he 'contributed more than any one, not only to his success, but still more to the evolution of public opinion with regard to

Meredith.' But the power that was greater than Henley and all the friendly critics to make for ultimate success is thus described by M. Schwob:

Summing up, we may say that because of the importance of the questions which Meredith raises in his works, by the impassioned strength of his heroes—than whom the seventeenth century poets have produced no finer figures—by the haunting spell cast over us by his women: Rose Jocelyn, Lucy Desborough, Clara Middleton, 'Sweet creatures, with sweet names, the girls of George Meredith,' as Stevenson says of them; and above all because his genius, so far from diminishing in strength, has never ceased to grow during the space of more than thirty years, in which time he has produced about twelve long novels and four volumes of poetry, he must prevail in the end.

As the train was bearing M. Schwob toward Dorking, he began to think of a phrase which might sum up Meredith and his works, and he found it in 'More brain, O Lord, more brain!' The need of woman to rise to the height of her possible intellectual power and so, on equal terms, to understand man her mate, and man's need to understand nature, seemed to be the lesson of the sage he was about to meet, as it shaped itself vaguely in the Frenchman's mind while on his way to Box Hill. But perhaps the greatest compliment M. Schwob pays to Meredith is not to be found in this critical Kit-Kat, but in his dialogue on 'L'Amour' in which he names one of the characters 'Sir Willoughby.'

It was Mme. Alphonse Daudet who reintroduced the name of Meredith into French periodical criticism by giving a racy sketch of her two meetings with him at Box Hill and in London in the spring of 1895, in her 'Notes on London,' contributed to the *Revue de Paris* of January 1, 1896. In the chapter on 'Home Life' we have already read Madame Daudet's vivacious description of the novelist at home and in society. From the point of view of criticism her notes are of less importance, for no doubt the late Hannah Lynch was within the mark in supposing that Madame Daudet had never read 'The Egoist' or 'Diana' and never puzzled over a line of 'Modern Love.' Her effort at criticism is to this effect:

When we French knew nothing of him beyond his hymn to France in 1870 ('France, December 1870'), the generosity of that page, offered on the morrow of the disasters, should have aroused our admiration of him; but all his work is full of human observation expressed in the highest manner; his poems, his novels: 'The

Egoist,' 'The Ordeal of Richard Feverel,' 'The Tragic Comedians.' I have heard him compared to our Mallarmé for his artistic inspiration, the originality and independence of his mind.

Quite obviously the charming wife of Daudet is here writing of what she does not fully understand. She had not read Meredith at all, I fancy, and spoke at second-hand. Miss Lynch, who from her long residence in Paris might almost be described as a Continental writer, took Madame Daudet to task in the *Bookman*, in this style:

She informs her French readers that he is the Mallarmé of England. Could ignorance run to more absurd length? If you must hunt for Mr. Meredith's brother on French soil, he is there under your eyes as Stendhal. The same ruggedness and obscurity of style and meaning; the same bewildering originality; the same daring conception and delineation of woman; the same wit and brilliance of epigram and dialogue; the same large interpretation of life, of motive, of character. The defects, too, run parallel in their separate tongues: excessive subtlety, an affectation of utterance never surprised into simplicity and directness; an abhorrence of the conventional and commonplace ever on active guard, a tendency to abuse comedy and reduce the life of fashion to a fine art eliminated of all nature and passion and common experiences.

Of course Madame Daudet only observed that she had heard Meredith compared to Mallarmé, and when we find a critic such as M. Firmin Roz discovering even a momentary suggestion of likeness between Meredith and Mallarmé, Madame Daudet's ignorance may not be so atrocious! As to Stendhal, is it not just possible that Miss Lynch found in him the French Meredith not because of any extraordinary fellowship in art, but because of a literary career that somewhat resembled Meredith's? These literary likenesses are most unsatisfactory aids to criticism. Madame Daudet's notes on Meredith have no critical value, yet they indicate that early in the nineties, if not before, Meredith was a celebrity to literary France. Naturally when in 1900, M. Charles Legras, a French *littérateur* who has made a special study of English letters, and was for two years on the staff of the *Westminster Gazette* in London, came to write his admirable series 'Chez nos Contemporains d'Angleterre' for the *Journal des Débats*, he began with George Meredith. M. Legras writes with a nice appreciation of every aspect of the master's work and the poise of a true critic. Even when his criticism tends to run on conventional lines it remains interesting as the

[*From the drawing by Hablot K. Browne* ('*Phiz*')
in '*Once a Week.*'

THE THREE MAIDENS.

Said they to the youngest 'Why walk you there so still?
  The land is dark, the night is late:'
'O, but the heart in my side is ill,
  And the nightingale will languish for its mate.'
—*George Meredith.*

[*To face p.* 360.

judgment of a foreign student who does not [illegible] but out of wide and deep knowledge of English [illegible]

It is suggestive of the French influence [illegible] dith has worked that of all his character[illegible] Croisnel, one of the heroines of [illegible] Frenchman were to propose to me, I'd tell [illegible] said to me laughing, "I should immediately [illegible] was a challenge which had a risk of being [illegible]

M. Legras then goes on to [illegible] order in which the [illegible] which in 1879 established his renown [illegible] Meredith." He touches upon the character [illegible] books and considers "Rhoda Fleming" the [illegible] that it could be easily translated [illegible] character he finds especially rich, but we [illegible] often requires an inordinate number of pages [illegible] for us the creatures of his brain."

In order to show us his heroes [illegible] in a quadrille, or [illegible] you this morning?" we have to [illegible] by living their life. When we add that [illegible] necessary to a conception of [illegible] we be able not to preserve in our minds [illegible] Loughby Patterne? Certainly there are [illegible] whom we remember in common with their [illegible] no striking originality and with whom we [illegible] much time.

Unfortunately, after having praised [illegible] romances, recognised the richness of the types [illegible] very unequal and a composition that is [illegible] shall be dazzled by the admirable [illegible] chapter of "Richard Feverel" entitled "A [illegible] Whistle," [illegible] elegance of these [illegible] fall into affectation and absurdity! In the [illegible] the excess of polish has banished all simplicity [illegible] is made to carry a metaphor, the images impinge [illegible] and the grammar abounds in idioms.

M. Legras then undertakes a minute anal[illegible] remarking that the work is at once human in its [illegible] sentiments, and essentially English in its setting [illegible] society it describes:

Unfortunately the construction of the book [illegible]

judgment of a foreign student who does not write at second-hand, but out of wide and deep knowledge of English literature:

It is suggestive of the French influence under which Mr. Meredith has worked that of all his characters he prefers Renée de Croisnel, one of the heroines of 'Beauchamp's Career.' 'If a Frenchman were to propose to her; tell me that he loved her,' he said to me laughing, 'I should immediately challenge him.' Here was a challenge which had a risk of being taken up.

M. Legras then goes on to mention Meredith's works in the order in which they appeared, saying that it was 'The Egoist' which in 1879 established his identity as distinct from that of 'Owen Meredith.' He touches upon the characteristics of the different books and considers 'Rhoda Fleming' the most dramatic, believing that it could be easily transferred to the stage. The types of character he finds essentially alive, but he observes that the author often requires an inordinate number of pages wherein to build up for us the creatures of his brain:

In order to show us his heroes mounting a horse or taking part in a quadrille, or even supping their soup and saying, 'How are you this morning?' we have to finish, whether we wish it or no, by living their life. When we add that at least fifteen days are necessary to a conscientious reading of 'The Egoist,' how shall we be able not to preserve in our mind the character of Sir Willoughby Patterne? Certainly there are too many of these figures whom we remember in common with their comrades as possessing no striking originality and with whom we have been forced to spend much time.

Unfortunately after having praised the subjects of these romances, recognised the fidelity of the types, we shall find a style very unequal and a composition that is lamentable. At times we shall be dazzled by the admirable pictures of nature, as in the chapter of 'Richard Feverel' entitled 'A Diversion on a Penny Whistle.' . . . But alongside of these excellences how deep is the fall into affectation and obscurity! In the later works especially, the excess of finish has banished all simplicity: nearly every word is made to carry a metaphor, the images impinge upon each other and the grammar abounds in idioms.

M. Legras then undertakes a minute analysis of 'The Egoist,' remarking that the work is at once human in its passions and general sentiments, and essentially English in its setting, its manners, the society it describes:

Unfortunately the construction of the book is a challenge to our

> good sense. Mr. Meredith does not understand the narrative art. As a rule he writes five pages when one would be sufficient. . . . In France there is an inclination to believe that this long-windedness and obscurity are common to the Anglo-Saxon genius; but this is somewhat of an error. Without doubt the novel among our English neighbours does not possess that brevity due to the judicious choice of details which is the glory of the great French romances: but we shall find a great difference of procedure between 'The Egoist' and 'Old Mortality' of Sir Walter Scott, 'The Woodlanders' of Thomas Hardy, 'The Jungle Book' of Rudyard Kipling. As regards the tendency to obscurity, there is one unfailing touchstone wherewith it may be tested: the theatre. A book that is obscure but may have other excellent qualities will possibly find many 'superior persons' ready to make it their gospel, but transport it to the stage and you will speedily learn whether it is in harmony with public taste. Mr. Meredith has once made this attempt, I believe, without, however, avowing his work, and the piece did not live. On the other hand, at the time of writing the three hundredth representation is taking place of 'The Second Mrs. Tanqueray,' a play that is clear and skilfully constructed.

To a Frenchman brought up in the faith of *une pièce bien faite* this opinion was inevitable. M. Legras's reference to Meredith's unavowed play I have been unable to confirm, and think it improbable.

> To me (he continues) the wit of Mr. Meredith is as strange as his humour. Thus, in 'The Egoist' we are presented with much pomp to a certain Mrs. Mountstuart Jenkinson, who possesses a wit so penetrating, so trenchant, so dazzling, 'that she could have ruled the county with an iron rod of caricature.' We see at once that she is going to pass on to young Willoughby one of these *mots* which stuck like an arrow between the shoulders of a man, and we find ourselves waiting for a remark such as that which she passed upon a certain prince of the best blood, 'A foot, a soul of a young lady;' or, if one wishes something more like caricature, one may recall the mordant epigram of Albert Millaud on Sarah Bernhardt when she was notably slim of figure: 'When she goes into her bath the water lowers.' Mrs. Mountstuart saw Sir Willoughby at a moment when the hero was engaging in a dance, the great lady opens her mouth, everybody pauses to receive her word, she speaks: 'You see, he has a leg!' Whereupon Mr. Meredith spreads himself out in twenty pages of admiration: he has sundry observations on the heart of Charles Stuart, on Buckingham and Rochester—I am left confounded.
>
> To-day Mr. Meredith's work is finished, or at least he is likely to add but little to his great performance: one can therefore attempt

to pass upon him a more complete judgment than on any of his contemporaries. To sum him up in a simile: he resembles the Victory of Samothrace, that statue without a head, without feet, and in every sense incomplete, but of such magnificent parts that it seems to tower above the greatest.

I have deemed it wise to devote especial attention to M. Legras's study for its intrinsic value as well as for its being the first fully-considered criticism of Meredith printed in French. It dates back a mere matter of nine years, but since then the name of Meredith has been much in evidence in the French reviews, and his work is engaging the French critics so earnestly that it cannot be long before some effort is made across the Channel worthily to present the best of his writings in the most literary language of Europe. But even more significant than occasional set studies of the master are the incidental references one discovers from time to time in the writings of French critics indicating an intimacy with the works of Meredith. In the brilliant sketch of 'Foules Anglaises' which M. André Chevrillon wrote in the *Revue de Paris*, December 1, 1902, there is, for example, a passing touch on Meredith which leaves us in no doubt as to M. Chevrillon's being one of the many French authors who have come under the influence of the great Englishman. He writes:

It was not until about 1880 that the English, who had always looked upon us as eager pleasure-seekers, frivolous merry-makers, followers of La Fontaine and Béranger, learnt to speak about 'French pessimism.' We, on the other hand, have come to speak of English optimism. The greatest of the writers who have helped to mould the mind of the people since 1870, such as Robert Browning, Ruskin, George Meredith, have preached and sung in praise of the willingness to live, the hope it breathes in the heart, the beauty with which it engages the eye, and how through all the trials of life it is a sustaining power and a source of beauty.

Ruskin, the æsthetic, has said that the most beautiful of all colours is the carnation-flush of human cheeks, and George Meredith, who has no peer for insight among the English novelists, the child of Shakespeare, a profound poet, a rare and delicately-adjusted philosopher, has flushed the cheeks of his heroines with that living carnation: they are healthy young girls, from the bosom of Nature. These maidens charm by their refined and unerring power, their courage, their sure instincts, divinations swift as the flight of birds, by the unconscious growth, apart from the deep questions of sex, of their emotions, in which we discern their dawning ideas—by the blossoming forth, in short, of all the united forces of their beings in the splendid flowering of their love.

He has full faith in Nature. In her he recognises the source of all wisdom and beauty; he considers her worthy of our love which, so far from being satisfied with the flight of the low-circling swallow, yields itself to the magic of an ascent that ceases not, even in the heavens. He is in love with our wonderful life, its changings and upliftings, its beauty when unspoiled, its unconscious or meaningful unfoldings of leaf and tender shoot, little by little, until the human plant, in all its ripe perfection, is revealed. Then, penetrating psychologist that he is, he takes in at a glance from crest to root, with its spiritual flower, the continuous play of its slightest shades of mind, its scintillations of thought, its ephemeral fragrances, maintained by the most subtle and mysterious distillation of the unseen essences which it receives from the dull earth. He knows that even the best of us living on this earth, unknown to ourselves, have still to spiritualise ourselves at the fire of our willingness.

Mr. Meredith, who never preaches, and whose following grows stronger day by day, is at heart a moralist, and the one to warn us most often and most hard to please. We might call him the apostle of an idealistic naturalism. Like Browning and Ruskin, he believes that the soul will rise to more and more lofty heights from the splendours disclosed to the world. He sees what is divine in that which is earthly; and believes that we can help this divinity to free itself from our nature if our life is pure and wholesome, our character firm and true.

'The Egoist' is, of course, the work which has most exercised the minds of Continental critics, and if any one book were to be chosen as significant of what Meredith has had to tell the thinkers across the Channel it would be this. To the Continent he is the author of 'The Egoist.' The most elaborate and painstaking study of the work which exists is that of M. Emile Légouis, published in the *Revue Germanique* of July–August 1905. No English writer has ever attempted so exhaustive an examination of any modern masterpiece. The learning and the specialised knowledge of English life and history which M. Légouis has contrived to weave into this paper are remarkable. For thoroughness his method is more German than French, but the spirit of the whole is eminently French. It is a piece of serious criticism that does infinite honour to its subject, in its earnestness and sincerity, and equally to French contemporary letters. M. Légouis read his paper in the first instance before the Société des Amis de l'Université de Paris in January, 1905, and he did not feel inclined to apologise for the tardiness of France in taking up the study of Meredith in view of his own countrymen having so long neglected him. He sketched the early life of the novelist, his travels on the Continent, and outlined something of his work in general before turning to the particular subject of his discourse. The novels he described as those of a man who had seen other peoples closely and deeply and, while full of the very pith of patriotism, had managed to look at his own country and his own people with the eyes of an outsider. He had come as a teacher at a time when England stood in need of such as he—the middle of the nineteenth century—when England was all ears to the doctrine of autophagy, or self-resource, which had been preached to her by Carlyle. That had been a doctrine of insularism, exclusiveness. Carlyle had adjured his countrymen to assert themselves, to be Germanic, to be Teutonic, to be Anglo-Saxon! But to be Anglo-Saxon, says M. Légouis, is to be doubly English; while this was certainly not all the counsel of Carlyle, it was at least the part of it most readily apprehended and observed. There were those who asked themselves what was the use of endeavouring to correct the insular haughtiness of the people, their disdain of the foreigner and their contempt for the finer issues of life doubly-dying their indigenous characteristics. Such remembered the culture of the south and what it had done and could still do to advance and clarify a national taste in the finer things of life. There was Matthew Arnold and his famous campaign against Philistinism, his holding up of Greece and France as examples, for the refining of the national character, against Carlyle's Anglo-Saxonism.

It was the time of increase in the followers of the æsthetic doctrine of Ruskin (says M. Légouis), whose aim was to cultivate the taste for the beautiful, whereas Carlyle had preached activity only; the pre-Raphaelites had withdrawn themselves from their own proper age, to look back across the years that had passed, seeking distractedly for delights of other days, deeming the people among whom they moved to be harsh and unsympathetic. It was the time that raised Swinburne, the *enfant terrible* of the group, to encourage the search after pleasure, Victor Hugo to show his pity for the poor, and raised to their highest the great Englishmen who had been Italianised by the Renaissance. It was, moreover, the period in which George Eliot gave a new depth to the ordinary novel, strengthened and enlivened moral philosophy by expending upon it a wider knowledge, and, without any of the narrowness of her countrymen, fixed her clear-sighted and kindly glance upon those who lived in other lands.

To this group of writers, informed with a wider or more refined culture, Meredith is allied. One of the first things to strike one when perusing his novels after those of his predecessors, is the sharpened intellect, the absence of haughtiness and prejudice; he has the deep interest in all minds and peoples which is common to psychologists. He is diligent in learning to understand them, or rather—for his analyses have not the appearance of being laboured—he has insight into the mode of life, action, and thought of each race; again, he seeks to offer to his fellow-countrymen, not in the guise of strangers, as a feast of raillery, but as food for their intelligence, objects on which they may lavish their affections, too often spent entirely on themselves, a greater variety, reality and wider outlook on life. Anything that seems to him to betray a British limitation rouses him to vigorous rebellion. It makes him feel angry and ashamed to see his country detracted from or made foolish by means of conceit or stupidity. So he goes on railing at what he calls the 'singular attraction amongst English people for thick-headedness,' directing their taste towards the arts, all the arts, for which he himself has a consuming passion. His countrymen may have humour, but he wishes them also to have intelligence.

This is all extremely well considered and shows a just appreciation of the *rôle* which Meredith was designed for as one of the great teachers of the English people; but in 'The Egoist' particularly his lesson is as much for Europe and all mankind as it is for his countrymen. Of all his books none is so elemental, so universal, in its appeal; hence M. Légouis could not have any hesitation in choosing it for his exposition of the real Meredith. After a minute and searching analysis of the work from every point of view, the French critic formulates the following opinions as to its philosophy:

It were truly superfluous to tack a moral on to this study. One, or rather two morals stand out quite clearly, I think; one in respect to women, the other for men.

Meredith reminds men that since the far-off times when they lived in woods and caves, they have altered only in the garbing of their primitive nature. The egoist of to-day is the primitive man. His egoism has only become more cultured without disappearing; it has abated nothing of its first primal strength. And he warns us that if we once retard our forward movement by one step we immediately fall back to our very starting-point. It is with us as with the rower against the stream: relax our effort and we drift back—to our common origin with seed and plant.

To women, Meredith expresses his desire that they should have 'more brain,' for he scarcely need say that the best among them to-day are those who yet sacrifice themselves to the egoist as his natural prey. He does not consider (this is another of his bold sayings) that clear-sightedness is unable to exist in harmony with true love. He sympathises with that feminist crusade which had already in 1879 passed its first infancy but had not yet attained the hardy growth we now observe in it. But on this subject he maintains a delicacy and caution which it is meet that we should consider. He who, among all the English novelists, has best known how to express in the most impassioned words, in the most glowing scenes, the emotions of love, young love that brightens and inflames, has not, even in that comedy of his, sacrificed love to the exigencies of his satirical mood, nor to the limits of a system. From the strength of true love his heroine Clara, the youthful rebel, borrows her power of resisting the advances of a false love. To the man who loves her in a true and noble manner she surrenders herself with the self-denial and renunciation that were—and doubtless will always be—the necessary signs by which she understands that she genuinely loves. Unbendable before Willoughby, before Vernon she is bendable, yielding, shy, abrupt and submissive. Vernon has for her that admiration which watches carefully and takes note.

What, then, according to Meredith, are the signs of the passion of love which he regards as genuine? First of all, a kind of humility common to the two lovers—the enraptured reflection of each in respect to the nature of the other, delight in seeing that nature unfold itself freely, fear of touching it lest it should be shaken or lessened, the feeling that one's own nature is of small account and that the nobler one is that which one contemplates. The true lover is he who loves the very soul of his adored one, who loves it in her and for her sake, who loves it distinct and sometimes wholly apart from her, as if by that means he could see her more perfectly as she is, and who delights in her variety.

It is fortunate that the background of the novel is lighted and warmed by the flame of genuine love, for the comedy which is acted in the front of the stage is sternly unmerciful, often with an undercurrent of pain in its laughter. The sharp instrument of the satirist pierces so fearlessly, so deeply that one wonders repeatedly if, in removing the diseased tissues, it does not affect the essential organs. It is a matter of doubt if there can be a name in any language which indicates a measurement slight enough to mark out the imperceptible distance which divides egoism from vitality. Does not a shiver run through one ceaselessly at the thought that the analyst is playing in his ironic fashion with the most intimate being of mankind: at the thought that the vice he so sternly condemns may be destroyed only by destroying life itself; for if it means life itself, it is curable only by death?

You have seen a spade dig deep into the earth around a sickly-looking stem at whose root the practised eye of the gardener has suspected there lives a never-dying worm. At each spade thrust one fears for the root as the iron comes so close to it. The smallest space, a fraction of an inch or so, and the tree is doomed. If the spade be handled by a La Rochefoucauld, we may be confident that the worm will not escape, but we may well tremble for the plant. The wonderful part of Meredith's philosophy and art is the fact that he knows so well, without cutting in any way the root, how to remove the hateful and formidable larva which has become encrusted there until it seems impossible to do anything without reckoning with it.

'La Femme dans L'Œuvre de Meredith' was the title of a remarkably well-informed article, also in the *Revue Germanique* (March–April 1906), from the pen of Mlle. Henriette Cordelet. This lady displays an extraordinary knowledge of women in English literature, from Shakespeare to Thomas Hardy, and her study ranks with the best criticism of Meredith, but it is an aspect of the novelist on which there is really nothing new to say; and in our chapter on 'His Heroines and Womenfolk' most that need be said has already found expression, so there is no call here to do more than mention the article of Mlle. Cordelet, who compares Meredith in 'The Egoist' to Molière in 'L'Ecole des Femmes.'

To the fine appreciation of Meredith with which M. Firmin Roz signalised the eightieth birthday celebration, in the *Revue des Deux Mondes*, of February, 1908, it would be difficult to devote undue attention; as a scholarly exposition of a foreign writer it ranks with M. Légouis's really great criticism of 'The Egoist,' showing every sign of a rich and scholarly mind and that splendid poise of judgment which seems native in all French men of letters, making of them the ideal critics. But M. Roz's essay occupies thirty-five pages of the *Deux Mondes*, which means that I can do no more than touch it in brief and sketchy outline. He begins by stating that no novelist is more open to misjudgment by reason of the very qualities which, once duly appreciated, are inherent in his greatness, and that a first essential to understanding Meredith is to forget all one has ever been accustomed to look for in fiction. He then goes on to contrast the non-conformity of English literature with the conformity of the French, and to point out that both have their virtues, though he naturally leans to that national taste and temper which go to the making of a consistent and equable literature. But Meredith is an arch-heretic, for he does not even conform to the commonest requirements of the medium he has chosen for his expression. Hence comparative criticism is useless as applied to him—though M. Roz is made to think of Mallarmé when he reads the prelude to 'The Egoist' and later does attempt comparisons.

By permission of Messrs. Bradbury, Agnew & Co.] [*From the drawing by Charles Keene in 'Once a Week.'*

EVAN'S ENCOUNTER WITH LAXLEY AND HENRY

Presently his horse's ears pricked, and the animal gave a low neigh. Evan's eyes fixed harder on the length of gravel leading to the house. There was no sign, no figure. Out from the smooth grass of the lane a couple of horsemen issued, and came straight to the gates.

—*Evan Harrington*. **Chapter XLV.**

[*To face p.* **368.**

There is arduous work before any one who essays to follow Meredith through the tangles and torrents of his stories! The individualism of our country, so strongly marked in the marriage relationship, so established in the home—an institution which M. Roz deems needful of explanation to French readers—and so characteristic of the national spirit, is *in excelsis* in Meredith. It is here the critic strikes the note that keys his whole study. As to the English devotion to 'character,' which finds expression in Meredith, he remarks:

There is a kind of wisdom which is above common sense and natural instincts: it is the quick perception of a strong, calm mind, the steadfastness of an upright will; it is 'character.' Mr. Meredith's noblest heroes, his favourite heroes, those who give to his books their most lasting impressions, as they would in real life, are strong characters: Merthyr Powys, Vernon Whitford, Redworth. We cannot help comparing them with those who have the whole-hearted sympathy of Thomas Hardy: Gabriel Oak, Winterborn, Diggory Venn. Tried in friendship, faithful in love, calm in their attitude towards life, they are strong and healthy specimens of Englishmen, active in body and mind, 'the typical Saxon,' as Diana calls one of them. Mr. Thomas Hardy has taken his models from the lowly country folk, Mr. Meredith from society people. The former are blunt, the latter more subtle; but the fundamental element is the same, and the refinement of sentiment belongs no less to the one group than to the other. This is because they are both brave enough to face life openly and to consider it in other ways than as merely ministering to their wishes, pleasures and whims. They see life as it really is; understand it and accept it. They are neither egoists nor creatures of passion. Their disinterestedness leads them to love; true love which gives up and forgets its own aspirations, surrenders everything, expects nothing, and triumphs in the end. Vernon marries Clara, Redworth weds Diana, and we have a presentiment and an earnest hope that some day Sandra will become the wife of Merthyr Powys.

In short, the whole 'philosophy' of life which we can gather from Mr. Meredith's novels is an essentially English vindication of character, prolonged and thoroughly examined. The heroes such as Merthyr, Redworth and Vernon are such as are in fullest accord with the facts of life, and that is why in the end they come out nobly from the great trial, 'ordeal,' in which Richard Feverel shows himself a failure.

In further consideration of Meredith's philosophy, M. Roz takes Mr. Trevelyan's phrase 'the prophet of sanity' for his text and approvingly expounds it thus:

He has brought to men some old truths shaped in a rejuvenated gospel that makes them seem to be but newly conceived. And in fact they are new, since they face the light in a new age, and one were at a loss how to distinguish them, except by the most artificial of abstractions, from the radiant intelligence which, in truth, does not merely accompany them, but inheres in them, and impresses them upon us. It is only by means of that illumination that we see clearly for the first time the things which have always been before our eyes without attracting our attention; it is by means of it that we at last understand, that we know. . . . So we must not rely upon finding very original ideas in Mr. Meredith's works: nor, indeed, is that the function of a novelist. Let us watch the movements of his characters, let us listen to their discourse. Behind the outward show on which we too often glance in a careless, indifferent and wearied fashion, there lurks an unknown meaning which will suddenly appear when the artist's hand draws aside the curtain. Genius does not invent: it simply points its finger at the very heart of things, and makes us tremble before the truths unveiled. Not that the truths are new, but that our comprehension of them is; it is on the mind of the beholder that they exert their influence, and in his mind are they created.

Mr. Meredith's novels seem to conjure up in our minds a vision of the world as it really exists, of life regarded as a concrete fact, with its necessary elements, and its true basis, of man and woman regarded in their proper relationship, in their real nature. All this, of course, not theoretically, arbitrarily, but seen by the simple light of observation, the results of experience, by the mere reflections of a courageous sincerity. Life is not regarded as an interesting system, but on the contrary it first of all impresses truths on the mind gathered by observation and these in turn react upon it, lighting up its secret recesses. Every exaggeration confutes itself by the disappointment which it involves, by the contradictions to which it gives rise, by its attendant consequences. To the man who looks upon life simply, frankly, there is no immoderation which does not reveal itself as such in the facts. The upright life stands between two opposing extremes. 'Our civilisation is founded in common sense. It is the first condition of sanity to believe it.'

Into the detail of M. Roz's most searching, but always appreciative criticism, one cannot here attempt to go, but this note as to the 'battle of the sexes,' of which Mlle. Cordelet has written so well in her study above mentioned, may be quoted:

The 'circumstances' of Mr. Meredith's novels are nearly always the same. When he makes his characters face great questions in 'Beauchamp's Career,' it is the radicalism of the English people; in 'The Tragic Comedians,' it is socialism; in 'Vittoria,' the revolutionary spirit; in 'Diana of the Crossways,' the social independence of women—he always and everywhere shows that they involve the battle of the sexes, in which prudence and happiness are the stakes. Man, indeed, never exposes himself more openly than in his opinions and attitude towards women. Take Willoughby as an example: his egoism never expands wholly, never unrolls all its folds and shows all its secrets until it is undergoing the test of love. Love is the great test of Richard Feverel. 'Women have us back to the conditions of primitive man,' he writes in 'The Egoist,' 'or they shoot us higher than the topmost star. But it is as we please. Let them tell us what we are to them: for us they are our back and front of life: the poet's Lesbia, the poet's Beatrice; ours is the choice . . . they are to us what we hold of best or worst within.'

As we choose: we are the artificers of their fate, so we are answerable for their degradation or their ennobling. Mr. Meredith wars on behalf of woman, but not for mere feminism. Although he may believe she ought to have her own rights, a mind, a soul, he is as far as possible from believing it would be an ideal thing for her to have the independence of isolated individuality. In his eyes, the fullest life exists only in union, in love. Woman brings into love that spontaneity which is seen in the poet, that beauty which compels us to cherish her as the purest mirror of beauty of the world, that spirituality which her less material and more subtle nature is able to maintain, so long as she is not turned aside from her natural destiny. Diana Warwick, Sandra Belloni, Clara Middleton, that is what you bring to those who are worthy of you, to those whom the test has shown to be the strongest and best, truly manly, in a word, men of character. These are they to whom is given the victory, and they alone are capable of achieving happiness since they alone live in the full sense of life.

Finally we have in the following M. Roz's own summing up of the great writer whose personality has within recent years awakened among the intellectuals of France an interest so deep and sincere that in the near future the influence of Meredith on French writers of the new generation cannot fail to be considerable:

He affects brevity when his wish is to gather himself together for a forward leap; a brevity that sharpens and betimes blunts the reader's perception; a briskness that engages us without affording any peace, and an energy that knows no repose. These qualities are all most effective in novels whose aim is not to amuse lazy minds nor to pamper idle fancies, but to rouse intelligent understandings and imprint upon them a clear and lasting impression of human life, its tragedies and comedies, its need of sympathy and its provocation to laughter. Gifted with so wide a sense of reality, equally capable of either irony or pathos, Mr. Meredith raises *sa figure d'aisée et superbe prépondérance* above all living English novelists. But in spite of all his disconcerting qualities, he does not exist among them in isolation. The tradition of the English novel is so strong that even the most independent or rebellious novelist never quite escapes it, and it would be interesting to follow its influence upon George Meredith. . . . He is not without qualities analogous with those of his great contemporaries; he is like Dickens in his wealth of detail, his humour and his feeling for caricature; like Thackeray in the delicacy and subtlety of his portrayal of womenkind, and in his irony; like George Eliot in the seriousness of the questions which he propounds and his deep knowledge of life. . . . There is no question as to the difficulty of his novels: they must be studied rather than read. But what a rich reward does the diligent reader reap from the subtle artist and close observer of life! What a lesson we should derive from him, we whose novels, if they have none of the blemishes which are the exact reverse of Mr. Meredith's good qualities, have too often a need of the good qualities which are the reverse of his blemishes! Let the mind but cleave its way through these thickets and accustom itself to the variations of light and shade in these enchanted woods: it will soon yield to their enchantment. Thus it is that we admire Meredith, and when we consider that he is also—some say, above all—a poet, and the author of 'Modern Love,' we would say that, even though his novels in their essentially human and English characteristics are too bedecked with personal fripperies to be universally recognised and loved as real masterpieces, they are yet very great novels, whose author discloses himself as a personality of the most remarkable kind; unquestionably the greatest man of letters in England at the present time, even in the eyes of those who hesitate or who refuse to own that he is England's greatest novelist.

In the *Mercure de France* of March 1, 1908, M. Henri D. Davray, who had already written so discerningly of Meredith's poetry in *Literature*, the short-lived weekly review issued by the *Times*, devoted his always scholarly article on 'Lettres Anglaises' to a review of Meredith's life and work, while a month later, in another Continental review, M. Stanislas Rzeuski published a long appreciation, declaring that 'Meredith is undoubtedly the most universally esteemed representative of English contemporary literature.' And shortly after the death of the novelist, M. L. Simons, the director of the Dutch Universal Library, Amsterdam, wrote an interesting letter to the *Westminster Gazette*, in which he stated that he had first been attracted to Meredith on the publication of 'The Amazing Marriage,' a reading of which induced him at once to secure a complete set of the author's works. He ended by reading all, and most of them twice He then wrote a study of Meredith for the benefit of his fellow countrymen. 'It took me,' he says, 'with my other work, little less than eighteen months to do this; but I have no recollection of my having spent another eighteen months in my life so full of intellectual, imaginative and literary enjoyment.'

From these somewhat sketchy notes, in which I have observed sequence of date rather than relativeness of criticism, it will be seen that in France at least there is a very intelligent and steadily widening appreciation of Meredith's art and philosophy. No such evidence of critical interest has come under my notice from Germany; but I am less familiar with German criticism and may have missed what others are acquainted with; though I do not think anything approaching in extent or importance to the French criticism I have quoted has yet appeared in Germany. [I have since been told that to the *Deutsche Rundschau*, in 1904-5, Dr. Sotteck contributed a fine appreciation of the novelist.] The German edition[1] of the novels is, however, something that France has to emulate; but I am persuaded that Meredith will never have finer interpreters than M. Légouis, Mlle. Cordelet, M. Roz, M. Davray, or indeed any of the French writers to whom in the foregoing pages I have had to draw attention. Certainly Mr. Trevelyan was less than just to France—whatever he may have been to Holland!—when he declared that it was the English world alone that honoured Meredith.

It should be noted that at the time when the first edition of the present work was in the press many articles appeared in the Continental journals and reviews—so many, indeed, that a survey of them would take this chapter beyond all bounds—called forth by the passing of the great poet-novelist. Of these none excelled in interest or beauty the tributes of M. Henri Davray in the *Mercure de France* and in the *Figaro*. But the 'Continental view' is, after all, the home view, for none of the foreign critics we have read differs vitally from English criticism, though they have all some fresh touch that adds to the completeness of our view of a great Englishman whose reputation has become European.

[1] A German friend informs me that Miss Ida L. Benecke's translation of 'The Tragic Comedians,' published soon after Meredith's death, is admirably done. Miss Benecke, I understand, actually made her translation of the novel no less than twenty-seven years before the author's death.

XVII

ILLUSTRATORS OF THE POEMS AND NOVELS

To all but collectors and connoisseurs it may be something of a surprise to know that the illustrators of Meredith are worthy of notice. Yet the illustrations of his poems and his novels, if collected, would make a large and interesting portfolio. The most important of them are also the least familiar; they take us back to that golden age of English wood-engraving in the early 'sixties,' when Millais, Holman Hunt, Sandys, Tenniel, Keene, and 'Phiz' were drawing their little pencil pictures for *Once a Week*, and the books of the period, now eagerly and wisely sought after by collectors. In the present work some of the most noteworthy of these engravings have been carefully reproduced, but the subject as a whole is of sufficient bibliographic importance to warrant more than can be conveyed in the 'legends' of the cuts.

There are several remarkable facts associated with the *débuts* of Meredith and his long survival. It was noted, for instance, that Mr. W. M. Rossetti, who reviewed 'Poems' of 1851 on the first appearance of the volume, was alive to congratulate the author, fifty-seven years later, on the attainment of his eightieth birthday, and now survives him. It may also be mentioned as an interesting fact that the first artist to illustrate anything written by Meredith was Sir John Tenniel, who made the admirable drawing of Sir Gawain and his bride that accompanied 'The Song of Courtesy,' the first contribution from the poet to *Once a Week*, dated July 9, 1859. Almost half a century later, Sir John was alive to sign the address presented to Meredith on February 12, 1908, though, oddly enough, his name was not among the signatures. This was Tenniel's only illustration to Meredith's words, and it is thoroughly characteristic of the artist's manner, which in his earlier career, as in his prime, was marked by a free line and a supple grace of figure that in later years tended to harden into certain rigid conventions.

The next poem in *Once a Week* was printed just three weeks

later, and Hablot K. Browne supplied the cut, which is not a success, and is quite unlike the familiar Frenchified style of 'Phiz.' Here and there it is out of drawing; the expressionless features of the women, the looseness of the grouping and the general feeling of emptiness, hardly make it a worthy pictorial interpretation of 'The Three Maidens,' but I reproduce it none the less, as it is not without interest to-day. To 'Phiz' was also allotted the illustrating of Meredith's next two poems, 'Over the Hills' (August 20, 1859), and 'Juggling Jerry' (September 3, 1859), in the same periodical. Here we find the illustrator more happily inspired. There is spirit and movement and a touch of atmosphere in the vignette to the first-named poem, while the simple pathos of Juggling Jerry's end is at least suggested with some imagination in the second woodcut. 'Phiz' was also the illustrator of 'A Story-telling Party,' signed 'Γ,' in *Once a Week*, December 24, 1859, which Sir Francis Burnand has told us was written by Meredith, to whom Burnand had related some of the stories; but though much more in the vein of the artist as we know him in his illustrations to Dickens, I have not reproduced either of the comic illustrations which accompany that merry fiction.

Most noteworthy of all these *Once a Week* woodcuts are the three next in succession, the work of Sir John Millais. 'The Crown of Love' (December 31, 1859) gave the artist good scope for a drawing informed with passion and poetic feeling, which, in a beautifully balanced composition, he has expressed to perfection. But 'The Head of Bran' (February 4, 1860) was an even better opportunity for the pencil of a master, and here we have a picture of real distinction, entirely worthy of its subject. There is less that is characteristic in Millais's woodcut to 'The Meeting' (September 1, 1860), but there is a quiet beauty and a homely touch in it that suits the subject admirably.

Of the other two illustrated poems in the same periodical, 'The Patriot Engineer' (December 14, 1861) has a typical illustration by Charles Keene, every touch of character being closely observed and portrayed with the precision we always expect and never miss in the work of that great genius in black and white. The decorative detail and studied beauty of line and composition of the pre-Raphaelite school find an excellent example in the masterly drawing by F. A. Sandys, with which 'The Old Chartist' was adorned in the issue of February 2, 1862.

Were these the sum total of the illustrations to Meredith, they would still be quite a noteworthy group; but while they are in many ways the most interesting, and contain at least three of the gems of the whole collection, their removal from the portfolio would have no appreciable effect on its bulk.

In going through the illustrations to 'Evan Harrington' to-day one feels that it was on the whole a happy chance when the editor of *Once a Week* gave the story to Charles Keene to illustrate. Of all the author's novels this is the only one in which Keene could possibly have felt at home. It moves at times along the same paths of character which the artist was wont himself to pursue, and if at times it rises into the rarer atmosphere of high comedy, demanding of the artist a conception of beauty rather than character, Keene does not altogether fail even then. Here I have chosen from the forty-one illustrations a selection, which is at once typical of the whole series and of intrinsic artistic interest.

There is quiet dignity and strength in the picture of the Great Mel on his deathbed, with Mrs. Mel and Lady Rosely standing by. In every sense this is a model of story illustration, the detail being carefully studied, and yet the result is an admirably balanced composition. But of course we have Keene in his element when he is showing us old Tom Cogglesby's arrival at Beckley Court in his donkey-cart, and perhaps best of all in his drawing of the two quaint brothers over their Madeira at the Aurora. The languorous, affected manner of the Countess de Saldar he suggests very cleverly in his cut for Chapter XIX of the novel, but perhaps he makes that remarkable woman a thought too fleshy. He was always less successful with women than with men, and any student of his work in *Punch* will remark how seldom he introduced women into his drawings. We do not feel, for instance, that the beauty of Rose Jocelyn is realised in either of the illustrations I reproduce, but Evan Harrington is conceived on the lines of the author in both, as again in the very striking picture of him on horseback awaiting the onset of Laxley and Harry. The vignette of Evan's meeting with Susan Wheedle I have also thought worthy of reproduction, for though it lacks definition in the lower part, and the hands of the girl are out of drawing very badly, it has a fine sense of vigour and dramatic colour.

On the whole, Keene's illustrations are not an impertinence to the novelist, as so many illustrations of fiction are to-day. Where they lose somewhat as pictures is in a too conscientious effort to

By permission of Messrs. Bradbury, Agnew & Co.] [*From the drawing by Sir John Tenniel in 'Once a Week.'*

THE SONG OF COURTESY.

'Like the true knight, may we
Make the basest that be
Beautiful ever by Courtesy!'

[*To face p.* 376.

stick to the text, but it is a fault that, save where he falls short of feminine grace, is to be accounted a virtue in an illustrator. None of these woodcuts have ever been printed in volume form, I think, and Mr. Bernard Partridge supplied the frontispiece to the story in the 'New Popular Edition.'

If we could have had a combination of Keene and Du Maurier to illustrate 'Evan Harrington' the result would have been as nearly perfect as it would be possible to attain; the one giving character, the other grace and that 'polite' touch which was foreign to Keene's work. But George Du Maurier—Meredith's most important illustrators, it will be noted, were both *Punch* men—did the illustrations for 'Harry Richmond' when the story appeared in *Cornhill*, and these charming drawings translate us at once into the realm of high comedy. By permission of Messrs. Smith Elder and Co., I am able to give a selection of Du Maurier's drawings.

The picture of Roy carrying his son Harry in his arms away from Riversley through the 'soft mild night,' that had witnessed the great storm between Squire Beltham and his son-in-law, is finely studied, and if that of Harry and Temple meeting the Princess Ottilia is on more conventional lines it is still instinct with grace and movement. Then, do we not see the very man, the splendid figure of romance, in the illustration of Richmond Roy, smoking his cigar and flipping idly the strings of his guitar, as he chats with Harry and Temple in 'High Germany'? And again, years later, when he re-introduces his son to Ottilia at Ostend? Then the picture of Ottilia, 'like a statue of Twilight,' makes one wish the same artist had given us his conception of the Countess de Saldar. The interest of the other drawings I have chosen centres in Richmond Roy—the figure of this great character having fascinated the artist as thoroughly as it does every reader of the book—and we see him in his strength and power at his meeting with Squire Beltham on the eve of his 'grand parade,' confounded when the squire 'has his last innings' and the grand parade is over, and towards his sunset when Harry returns to find Janet Ilchester the stay of his sinking father.

In the 'New Popular Edition' Mr. William Hyde has drawn a frontispiece for 'Harry Richmond' which is totally unlike anything of Du Maurier's. Instead of high comedy, which is always the note of Du Maurier, Mr. Hyde has given us a dramatic and masterly picture of Riversley on the great night when Roy came hammering at the door; the lighted windows, the stormy sky, and full moon, are all suggestive of the tragic, but the picture is wholly admirable. A few notes on the other illustrators of the edition may here be added. Mr. C. O. Murray imparts a fine old-fashioned touch to his picture of 'The Magnetic Age' for 'Richard Feverel,' which was drawn in 1878; there is but little character in the frontispiece to 'The Egoist' by Mr. John C. Wallis, and Mr. Leslie Brooke's rather feeble line drawing of Robert and Aminta at the death-bed of Mrs. Armstrong is no great adornment to 'Lord Ormont and his Aminta,' while Mr. Sauber's plate to 'The Tale of Chloe' is distinctly conventional, illustrating the lines:

> 'Fear not, pretty maiden,' he said, with a smile;
> 'And pray let me help you in crossing the stile.'
> She bobbed him a courtesy so lovely and smart,
> It shot like an arrow and fixed in his heart.

Unique among the illustrations of Meredith's poetry is the edition of 'Jump-to-Glory Jane' produced by the late Harry Quilter in 1892. This contains 'forty-four designs invented, drawn and written by Lawrence Housman.' The mis-spelling of Mr. Housman's name, which is printed in bold type on the title page and occurs again in the text, cannot have been a printer's error; but whether Mr. Laurence Housman used to spell his name with a 'w' I cannot say. That is a minor point. Here the pictures are the thing, rather than the poem or the critical notes wherewith the editor prefaced the little work.

The poem itself was first published in the *Universal Review*, in 1889, and the editor would seem to have endeavoured in vain to get an artist to illustrate it suitably there, but having determined that it was capable of imaginative treatment in black and white he carried out his idea a year or two later by entrusting Mr. Housman, then a young and promising artist, with the work. He had suggested Mr. Linley Sambourne to Meredith in 1889, as the right man to do the drawings, and the poet replied: 'Sambourne is excellent for *Punch,* he might hit the mean. Whoever does it should be warned against giving burlesque outlines.' For some reason or other Mr. Sambourne could not undertake it and Mr. Bernard Partridge was next applied to, but 'his heart failed him'—he was surely the last man to do the drawings, so that his heart did not misguide him!—and consequently the poem first appeared without illustrations. Later when Mr. Housman undertook the commission, the artist, whose imaginative touch is seen in all his line work, as it has later found expression in both prose and verse, complete the series.

Here was the man for the work: he had just that restrained notion of the comic which blends into the weird, the imaginative, the mystic, the spiritual, and is so rare among artists. Mr. Sambourne would certainly not have made a success of the drawings, had he been so misguided as to undertake them. Mr. Housman did, so far as success was attainable.

Quilter very frankly criticises the drawings. 'They are not perfect by any means,' he says, 'and in many points open to serious criticism, but the root of the matter is in them—they have the rare qualities of imagination and sympathy, and from the technical point of view, they show that this artist has only to work to become an admirable designer.' They fail only in certain details of pen-work, it seems to me, indicating no weakness of the artist, but an in-acquaintance with the limitations of process engraving, then less advanced than it is to-day, and the technique of which he speedily mastered.

As imaginative pictorial presentments of the poem they are wholly admirable. The 'wistful eyes, in a touching but bony face,' and the whole gaunt, pathetic figure of Jane are successfully realised. The subtle suggestion of the stained-glass saint in the jumping figure of Jane, as in the plate, showing the prophetess appearing before her first convert, 'Winny Earnes, a kind of woman not to dance inclined,' has a firmness and confidence of line which would have strengthened some of the other designs, while that illustrating the verse 'Those flies of boys disturbed them sore,' has a quaint touch of friendly humour in the figure of Daddy Green, in whom the boys seem chiefly interested.

Mr. Housman's drawings are certainly among the most interesting of all the Meredith illustrations, and one cannot but think that they must have had the approval of the poet himself, as they fully conform to the lines he had laid down for the illustrating of the poem, being charged with quiet but sympathetic satire of the religious mania he sought to expose, and never remotely leaning to burlesque: indeed, there is pity in them, as in the poem, and pity, as a rule, is no friend of satire.

To Mr. William Hyde are due some of the finest of recent illustrations to Meredith, and these entirely of nature scenes. Mr. Hyde's work is of a rare quality in nature-feeling and repose, with just that touch of indefiniteness that leaves us still with a little of the mystery to colour our vision of the scene, so that no better illustrator of Meredith's poems could be imagined. The collection of 'Nature Poems of George Meredith,' published in 1898, with twenty full-page pictures in photogravure and an etched frontispiece by Mr. Hyde, is a real artistic treasure. For the two volumes of poems in the edition of 1898, Mr. Hyde drew the Châlet and Flint Cottage, and London Bridge as the frontispiece to 'One of Our Conquerors.' The view of Oxshott Woods which adorns 'Sandra Belloni' is also, I suspect, by Mr. Hyde, and he too may have drawn 'Off the Needles' which accompanies 'Beauchamp's Career,' but if so it is not quite in his usual style. There is a pretty wash drawing of Queen Anne's Farm to 'Rhoda Fleming' and 'The Old Weir,' finely suggestive of the romantic quietude of the scene, to 'Richard Feverel,' both by Mr. Harrison Miller, while Mr. Maxse Meredith contributes a dainty little line drawing of 'Crossways Farm' to 'Diana,' and there is a fine sunny wash of La Scala by Mr. Edward Thornton as frontispiece to 'Vittoria.' For 'The Amazing Marriage' a photographic view of a scene in Carinthia is thought sufficient, and a dignified, virile bust of Lassalle, evidently of German origin, is given as frontispiece to 'The Tragic Comedians.' One of the earliest and best of all the illustrations to Meredith is included in the 'New Popular Edition.' This is F. Sandys's well-known picture of 'Bhanavar among the Serpents of Lake Karatis,' a fine decorative work which was first engraved on steel for the 1865 edition of 'Shagpat' and the original of which in oils was exhibited at the Royal Acadamy show of English painters some years ago.

In the autumn of 1908 a most noteworthy addition was made to the gallery of Meredith illustrations in the shape of Mr. Herbert Bedford's fine series of miniature portraits of 'Meredith Heroines,' exhibited at the Doré Gallery from October 23 to November 18. Mr. Bedford takes eminent rank among the illustrators of Meredith by virtue of these exquisite little paintings on ivory. For many years the thoughts of this well-known miniaturist had been so engaged with Meredith's womenfolk that he set himself the delightful task of searching out fair sitters who already possessed many of the physical charms of the heroines, determined to interpret in a series of beautiful ivories the Meredithian women who had most captured his fancy. His paintings are thus idealised portraits of actual ladies who, more or less, 'fill the bill' of the novelist in the

[From the drawing by Hablot K. Browne ('Phiz') in 'Once a Week.'

OVER THE HILLS.

The torrent glints under the rowan red,
  And shakes the bracken spray:
What joy on the heather to bound, old hound,
  Over the hills and away.
—*George Meredith.*

[*To face p.* 380.

matter of good looks, and few who saw Mr. Bedford's exhibition will deny the genuine feeling for character which he displays in his interpretation of these famous figures of the novelist's imagination.

In all, fifteen subjects have been exhibited by the artist, and where the quality of all is so even it is not easy to indicate preferences. His Lucy is certainly worthy of Ripton Thompson's 'She's an angel!' and Mrs. Mount is admirably caught, in a way to justify her creator's declamation that 'she could read men with one quiver of her half-closed eyelashes.' If anything, I prefer Keene's Louisa, Countess de Saldar—although Keene so often failed in depicting women—to Mr. Bedford's. There is, of course, no real comparison of the two pictures; Keene's easy, confident pencil lines against Mr. Bedford's meticulous brush and colours. But I feel that Mr. Bedford's is too charming a face—it is a little gem of painting, the black of the Portuguese head-dress against the delicate flesh tints being perfectly contrived—too charming for that lady, whose affectation of indolence is so happily suggested by Keene. On the other hand, Mr. Bedford's Rose Jocelyn is as successful as Keene's is stodgy and ungraceful, while his Caroline makes one almost willing to agree with George Uploft, when he said of her, 'The handsomest gal, I think, I ever saw!'

From 'The Egoist' Mr. Bedford has taken, of course, Clara and Lætitia, and he is more successful, I fancy, with the latter, more to the book, that is to say, giving us some real hint of the character, for which he has chosen the words of Mrs. Mountstuart Jenkinson, 'Here she comes with a romantic tale on her eyelashes.' This Mr. Bedford has used as his text and applied admirably. But Clara seems to me too literally the 'dainty rogue in porcelain,' with a shortage of character in her girlishly pretty face. The three subjects from 'Rhoda Fleming,' however, are all brilliantly successful. Dahlia is a blonde beauty of the freshest, and caught in that moment when, before her mirror, she herself has said, 'There were times when it is quite true I thought myself a Princess.' Rhoda, if she has a fault in Mr. Bedford's hands, seems too capable of sympathy, she lacks suggestion of hardness, but certainly 'she has a steadfast look in her face.' Mrs. Lovell, fair and fascinating, is as surely the imaged figure of Meredith's imagination as Diana, with her dark hair and dignified mien is curiously suggestive both of the fact and the fiction of that character. The serene-minded Lady Dunstane companions Diana, and from 'The Amazing Marriage'

Mr. Bedford has chosen Carinthia, Livia, and Henrietta, which complete the series.

I believe that he contemplates pursuing his most praiseworthy labours, to the end that he may produce a gallery of similar miniatures representative of the leading feminine characters in all the novels. Whether this be achieved or not, Mr. Bedford has already done a very notable work, which gives him an unique place among the illustrators of Meredith.

INDEX